AN ANNOTATED BIBLIOGRAPHY OF 1 AND 2 THESSALONIANS

NEW TESTAMENT TOOLS AND STUDIES

EDITED BY

BRUCE M. METZGER, Ph.D., D.D., L.H.D., D. Theol., D. Litt.
Professor of New Testament Language and Literature, Emeritus
Princeton Theological Seminary
and
Corresponding Fellow of the British Academy

AND

BART D. EHRMAN, Ph.D.
Associate Professor, Department of Religious Studies
University of North Carolina at Chapel Hill

VOLUME XXVI

AN ANNOTATED BIBLIOGRAPHY OF 1 AND 2 THESSALONIANS

BY

JEFFREY A.D. WEIMA
AND
STANLEY E. PORTER

TUTA SUB AEGIDE PALLAS · 1683 ·

BRILL
LEIDEN · BOSTON · KÖLN
1998

This book is printed on acid-free paper.

ISSN 0077-8842
ISBN 90 04 10740 1

PRINTED IN THE NETHERLANDS

Contents

Acknowledgements

This project, by its very nature, has required a significant amount of work by the two authors in producing and coordinating the production of bibliographical annotations for a number of different languages, some of them only sparsely represented in the secondary literature on the Thessalonian letters. Whereas the authors assume responsibility for the work in its entirety, we freely acknowledge the help of several other individuals from around the world whose assistance has been instrumental to this project's success: Prof. Carl Bosma, Calvin Theological Seminary, Michigan (Portuguese), Rev. Huascar de la Cruz, Presbyterian Theological Seminary, Mexico (Spanish), Dr. Brook W. R. Pearson, Roehampton Institute London, UK (French), Rev. Gary Roest, Daosheng Theological Seminary, Taiwan (Dutch), Prof. Dwight Ten Huizen, Calvin College, Michigan (Italian), Dr. Fika J. Van Rensburg, Potchefstroom, South Africa (Afrikaans), and Dr. Al Wolters, Redeemer College, Canada (Latin). Thanks are also extended to Miss Kathleen Struck of the Interlibrary Loan department at Calvin College for her assistance in obtaining a hard copy of many of the sources listed in the bibliography, and to the librarians of the Bodleian Library, Oxford, for their help in tracking down several obscure sources.

Preface

Some 1200 bibliographic references related to the study of the Thessalonian letters were collected for this project, including virtually all relevant works written in the twentieth century, as well as a sizable number of important sources from the nineteenth century. The decision to publish an annotated version of this bibliography stemmed from a desire to assist the research of scholars, pastors, students, and others who are interested in these early Pauline letters.

Format and Use of the Bibliography

The bibliography consists of four major sections. The first section contains a wide variety of sources related to 1 and 2 Thessalonians: commentaries, dictionary and encyclopedia articles, general treatments of the Thessalonian letters, surveys of research, meditations, and bibliographic references. No annotations have been written for the sources listed in this first section due to the difficulty of such a task and the small benefit that annotations for these kinds of sources would be for the typical user of this bibliography.

The second section contains sources which deal with various special topics concerning 1 and 2 Thessalonians--topics typically treated in the introduction to commentaries on these letters: the city of Thessalonica (including issues of archeology, history, and culture), the church of Thessalonica (including the use of Acts in the reconstruction of the church and Pauline chronology), the text of the Thessalonian letters, authenticity, unity, order, date, form (including epistolary and rhetorical analyses of the letters), purpose, and theology.

The third and fourth sections list sources according to their relevance for the major passages or pericopes of the two letters (e.g., 1 Thess 1:1; 1:2-10; 2:1-12; 2:13-16; etc.). Happily, there is relatively wide agreement among scholars over the major divisions in 1 and 2 Thessalonians. Sources dealing with the disputed issue of whether the first person plurals in the letter are real plurals (reflecting the authorship of all three letter senders: 1 Thess 1:1; 2 Thess 1:1-2) or literary plurals (reflecting the authorship of Paul alone) are listed under the section "1 Thessalonians 1:1."

Many of the listed sources are relevant for topics or passages in the Thessalonian letters beyond the one section where they are cited in full in the bibliography. These sources are listed by their reference number at the end of each section under the heading "Other Relevant Sources."

All the sources listed in the bibliography are cited as fully as possible so as to avoid forcing the user to look elsewhere for the meaning of an abbreviated journal title or series. Details of the original have been followed whenever possible in every particular. This affects especially the capitalization and punctuation found in foreign sources.

I. Commentaries and Other Materials Related to 1 and 2 Thessalonians

A. Commentaries

1 Adeney, Walter Frederic. *The Epistles of Paul the Apostle to the Thessalonians and Galatians* (New York: Oxford University Press, 1902).

2 Adinolfi, Marco. *La prima lettera ai Tessalonicesi nel mondo greco-romano* (Bibliotheca Pontificii Athenaei Antoniani 31; Rome: Pontificium Athenaeum Antonianum, 1990).

3 Alford, Henry. "The First Epistle to the Thessalonians," *The Greek Testament: With a Critically Revised Text and a Critical and Exegetical Commentary* (4 vols.; London: Rivingtons, 1857) 3.43-50, 236-269.

4 ---. "The Second Epistle to the Thessalonians," *The Greek Testament: With a Critically Revised Text and a Critical and Exegetical Commentary* (4 vols.; London: Rivingtons, 1857) 3.51-69, 270-284.

5 Amiot, François. *Épîtres aux Galates, Épîtres aux Thessaloniciens: Traduction et Commentaire* (Verbum Salutis 14; Paris: Beauchesne et Ses Fils, 1956).

6 Aquinas, Thomas. *Commentary on Saint Paul's First Letter to the Thessalonians and the Letter to the Philippians* (trans. Michael J. Duffy; Aquinas Scripture Series 3; Albany, NY: Magi Books, 1969).

7 Arvidsson, E. *Till Tessaloniki. En studiebok över första brevet till Tessalonikerna* (Stockholm: Diakonistyrelsen, 1966).

8 Auberlen, Charles A. *The Two Epistles of Paul to the Thessalonians* (Lange's Commentary on the Holy Scriptures 3; New York: Scribners, 1868).

9 Bailey, John W., and J. W. Clarke. "The First and Second Epistles to the Thessalonians," *The Interpreter's Bible* (12 vols.; Nashville: Abingdon, 1955) 11.243-339.

10 Balthasar, Hans U. von. *Thessalonicher- und Pastoralbriefe des Heiligen Paulus* (Einsiedeln: Johannes, 1955).

11 Barclay, William. "The Letters to the Thessalonians," *The Letters to the Philippians, Colossians, and Thessalonians. Translated with an Introduction and Interpretation* (Daily Study Bible; Philadelphia/Edinburgh: Westminster, 1975) 177-219.
Republished in Spanish as *Filipenses, Colosenses y I-II Tesalonicenses* (Nuevo Testamento comentado 11; Buenos Aires: La Aurora, 1973).

12 Barnhouse, Donald Grey. *Thessalonians. An Expositional Commentary* (Grand Rapids: Zondervan, 1977).

13 Barrat, Trenchard. *I y II Tesalonicenses* (Madrid: Literatura Bíblica, 1979).

14 Bassin, François. *Les Épîtres de Paul aux Thessaloniciens* (Commentaires Évangéliques de la Bible 13; Vaux-sur-Seine: Edifac, 1991).

15 Baumgarten-Crusius, Ludwig Friedrich Otto. *Commentar über die Briefe Pauli und die Philipper und Thessalonicher* (Jena: Druck und Verlag von Friedrich Manke, 1848).

16 Becker, Jürgen, Hans Conzelmann, and Gerhard Friedrich. *Die Briefe an die Galater, Epheser, Philipper, Kolosser, Thessalonicher und Philemon* (Das Neue Testament Deutsch 8; Göttingen: Vandenhoeck & Ruprecht, 1976).

17 Best, Ernest. *A Commentary on the First and Second Epistles to the Thessalonians* (Black's New Testament Commentaries; London: Adam & Charles Black, 1972).

18 Bicknell, Edward John. *The First and Second Epistles to the Thessalonians* (Westminster Commentaries; London: Methuen, 1932).

19 Bisping, August. *Exegetisches Handbuch zu den Briefen des Apostels Paulus.* III. *Erklärung des zweiten Briefes an die Thessalonicher, der drei Pastoralbriefe und des Briefes an Philemon* (Münster: Aschendorff, 1858).

20 Blackwelder, Boyce W. *Toward Understanding Thessalonians: An Introduction, Exegetical Translation and Commentary* (Anderson, IN: Warner Press, 1965).

21 Bolkestein, Marinus Hendrik. *De Brieven aan de Tessalonicenzen* (De Prediking van het Nieuwe Testament; Nijkerk: G. F. Callenbach, 1970).

22 Boor, Werner de. *Die Briefe des Paulus an die Thessalonicher* (Wuppertaler Studienbibel; Wuppertal: Brockhaus, 1959).

23 Bristol, Lyle O. *Paul and Thessalonians* (Valley Forge, PA: Judson, 1965).

24 Bruce, F. F. "1 and 2 Thessalonians," *The New Bible Commentary* (ed. Donald Guthrie and J. A. Motyer; Grand Rapids: Eerdmans, 1970) 855-864.

25 ---. *1 and 2 Thessalonians* (Word Biblical Commentary 45; Waco, TX: Word, 1982).

26 ---. *Paul and His Converts. 1 and 2 Thessalonians. 1 and 2 Corinthians* (Bible Guides 17; New York/Nashville: Abingdon, 1962).

27 Buzy, Denis. "Deuxième épître aux Thessaloniciens," *La Sainte Bible* (ed. Louis Pirot and Albert Clamer; 12 vols.; Paris: Letouzey & Ané, 1946) 12.175-190.

28 ---. "Première épître aux Thessaloniciens," *La Sainte Bible* (ed. Louis Pirot and Albert Clamer; 12 vols.; Paris: Letouzey & Ané, 1946) 12.129-174.

29 Cantinat, Jean. *Les épîtres de saint Paul expliquées* (Paris: Gabalda, 1960).
Republished in English as *The Epistles of Saint Paul Explained* (Staten Island, NY: Alba House, 1966).

30 Carroll, Benajah Harvey. *I and II Thessalonians and I and II Corinthians* (Nashville: Broadman, 1942).
Republished in Spanish as *1 y 2 Tesalonicenses; 1 y 2 Corintios* (Barcelona: CLIE, 1987).

31 Chrysostom, John. "Homilies on Thessalonians," *The Nicene and Post-Nicene Fathers* (ed. Philip Schaff; Grand Rapids: Eerdmans, 1956) 13.323-375.

32 Clark, Gordon H. *First and Second Thessalonians* (Jefferson, MD: Trinity Foundation, 1986).

33 Cook, F. C. *Speaker's Bible Commentary: I and II Thessalonians by Lord Bishop of Derry* (Cambridge/London: The Holy Bible, 1881).

34 Cunchillos, Jesús-Luis. "Première épître aux Thessaloniciens," *La Bible. Première lecture de Saint Paul* (Le Point théologique 13; Paris: Éditions Beauchesne, 1975) 21-53.

35 Cürlis, Peter. *Die Briefe Pauli an die Thessalonicher* (Holstein: G. Ihloff, 1925).

36 da Spinetoli, Ortensio. *Lettere ai Tessalonicesi* (Nuovissima Versione della Bibbia dai Testi Originali 38; Rome: Edizioni Paoline, 1971).

37 ---. *Le Lettere di San Paolo* (Parola di Dio 16; Rome: Edizioni Paoline, 1978).

38 Davies, Mervyn. "1 and 2 Thessalonians," *Paul I* (Mervyn Davies, Duncan Macpherson, and Lionel Swain *et al.*; Scripture Discussion Commentary 10; London/Chicago: Sheed and Ward/ACTA Foundation, 1972) 29-69.

39 Demarest, Gary W. *1, 2 Thessalonians, 1, 2, Timothy, Titus* (Communicator's Commentary Series 9; Waco, TX: Word, 1984).

40 Dewailly, Louis-Marie. *La jeune église de Thessalonique. Les Deux Premières Épîtres de Saint Paul* (Lectio Divina 37; Paris: Cerf, 1963).
Republished in Spanish as *La joven iglesia de Tesalónica* (Madrid: Studium, 1971).

41 Dewailly, Louis-Marie, and Beda Rigaux. *Les épîtres de saint Paul aux Thessaloniciens* (La Sainte Bible: Traduite en français sous la direction de l'École biblique de Jérusalem; Paris: Cerf, 1954).

42 Dibelius, Martin. *Die Briefe des Apostels Paulus*. II. *Die neun kleinen Briefe* (Tübingen: Mohr/Siebeck, 1913).

43 ---. *An die Thessalonicher I, II* (Handbuch zum Neuen Testament 11; Tübingen: Mohr, 1937).

44 Dobschütz, Ernst von. *Die Thessalonicherbriefe* (Kritisch-Exegetischer Kommentar über das Neue Testament 10; Göttingen: Vandenhoeck & Ruprecht, 1909).

45 Doyle, Stephen C. *1-2 Thessalonians and Galatians* (Read and Pray 10; Chicago: Franciscan Herald Press, 1980).

46 Du Preez, J. *Die briewe aan die Tessalonisense* (Cape Town: N. G. Kerk-Uitgewers, 1981).

47 Dunlop, R. V. *Lectures on St. Paul's First Epistle to the Thessalonians* (Edinburgh: Grant, 1882).

48 Eadie, John. *Commentary on the Greek Text of the Epistles of Paul to the Thessalonians* (New York: Macmillan, 1877).

49 Egenolf, Hans-Andreas. *Der zweite Brief an die Thessalonicher* (Geistliche Schriftlesung: Erläuterungen zum Neuen Testament für die Geistliche Lesung 14; Düsseldorf: Patmos Verlag, 1965).
Republished in English as *The Second Epistle to the Thessalonians* (trans. William Glen-Doepel; New Testament for Spiritual Reading 18; London: Burns & Oats, 1969) and in Spanish as *Segunda carta a los Tesalonicenses* (El Nuevo Testamento y su mensaje 14; Barcelona: Editorial Herder, 1970).

50 Elias, Jacob W. *1 and 2 Thessalonians* (Believers Church Bible Commentary; Scottdale, PA: Herald, 1995).

51 Ellicott, Charles John. *A Critical and Exegetical Commentary on St. Paul's Epistles to the Thessalonians* (Boston: Gould & Lincoln, 1864).

52 Ellingworth, Paul, and Eugene A. Nida. *A Translator's Handbook on Paul's Letters to the Thessalonians* (Helps for Translators 16; Stuttgart: United Bible Society, 1975).

53 Ellis, Peter F. "The First Letter of Paul to the Thessalonians," *Seven Pauline Letters* (Collegeville, MN: Liturgical Press, 1982) 4-37.

54 Erdman, Charles Rosenbury. *The Epistles of Paul to the Thessalonians: An Exposition* (Erdman Commentaries on the New Testament; Philadelphia: Westminster, 1935). Republished in Spanish as *La primera y la segunda epístolas a los Tesalonicenses* (Grand Rapids: T.E.L.L., 1976).

55 Exell, Joseph Samuel. *Thessalonians* (The Biblical Illustrator; New York: Revell, 1900).

56 Fausset, Andrew Robert. "I Thessalonians," *A Commentary Critical, Experimental and Practical on the Old and New Testaments* (ed. Robert Jamieson, Andrew Robert Fausset and David Brown; Glasgow: W. Collins, Sons & Co., 1869) 457-470.

57 Faye, Eugène de. *De vera indole Pauli apostoli epistolarum ad Thessalonicenses* (Paris: N.P., 1892).

58 Fergusson, James. *A Brief Exposition of the Epistles of Paul to the Galatians, Ephesians, Philippians, Colossians and Thessalonians* (London: Thomas Ward, 1649).

59 Findlay, George Gillanders. *The Epistles to the Thessalonians* (Cambridge Bible for Schools and Colleges 44; Cambridge: Cambridge University Press, 1891).

60 ---. *The Epistles of Paul the Apostle to the Thessalonians* (Cambridge Greek New Testament for Schools and Colleges; Cambridge: Cambridge University Press, 1991; republished, Grand Rapids: Baker, 1982).

61 Flatt, Johann Friedrich von. *Vorlesungen über die Briefe Pauli an die Philipper, Kolosser, Thessalonicher und an Philemon* (Tübingen: L. F. Fues, 1829).

62 Frame, James Everett. *A Critical and Exegetical Commentary on the Epistles of St. Paul to the Thessalonians* (International Criticial Commentary; Edinburgh: T. & T. Clark, 1912).

63 Frede, Hermann Josef. *Epistulae ad Thessalonicenses, Timotheum, Titum, Philemonem, Hebraeos* (Vetus Latina 25; Freiburg: Herder, 1975).

64 Friedrich, Gerhard. "Der Erste Brief an die Thessalonicher und Der Zweite Brief an die Thessalonicher," *Die Briefe an Die Galater, Epheser, Philipper, Kolosser, Thessalonicher, und Philemon* (Jürgen Becker, Hans Conzelmann, and Gerhard Friedrich; Das Neue Testament Deutsch 8; Göttingen: Vandenhoeck & Ruprecht, 1976) 202-251.

65 Galanis, John L. *The Second Letter of the Apostle Paul to Thessalonica* [in Greek] (Thessaloniki: Pournaras, 1989).

66 Galizzi, Mario. *Una chiesa giovane. Le due lettere di Paolo ai Tessalonicesi* (Commenti al Nuovo Testamento; Turin-Leumann: Elle di Ci, 1973).

67 García, Míguel Salvador. *San Pablo: Tesalonicenses y grandes cartas* (Madrid: PPC, 1983).

68 Garrod, George Watts. *The First Epistle to the Thessalonians: Analysis and Notes* (London: Macmillan, 1899).

69 ---. *The Second Epistle to the Thessalonians: Analysis and Notes* (London: Macmillan, 1900).

70 Gaventa, Beverly Roberts. *First and Second Thessalonians* (Interpretation; Louisville: John Knox, 1998).

71 Ghini, Emanuela. *Lettere di Paolo ai Tessalonicesi: Commento pastorale* (Collana Lettura pastorale della Bibbia 9; Bologna: Dehoniane, 1980).

72 Gingrich, Raymond E. *First and Second Thessalonians: The Epistles of the Blessed Hope* (Winona Lake, IN: BMH Books, 1985).

73 Gloag, Paton James. *I Thessalonians* (The Pulpit Commentary; London: Kegan Paul, Trench & Co., 1887).

74 ---. *II Thessalonians* (The Pulpit Commentary; London: Kegan Paul, Trench & Co., 1887).

75 Gorrín Castellanos, Obed. *Primera a los Tesalonicenses--una lectura cubana* (Havana: Consejo Ecuménico de Cuba, 1989).

76 Grayston, Kenneth. *The Letters of Paul to the Philippians and to the Thessalonians* (The Cambridge Bible Commentary: New English Bible; London: Cambridge University Press, 1967).

77 Harris, William Burleigh. *1 & 2 Thessalonians* (Epworth Preacher's Commentary; London: Epworth, 1968).

78 Havener, Ivan. "1 and 2 Thessalonians," *First Thessalonians, Philippians, Philemon, Second Thessalonians, Colossians, Ephesians* (ed. Dianne Bergant and Robert J. Karris; Collegeville Bible Commentary 8; Collegeville, MN: Liturgical Press, 1983) 9-26. Republished in Spanish as *Primera Tesalonicenses, Filipenses, Filemón, Segunda Tesalonicenses, Colosenses, Efesios* (Comentario bíblico de Collegeville; Collegeville, Liturgical Press, 1995).

79 Hendriksen, William. *Exposition of I and II Thessalonians* (New Testament Commentary; Grand Rapids: Baker, 1955).
Republished in Spanish as *1 y 2 Tesalonicenses* (Grand Rapids: Subcomisión de Literatura Cristiana de la Iglesia Cristiana Reformada, 1980).

80 Hendrix, John Dillard. *To Thessalonians with Love* (Nashville: Broadman, 1982).

81 Hiebert, David Edmond. *The Thessalonian Epistles: A Call to Readiness* (Chicago: Moody, 1971).
Republished as *1 & 2 Thessalonians; First Peter; James* (Chicago: Moody, 1982, 1992).

82 Hobbs, Herschel H. "1-2 Thessalonians," *The Broadman Bible Commentary* (ed. Clifton J. Allen; 12 vols.; Nashville: Broadman Press, 1971) 11.257-298.

83 Hogg, Charles Frederick. *The Epistles of Paul the Apostle to the Thessalonians* (Glasgow: Pickering & Inglis, 1914).

84 Holmes, Michael W. *1 & 2 Thessalonians* (NIV Application Commentary; Grand Rapids: Zondervan, 1998).

85 Holtz, Traugott. *Der erste Brief an die Thessalonicher* (Evangelisch-Katholischer Kommentar zum Neuen Testament 13; Zürich: Benziger, 1986).

86 Holtzmann, Heinrich Julius. "Die Briefe an die Thessalonicher," *Handkommentar zum Neuen Testament* (ed. Richard A. Lipsius, Paul W. Schmiedel, and Hans von Soden; Freiburg: Mohr, 1889) 1-46.

87 Horne, Charles M. *The Epistles to the Thessalonians: A Study Manual* (Shield Bible Study Series; Grand Rapids: Baker, 1961).

88 Hubbard, David Allan. *Thessalonians: Life That's Radically Christian* (Waco, TX: Word, 1977).

89 Iovino, Paolo. *La prima lettera ai Tessalonicesi. Introduzione, versione, commento* (Scritti delle origini cristiane 13; Bologna: Dehoniane, 1992).

90 Ironside, Henry Allan. *Addresses on the First and Second Epistles to the Thessalonians* (Nepture, NJ: Loizeaux Brothers, 1947).

91 Jewell, John. *An Exposition upon the Two Epistles of the Apostle Paul to the Thessalonians* (London: B. Wertheim, Aldine Chamers, 1583, 1891).

92 Jowett, Benjamin. *The Epistles of St. Paul to the Thessalonians, Galatians and Romans* (London: J. Murray, 1894).

93 Juel, Donald H. "I Thessalonians," *Galatians, Philippians, Philemon, I Thessalonians* (Edgar Krentz, John Koenig, and Donald H. Juel; Augsburg Commentary on the New Testament; Minneapolis: Augsburg, 1985) 213-255.

94 Kelcy, Raymond C. *The Letters of Paul to the Thessalonians* (The Living Word Commentary 13; Austin, TX: R. B. Sweet, 1968).

95 Kelly, William. *The Epistles of Paul the Apostle to the Thessalonians* (London: Race, 1912).

96 Knoch, Otto B. *1. und 2. Thessalonicherbrief* (Stuttgarter Kleiner Kommentar NT 12; Stuttgart: Verlag Katholisches Bibelwerk, 1987).

97 Koch, August. *Commentar über den ersten Brief des Apostels Paulus an die Thessalonicher* (Berlin: L. Oehmigke, 1849).

98 Krodel, Gerhard. "2 Thessalonians," *Ephesians, Colossians, 2 Thessalonians, The Pastoral Epistles* (J. Paul Sampley, Joseph Burgess, Gerhard Krodel, and Reginald H. Fuller; Proclamation Commentaries; Philadelphia: Fortress, 1978) 73-96.
Republished in a slightly revised version as *The Deutero-Pauline Letters. Ephesians, Colossians, 2 Thessalonians, 1-2 Timothy, Titus* (Minneapolis: Fortress, 1993) 39-58.

99 Kuske, David P. *Thessalonians* (The People's Bible; Milwaukee: Northwestern Publishing, 1984).

100 Kuss, Otto. *Die Thessalonicherbriefe* (Regensburger Neues Testament 7; Regensburg: Pustet, 1959).

101 Laub, Franz. *1. und 2. Thessalonicherbrief* (Die Neue Echter Bibel: Kommentar zum Neuen Testament mit der Einheitsübersetzung 13; Würzburg: Echter, 1985).

102 LaVerdiere, Eugene A. *Invitation to the New Testament. Epistles II. A Commentary on 1 Thessalonians, 2 Thessalonians, 1 Corinthians, 2 Corinthians, Philippians and Philemon with Complete Text from the Jerusalem Bible* (Garden City, NY: Image Books, 1980).

103 Leal, Juan. "Cartas a los Tesalonicenses," *La Sagrada Escritura: Nuevo Testamento* (ed. Professores de la Compañía de Jesús; Biblioteca de Autores Cristianos; 3 vols.; Madrid: La Editorial Católica, 1962) 2.875-952.

104 Lecompte, Cesar. *1 Thessalonicenzen* (Verklaring van een Bijbelgedeelte; Kampen: Kok, 1983).

105 ---. *2 Thessalonicenzen* (Verklaring van een Bijbelgedeelte; Kampen: Kok, 1983).

106 Leeuwen, Jacobus Adrien Cornelius van. *De brievan aan de Thessalonicensen* (Korte verklaring der Heilige Schrift; Kampen: Kok, 1923).

107 Lenski, R. C. H. *The Interpretation of St. Paul's Epistles to the Colossians, to the Thessalonians, to Timothy, to Titus and to Philemon* (Minneapolis: Augsburg, 1937).

108 Lightfoot, Joseph Barber. *Notes on the Epistles of St. Paul* (London/New York: Macmillan, 1904).

109 Lillie, John. *Lectures on the Epistles of Paul to the Thessalonians* (Edinburgh: William Oliphant, 1863).

110 Lineberry, John. *Vital Word Studies in 1 Thessalonians. A Sound Scriptural Presentation based upon the Original Greek Text* (Grand Rapids: Zondervan, 1960).

111 Lueken, Wilhelm. *Der erste Brief an die Thessalonicher* (Die Schriften des Neuen Testaments neu übersetzt und für die Gegenwart erklärt 2; Göttingen: Vandenhoeck & Ruprecht, 1917).

112 ---. *Der zweite Brief an die Thessalonicher* (Die Schriften des Neuen Testaments neu übersetzt und für die Gegenwart erklärt 2; Göttingen: Vandenhoeck & Ruprecht, 1917).

113 Lünemann, Gottlieb. *Critical and Exegetical Handbook to the Epistles of St. Paul to the Thessalonians* (trans. Paton J. Gloag; Critical and Exegetical Commentary on the New Testament; Edinburgh: T. & T. Clark, 1880).
Originally published in German as *Kritisch exegetisches Handbuch über die Briefe an die Thessalonicher* (Kritisch-Exegetischer Kommentar über das Neue Testament 10; Göttingen: Vandenhoeck & Ruprecht, 1878).

114 Macdonald, William. *Letters to the Thessalonians* (Kansas City: Walterick, 1969).

115 Mackintosh, Robert. *Thessalonians and Corinthians: Introduction and Notes* (The Westminster New Testament; New York: Fleming H. Revell, 1909).

116 Maclaren, Alexander. *Second Corinthians, Galatians, Philippians, Colossians, Thessalonians and First Timothy* (Expositions of Holy Scripture 14; Grand Rapids: Eerdmans, 1932).

117 Marín, Francisco. *Evangelio de la Esperanza. Evangelio de la Unidad. Cartas de San Pablo a los Tesalonicenses y a los Filipenses* (Publicaciones de la Universidad Pontificia Comillas; Estudios 13; Madrid: Universidad Pontificia Comillas, 1979).

118 Marshall, I. Howard. *1 and 2 Thessalonians* (New Century Bible; London: Marshall, Morgan & Scott, 1983).

119 Martin, D. Michael. *1, 2 Thessalonians* (New American Commentary 33; Nashville: Broadman & Holman, 1995).

120 Martin, Sydney. *Thessalonians, Timothy, Titus* (Beacon Bible Expositions 10; Kansas City: Beacon Hill, 1977).

121 Marxsen, Willi. *Der erste Brief an die Thessalonicher* (Zürcher Bibelkommentare 11.2; Zürich: Theologischer Verlag, 1979).

122 ---. *Der zweite Thessalonicherbrief* (Zürcher Bibelkommentare 11.2; Zürich: Theologischer Verlag, 1982).

123 Masson, Charles. *Les deux Épîtres de Saint Paul aux Thessaloniciens* (Commentaire du Nouveau Testament 11; Neuchâtel: Delachaux et Niestlé, 1957).

124 McGarvey, John William. *Thessalonians, Corinthians, Galatians and Romans* (The Standard Bible Commentary 3; Cincinnati: Standard Publishing, 1916).

125 Menken, Maarten J. J. *2 Thessalonians: Facing the End with Sobriety* (New Testament Readings; London/New York: Routledge, 1994).

126 Milligan, George. *St. Paul's Epistle to the Thessalonians: The Greek Text with Introduction and Notes* (London: Macmillan, 1908).

127 Moffatt, James. "The First and the Second Epistles of Paul the Apostle to the Thessalonians," *The Expositor's Greek New Testament* (ed. W. Robertson Nicoll; vol. 4;

London/New York: Hodder & Stoughton, 1897; republished, Grand Rapids: Eerdmans, 1980).

128 Montague, George T. "The Letters to the Thessalonians," *The Living Thought of Saint Paul. An Introduction to Pauline Theology through Intensive Study of Key Texts* (Contemporary College Theology Series; Milwaukee: Benzinger, 1966) 13-44.

129 Moore, Arthur Lewis. *1 and 2 Thessalonians* (New Century Bible; Camden, NJ: Nelson, 1969).

130 Morris, Leon. *The Epistles of Paul to the Thessalonians* (Tyndale New Testament Commentaries; Grand Rapids: Eerdmans, 1958).
Republished in Spanish as *Las Cartas a los Tesalonicenses* (Buenos Aires: Ediciones Certeza, 1976).

131 ---. *The First and Second Epistles to the Thessalonians: The English Text with Introduction, Exposition and Notes* (New International Commentary on the New Testament; Grand Rapids: Eerdmans, 1959).

132 *The Navarre Bible: St. Paul's Epistles to the Thessalonians and Pastoral Epistles in the Revised Standard Version and the New Vulgate* (Dublin: Four Courts Press, 1992).
Originally published as *Epístolas de San Pablo a los Tesalonicenses y Epístolas pastorales* (Sagrada Biblia 9; Ediciones Universidad de Navarra, 1989).

133 Neil, William. *The Epistles of Paul to the Thessalonians* (Moffatt New Testament Commentary; London: Hodder & Stoughton, 1950).

134 Núñez, Emilio Antonio. *Constantes en la esperanza. Primera carta a los Tesalonicenses* (Guatemala: TEMA, 1976).

135 Oepke, Albrecht. *Die Briefe an die Thessalonicher* (Göttingen: Vandenhoeck & Ruprecht, 1933).
Republished with minor changes in *Die kleineren Briefe des Apostels Paulus* (Das Neue Testament Deutsch 8; Göttingen: Vandenhoeck & Ruprecht, 1965) 157-187.

136 Olshausen, Hermann. *Biblical Commentary on St. Paul's Epistles to the Galatians, Ephesians, Colossians, and Thessalonians* (Clark's Foreign Theological Library 21; Edinburgh: T. & T. Clark, 1856).

137 Palmer, Earl F. *1 and 2 Thessalonians* (Good News Commentary; San Francisco: Harper & Row, 1983).

138 Parker, Joseph. *The Epistles to the Colossians, Philemon, and Thessalonians* (The Expositor's Library; London: Hodder & Stoughton, 1900).

139 Patterson, Alexander Simpson. *A Brief Commentary on the First Epistle of St. Paul to the Thessalonians* (Edinburgh: Thomas Clark, 1846).

140 Picirilli, Robert E. *1 Thessalonians through Philemon* (Randall House Bible Commentary; Nashville: Randall House, 1990).

141 Plummer, Alfred. *A Commentary on St. Paul's First Epistle to the Thessalonians* (London: Robert Scott, 1918).

142 ---. *A Commentary on St. Paul's Second Epistle to the Thessalonians* (London: Robert Scott, 1918).

143 Ragnarsson, Per-Erik. *Thessalonikerbreven* (Kommentar zum Neuen Testament 13; Stockholm: EFS-Förlaget, 1983).

144 Reese, James M. *1 and 2 Thessalonians* (New Testament Message 16; Wilmington: Michael Glazier, 1979).

145 Reiss, Hermann. *Die beiden Thessalonicherbriefe* (Stuttgarter Bibelhefte; Stuttgart: Quell, 1960).

146 Richard, Earl J. *First and Second Thessalonians* (Sacra Pagina 11; Collegeville, MN: Liturgical Press, 1995).

147 Rigaux, Béda. *Les épîtres aux Thessaloniciens* (Études bibliques; Paris: Gabalda, 1956).

148 Rollock, Robert. *Lectures upon the First and Second Epistles of Paul to the Thessalonians* (Edinburgh: Robert Charteris, 1606).

149 Rolston, Holmes. *The First and Second Letter of Paul to the Thessalonians, the First and Second Letter of Paul to Timothy, the Letter of Paul to Titus, the Letter of Paul to Philemon* (The Layman's Bible Commentary 23; Atlanta: John Knox, 1976).
Originally published as *Thessalonians. Timothy. Titus, Philemon* (London: SCM Press, 1963).

150 Roosen, Antoon. *De Brieven van Paulus aan de Tessalonicenzen* (Het Nieuwe Testament; Rome: Roermond, 1971).

151 ---. *Kerk, Apostolaat, Christelijk Leven. De Tessalonicenzenbrieven* (Van Exegese tot Verkondiging 28; Leuven: Vlaamse Bijbelstichting, 1976).

152 Rossano, Piero. *Lettere ai Tessalonicesi* (La Sacra Bibbia; Rome: Marietti, 1965).

153 Ryrie, Charles Caldwell. *First and Second Thessalonians* (Chicago: Moody, 1959). Republished in Spanish as *1 y 2 Tesalonicenses* (Barcelona: Portavoz Evangélico, 1980).

154 Sadler, Michael Ferrebee. *The Epistles of St. Paul to the Colossians, Thessalonians, and Timothy* (London: George Bell & Sons, 1899).

155 Samuel, Leith. *Awaiting Christ's Return. Study Outlines in Thessalonians* (London/Edinburgh: Marshall, Morgan & Scott, 1961).

156 Saunders, Ernest W. *1 Thessalonians, 2 Thessalonians, Philippians, Philemon* (Knox Preaching Guides; Atlanta: John Knox, 1981).

157 Sánchez, Benjamín Martín. *Primera carta de San Pablo a los Tesalonicenses* (Madrid: Ediciones Paulinas, 1960).

158 Schäfer, Aloys. *Erklärung der zwei Briefe an die Thessalonicher und des Briefes an die Galater* (Die Bücher des Neuen Testamentes 1; Münster: Aschendorff, 1890).

159 Schlatter, D. *Die Briefe an die Kolosser und Thessalonicher* (Stuttgart: Verlag der Vereinsbuchhandlung, 1913).

160 Schmidt, Johann Ernst Christian. *Vermutungen über die beiden Briefe an die Thessalonicher* (Bibliothek für Kritik und Exegese des Neuen Testaments und ältesten Christengeschichte 2/3; Hadamar: Gelehrtenbuchhandlung, 1801).

161 Schmidt, Paul Wilhelm. *Der erste Thessalonicherbrief, neu erklart, nebst einem Excurs über den zweiten gleichnamigen Brief* (Berlin: Georg Reimer, 1885).

162 Schmiedl, Paul Wilhelm. *Die Briefe an die Thessalonicher und an die Korinther* (Freiburg: Mohr, 1891).

163 Schürmann, Heinz. *Der Erste Brief an die Thessalonicher* (Geistliche Schriftlesung 13; Düsseldorf: Patmos, 1962).
Republished in English as *The First Epistle to the Thessalonians* (trans. William Glen-Doepel; London: Burns & Oats, 1969) and in Spanish as *Primera carta a los Tesalonicenses* (Barcelona: Herder, 1984).

164 Simpson, Albert B. *The Epistles of Thessalonians, Timothy, and Titus* (Harrisburg, PA: Christian Publications, 1886).

165 Staab, Karl, and Joseph Freundorfer. *Die Thessalonicherbriefe, die Gefangenschaftsbriefe und die Pastoralbriefe* (Regensburger Neues Testament 7; Regensburg: Friedrich Pustet, 1950).
Republished in Spanish as *Cartas a los Tesalonicenses, cartas de la cautividad, cartas pastorales* (Barcelona: Herder, 1974).

166 Stam, Cornelius Richard. *Commentary on the Epistles of Paul to the Thessalonians* (Chicago: Berean Bible Society, 1984).

167 Steinmann, Alphons. *Die Briefe an die Thessalonicher und Galater* (Die Heilige Schrift des Neuen Testamentes 5; Bonn: Peter Hanstein, 1935).

168 Stevens, William Arnold. *Commentary on the Epistles to the Thessalonians* (American Commentary on the New Testament; Philadelphia: American Baptist Publication Society, 1890).

169 Stott, John R. W. *The Gospel and the End of Time: The Message of 1 & 2 Thessalonians* (Downers Grove, IL: InterVarsity, 1991).

170 Tarazi, Paul Nadim. *1 Thessalonians: A Commentary* (Orthodox Biblical Studies; Crestwood, NY: St. Vladimir's Seminary Press, 1982).

171 Tatford, Frederick A. *Paul's Letters to the Thessalonians* (Neptune, NJ: Loizeaux Brothers, 1919).

172 Thomas, Robert L. "1-2 Thessalonians," *Expositor's Bible Commentary* (ed. Frank E. Gaebelein; 12 vols.; Grand Rapids: Zondervan, 1981) 11.227-337.

173 Thurston, Bonnie Bowman. *Reading Colossians, Ephesians, and 2 Thessalonians. A Literary and Theological Commentary* (Reading the New Testament Series; New York: Crossroad, 1995).

174 Tolbert, Malcolm. *Colossians, Philippians, 1 & 2 Thessalonians, 1 & 2 Timothy, Titus, Philemon* (Layman's Bible Book Commentary 22; Nashville: Broadman, 1980).

175 Trilling, Wolfgang. *Der zweite Brief an die Thessalonicher* (Evangelisch-Katholischer Kommentar zum Neuen Testament 14; Neukirchen-Vluyn: Neukirchener, 1980).

176 Trimaille, Michel. *La première lettre aux Thessaloniciens* (Cahiers évangéliques 39; Paris, 1982).
Republished in Spanish as *La primera carta a los Tesalonicenses* (Cuadernos bíblicos 39; Estella [Navarra]: Verbo Divino, 1982).

177 Vanhoye, Albert. *Esegesi della Prima Lettera ai Tessalonicesi* (Rome: Pontifical Biblical Institute, 1987).

178 Vawter, Bruce. *Introduction to the Pauline Epistles: I Thessalonians. II Thessalonians* (Collegeville, MN: Liturgical Press, 1965).
Republished in Spanish as *Introducción a las cartas paulinas. Primera y Segunda a los Tesalonicenses* (Santander: Sal Terrae, 1966).

179 Verhoef, Eduard. *Tessalonicenzen. Een praktische bijbelverklaring* (Tekst en Toelichting; Kampen: Kok, 1995).

180 Vosté, Jacques-Marie. *Commentarius in epistolas ad Thessalonicenses* (Rome: F. Ferrari, 1917).

181 Walvoord, John F. *The Thessalonian Epistles* (Findlay, OH: Dunham, 1955).

182 Wanamaker, Charles A. *The Epistles to the Thessalonians* (New International Greek Testament Commentary; Grand Rapids: Eerdmans, 1990).

183 Ward, Ronald A. *Commentary on 1 & 2 Thessalonians* (Waco, TX: Word, 1973).

184 Weatherly, Jon Allen. *1 & 2 Thessalonians* (The College Press NIV Commentary; Joplin: MO: College Press, 1996).

185 Weider, Bjarne O. *Fortolkning til Tessalonikerbrevene* (Oslo: Luther Forlag/Lunde Forlag, 1974).

186 Weinrich, George. *Explicatio Posterioris Epistolae D. Pauli, Quam Thessalonicensibus inprimis nuncupavit Apostolus* (Lipsiae: Sumptibus Thomae Schüreri, 1615).

187 Whiteley, Denys Edward Hugh. *Thessalonians in the Revised Standard Version, With Introduction and Commentary* (New York/London: Oxford University Press, 1969).

188 Williams, David John. *1 and 2 Thessalonians* (New International Biblical Commentary 12; Peabody, MA: Hendrickson, 1992).

189 Wilson, Geoffrey B. *1 & 2 Thessalonians: A Digest of Reformed Comment* (Carlisle, PA: Banner of Truth, 1982).

190 Wohlenberg, Gustav. *Der erste und zweite Thessalonicherbrief* (Kommentar zum Neuen Testament 12; Leipzig: Deichert, 1903).

191 Wrightman, Paul. "I and II Thessalonians," *Paul's Early Letters. From Hope through Faith to Love. A Study Guide to I and II Thessalonians, Galatians, I & II Corinthians* (New York: Alba House, 1983) 3-12.

192 Zedda, Silverio P. *Prima Lettura di San Paolo.* II. *Lettere ai Tessalonicesi, Prima ai Corinti, Galati, Romani* (Turin: Tecnograph, 1958).

B. Dictionary and Encyclopedia Articles

193 Bassler, Jouette M. "I and II Thessalonians," *The Books of the Bible* (New York: Scribners, 1989) 311-318.

194 ---. "The Second Letter of Paul to the Thessalonians," *The HarperCollins Study Bible. New Revised Standard Version. With the Apocryphal/Deuterocanonical Books* (ed. Wayne A. Meeks; New York: HarperCollins, 1993) 2225-2228.

195 Beare, F. W. "Thessalonians, Second Letter to the," *The Interpreter's Dictionary of the Bible* (ed. George Arthur Buttrick; 12 vols.; Nashville: Abingdon, 1962) 4.625-629.

196 ---. "Thessalonians, First Letter to the," *The Interpreter's Dictionary of the Bible* (ed. George Arthur Buttrick; 12 vols.; Nashville: Abingdon, 1962) 4.621-625.

197 Beavis, Mary Anne. "2 Thessalonians," *Searching the Scriptures. Volume Two: A Feminist Exegetical Commentary* (ed. Elisabeth Schüssler Fiorenza; New York: Crossroad, 1994) 265-271.

198 Collins, Raymond F. "The First Letter to the Thessalonians," *The New Jerome Biblical Commentary* (ed. Raymond E. Brown, Joseph A. Fitzmyer, and Roland E. Murphy; Englewood Cliffs, NJ: Prentice Hall, 1989) 772-779.

199 Donfried, Karl Paul. "Thessalonians, the First Letter of Paul to the," *Harper's Bible Dictionary* (ed. Paul J. Achtemeier *et al.*; San Francisco: Harper & Row, 1985) 1063-1064.

200 ---. "Thessalonians, the Second Letter of Paul to the Thessalonians," *Harper's Bible Dictionary* (ed. Paul J. Achtemeier *et al.*; San Francisco: Harper & Row, 1985) 1064-1065.

201 ---. "Thessalonica," *Harper's Bible Dictionary* (ed. Paul J. Achtemeier *et al.*; San Francisco: Harper & Row, 1985) 1065-1066.

202 Fatum, Lone. "1 Thessalonians," *Searching the Scriptures. Volume Two: A Feminist Commentary* (ed. Elisabeth Schüssler Fiorenza; New York: Crossroad, 1994) 250-264.

203 Feuillet, André. "Parousie," *Supplément au Dictionnaire de la Bible* (Paris: Letouzey et Ané, 1960) 6.1331-1419.

204 Forestell, J. Terence. "The Letters to the Thessalonians," *The Jerome Biblical Commentary* (ed. Raymond E. Brown, Joseph A. Fitzmyer, and Roland E. Murphy; London: Geoffrey Chapman, 1968) 227-235.
Republished in Spanish as "Cartas a los Tesalonicenses," *Comentario Bíblico San Jerónimo* (ed. Raymond E. Brown, Joseph A. Fitzmyer, and Roland E. Murphy; Madrid: Ediciones Cristiandad, 1972) 575-596.

205 Giblin, Charles Homer. "1 Thessalonians," *In Hope of God's Glory. Pauline Theological Perspectives* (New York: Herder & Herder, 1970) 3-26.

206 ---. "2 Thessalonians," *In Hope of God's Glory. Pauline Theological Perspectives* (New York: Herder & Herder, 1970) 27-44.

207 ---. "The Second Letter to the Thessalonians," *New Jerome Biblical Commentary* (ed. Raymond E. Brown, Joseph A. Fitzmyer, and Roland E. Murphy; Englewood Cliffs, NJ: Prentice Hall, 1989) 871-875.

208 Hurd, John C., Jr. "Thessalonians, First Letter to the," *Interpreter's Dictionary of the Bible* (ed. K. Crim; Nashville: Abingdon, 1976) 4.900.

209 ---. "Thessalonians, Second Letter to the," *Interpreter's Dictionary of the Bible* (ed. K. Crim; Nashville: Abingdon, 1976) 4.900-901.

210 Krentz, Edgar. "1 Thessalonians," *The HarperCollins Study Bible. New Revised Standard Version. With the Apocryphal/Deuterocanonical Books* (ed. Wayne A. Meeks; New York: HarperCollins, 1993) 2218-2224.

211 Marxsen, Willi. "The First & Second Epistles to the Thessalonians," *Introduction to the New Testament: An Approach to its Problems* (trans. G. Buswell; Oxford: Blackwell, 1968) 30-44.

212 McKinnish Bridges, Linda. "First Thessalonians," *Mercer Commentary on the Bible* (ed. Watson E. Mills and Richard F. Wilson; Macon, GA: Mercer University Press, 1995) 1241-1246.

213 ---. "Second Thessalonians," *Mercer Commentary on the Bible* (ed. Watson E. Mills and Richard F. Wilson; Macon, GA: Mercer University Press, 1995) 1247-1251.

214 Neil, William. "I and II Thessalonians," *Peake's Commentary on the Bible* (ed. Matthew Black and Harold H. Rowley; London/New York: Nelson, 1962) 996-1000.

215 Oberhummer, Eugen. "Thessalonike," *Paulus Realencyclopädie für der classischen Altertumswissenschaft* (ed. W. Kroll and K. Mittelhaus; Stuttgart: Metzler, 1936) 143-163.

216 Orchard, J. Bernard. "1 and 2 Thessalonians," *A New Catholic Commentary on Holy Scripture* (ed. Reginald C. Fuller; London: Nelson, 1969) 1204-1208.

217 Reicke, Bo. "Thessalonicherbriefe," *Die Religion in Geschichte und Gegenwart* (ed. K. Galling; Tübingen: Mohr/Siebeck, 1962) 851-853.

218 Simpson, John W., Jr. "Thessalonians, Letters to the," *Dictionary of Paul and His Letters* (ed. Gerald F. Hawthorne, Ralph P. Martin, and Daniel G. Reid; Downers Grove, IL: InterVarsity, 1993) 932-939.

C. General Treatments

219 Beare, F. W. "The First Letter of St. Paul to the Thessalonians," *Canadian Journal of Theology* 8.1 (1962) 4-11.

220 Blair, Edward P. "The First Epistle to the Thessalonians," *Interpretation* 2 (1948) 208-217.

221 Flood, Edmund. "Reading Thessalonians," *Clergy Review* 69 (1984) 87-91.

222 Fransen, Iréné. "Der Tag des Herrn. Erster und zweiter Brief an die Thessalonicher," *Bibel und Liturgie* 25 (1957) 7-13; 67-74.

223 Godet, Fréderic Louis. "The First Love and Hope in Thessalonica," *The Expositor, 3rd Series* 1 (1885) 81-101.

224 Goodspeed, Edgar J. "The Epistles to the Thessalonians," *Biblical World* 34 (1909) 48-56.

225 Havener, Ivan. "First and Second Thessalonians: An Introduction," *Bible Today* 26 (1988) 324-327.

226 Howard, W. F. "The Message of the Epistles. I Thessalonians," *Expository Times* 44 (1933) 357-362.

227 Krentz, Edgar. "Roman Hellenism and Paul's Gospel," *The Bible Today* 26.6 (1988) 328-337.

228 LaVerdiere, Eugene A. "Introducing First Thessalonians," *The Bible Today* 12 (1974) 95-103.

229 Marxsen, Willi. "Unterwegs. Gedanken zum 1. Thessalonicherbrief," *Mutuum Colloquium. Festschrift für H. Kittel* (P. C. Block *et al.*; Dortmund, 1972) 241-245.

230 Míguez, Néstor O. "La misión de Pablo entre los gentiles--La 'autobiographia' de Pablo y la estrategia evangelizadora," *El Estandarte Evangélico* 107.4 (1989) 6-7.

231 ---. "La misión de Pablo entre los gentiles--Primera epistola a los Tesalonisences," *El Estandarte Evangélico* 107.3 (1989) 7-8.

232 Moretti, A. "Le due lettere ai Tessalonicesi," *Il messaggio della salvezza. Corso complete di studi biblici* (ed. Giovanni Canfora; Turin: Editrice Elle Di Ci, 1964) 5.748-785.

233 Robertson, J. Armitage. "The Message of the Epistles. 2 Thessalonians," *Expository Times* 44 (1933) 407-408.

234 Spadafora, Francesco. "I e II lettera ai Tessalonicesi," *Revista bíblica* 1 (1953) 5-24.

235 ---. "San Paolo: Le lettere (Parte I)--Le due lettere ai Tessalonicesi," *Renovatio* 21.1 (1986) 115-137.

D. Surveys of Research

236 Collins, Raymond F. "Recent Scholarship on the First Letter to the Thessalonians," *Studies on the First Letter to the Thessalonians* (Bibliotheca ephemeridum theologicarum lovaniensium 66; Leuven: Leuven University Press, 1984) 3-75.

237 Hilgenfeld, Adolf H. "Die Paulus-Briefe und ihre neuesten Bearbeitungen," *Zeitschrift für wissenschaftliche Theologie* 9 (1866) 293-316.

238 Richard, Earl J. "Contemporary Research on 1 (& 2) Thessalonians," *Biblical Theology Bulletin* 20.3 (1990) 107-115.

239 Trilling, Wolfgang. "Die beiden Briefe des Apostels Paulus an die Thessalonicher: Eine Forschungsübersicht," *Aufstieg und Niedergang der römischen Welt. II* (ed. Wolfgang Haase; Berlin: de Gruyter, 1987) 25.3365-3403.

E. Meditations

240 Assonville, Victor Eduard. *Sy koms om middernag. 10 preke uit die Thessalonisense-briewe* (Potchefstroom: Marnix, 1977).

241 Barth, Gerhard. "Meditation über 1 Thessalonicher 1,2-10," *Göttinger Predigtmeditationen* 30 (1975/76) 377-383.

242 Blum, Paul. "Estudios homiléticos," *Vox Concordiana--Suplemento Teológico* 4.2 (1988) 48-49.

243 Brillet, G. "(1 Th 4,1-7) Dieu veut nous sanctifier dans le Christ," *Assembleés du Seigneur* 28 (1963) 16-26.

244 Casalis, Georges. "Meditation über 1 Thessalonicher 5,1-11," *Göttinger Predigtmeditationen* 18 (1963/64) 9-12.

245 Charpentier, Étienne. "La foi vécue est contagieuse. 1 Th 1,5c-10," *Assemblées du Seigneur* 61 (1972) 10-17.

246 ---. "L'action de grâce du pasteur. 1 Th 1,1-5b," *Assemblées du Seigneur* 60 (1975) 10-15.

247 Cullmann, Oscar. "Andacht zur Eröffnung der S.N.T.S. am 30. August 1965 in Heidelberg," *New Testament Studies* 12 (1966) 140-144.

Republished in English as "Meditation," *Concordia Theological Monthly* 39 (1968) 6-9, and French as "Méditation sur I Th. 5.19-21," in Oscar Cullmann, *Des sources de l'Évangile à la formation de la théologie chrétienne* (Neuchatel: Delachaux et Niestlé, 1969) 176-180.

248 Delorme, Jean. "Sur un texte de S. Paul (I Thess. IV, 13-17). L'avènement du Seigneur et la présence des fidèles," *L'Ami du Clergé* 65 (1955) 247-251.

249 Fuchs, Ernst. "Meditation über 1 Thessalonicher 1,2-10," *Göttinger Predigtmeditationen* 18 (1963/64) 299-303.

250 Gloege, G. "Meditation über 1 Thess 4,1-7,(8)," *Göttinger Predigtmeditationen* 22 (1967/68) 142-154.

251 Hempel, J. "Meditation über 1 Thess 4,13-18," *Göttinger Predigtmeditationen* 22 (1967/68) 438-443.

252 ---. "Meditation über 1 Thess 5,1-11," *Göttinger Predigtmeditationen* 24 (1969/70) 4-9.

253 Krause, O. "Meditation über 1 Thessalonicher 1,2-10," *Göttinger Predigtmeditationen* 24 (1969/70) 353-359.

254 ---. "Meditation über 1 Thess 4,1-7," *Göttinger Predigtmeditationen* 28 (1973/74) 147-154.

255 Langevin, Paul-Émile. "Conseils et prière. 1 Thess 5,16-24," *Assemblées du Seigneur* 7 (1969) 34-39.

256 ---. "Nous serons pour toujours avec le Seigneur: 1 Th 4,13-18," *Assemblées du Seigneur* 63 (1971) 13-19.

257 Reicke, Bo. "Paulus über den Tag des Herrn: Homiletisch orientierte Auslegung von 1 Thess 5:1-11," *Theologische Zeitschrift* 44 (1988) 91-96.

258 Rigaux, Béda. "L'Antichrist," *Assemblées du Seigneur* 6 (1965) 97-108.

259 Schellong, D. "Meditation über 1 Thess 4,13-18," *Göttinger Predigtmeditationen* 28 (1973/74) 460-467.

260 Schmithals, Walter. "1. Thessalonicher 4,13-14," *Göttinger Predigtmeditationen* 77 (1988) 194-198.

261 ---. "Meditation über 1 Thess 5,1-5," *Göttinger Predigtmeditationen* 30 (1975/76) 7-12.

262 Traub, H. "Meditation über 1 Thess 4,1-7," *Göttinger Predigtmeditationen* 16 (1961/62) 125-130.

263 Vanderhaegen, Jean. "Le désir de l'Apôtre. 1 Th 3,12-4,2," *Assemblées du Seigneur* 5 (1969) 62-70.

264 Weber, Otto. "2. Thessalonicher 3,6-13," *Göttinger Predigtmeditationen* 30 (1975/76) 383-386.

F. Bibliographic References

265 Collins, Raymond F. "Bibliography," *Studies on the First Letter to the Thessalonians* (Bibliotheca ephemeridum theologicarum lovaniensium 66; Leuven: Leuven University Press, 1984) 385-401.

266 ---. "1 Thessalonians," *Pauline Theology 1: Thessalonians, Philippians, Galatians, Philemon* (ed. Jouette M. Bassler; Minneapolis: Fortress, 1991) 272-276.

267 Krentz, Edgar. "2 Thessalonians," *Pauline Theology 1: Thessalonians, Philippians, Galatians, Philemon* (ed. Jouette M. Bassler; Minneapolis: Fortress, 1991) 276-279.

II. Special Topics Related to 1 and 2 Thessalonians

A. The City of Thessalonica

268 Burton, Ernest DeWitt. "The Politarchs," *American Journal of Theology* 2 (1898) 598-632.

Although the word πολιτάρχης, used twice in Acts' description of Paul's ministry in Thessalonica (Acts 17:6, 8), does not occur elsewhere in extant Greek literature, this noun and its verb form have been found in seventeen (plus likely two more) inscriptions. With respect to geographic distribution, thirteen of these inscriptions belong to Macedonia and five specifically to Thessalonica. It is clear that Thessalonica had politarchs from the beginning of the first century to the middle of the second. Five or six politarchs served in office at any given time.

269 Davies, Paul E. "The Macedonian Scene of Paul's Journeys," *Biblical Archaeologist* 26.3 (1963) 91-106.

A review of the historical and archaeological data relating to the cities of Neapolis, Philippi, Amphipolis, Apolonia and Thessalonica illumines Paul's travels and ministry activities in Macedonia. The complex world which Paul experienced in Macedonia possessed a rich civilization and a developed pagan society.

270 Donfried, Karl Paul. "The Cults of Thessalonica and the Thessalonian Correspondence," *New Testament Studies* 31.3 (1985) 336-356.

The starting point for interpreting the Thessalonian correspondence is the reconstruction of the interrelated cultic (both religious and civic) and historical background of Thessalonica, particularly the strong Roman presence and domination at the time of Paul. The Thessalonians who were attracted to the Pauline mission grew up in a city filled with mystery cults and royal theology. For this reason Paul skillfully selects his terminology for protreptic purposes, involving both continuities and discontinuities with his readers' past pagan practices.

271 Edson, Charles. "Cults of Thessalonica (Macedonia III)," *Harvard Theological Review* 41.3 (1948) 153-204.

This survey of Greek inscriptions illumines the history, membership, practices, and significance of four cults of Thessalonica: (1) the Asiani--a cult likely associated with Dionysus; (2) the cult of Dionysus; (3) the Ἱεραφόροι συνκλῖται--a well-defined group of functionaries associated with the municipal cult of the Egyptian gods at Thessalonica who chose to form themselves also into a private club for purposes of social interaction under the tutelage of the god Anubis; and (4) the Cabiric cult.

272 ---. "Macedonia," *Harvard Studies in Classical Philology* 51 (1940) 125-136.

An inscription by Philip V is the first certain evidence for the cult of Heracles

Kynagidas in pre-Roman Macedonia. A survey of other inscriptions reveals the presence of the following five state cults and priesthoods in Thessalonica and their probable date of origin: (1) Priest of the Gods (316 BCE); (2) Priest of Zeus Eleutherios and Rome (148 BCE); (3) Priest of Rome and the Benefactor Romans (42-41 BCE); (4) Priest and Agonothete of Augustus (27 BCE); and (5) Priest and Agonothete of the Divine (Aurelius) Fulvus (138-139 CE).

273 Elliger, Winfried. "Thessaloniki," *Paulus in Griechenland: Philippi, Thessaloniki, Athen, Korinth* (Stuttgarter Bibelstudien 92/93; Stuttgart: Verlag Katholisches Bibelwerk, 1978) 78-116.

The discussion of Thessalonica includes the following subjects: the founding of the city, inscriptions of Egyptian cults, the city under Roman rule, politarchs, cults, archaeology, the palace of Galarius, and the early Christian basilica. The city of Berea is also discussed.

274 Evans, Robert Maxwell. *Eschatology and Ethics: A Study of Thessalonica and Paul's Letters to the Thessalonians* (Princeton, NJ: McMahon, 1968).

A thorough examination of Thessalonica--its history, geography, political situation, economic structure, social and religious context--explains why some in that city responded to the eschatological aspect of Paul's preaching as an answer to their frustrations and fears. The pressure to which the young church was subjected led them to emphasize eschatology and also to distort it. Although an eschatological consciousness provided a positive incentive to the church to perform its daily tasks in a manner appropriate to its returning Lord, it also caused some in the congregation to withdraw from the responsibilities of human life. In spite of the dangers evident in Thessalonica, Paul makes it plain that eschatology and ethics belong together.

275 Gill, David W. J. "Macedonia," *The Book of Acts in Its First Century Setting*. II. *The Book of Acts in Its Graeco-Roman Setting* (ed. David W. J. Gill and Conrad Gempf; Grand Rapids: Eerdmans, 1994) 397-417.

Paul's travels through Macedonia helped to establish key Christian communities at Philippi, Thessalonica, and Berea. The first two of these cities, located on the *Via Egnatia*, were strategic locations and would have helped the spread of the Christian message westward to Rome. Macedonians are also key figures as Paul's companions, and their names suggest that they may have come from the elite of the province.

276 Hammond, Nicholas Geoffrey Lempriére. *A History of Macedonia, I-II* (Oxford: Clarendon Press, 1979).

277 Hemberg, Bengt. *Die Kabiren* (Uppsala: Almquist & Wiksells, 1950).

Although there is limited inscriptional evidence concerning the Cabiric cult, it was known from 200 BCE in Larisa. It later spread to Thessalonica, where it probably was taken over in later Christian worship. By the third century CE, the Cabiric cult became the chief cult of the city.

278 Hendrix, Holland Lee. "Benefactor/Patron Networks in the Urban Environment: Evidence from Thessalonica," *Semeia* 56 (1991) 39-58.

Network analysis provides a useful means of evaluating both the structures and the dynamics of social relations in Greco-Roman society. In so doing, it may also offer further insights on the development of Christianity, particularly the extent to which it did or did not adapt socially to organizational patterns in the environment. A study of four cases of benefactor/patron networks known from epigraphic or literary remains shows that in Roman Thessalonica there developed specific hierarchies of benefaction structures which operated as networks between individuals, groups and/or institutions, and the Roman imperial power. Significantly, the inscriptions also show religious elements in linking these networks of social relations to the divine realm. Finally, the dynamic qualities of these network relations serve to promote the individual actors within them by connecting them to larger spheres of influence and power.

279 ---. "Beyond 'Imperial Cult' and 'Cults of Magistrates,'" *SBL 1986 Seminar Papers* (ed. Kent Harold Richards; SBL Seminar Papers 25; Atlanta: Scholars Press, 1986) 301-308.

However much Greeks may have modeled honors for Romans and emperors on cults of the gods, in most cases, they were careful in distancing emperors from gods. In Thessalonica, whether the honoree was a magistrate, important Roman or even an emperor, it was the norm to honor that person as human and not divine. Terms such as "imperial cult," "emperor worship," and "cults of magistrate" wrongly emphasize primarily divine or divine-like honors, only one dimension of the larger phenomenon of honorific traditions extended to include Romans. To continue to use these terms invites an unwarranted bifurcation between specific religious activity and the more inclusive cultural processes from which such practices derived their significance.

280 ---. "Thessalonians Honor Romans" (Unpublished Ph.D. Dissertation; Cambridge, MA: Harvard University, 1984).

The history of honors given to Romans by inhabitants of Thessalonica during the second and first centuries BCE and the first century CE sheds light on the city's religious history and, in particular, on religious aspects of the residents' regard for Romans. Terms such as "cults of magistrates" and "imperial cult" are of limited value in describing and explaining the history of Thessalonica's honors for Romans. These terms obscure the precise objects of honors and the reasons they were granted. The use of these terms may also misrepresent the nature of religious activity undertaken for particular Romans and emperors, and disregards the honorific context of such religious behavior. Categories of Roman honorands at Thessalonica became increasingly differentiated as part of complex but broadly unified traditions derived ultimately from civic honors to foreign benefactors.

281 ---. "Thessalonica," *Archaeological Resources for New Testament Studies. A Collection of Slides on Culture and Religion in Antiquity* (ed. Helmut Koester and Holland L. Hendrix; Philadelphia: Fortress, 1987) 1.1-49.

This slide set contains pictures and accompanying descriptions and bibliography of various ruins, inscriptions, maps and reconstructions related to Thessalonica.

282 Horsley, Greg H. R. "The Politarchs," *The Book of Acts in Its First Century Setting.* II. *The Book of Acts in Its Graeco-Roman Setting* (ed. David W. J. Gill and Conrad Gempf; Grand Rapids: Eerdmans, 1994) 419-431.

The wealth of archaeological discoveries in Macedonia in the past quarter-century has added considerably to our knowledge of the office of politarchs. In fact, the discoveries have been so great that publications about the politarchs prior to 1960 are now largely superseded. There are as many as seventy non-literary references to politarchs, twenty eight of which are attested from Thessalonica. This office was an annual magistracy which could be held more than once. In terms of function, politarchs had administrative responsibilities (e.g., convening the βουλή ["council"] and introducing motions to it) and judicial authority to maintain peace and order. Although the number of politarchs serving simultaneously in Thessalonica was five until the late first century BCE, after this time the size of the college varied from three to perhaps seven. It is most unlikely that the Aristarchus of Acts 19:29 and 20:4 was the politarch of this same name listed in several inscriptions from Thessalonica.

283 Johnson, Sherman E. "The Apostle Paul in Macedonia," *Lexington Theological Quarterly* 18.3 (1983) 75-83.

A survey of the geographical, political, archaeological and cultural data of Macedonia illumines the historical and religious context of the churches founded in Macedonia by Paul, especially the churches in Philippi and Thessalonica.

284 Koester, Helmut. "Archäologie und Paulus in Thessalonike," *Religious Propoganda and Missionary Competition in the New Testament World: Essays Honoring Dieter Georgi* (ed. Lukas Bormann, Kelly Del Tredici, and Angela Standhartinger; Novum Testamentum Supplements 74; Leiden: Brill, 1994) 393-404.

The archaeological finds from Thessalonica are slim. The often-referred to inscriptions about the politarchs of Thessalonica show that the author of Acts had a good local knowledge, but says nothing about the mission of Paul. The evidence for the existence of a Jewish community in Thessalonica is a fourth-century Greek inscription with two letters in Hebraic/Samaritan script. The inscription is important for showing the establishment of a diaspora Samaritan community in early Christian times, but it has no bearing on whether Paul preached in a Samaritan synagogue. Our knowledge of Gentile religion at the time of Paul is not much better. Attempts to create a direct line from archaeology to the New Testament or other early Christian texts fail in three fundamental and fatal ways: these attempts lack factual statements coming from archaeology; they fail to understand the cultural and religious dimensions of the Greco-Roman world; and it remains unclear what early Christian texts such archaeological finds are supposed to be able to interpret. Examples from Thessalonica such as the third-century CE bronze statue of Caesar, the relief of the triumphal arch of Galerius, the Roman market from the second century, or certain inscriptions, while they may prove the existence of certain types of Hellenistic religions, provide no key to the rituals and popularity of these religions.

285 Laourdas, B., and C. I. Makaronas, ed. *Ancient Macedonia I: Papers Read at the First International Symposium Held in Thessaloniki, 26-29 August 1968* (Thessaloniki: Institute for Balkan Studies, 1970).

286 ---. *Ancient Macedonia II: Papers Read at the Second International Symposium Held in Thessaloniki, 19-24 August 1973* (Thessaloniki: Institute for Balkan Studies, 1977).

287 ---. *Ancient Macedonia III: Papers Read at the Third International Symposium Held in Thessaloniki, 21-25 September 1977* (Thessaloniki: Institute for Balkan Studies, 1983).

288 Lifschitz, B., and J. Schiby. "Une synagogue samaritaine à Thessalonique," *Revue Biblique* 75 (1968) 368-378.

A bilingual inscription in Samaritan characters and Greek, carved on marble, dating to the fourth century and discovered in 1954, attests to a Samaritan community in Thessalonica. Lines 1 and 15 are in Samaritan, but the bulk of the inscription is a quotation from Num 6:22-27, which follows the Samaritan Pentateuch rather than the Septuagint. An edition with textual notes is offered here.

289 Makaronas, Charles I. "Via Egnatia and Thessalonike," *Studies Presented to David Moore Robinson on His Seventieth Birthday* (ed. George E. Mylonas; 2 vols.; St. Louis: Washington University Press, 1951) 1.380-388.

The *Via Egnatia*, in its course from Pella, crossed the Echedoros river at the point where the modern bridge now stands and reached the Golden Gate, near the modern Vardar square. The eastern section of the ancient highway followed the same course as the modern road of Thessalonica-Kavala. The *Via Egnatia* did not go through the center of the city of Thessalonica. The great thoroughfare which today traverses the city from west to east nowhere in our traditions is referred to by the name of *Egnatia*, that is, by the name, which it now bears, and which is due to an error that has prevailed to our own day.

290 Merkelbach, Reinhold. "Zwei Texte aus dem Serapeum zu Thessalonike," *Zeitschrift für Papyrologie und Epigraphik* 10 (1973) 45-54.

Two new inscriptions have been published in *IG* X 2.1. They are both from the Serapeum of Thessalonica, one concerning Osirus and the other Serapis, recounting his wonderful deeds in healing others.

291 Papazoglou, Fanoula. *Les villes de Macédoine à l'époque romaine* (Bulletin de correspondance hellénique; Supplement 16; Paris: de Boccard, 1988).

292 ---. "Quelques aspects de l'histoire de la province de Macédoine," *Aufstieg und Niedergang der römischen Welt* 2.7.1 (ed. H. Temporini and W. Haase; Berlin: de Gruyter, 1979) 302-369.

Economic prosperity, commercial development, and widespread peace characterized the Macedonian area, including the city of Thessalonica, after the civil war between Mark Antony and Octavian through the first century, with the city and region being reorganized in a major administrative move in 27 BCE and then returned to senatorial control with Thessalonica, the capital of the region, in 44 CE. Also discussed are the governors of the province during the Republican period, the army, and city and regional development.

293 Purvis, James D. "The Paleography of the Samaritan Inscription from Thessaloniki," *Bulletin of the American Schools of Oriental Research* 221 (1976) 121-123.

The Samaritan inscription from Thessalonica is bilingual, with seventeen lines in Greek (lines 2-14, 16-19) and two in Samaritan Hebrew (lines 1, 15). The text consists of the priestly benediction from Num 6:22-27 and a concluding eulogia by a person named "Sirika." There are a sufficient number of forms corresponding to types known from early inscriptions to place this inscription in the Byzantine period, ca. the fourth-sixth century.

294 Robert, Louis. "Les Inscriptions de Thessalonique," *Revue de Philologie* 34 (1974) 180-246.

This review of *Inscriptiones Graecae*, X, part 2, fascicule 1, *Inscriptiones Thessalonicae et viciniae* (ed. Charles Edson; Berlin: de Gruyter, 1972), examines the contribution of the volume and offers numerous comments of various types. These observations not only address the edition itself but also individual texts, proposing other readings and interpretations. There is a transcription of No. 126, which is an inscription that refers to a politarch at Thessalonica (see Acts 17:5-6). The editor of the volume claims that the inscription was written in the second century CE.

295 Rossano, Piero. "Note archeologiche sulla antica Tessalonica," *Revista bíblica* 6.3 (1958) 242-247.

Archaeological data confirm, despite the errors of previous scholars, the location of Thessalonica and the fact that Paul and his co-workers followed the *Via Egnatia* to this key Macedonian city. It also confirms the existence of a temple erected in the third century BCE and dedicated to Serapis and other Egyptian gods (Isis, Osiris, Anubis), as well as the existence of a Roman necropolis. The dimensions of the remains as well as the inscriptions in the temple attest to the large number of devotees to the Egyptian gods and also demonstrate that the city was the regional center of the Imperial cult of Rome (see Acts 18:12-17; 1 Thess 2:14; 5:3; 2 Thess 2:4). These archaeological data explain and underline the difficult situation which the first preachers of the gospel encountered in Thessalonica.

296 Sakellariou, M. B., ed. *Macedonia: 4000 Years of Greek History and Civilization* (Greek Lands in History; Athens: Ekdotike Athenon, 1983).

297 Schuler, Carl. "The Macedonian Politarchs," *Classical Philology* 55 (1960) 90-100.

The number of inscriptions testifying to the ancient Macedonian office of the politarchs has more than doubled since the turn of the century. An examination of these inscriptions reveals much about this office. The politarchate was widespread in Macedonia and the number of politarchs varied from city to city and from time to time. Where there were colleges of politarchs, there was likely to be a presiding officer. The politarchs, who could simultaneously hold other offices, were the chief administrative and executive officers of their respective cities or communities. They had some kind of judicial authority, although the precise nature of this authority cannot be ascertained. The politarchate was an annual magistracy and the same person could hold office more than once. An unresolved issue concerns the date when the politarchate was instituted in Macedonia: either the monarchical period or, more likely, that of the Romans.

298 Tov, E. "Une inscription grecque d'origine samaritaine à Thessalonique," *Revue Biblique* 81 (1974) 394-399.

The character of the biblical text (Num 6:22-27) of the bilingual (Greek and Hebrew) inscription found in a synagogue at Thessalonica and published by Lifschitz and Schiby (288) is such that it is a revised version of the Septuagint, very near that of the Hebrew text, but occasionally different from the Masoretic Text.

299 Vickers, Michael J. "Hellenistic Thessaloniki," *Journal of Hellenic Studies* 92 (1972) 156-170.

The plan of Thessalonica was laid out at the time of the city's foundation by Cassander in ca. 316 BCE and has close parallels with the plans of other early Hellenistic cities. There was possibly an agora in the upper city from the beginning, but the principal, commercial agora of the Hellenistic city was probably closer to the sea. A large open space to the west was possibly a "sacred area" in Hellenistic times, but the only religious center whose site is known with any degree of certainty is the Serapeum. A gymnasium is known to have existed to the north of the city from the late Hellenistic period at least, and a nearby stadium probably goes back to this time period as well. In common with many other Hellenistic cities there is an acropolis incorporated in the city wall, but the fortifications of Thessalonica are slightly anomalous in that the lower stretches of the east and west walls run parallel with some of the streets of the city plan.

300 ---. "Therme and Thessaloniki," *Ancient Macedonian Studies in Honor of Charles F. Edson* (Thessaloniki: Institute for Balkan Studies, 1981) 327-333.

301 ---. "Towards Reconstruction of the Town Planning of Roman Thessaloniki," *Ancient Macedonia I: Papers Read at the First International Symposium Held in Thessaloniki, 26-29 August 1968* (ed. B. Laourdas and C. I. Makaronas; 2 vols.; Thessaloniki: Institute for Balkan Studies, 1970) 239-251.

Thessalonica was planned as a Hellenistic city, according to the two principles that seaports were usually built following the line of the seafront and that main streets follow contour lines. The alignment of the streets in the northern part of the city departs noticeably from that of the southern part, due to an expansion of the city during the Roman period. In establishing a relative chronology of the planning of the various parts of the city, the following building structures need to be considered: Serapeion, Temple of the Imperial Cult, North Agora, Galerian building, Exedra, Vardar Gate, Palace, Arch of Galerius, Nymphaeum, Rotunda, Hippodrome, Galerian walls, and Theodosian walls.

302 Witt, Rex E. "The Egyptian Cults in Ancient Macedonia," *Ancient Macedonia II: Papers Read at the Second International Symposium Held in Thessaloniki, 19-24 August 1973* (ed. B. Laourdas and C. I. Makaronas; 2 vols.; Thessaloniki: Institute for Balkan Studies, 1977) 1.324-333.

There can be no doubt that the religion of Egypt had taken firm hold in northern Greece, as it did elsewhere in Greek territory. The god-fearing Greeks whom Paul is stated to have converted at Thessalonica would have reason to compare his new gospel in closest detail with the old cults which they had forsaken. His terminology, most skillfully chosen for protreptic purposes, would have reminded them of Egyptian worship. It may well be that Paul's reference to the "lawless one" in 2 Thess 2:3-5 has in mind a Thessalonian cult in which emperor worship was combined with the cult of Isis and Serapis.

303 ---. "The Kabeiroi in Ancient Macedonia," *Ancient Macedonia II: Papers Read at the Second International Symposium Held in Thessaloniki, 19-24 August 1973* (ed. B. Laourdas and C. I. Makaronas; 2 vols.; Thessaloniki: Institute for Balkan Studies, 1977) 2.67-80.

Although much information has been gleaned from literary texts, archaeological finds, inscriptions, and coins, much about the Cabiric cult remains a mystery. The Cabiri were worshipped at Thessalonica, Pella, Olynthus, and on the islands of Lemnos and Imbros. With respect to attitudes toward the cult in Thessalonica, the numismatic evidence makes it clear that, from the Flavian period at the latest, the Cabiric cult was the chief cult.

Other Relevant Sources:

328, 356, 994.

B. The Church of Thessalonica

304 Barclay, John M. G. "Conflict in Thessalonica," *Catholic Biblical Quarterly* 55 (1993) 512-530.

The opposition experienced by the believers in Thessalonica is best understood as social harassment from non-Christians due to the converts' refusal to take part in normal social and cultic activities. The Thessalonian Christians found their social experience to tally remarkably well with an apocalyptic ideology of social distinction and imminent judgment. Their reaction to such social harassment, however, was not entirely passive and Paul was concerned that his converts' actions of giving up work (1 Thess 4:11-12) in order to engage in aggressive evangelistic activity would further provoke non-Christians. This understanding of 1 Thessalonians suggests that 2 Thessalonians is Paul's response to a feverish church which was convinced that the day of wrath (see 1 Thess 5:2-3; 2 Thess 2:1-12) had already come.

305 ---. "Thessalonica and Corinth: Social Contrasts in Pauline Christianity," *Journal for the Study of the New Testament* 47 (1992) 49-74.

Although only a short interval separated the founding of the Christian communities in Thessalonica and Corinth by Paul, these communities developed remarkably different interpretations of the Christian faith. These differences can be especially seen in the area of social relations between Christians and non-Christians. The Thessalonian church received Paul's apocalyptic message with enthusiasm and found its dualistic symbolic structure confirmed in their experience of hostility from non-believers in Thessalonica. By contrast, the Corinthian Christians enjoyed friendly relations with non-Christians and were more at ease in society than Paul thought proper. The dominant ethos in the Corinthian church emphasized knowledge, imparted by the Spirit, and it appears that the Corinthians themselves were responsible for interpreting Paul's apocalyptic message in this way. This style of faith, which imparted a sense of superiority without entailing hostility or exclusivity, correlates well with their peaceful social experience in Corinth. Thus the presence (at Thessalonica) or absence (at Corinth) of conflict in social interaction with outsiders had an important influence on the development of these two churches and on their perception of their Christian identity.

306 Bercovitz, J. Peter. "Paul and Thessalonica," *Proceedings: Eastern Great Lakes and Midwest Biblical Societies* 10 (1990) 123-135.

Quite independently from Acts, and at a number of points correcting Acts, the pre-history of 1 Thessalonians based exclusively on the letters offers a wealth of information about Paul's relationships with the Thessalonian Christians. This pre-history not only provides crucial links in the construction of the letter's chronology but also raises serious questions about the authenticity of 2 Thessalonians.

307 Bruce, F. F. "St. Paul in Macedonia," *Bulletin of the John Rylands University Library of Manchester* 61 (1979) 337-354.

Information from Paul's letters, Acts and other secondary sources illumines the apostle's movements in Macedonia (Philippi, Thessalonica and Berea) as well as the general history of Macedonia up to his time. This information also supports the following conclusions: (1) E. A. Judge's proposal (325) that the "decrees of Caesar" refer to the prohibition against predicting a change of ruler is likely correct. (2) Paul may well have planned to travel the *Via Egnatia* from Philippi and Thessalonica on to Rome before opposition at Thessalonica forced a change of plans. (3) Paul's later relations and travel in Macedonia, including his visit to Illyricum, may have provided him the opportunity to learn Latin in preparation for his future missionary activity in Spain.

308 ---. "St. Paul in Macedonia: 2. The Thessalonian Correspondence," *Bulletin of the John Rylands University Library of Manchester* 62 (1980) 328-345.

The study of a number of introductory issues associated with 1 and 2 Thessalonians leads to the following conclusions: (1) Although Silvanus and Timothy are named as Paul's associates, Paul is the effective author of both letters. (2) 2 Thessalonians was originally sent to the church in Thessalonica and not to the church in Berea or Philippi or to distinct groups within the Thessalonian church. (3) There is not enough evidence to warrant reversing the canonical order of the Thessalonian letters.

309 Clemen, Carl D. "Paulus und die Gemeinde zu Thessalonike," *Neue kirchliche Zeitschrift* 7 (1896) 139-164.

Paul wrote both letters to the Thessalonians while he was in Corinth, after which he traveled by sea back to Antioch and then on to Ephesus. An analysis of both letters, in conjunction with the book of Acts, provides valuable information regarding the relationship of Paul to the community of Christians in Thessalonica.

310 Collins, Raymond F. *The Birth of the New Testament. The Origin and Development of the First Christian Generation* (New York: Crossroad, 1993).

This volume engages in a detailed textual, historical-critical, rhetorical, and social analysis of 1 Thessalonians. As the earliest complete writing in the New Testament canon, this letter provides an important key to understanding the historical setting and theological concerns of early Christians. By writing 1 Thessalonians and instructing the believers there to read it in their assembled gatherings, Paul transformed the medium through which the gospel is communicated. This letter represents the birth of the New Testament that extends the apostolic presence and writers.

311 ---. "The Christian Community, Servant of the Word," *Studies on the First Letter to the Thessalonians* (Bibliotheca ephemeridum theologicarum lovaniensium 66; Leuven: Leuven University Press, 1984) 371-382.

The church at Thessalonica was called into being by the word of God conveyed as a powerful force to that group of people by Paul, the apostle of Christ. As such, the church of Thessalonica is a model of what every parish today ought to be: a Christian community, servant of the Word.

312 deSilva, David A. "'Worthy of His Kingdom': Honor Discourse and Social Engineering in 1 Thessalonians," *Journal for the Study of the New Testament* 64 (1996) 49-79.

Honor discourse was an effective means by which Paul sustains the group values and commitment of the Thessalonian church and so equips it to meet the challenges faced from the surrounding majority culture. Paul insulates the believers in Thessalonica from concern for the opinion and approval of non-Christians by censuring outsiders as unreliable guides to honorable behavior. Consequently, society's censure of the believers should carry no weight. Paul directs their ambitions to the eternal honor to be gained by securing God's approval. The group members are called to reinforce one another's commitment to those distinctive Christian values which will result in honor on the last day.

313 Donfried, Karl Paul. "1 Thessalonians, Acts, and the Early Paul," *The Thessalonian Correspondence* (ed. Raymond F. Collins; Bibliotheca ephemeridum theologicarum lovaniensium 87; Leuven: Leuven University Press, 1990) 3-26.
Republished with minor changes in Karl Paul Donfried and I. Howard Marshall, *The Theology of the Shorter Pauline Letters* (Cambridge: Cambridge University Press, 1993) 64-72.

Recent studies of Pauline chronology have convincingly suggested an earlier date for 1 Thessalonians: the early forties of the first century. This earliest Pauline letter contains a fair amount of traditional material--material which has much in common with the Hellenistic church and the Antiochene tradition. This tradition and its transformation, rather than the late Paul represented in Galatians and Romans, ought to be the starting point for understanding the evolution of Pauline theology. 1 Thessalonians illustrates how Paul's coherent theology of the gospel of the eschatological triumph of God in Jesus and its imminent conclusion shaped his inherited theological framework in light of the contingent situation he encountered in Thessalonica. This can be seen with particular clarity in the amplification of 1 Thess 1:9-10 in 4:13-18 and in the reshaping of the phrase "in Christ." Luke does present some accurate accounts of the early Paul as well as some fleeting views of their common inheritance from the Antiochene tradition.

314 ---. "2 Thessalonians and the Church of Thessalonica," *Origins and Method. Towards a New Understanding of Judaism and Christianity. Essays in Honour of John C. Hurd* (ed. Bradley H. McLean; Journal for the Study of the New Testament Supplement Series 86; Sheffield: JSOT Press, 1993) 128-144.

The Thessalonian church is faced with a variety of dilemmas in the midst of an over-all situation of increased persecution. Even though one of Paul's co-workers (probably Timothy) rather than the apostle himself is the author of the letter, there is good justification for reading it as addressed to the Thessalonian church sometime after the writing of 1 Thessalonians. The presence of the κατέχον/ων references, the refutation of the belief that the "day of the Lord is already here," and the tendency toward a charismatic authority by a few in this letter all strongly suggest the influence of the pagan cults in this crisis. The paraenetic intention of the author of 2 Thessalonians becomes evident as one observes the manner in which he addresses and refutes these unsettling circumstances current in the Thessalonian church.

315 Ferreira, Joel A. "Sociologa da comunidade de Thessalônica," *Estudios bíblicos* 25 (1990) 9-20.

A sociological reading of 1 Thessalonians leads to the following conclusions about both the letter itself and the church to which it is addressed. 1 Thessalonians is an apocalyptic letter of encouragement to a newly organized church which consists primarily of poor and oppressed Christians. They had readily accepted Paul's apocalyptic gospel of Jesus because it was a natural substitute for the worship of the Cabiri. Although the Cabiric cult had originally been popular with the poor, the worship of the Cabiri was taken over by the rich during the reign of Augustus. Consequently, Paul's preaching of the apocalyptic gospel of Jesus filled a natural void among the poor and working class citizens. The newly organized church faced opposition from three sources: Satan, rich pagans, and Jews.

316 Galanis, John L. "The Apostle Paul and Thessalonica [in Greek]," *Deltio Biblikon Meleton* 14.2 (1985) 61-72.

A review of the events which took place immediately prior to and during Paul's journey to Thessalonica demonstrates the importance of his visit to this city.

317 Hadorn, W. "Die Abfassung der Thessalonicherbriefe auf der dritten Missionsreise und der Kanon des Marcion," *Zeitschrift für die neutestamentliche Wissenschaft* 19 (1919/20) 67-72.

The only time that Paul, Silvanus, and Timothy were all together during the second missionary trip was in Corinth, from where the apostle wrote his first letter to the Thessalonians. This letter is probably authentic.

318 ---. *Die Abfassung der Thessalonicherbriefe in der Zeit der dritten Missionsreise des Paulus* (Beiträge zur Förderung christlicher Theologie 24; Gütersloh: Bertelsmann, 1919).

This discussion of the historical circumstances of the Thessalonian letters focuses on the writing of these documents. The authenticity of 1 Thessalonians is already established. It was probably written from Achaia after Paul left Athens, soon after the founding of the Christian community in Thessalonica, although the letter provides little information in this regard. The letter addresses issues which caused some to oppose Paul and which also were problematic in Corinth. These issues include the return of Christ, libertine tendencies, admonitions relating to the grace gifts, the nearness of the day of the Lord, and disorderliness. 2 Thessalonians is a self-contained document, with wording apparently different from that in other Pauline letters. The issue of the Antichrist in 2 Thess 2:1-12 provides the key to establishing the letter's authenticity. The "restrainer" seems to be Caesar. There are good grounds for thinking 2 Thessalonians was written before 1 Thessalonians.

319 Hainz, Josef. *Ekklesia. Strukturen paulinischer Gemeinde-Theologie und Gemeinde-Ordnung* (Biblische Untersuchungen 9; Regensburg: Pustet, 1972) 31-47.

Several passages from 1 Thessalonians, probably the earliest of the Pauline letters, are important in discussing elements of community life. These include 1:1 and 2:4-12 on Paul's relationship with the Thessalonians despite misunderstandings; 4:2, 8, which contain his commands and prayers for them; and 2:13-14, which deals with his word of preaching. A number of passages address the fellow work of the apostle and his community, including 3:2. The structuring of the community in terms of authority is addressed in 5:12-14. Finally, the reciprocal nature of the building up of the community is addressed in 5:11ff, including the goal of every effort being one of service to the community.

320 Hill, Judith Lynn. "Establishing the Church in Thessalonica" (Unpublished Ph.D. Dissertation, Durham, NC: Duke University, 1990).

The evidence of 1 Thessalonians and the relevant data from history, archeology, and sociology reveal the various strategies used by Paul and his fellow missionaries to establish the Thessalonian church. Their nonverbal means of attracting listeners and communicating their message included their housing, jobs, character, and use of miraculous signs. Their verbal means involved concentrating on a few basic facts of the Christian truth. This verbal communication took place in both formal and informal ways and was coupled with a challenge to the audience, urging them to convert from paganism to Christianity. When appropriate, Paul made use of Hellenistic, Jewish, or Christian materials in his communication with them. The Thessalonians whom Paul reached with the gospel were primarily non-slave, working class members, both men and women. Few in the congregation were rich, but a small contingent of "patrons" may have held leadership positions. The letter indicates that the majority of the church were Thessalonians who came from a pagan background and used *koine* Greek as their primary language. Although the group was limited in size and ethnic scope, it was a significant gathering because it was representative of the largest group of people in the city.

321 Holland, Glenn Stanfield. "Let No One Deceive You in Any Way: 2 Thessalonians as a Reformulation of the Apocalyptic Tradition," *SBL 1985 Seminar Papers* (ed. Kent H. Richards; SBL Seminar Papers 24; Atlanta: Scholars Press, 1985) 327-341.

2 Thessalonians is representative of several currents of thought of the second Christian generation. It offers a definitive reinterpretation of an earlier, misunderstood

eschatological tradition, and uses traditional elements of Jewish apocalyptic to achieve this end. It was written to refute the erroneous interpretation of the eschatological tradition which had arisen in part from the delay of the parousia. Following the lead of Paul in Rom 1:18-32, the pseudepigraphal author makes a close connection between doctrinal error and "deception" in regard to morality, attacking his opponents (the ἄτακτοι) both on the grounds of their false teaching and on that of their "disorderly" behavior. The letter serves an eschatological function because it serves as a shield against the deceptions of eschatological evil, both by offering the "correct" apocalyptic scenario and by insisting upon obedience to the inherited Pauline tradition of doctrinal and moral instruction.

322 Hong, Sung Kook. "Paul's Efforts at Consolidation of Conversion: A Sociological Study of First Thessalonians and Philippians" (Unpublished Th.D. Dissertation; Boston: Boston University, 1994).

Three social theories which explain well particular issues in the three stages (construction, preservation, and transmission) of new religious movements include the theory of the construction of social reality, the theories of cognitive dissonance and commitment enhancement, and the theory of religious involvement. When these theories are applied to 1 Thessalonians and Philippians, the following conclusions are reached: (1) Paul's activity and message find different emphases depending on the social context of each city at the initial stage of constructing the conversion reality; (2) the problems within the two churches are connected to the peculiar ethos of each church; (3) Paul perceives the problems in terms of their potential dissonance and controls them in order to prevent the converts from defection; (4) the converts of the two cities identify differently with their role of conversion and begin their commitment imitating Paul's example and how Paul tries to consolidate their continuing commitment; (5) one can derive Paul's pattern of institutionalized order of conversion from his previous effort to construct a conversion reality and confirm the converts' identity and role; and (6) Paul's conviction and behavior serve as the archetypal example for the gentile converts in their constructing biography.

323 Jewett, Robert. "Enthusiastic Radicalism and the Thessalonian Correspondence," *SBL 1972 Proceedings* (ed. Lane C. McGaughy; 2 vols.; N.P.: Society of Biblical Literature, 1972) 1.181-232.

The thesis of Wilhelm Lütgert, with some modification, explains the situation in Thessalonica which Paul was addressing in 1 and 2 Thessalonians (both of which are authentically Pauline). Some in the church developed a radical enthusiastic self-consciousness in which they identified their experience of the Spirit with the parousia. Consequently, they believed that the resurrection was already past and that they had no future expectation. The mindset of having been freed from earthly ties and limitations led to living in sexual license, idleness, and liberation from societal order. They were consequently shocked by the persecution which was disturbing the church and also by the deaths of some of the members which contradicted their belief that they already were living in the new age. These radical enthusiasts demonstrate a number of similarities with the "divine men" whose activities have been suspected in Corinth.

324 ---. *The Thessalonian Correspondence: Pauline Rhetoric and Millenarian Piety* (Foundations and Facets: New Testament; Philadelphia: Fortress, 1986).

Paul was faced with a unique situation of millenarian radicalism in Thessalonica, concerning the actual arrival of the millennium and subsequent behavior based on that assumption. Despite the claimed problems in 1 and 2 Thessalonians concerning authenticity, sequence, recipients, literary integrity, and chronology, a survey of these issues demonstrates that both documents are authentic Pauline letters. A rhetorical analysis of these letters shows that 1 Thessalonians is an example of demonstrative/epideictic rhetoric, while 2 Thessalonians belongs to the genre of deliberative rhetoric. The literary, historical, and sociological evidence shows that the Thessalonian community was (1) perturbed that persecution would be a part of their new life in Christ; (2) perplexed because some of its members died before the parousia; (3) attracted to a radical kind of realized eschatology; (4) struggling with conflicts stemming from ecstatic manifestations of the Spirit; and (5) critical of Paul's own lack of charismatic qualities. Within the community were the ἄτακτοι, the "obstinate resisters of authority," who believed in the present possession of immortal existence in the Spirit and challenged both work and sexual ethics.

325 Judge, Edwin A. "The Decrees of Caesar at Thessalonica," *Reformed Theological Review* 30 (1971) 1-7.

No satisfactory explanation has yet been given of the charges brought against the apostles at Thessalonica (Acts 17:5-7). The traditional view that the "decrees of Caesar" refer to a breach of the Roman law of treason (*maiestas*) does not satisfactorily account for the behavior of either Paul or his Thessalonian critics. Another possibility is that the "decrees of Caesar" refer to prohibitions against forecasting the emperor's health and death--prohibitions which carried severe penalties. Against this background, the strong eschatological nature of Paul's preaching in Thessalonica concerning a crucified, risen, and exalted king who would soon appear on earth as universal judge could have been interpreted as a *prediction of a change of ruler*--an act which violated the "decrees of Caesar." Another possibility is that there may have been an imperial edict prohibiting Jewish messianic agitation which the Thessalonian informers invoked.

326 Keightley, Georgia Masters. "The Church's Memory of Jesus: A Social Science Analysis of 1 Thessalonians," *Biblical Theology Bulletin* 17 (1987) 149-156.

The collective memory theory of the social theorist Maurice Halbwachs shows that the memory traditions of Jesus recorded in the New Testament have a function beyond the mere provision of factual information about this historical figure. From this perspective, the memory of Jesus is understood to be constitutive of the Christian community and to be normative for the collective self-definition: the church is the community which remembers Jesus. To participate in the Christian life is to participate in all that Jesus has meant and continues to mean to those who are his followers. A study of 1 Thessalonians demonstrates the extent to which the memory of Jesus is constitutive of Christian corporate life and is determinative of ecclesial identity.

327 Lake, Kirsopp. "The Epistles to the Thessalonians," *The Earlier Epistles of St. Paul: Their Motive and Origin* (London: Rivingtons, 1911) 61-101.

The order of events which occurred in connection with Paul's ministry in Thessalonica can be reconstructed from the book of Acts--an account which is essentially supported by the testimony of 1 Thessalonians. Even though the authenticity of 2 Thessalonians has frequently been questioned, it too is a genuine Pauline letter. The claimed problems with this letter are solved by Harnack's proposal that 1 Thessalonians is addressed to the Gentile Christian community in Thessalonica, while 2 Thessalonians is written to the Jewish Christian community there. Thus both Thessalonian letters can be used to reconstruct the situation of the Thessalonian church and the items likely included in Timothy's report to Paul: (1) Christians in Thessalonica were being persecuted and probably even martyred; (2) a division existed between the Gentile and Jewish parts of the community; (3) believers were anxious about the parousia and the fate of those Christians who died before this event would take place; (4) the presence of forged letters created doubt and confusion about the Day of the Lord; and (5) the community was struggling with problems of immorality (especially the Gentile section) and idle restlessness (especially, but not exclusively, the Jewish section).

328 Lightfoot, Joseph Barber. "The Church of Thessalonica," *Biblical Essays* (London/New York: Macmillan, 1893) 253-269.

The natural advantages of Thessalonica with respect to both land and sea guaranteed the wealth and political importance of this city. Its status as a free city further enhanced the success of Thessalonica and also allowed it to keep its existing political structure (the offices of the politarchs, city steward, gymnasiarch, and popular assembly). The moral and religious condition of Thessalonica was not much different from that of other major cities in that day, except for its support of the Cabiric cult. Acts is a largely reliable source for reconstructing the events of Paul's original missionary activity in Thessalonica. 1 Thessalonians highlights some of issues with which the church was struggling: persecution, neglect of ordinary business, anxiety over church members who had died, overemphasis and neglect of certain spiritual gifts, a tendency to despise authorities, and a danger of relapsing into former pagan practices. 2 Thessalonians shows that there was some confusion over the Day of the Lord and that the restless and unruly spirit, which Paul had rebuked in the first letter, was gaining ground.

329 ---. "The Churches of Macedonia," *Biblical Essays* (London/New York: Macmillan, 1893) 237-250.

The three Macedonian churches of Philippi, Thessalonica, and Berea are so closely linked together in terms of their foundation and membership that it is especially instructive to consider their history and character collectively. Standing sufficiently apart from each other and commanding three separate districts, these three cities recommended themselves to Paul by their geographical position as good missionary centers. It was also necessary that there should be a sufficient Jewish population in each city which could serve as the nucleus for the new churches. Paul's communications with the Macedonian churches were very close and frequent as evidenced in his personal visits, the sending of his representatives, the more or less constant presence of Macedonian Christians with the apostle, and his three letters (1 and 2 Thessalonians, Philippians).

330 Lührmann, Dieter. "The Beginnings of the Church at Thessalonica," *Greeks, Romans, and Christians. Essays in Honor of Abraham J. Malherbe* (ed. David L. Balch, Everett Ferguson, and Wayne A. Meeks; Minneapolis: Fortress, 1990) 237-249.

Luke's account shows how, according to his view, the beginnings in Thessalonica were the same as beginnings in every other city. Paul's letter to the Thessalonians confirms in general the details told by Luke but at some points contradicts that account. An analysis of 1 Thessalonians also leads to two surprising results about the content of the gospel which Paul originally preached in Thessalonica. First, contrary to what form criticism has commonly claimed about the essentials of the kerygma, it is clear that the imminent judgment and the parousia of Christ were key elements of Paul's preaching (1:9-10). Second, ethics was by no means only a topic in early Christian theology due to the delay of the parousia but rather an important part of Paul's initial preaching in Thessalonica (4:1-12).

331 Lütgert, E. Wilhelm. "Die Volkommenen im Philipperbrief und die Enthusiasten in Thessalonich," *Beiträge zur Förderung christlicher Theologie* 13.6 (1909) 547-654.

Paul's opponents in Thessalonica consisted of "spiritual enthusiasts." As a result of their spiritual enthusiasm, combined with a radicalization of Paul's teaching and their lack of eschatological understanding, they encouraged and developed libertinism, and misunderstood Christian morality such that many were idle, thinking that they were spiritually superior. They believed that the eschaton had already occurred for those who had received the Spirit, with the benefits of the resurrection to be experienced by them.

332 Malherbe, Abraham J. "Did the Thessalonians Write to Paul?" *The Conversation Continues: Studies in Paul and John in Honor of J. Louis Martyn* (ed. Robert T. Fortna and Beverly R. Gaventa; Nashville: Abingdon, 1990) 246-257.

Although Paul does not mention earlier correspondence between himself and the Thessalonians, it is quite possible that he had written to them when he first sent Timothy to them, and it is highly probable that they in return wrote him for advice. 1 Thessalonians contains a number of epistolary clichés which strongly suggest the existence of previous letters. That Paul does not mention these letters, especially the one from

Thessalonica, should not be surprising, for he elsewhere does not mention letters where he could have been expected to do so (1 Cor 16:17; Phil 2:25-30).

333 ---. "God's New Family in Thessalonica," *The Social World of the First Christians: Essays in Honor of Wayne A. Meeks* (ed. L. Michael White and O. Larry Yarbrough; Minneapolis: Fortress, 1995) 115-125.

Paul's consistent description of the Thessalonian church and his relationship to them in familial terms ("beloved," "wet nurse," "father," "orphan," "brothers") is probably not simply due to his use of those traditions which employed kinship language. Instead it appears that the experience of new converts, who underwent a painful reorientation of social relationships, made Paul's approach particularly appropriate to their situation. Paul is aware of the domestic problems caused by the new missionary religion and addresses them in this finely crafted pastoral letter by using language of kinship to describe God's new family in Thessalonica.

334 ---. *Paul and the Thessalonians: The Philosophical Tradition of Pastoral Care* (Philadelphia: Fortress, 1987).

1 Thessalonians illustrates well Paul's method of forming a Christian community among Greek manual laborers. This method of the apostle shares much in common with that employed by contemporary moral philosophers who were engaged in a similar enterprise. The workshop as a semiprivate setting in which Paul led his listeners to conversion, the presentation of himself as a model to be imitated, and his adaptation to the psychological conditions of individuals in Thessalonica represented the ideal to many of Paul's contemporaries. The writing of a letter in a hortatory style is also conventional. Among the many ancient authors used, Philodemus, Plutarch, and Seneca figure prominently.

335 ---. "Paul: Hellenistic Philosopher or Christian Pastor?" *American Theological Library Association: Proceedings* 39 (1985) 86-98.
Republished in *Anglican Theological Review* 68.1 (1986) 3-13.

Paul's letters, particularly 1 Thessalonians, reveal that there are striking similarities between the apostle and the Hellenistic philosophers of his day. The function to which Paul put that which he has received from the moral philosophers is essentially pastoral. The apostle is so familiar with the rich Greek traditions of pastoral care and uses them in so unstudied a fashion that it would be wrong to think that he only superficially mined the lode for his own purposes. He is as consistent and unconscious in his appropriation of the pastoral tradition as any of his pagan contemporaries. At the same time, his apostolic self-understanding and theology so completely informed his pastoral care that it would be wrong to posit an antithesis between Paul as Hellenistic philosopher and as Christian pastor.

336 Manus, Chris Ukachukwu. "Luke's Account of Paul in Thessalonica (Acts 17,1-9)," *The Thessalonian Correspondence* (ed. Raymond F. Collins; Bibliotheca ephemeridum theologicarum lovaniensium 87; Leuven: Leuven University Press, 1990) 27-38.

A comparative analysis of Luke's and Paul's account of the founding of Christianity in Thessalonica shows that there are obvious discrepancies between them. Luke, for example, attributes the persecution originally faced by the church to the Jews alone, whereas Paul in 1 Thess 2:14-16 has Gentiles in view. Luke's portrayal of the Jewish opposition to the gospel in contrast to the city authorities' willingness to free the missionaries functions to emphasize the *religio licita* status of Christianity in the Roman Empire of his time. This is in line with Luke's larger concern in Acts to demonstrate that Christianity was a religion acceptable to the Romans.

337 Martínez, Aquiles Ernesto. "El apóstol Pablo y la comunidad de Tesalónica: Lecciones sobre el uso del poder," *Apuntes. Reflexiones Teológicas desde el Margen Hispano* 15 (1995) 3-13.

The way in which Paul relates to the Thessalonian church mirrors the constructive use of his apostolic power. To a community which faces alienation and oppression from the dominant Greco-Roman culture, Paul responds pastorally rather than authoritatively. First, he establishes and cultivates a fraternal relationship with the congregation. Second, he uses his missionary work in Thessalonica as a model to be imitated. Third, he cares for the Thessalonians and demonstrates his love for them. Fourth, he encourages the faith and praxis of the community by appealing to and celebrating the outstanding actions of the Thessalonians' religious pilgrimage. Finally, he reaffirms the identity of the church by providing a message of hope in the midst of death and despair. Paul's use of his apostolic power, therefore, represents a challenging paradigm for church leaders today.

338 McDonald, William A. "Archaeology and St. Paul's Journeys in Greek Lands," *Biblical Archaeologist* 3 (1940) 18-24.

A study of the cities of Northern Greece where Paul travelled (Troas, Neapolis, Philippi, Amphipolis, Apollonia, Thessalonica, Berea) demonstrates the way in which archaeology illumines the missionary activity of the apostle.

339 Meeks, Wayne A. "The Circle of Reference in Pauline Morality," *Greeks, Romans, and Christians. Essays in Honor of Abraham J. Malherbe* (ed. David L. Balch, Everett Ferguson, and Wayne A. Meeks; Minneapolis: Fortress, 1990) 305-317.

Sociological theory has introduced the notion of "reference groups"--groups or individuals who act on people either normatively, by affecting their motivations, or comparatively, by affecting their perceptions and giving them a standard for self-evaluation. This notion of reference groups and reference individuals help us understand how broad the moral horizons of Pauline Christianity were. In 1 Thessalonians, the apostles, the other churches which Paul has founded, and the earlier Christian groups in Judea, as well as the idealized picture of themselves at the beginning, constitute the reference groups with which the Thessalonian Christians ought to compare themselves and within which the norms that Paul states and implies in the admonitions of the letter are validated. Paul also introduces in this letter reference individuals: himself, his co-workers, local leaders, Christ, and God. Non-Christians also function as a reference group but in a negative manner.

340 ---. "'Since Then You Would Need to Go Out of the World': Group Boundaries in Pauline Christianity," *Critical History and Biblical Faith: New Testament Perspectives* (ed. Thomas J. Ryan; College Theology Society Annual Publication Series; Villanova, PA: Villanova University, 1979) 4-23.

A much greater appreciation is needed of the social factors at work in early Christian communities. The Pauline churches experienced a tension between the desire for separation and the desire to attract new converts. The first desire was realized by a variety of factors which highlighted the boundaries which separated the church from those "outside": (1) special language emphasizing separation; (2) rules and rituals of purity; (3) membership sanctions, especially the process for excluding non-conformists; (4) the development of autonomous institutions; and (5) reports of specific kinds of interaction with the macrosociety. Yet there were forms of self-description and basic symbols which stressed universality and comprehensiveness.

341 ---. "Social Functions of Apocalyptic Language in Pauline Christianity," *Apocalypticism in the Mediterranean World and the Near East. Proceedings of the International Colloquium on Apocalypticism. Uppsala, August 12-17, 1979* (ed. David Hellholm; Tübingen: Mohr/Siebeck, 1983) 687-705.

Apocalyptic language in 1 Thessalonians, Galatians, and 1 Corinthians performs a variety of functions in the lives of Paul's congregations: e.g., to emphasize and legitimate boundaries between the Christian groups and the larger society, to enhance internal cohesion and solidarity, to provide sanctions for normative behavior, to legitimate the leadership of Paul and his associates against challenges. There are important aspects of Pauline Christianity which are best understood by comparison with analogous forms and functions of apocalyptic movements. At the same time, however, it would be wrong to conclude too quickly that Pauline Christianity was identical to these apocalyptic movements.

342 Míguez, Néstor O. "La composición social de la Iglesia en Tesalónica," *Revista Bíblica* 51.34 (1989) 65-89.

Against the recent idea that the Gentile Christian primitive church was a policlassist group and that the reference in 2 Cor 8:2 to the poverty of the Thessalonian church is merely a rhetorical expression, the letter to the Thessalonians confirms that this early Christian community was composed of a group of poor artisans who lacked access to the benefits of the upper class. Paul chose to work among the artisans (1 Thess 2:9) and this identification with them provided him a good opportunity to preach an incarnated gospel, something that will be developed in a Christological basis. His exhortations concerning work and rest in 1 Thess 4:7-12 flow from his concrete experience among them and reveal one of the main tenets of his gospel: participation in the life of the poor. It is an announcement in the midst of grief and persecution of those who have no influence or authority, and for those who have to live from hard and difficult work.

343 Morgan-Gillman, Florence. "Jason of Thessalonica (Acts 17,5-9)," *The Thessalonian Correspondence* (ed. Raymond F. Collins; Bibliotheca ephemeridum theologicarum lovaniensium 87; Leuven: Leuven University Press, 1990) 39-49.

The Jason of Thessalonica mentioned in Acts 17:5-9 is to be identified with the similarly named person of Rom 16:21. Jason was a relatively well-off Hellenistic Jew who was converted by Paul's preaching in the local synagogue and became one of the leaders in the predominantly Gentile church. The traditional view that Jason was left "holding the bag" because Paul could not be found by the city leaders is probably not correct. Instead it appears as if Jason continued to sponsor church meetings after Paul had moved on and was thus held liable for the actions of his congregants.

344 Patte, Daniel. "First Thessalonians: Beloved and Chosen by God," *Paul's Faith and the Power of the Gospel. A Structural Introduction to the Pauline Letters* (Philadelphia: Fortress, 1983) 122-154.

The main objective of 1 Thessalonians is to exhort the Thessalonians to lead a sanctified Christian life. The letter contains two types of statements: those which express the main argument, in this case the exhortations (the "dialogic" level), and those which justify the validity of the statements of the main argument (the "warranting" level). The first part of the letter (1:3-3:6) belongs, generally speaking, to the warranting level, while the second part (3:7-5:22) to the dialogic level. The warranting level has two functions: it establishes the fundamental convictional pattern which sets the believers in a right relationship with God; and it proposes example(s) of the way in which this pattern can be applied. The dialogic level aims at causing the readers to apply the convictional pattern in their daily life.

345 Perkins, Pheme. "1 Thessalonians and Hellenistic Religious Practices," *To Touch the Text: Biblical and Related Studies in Honor of Joseph A. Fitzmyer* (ed. Maurya P. Horgan and Paul J. Kobelski; New York: Crossroad, 1989) 325-334.

1 Thessalonians shows the precarious process by which a new Christian community carved out its place among the cults and associations of a Greco-Roman city. The conversion of the Thessalonian Christians does not appear to involve intellectual enlightenment as much as a decisive shift in cultic practice. Since Christianity required withdrawal from all forms of cultic association, its new adherents could not but offend the civic sentiments of their fellow citizens. The resulting opposition faced by the church did not weaken the new Christian community but strengthened its perception of a divine calling to holiness and salvation. The most basic categories and images which Paul gives

his readers to understand their common experience stem not from Greco-Roman philosophic and religious thought but from his Jewish heritage.

346 Perkins, William James. "A Sociological Exegesis of Pauline Paraeneses Pertaining to the Formation of the Community of Believers in Romans, 1 and 2 Corinthians, Galatians, and 1 and 2 Thessalonians" (Unpublished Ph.D. Dissertation; Waco, TX: Baylor University, 1992).

When aspects from sociological theory are applied in an exegetical study of passages from Paul's authentic letters containing "situational" paraenesis, the result is a better understanding of the function of these texts in establishing boundaries--both boundaries of inclusion (Rom 14:1-15:13; 1 Cor; Gal 5:13-6:10; 1 Thess 4:1-12; 5:11-15; 2 Thess 3:6-15) and boundaries of exclusion (1 Cor; 2 Cor 6:14-7:1; Gal 5:16-25; 1 Thess 5:1-11; 2 Thess 3:6-15)--for the group or "community of believers." The incorporation of sociological theory in such an exegetical study also demonstrates the value of this methodology in providing a better understanding of Paul's paraenetic material, especially as it pertains to the formation of recognizable groups called "communities of believers."

347 Plevnik, Joseph. "Pauline Presuppositions," *The Thessalonian Correspondence* (ed. Raymond F. Collins; Bibliotheca ephemeridum theologicarum lovaniensium 87; Leuven: Leuven University Press, 1990) 50-61.

Pauline presuppositions are what Paul takes for granted with respect to the community's knowledge about the gospel, about Christian living in the light of the gospel, and about the manner of his ministry. References to the presuppositions bridge the issues raised in Paul's letters with the foundation of faith which he has laid down during his earlier preaching in the community. Although references to these presuppositions can be found in all Pauline writings, they are especially predominant in 1 Thessalonians. These many references reflect the closeness of the letter to his mission in Thessalonica and the need both to supplement that original instruction and to affirm the believers in their young faith amidst trials.

348 Riesner, Rainer. *Die Frühzeit des Apostels Paulus: Studien zur Chronologie, Missionsstrategie und Theologie* (Wissenschaftliche Untersuchungen zum Neuen Testament 71; Tübingen: Mohr/Siebeck, 1994).
Republished in English as *Paul's Early Period: Chronology, Mission Strategy, and Theology* (Grand Rapids: Eerdmans, 1997).

This chronological analysis of Paul's career from the time of his conversion to the founding of the church in Corinth involves four major sections. The first section or introduction surveys how scholarship has handled the issue of Pauline chronology. The second section uses information from the Pauline letters, the book of Acts, and early Christian traditions, along with material gathered from archeology, history, and geography of the first-century world, to ascertain relative or absolute dates for key events in Paul's life. The third section shifts from a study of events treated in isolation to the overall framework of Paul's missionary activity. The fourth and final section addresses the connection between chronology and theology, using 1 Thessalonians as a case study. Contrary to the view of Lüdemann and others, there is no need to resort to developmental theories with respect to Paul's theology. Rather, the distinctive elements of 1 Thessalonians are situationally produced.

349 Roberts, Mark David. "Images of Paul and the Thessalonians" (Unpublished Ph.D. Dissertation; Cambridge, MA: Harvard University, 1992).

A variety of images of Paul can be found in Acts 17 and 1 Thessalonians 1-3. In Acts 17 Paul stars as a philosopher/apologist who utilizes logic and rhetoric to persuade his listeners. Luke's portrayal of Paul in Thessalonica functions apologetically, exonerating Christians in Roman eyes, while edifying the church. In 1 Thessalonians images of Paul abound: he is the traveler, missionary, philosopher, victim, nurse, and imitator of Christ. These images of Paul build and form the church in response to the experiences of the new converts, especially persecution. By telling the story of the ministry of Paul and his co-workers, the converts' identity as God's assembly is shaped, while rhetorically an experience of Christian *communitas* is created.

350 Rodríguez Carmona, Antonio. "El nacimiento de una comunidad cristiana entre paganos: El testimonio de 1 Tesalonicenses," *Proyección* 25.108 (1978) 13-22.

351 Schmitz, John R. "Generativity in 1 Thessalonians," *Emmanuel* 90 (1984) 560-566.

Generativity is primarily the concern for establishing and guiding the next generation. Paul was a generative person and his first letter to the Thessalonians illustrates well his parental drive towards establishing and nurturing this Christian community.

352 Smith, Abraham. "The Social and Ethical Implications of the Pauline Rhetoric in I Thessalonians" (Unpublished Ph.D. Dissertation; Nashville, TN: Vanderbilt University, 1990).

A cross-disciplinary method integrating the theory of New Rhetoric with that of the Sociology of Knowledge leads to a better understanding of the resocialization process at work in the early Christian community in Thessalonica. In 1 Thessalonians Paul masterfully weaves social and ethical concerns together to help the community deal with the fragmenting forces in its midst. In this letter Paul draws not only from the Hellenistic consolatory tradition but from the Greco-Roman philosophical moral tradition as well. A rhetorical analysis of the letter reveals much about the complexities of the Thessalonian church: its social constituency (a Gentile congregation), its social relations (non-hierarchical), its social forms of legitimation (three symbolic myths: the death and resurrection of Jesus, the parousia, and the day of the Lord) and its social world (a semi-dualistic world view).

353 Stowers, Stanley Kent. "Social Status, Public Speaking and Private Teaching: The Circumstances of Paul's Preaching Activity," *Novum Testamentum* 26 (1984) 59-82.

The following conclusions may be asserted with respect to Paul's preaching activity. First, he used the synagogue on numerous occasions, although this often led to conflict and thus could not be a permanent locus for his preaching. Second, the private home provided the most important place for his work. Here Paul followed the pattern of Hellenistic teachers, a pattern which was continued by Christian teachers in the second century and later. The widespread picture of Paul the public orator, sophist or street-corner preacher is a false one. Finally, these conclusions must be related to the close and open life lived in the ancient cities of the eastern Mediterranean. But while the physical distance between the market, stoa, gymnasium, synagogue, and private house might be very small, the social and cultural distance between them might be very great. It is not surprising, then, that the gymnasium and synagogue were places of ambiguous status for Paul and that the private home became the major platform for his preaching activity.

354 Suhl, Alfred. *Paulus und seine Briefe. Ein Beitrag zur paulinischen Chronologie* (Studien zum Neuen Testament 11; Gütersloh: Gütersloh Verlagshaus, 1975).

In reviewing Paul's chronological relationship to Thessalonica and the writing of his two letters to the church there, it appears that the apostle intended to go to Rome from Thessalonica but was forced to go out of his way to Corinth, thereby drawing upon the financial resources he had gathered in Macedonia. He wrote 1 Thessalonians in early 50 CE. His writings to the church there do not include partitioned forms of the canonical letters, against the claims of Schmithals (433). Many of the literary features which Schmithals appeals to as evidence for his partition theory can be explained in other ways.

355 Tajra, Harry William. "Saint Paul à Thessalonique," *Positions luthériennes* 33 (1985) 233-244.

Acts 17:1-10a, although a rather brief description of Paul's ministry in Thessalonica, provides important information about the apostle's life and work.

356 ---. "Thessalonica: Paul, Jason and the Politarchs," *The Trial of St. Paul. A Juridical Exegesis of the Second Half of the Acts of the Apostles* (Wissenschaftliche Untersuchungen zum Neuen Testament 2; Tübingen: Mohr/Siebeck, 1989) 30-44.

Thessalonica enjoyed the status of a "free" city, which allowed it a number of special privileges. Paul's stay here may well have been longer than three Sabbaths. Luke's description of the events which Paul experienced in Thessalonica makes use of a number of unusual and powerful words to highlight the dramatic setting. The Jews instigated a riot in which Paul and his fellow missionaries were charged with the serious crimes of sedition and rebellion against the reigning emperor. Even after Paul's departure, the young church continued to be persecuted. Indeed, a reading of 1 Thess 2:14-16 shows that the riot in Thessalonica was considerably more serious than the language in the Acts narrative suggests.

357 Unger, Merrill F. "Historical Research and the Church at Thessalonica," *Bibliotheca Sacra* 119 (1962) 38-44.

Information from archaeology and historical research, together with the account of Acts 17, provides a clearer picture of the events surrounding Paul's original mission in Thessalonica.

358 Wanamaker, Charles A. "Apocalypticism at Thessalonica," *Neotestamentica* 21 (1987) 1-10.

Although it is commonly recognized that Paul's theology has an apocalyptic character, the social dimensions of Paul's apocalypticism are typically ignored. The creation of the apocalyptic Christian community at Thessalonica can be helpfully understood by recognizing the three essential components involved in the formation of millenarian movements: dissatisfaction with the current system; the appearance of an individual, normally referred to as a prophet, who articulates a new set of beliefs and values for this frustrated group; and the formation of a new symbolic and social world, which reinforces commitment to the new group. Thus Pauline Christianity can usefully be understood as a millenarian movement for the purpose of describing and explaining its development and character.

Other Relevant Sources:

406, 439, 446, 651, 814, 863.

C. The Text of the Thessalonian Letters

359 Asso, Cecilia. "A proposito di Paolo, I Thess., II 7," *Maia* [Messina] 38 (1986) 233-234.

The change in the twenty-sixth edition of the Nestle-Aland text from the reading ἤπιοι ("gentle") to νήπιοι ("babes") is not warranted. The previous reading of "gentle" not only makes more rhetorical sense in the context but also is supported by its one other occurrence in 2 Tim 2:24.

360 Baarda, Tjitze. "1 Thess. 2:14-16. Rodrigues in 'Nestle-Aland'," *Nederlands theologisch tijdschrift* 39 (1985) 186-193.

The critical apparatus in Nestle-Aland's *Novum Testamentum Graece* contains a note that, according to H. Rodrigues, 1 Thess 2:15-16 is an interpolation and should be eliminated. The note should be amended, however, since it is verses 14 and 15 (plus 16?) which Rodrigues suggested were a late insertion (after 135 CE) of an anti-Jewish "Johannine" type. In fact, it would be better to omit the mention of Rodrigues altogether and retain only A. Ritschl's suggestion that just verse 16c is an interpolation.

361 Baljon, J. M. S. "De 1 brief aan de Thessalonicensen," *Theologische Studiën* 6 (1888) 188-195.

Text-critical comments are made on the following fourteen passages in 1 Thessalonians (the key words are given within the brackets): 2:3 (ἀρεσκίας); 2:4 (λαλοῦμεν); 2:5-6 (μάρτυς); 2:8 (ὁμειρόμενοι); 2:12 (ὑμᾶς – παραμυθούμενοι); 2:13 (τοῦ θεοῦ); 2:14 (αὐτοὶ – αὐταί); 2:16 (ἔφθασεν); 3:3 (σαλεύεσθαι – σαίνεσθαι); 3:5 (γένηται – ἐγένετο); 3:12 (καὶ ἡμεῖς εἰς ὑμᾶς); 4:4 (σκεῦος); 4:6 (ἐν τῷ πράγματι); 4:14 (δοξάσει – δοξάζειν).

362 Collins, Raymond F. "The Text of the Epistles to the Thessalonians in Nestle-Aland[26]," *Studies on the First Letter to the Thessalonians* (Bibliotheca ephemeridum theologicarum lovaniensium 66; Leuven: Leuven University Press, 1984) 79-95.

There are a number of ways in which the twenty-sixth edition of the Nestle-Aland text of 1 and 2 Thessalonians differs from the twenty-fifth edition. The new edition contains nine different readings in the main text, a number of orthographic changes, a greater sophistication in the use made of papyri, and considerable differences in the marginal references as well as in the presentation of the text (paragraph divisions, the printing of strophes, and punctuation).

363 Fee, Gordon D. "On Text and Commentary on 1 and 2 Thessalonians," *SBL 1992 Seminar Papers* (ed. Eugene H. Lovering; SBL Seminar Papers 31; Atlanta: Scholars Press, 1992) 165-183.

A survey of the way in which textual variants are typically handled in English language commentaries leads to the following two recommendations. First, the textual discussion in the footnotes should be as complete as possible, so that, on the one hand, it can stand by itself as a form of "textual commentary," and that, on the other hand, one can comment on the resultant Greek text in the exposition, without cluttering the exposition with reasons for and against. Second, for all of the more significant variants, as well as for many of the lesser ones, some form of further comment is needed in the exposition itself, so that the reader can see the exegetical significance of the textual choices made in the footnotes. These two recommendations are then illustrated by a treatment of four textual variations, two of lesser significance (1 Thess 1:5; 1 Thess 4:8) and two of greater significance (1 Thess 2:7; 2 Thess 2:13).

364 Frede, Hermann Josef. "Ein Paulustext aus Burgund," *Biblica* 54 (1973) 516-536.

The handwritten manuscript of various texts in Verona, Biblioteca Capitolare LII, dates from the end of the eighth century and contains 277 parchment pages. Among these, on pages 21R-26V, between homilies for Epiphany and for the feast for the purification of Mary on February 2, is the only biblical text, that of 1 Thessalonians in a Latin Vulgate hand. The text probably represents a local text from Lyon and was likely written about the tenth century.

365 ---. "Eine neue Handschrift des Pauluskommentars von Pelagius," *Revue bénédictine* 73 (1963) 307-311.

A small fragment of parchment in the Göttingen University library, written in a minuscule hand in the eighth or ninth century, appears to be a fragment of Pelagius' commentary on 1 Thess 4:6-8 and 4:10-13.

366 Katz, Peter. "Ἐν πυρὶ φλογός," *Zeitschrift für die neutestamentliche Wissenschaft* 46 (1955) 133-138.

In the twenty-first edition of Nestle (1952) one finds in 2 Thess 1:8 the reading ἐν πυρὶ φλογός, while Acts 7:30 reads ἐν φλογὶ πυρός, with the same variants listed in both passages. Exod 3:2 agrees with Acts 7:30. 2 Thess 1:8 makes a fragmentary allusion to five biblical passages. The first is with ἐν πυρὶ φλογός where the reference to Exod 3:2 cannot be missed: Christ's parousia in a fiery flame corresponds to the theophany before Moses. With Acts 7:30 begins an abbreviated but rather wordy summary of Exodus 3. That the phrasing reads differently in the two places is not justifiable. This does not mean, however, that the reading in Acts should be followed. It is an improvement that Nestle in the apparatus includes ἐν πυρὶ φλογός.

367 Koester, Helmut. "The Text of 1 Thessalonians," *The Living Text: Essays in Honor of Ernest W. Saunders* (ed. Dennis E. Groh and Robert Jewett; Lanham, MD: University Press of America, 1985) 219-227.

The twenty-sixth edition of the Nestle-Aland, *Novum Testamentum Graece*, has changed the text of 1 Thessalonians from its predecessor, the twenty-fifth edition, in thirteen instances. In the five instances where words in brackets were added (1:5; 1:8; 3:13; 4:11; 5:15) it can be said with great certainty that these words are not part of the original text. Of the three instances in which words of the Nestle text were bracketed, two are not justified (1:5; 1:10) and, in the third case (4:8), brackets do not solve the textual problem. Of the five other changes, two are a definite improvement (5:10; 5:13); one can be disputed (2:13); one is justified but does not bring us closer to the original text (2:8); and one is clearly wrong (2:7). Thus, though the text has been improved in three cases, it is still problematic in two instances (2:8; 4:8) and inferior to its predecessor in eight instances.

368 Molitor, Joseph. "Die altgeorgische Version des Philipper-, Kolosser- und des 1. und 2. Thessalonichersbriefs ins Lateinische übertragen und nach Syriazismen untersucht," *Oriens Christianus* 60 (1976) 14-23.

369 ---. "Die syrische Übersetzung des 1 and 2 Thessalonicherbriefes," *Oriens Christianus* 56 (1972) 150-163.

After presenting the text of 1 and 2 Thessalonians, the conclusion discusses the Peshitta and Christian-Palestinian fragments, the Peshitta and Harclensis, and the Old Armenian Version.

370 Nellessen, Ernst. *Untersuchung zur altlateinischen Überlieferung des ersten Thessalonicherbriefes* (Bonner biblische Beiträge 22; Bonn: Hanstein, 1965).

The Old Latin tradition of 1 Thessalonians is examined, as it is found in the *Liber de divinis scripturis*, the Book of Armagh, and the commentaries of a number of Latin church fathers, including Ambrosiaster, Theodore of Mopsuestia, Pelagius, as well as the ninth-century poet Sedulius Scotus.

371 Ross, Arthur M. "Studies in the Thessalonian Epistles in Syriac" (Unpublished Ph.D. Dissertation; Chicago, IL: Lutheran School of Theology, 1983).

A comparison of the important Syriac manuscripts of the Thessalonian letters with the Syriac Vulgate (Peshitta Version) shows, among other things, a vigorous interest by the copyists in the eschatological passages of these Pauline letters (1 Thess 4:13-18; 2 Thess 2:1-12). Yet there are also frequent references to the sufferings of the Thessalonians and their strong faith as an example and encouragement to the Christians of later centuries. While there is considerable fidelity to the ideas and wording of the Greek text, there was a freedom on the part of the Syrian translations and commentators to adapt the text and apply it to a certain situation in the spirit of the original writer.

372 Schippers, R. "De papyrusfragmenten van I en II Thessalonicenzen," *Gereformeerd Theologisch Tijdschrift* 57 (1957) 121-127.

There are presently four papyrus fragments which contain the text of the Thessalonian letters: P30, P46, P61, and P65. All four fragments are badly damaged, including the text of 1 Thessalonians in P46 which is the most important papyrus for establishing the text of this letter. Some of the variations found in P30 have been incorporated in the Nestle-Aland text. P61 contains only some six words or fragments of words from 1 Thess 1:2. P65 contains the text of the first two chapters of 1 Thessalonians and clearly demonstrates its independence from the Western text.

373 Zimmer, Friedrich. *Der Text der Thessalonicherbriefe: samt textkritischem Apparat und Kommentar* (Güdlimburg: Chr. Friedr. Viewegs, 1893).

Readings from the various Greek manuscripts, versions and Patristic sources are conveniently collected.

374 ---. "Zur Textkritik des zweiten Thessalonicherbriefes," *Zeitschrift für wissenschaftliche Theologie* 31 (1888) 347-352.

Consideration is given to the major textual variants in 2 Thessalonians, including 1:2, 4, 7, 8; 2:1, 2, 3, 4, 6, 8, 12, 13, 14, 17; 3:3, 6, 8, 13.

Other Relevant Sources:

711, 726, 727, 730, 731, 735, 753, 832.

D. The Authenticity of the Thessalonian Letters

375 Aarde, Andries G. van. "The Struggle against Heresy in the Thessalonian Correspondence and the Origin of the Apostolic Tradition," *The Thessalonian Correspondence* (ed. Raymond F. Collins; Bibliotheca ephemeridum theologicarum lovaniensium 87; Leuven: Leuven University Press, 1990) 418-425.

Paul did not make use of his apostolic authority to convince the Thessalonians. In fact, nowhere in the authentic letters is Paul's claim to authority based on his apostleship. The rhetoric of his kerygma was based rather on his own person as an ideal figure who, by his suffering, imitates the suffering and fate of the prophets and that of the Lord Jesus Christ. Thus the appeal to apostleship in 2 Thessalonians in order to combat heresy (2:1-12) shows this letter to be non-Pauline.

376 Askwith, Edward Harrison. *An Introduction to the Thessalonian Epistles: Containing a Vindication of the Pauline Authorship of both Epistles and an Interpretation of the Eschatological Section of 2 Thess. ii* (London/New York: Macmillan, 1902).

Despite objections based on the claimed non-Pauline character of certain phrases and passages, the perceived incongruities in the letter itself, and some possible anachronisms, a careful evaluation of such factors reaffirms the Pauline authorship of 1 Thessalonians. Although the objections raised against the second letter are more numerous and forceful, especially those objections that highlight differences and supposed contradictions between the eschatology of 2 Thess 2:1-12 with that of the first letter, the Pauline authorship of 2 Thessalonians is similarly vindicated. The key exegetical issues in 2 Thess 2:1-12 should be interpreted as follows: the "apostasy" is not a religious falling away in the church but probably a political rebellion of the Jews against the Romans; the "man of lawlessness" is the Roman emperor claiming divine honors; "the restraining force" and the "restrainer" are also the Roman empire and its leader.

377 Bailey, John A. "Who Wrote II Thessalonians?," *New Testament Studies* 25.2 (1978/79) 131-145.

Although no single argument against Pauline authorship is decisive, the cumulative effect of the literary considerations (particularly the structural similarity), the eschatological differences, the change in tone between the two letters, and non-Pauline usages in the second letter (particularly the autograph greeting in 2 Thess 3:17) is the clear conclusion that 2 Thessalonians is pseudepigraphal. The pseudonymous author was opposing the view that the day of the Lord has already come (2 Thess 2:2: ἐνέστηκεν does not mean "to be at hand," against the RSV). His opponents were Gnostics (see 2 Tim 2:17b-18) who cited 1 Thess 5:4-8 in support of their position. This explains why the author addressed his letter to the Thessalonians, though he released it elsewhere. The letter is to be dated sometime between the death of Paul in the early sixties and the writing of Polycarp's letter to the Philippians in 135 CE.

378 Baur, Ferdinand Christian. "Appendix III. The Two Epistles to the Thessalonians: Their Genuineness and Their Bearing on the Doctrine of the Parousia of Christ," *Paul, the Apostle of Jesus Christ. His Life and Work, His Epistles and His Doctrine* (trans. A. Menzies; 2 vols.; Edinburgh: Williams and Norgate, 1875) 2.314-340.
Originally published as "Die beiden Briefe an die Thessalonicher, Ihre Echtheit und Bedeutung für die Lehre de Parusi Christie," *Theologische Jahrbücher* 14 (1855) 141-168.

In response to the criticisms forwarded by Lipsius (398), Baur defends his earlier claim (379) that the two Thessalonian letters cannot have come from the hand of Paul. In contrast to his previous position, however, Baur argues that 1 Thessalonians must have been written after 2 Thessalonians.

379 ---. "The Two Epistles to the Thessalonians," *Paul, the Apostle of Jesus Christ. His Life and Work, His Epistles and His Doctrine* (trans. A. Menzies; 2 vols.; Edinburgh: Williams and Norgate, 1875) 2.85-97.

Both 1 Thessalonians and 2 Thessalonians differ so much from the authentic Pauline letters that they cannot be ascribed to the apostle Paul. The main purpose of the first letter is to give a comforting view of the second coming, such as the Christians of a later age required. The second letter is intended to correct the nearness of the parousia as it has been presented in the first letter.

380 Braun, Herbert. "Zur nachpaulinischen Herkunft des zweiten Thessalonicherbriefes," *Zeitschrift für die neutestamentliche Wissenschaft* 44 (1952) 152-156.

Rather than treating the question of the inauthenticity of 2 Thessalonians on the basis of its eschatology (2:1-12) or its literary dependence on 1 Thessalonians, questions regarding the letter's theological concepts must be raised. Such topics as judgment (1:5), the kingdom (1:5), tribulation (1:6, 8, 9) and the letter's concern for morality, indicate that 2 Thessalonians was written during the generation after Paul, separated by a number of decades from 1 Thessalonians. In light of the community which still awaits the return of Christ and similarities to Polycarp, a date of 107-117 CE can be proposed.

381 Collins, Raymond F. "'The Gospel of Our Lord Jesus Christ' (2 Thes 1,8): A Symbolic Shift of Paradigm," *The Thessalonian Correspondence* (ed. Raymond F. Collins; Bibliotheca ephemeridum theologicarum lovaniensium 87; Leuven: Leuven University Press, 1990) 426-440.

A comparison of the two letters to the Thessalonians indicates that the language of 2 Thessalonians is much less characteristically kerygmatic than is the language of 1 Thessalonians. This shift in language usage goes hand in hand with 2 Thessalonians' total neglect of the verb κηρύσσω and the relative infrequency of the use of εὐαγγέλιον. Although both letters contain "retrospection" (a looking back to the past), this feature is much less personal and extensive in 2 Thessalonians. The retrospection of 2 Thessalonians also completely omits any explicit reference to the death and resurrection of Jesus and any clearly identifiable creedal formulae. The author of 2 Thessalonians has chosen to ground his exhortation in a tradition attributed to Paul rather than in the common and traditional faith of the church. Thus 2 Thessalonians represents a paradigmatic shift away from the past and the Pauline proclamation to the future and the expectation of the coming Lord.

382 ---. "The Second Epistle to the Thessalonians," *Letters That Paul Did Not Write. The Epistle to the Hebrews and the Pauline Pseudepigrapha* (Good News Studies 28; Wilmington, DE: Michael Glazier, 1988) 209-241.

A historical survey of scholarly opinion regarding the authorship of 2 Thessalonians shows that the heart of the issue concerning this letter's authenticity lies in the document's relationship to 1 Thessalonians. Although some have tried to solve the difficulties in the relationship of the two letters by proposing a different canonical order, different addressees, or different secretaries, the majority of contemporary scholarship considers 2 Thessalonians not to be from the hand of Paul. This conclusion is confirmed by a variety of factors: remarkable similarities of vocabulary with 1 Thessalonians, which are accompanied at the same time by striking departures from Paul's normal writing style; differences in eschatology, tone, christology, paraenesis, and the image of Paul; and the presence of problematic statements in 2 Thessalonians.

383 Deeleman, C. F. M. "2 Thess. 2:1-12," *Tijdschrift* 23 (1905) 252-276.

A consideration of the authenticity of 2 Thessalonians leads to the following two conclusions: (1) 2:1-12 is not from the hand of Paul; (2) this fact by no means repudiates the genuineness of the letter as a whole. The eschatology of Paul in 2:1-12 clearly is at odds with that of his first letter to the Thessalonians as well as his other letters. The author uses genuine Pauline form and words to bolster his argument and assure its acceptance from his readers. It is impossible to believe that Paul, writing to persecuted Gentile believers, would attempt to comfort them with speculations about a Jewish Antichrist who would be destroyed at Christ's appearance. Nowhere else in the New Testament is there a tradition of a Jewish Antichrist who is being restrained by the Roman state. Such a view, however, is found in such church fathers as Irenaeus, Hippolytus, Victorinus, and Tertullian. By comparing various apocalyptic traditions in Jewish, New Testament, and early church sources, it can be determined that 2:1-12 is dependent on the Didache and was written around 130 CE.

384 Findlay, George G. "Recent Criticism of the Epistles to the Thessalonians," *The Expositor, 6th Series* 2 (1900) 252-261.

Several recent works challenge in various ways the authenticity of 2 Thessalonians. Most of these challenges involve some kind of claim about 2 Thess 2:1-12: e.g., that a Nero legend lies behind this passage; that this passage contradicts 1 Thess 5:1-11; that this passage ought to be seen as a later interpolation. None of these arguments, however, warrants the conclusion that 2 Thessalonians was written by someone other than Paul.

385 Friedrich, Gerhard. "1. Thessalonicher 5,1-11, der apologetische Einschub eines Späteren," *Zeitschrift für Theologie und Kirche* 70.3 (1973) 288-315.
Republished in *Auf das Wort kommt es an. Aufsätze sum 70. Geburtstag J. H. Friedrich* (ed. Johannes H. Friedrich; Göttingen: Vandenhoeck & Ruprecht, 1978) 251-278.

1 Thess 5:1-11 was not written by Paul but by a later redactor who corrects the apostle's view of an imminent parousia in light of its delay. The problem being dealt with in 5:1-11 is not anxiety, as in 4:13-18, but false security. The expressions used are general and formalized rather than concrete, as in the rest of the letter, with few distinctly Pauline features. In content the passage appears to be a further development of ideas found in Rom 13:11-14, but without the same sense of imminency. It may have originated in Lukan circles (see Acts 1:7 and especially Luke 21:24, 36). A major purpose of the insertion seems to have been to correct the impression left by 4:15 that Paul expected to live until the parousia. This is done by showing that he reckoned with delay (5:1, "times and seasons") and therefore with the possibility of his own death (5:10). If 5:1-11 is deleted, a smooth transition can be made from 4:18 to 5:12.

386 Graafen, J. *Die Echtheit des zweiten Briefes an die Thessalonicher* (Neutestamentliche Abhandlungen 14; Münster: Aschendorff, 1930).

The authenticity problem of 2 Thessalonians has been discussed by a number of scholars (ch 1). The city was one where Jews and Greeks lived, although there were social differences. The Christians had the expectation of the parousia, and were experiencing tribulations, as reflected in 1 Thessalonians. 2 Thessalonians is not a Jewish-Christian letter, and has its own eschatology (ch 2). The literary and theological characteristics of the letters are difficult to account for by those who think that 2 Thessalonians is inauthentic. Despite small problems with the text, the unity of the text of 2 Thessalonians can be maintained (ch 3). The eschatology of the second letter (see 2 Thess 2:1-17) shows many actual Pauline characteristics when compared to 1 Thess 5:1-11 (ch 4). Thus the authenticity of 2 Thessalonians can be defended.

387 Grimm, Carl Ludwig Wilibald. "Die Echtheit der Briefe an die Thessalonicher gegen Baur's Angriff vertheidigt," *Theologische Studien und Kritiken* 23 (1850) 753-816.

In opposition to the arguments of F. C. Baur and his school, it can be shown that both 1 and 2 Thessalonians are authentic. This can be demonstrated on virtually all the grounds forwarded by Baur and others in his camp. This includes discussion of certain vocabulary, the influence of later theologians, developed church structure, attestation of church fathers, the relationships of faith and works and Jews and Christians as showing parties in the church, Paulinism and Petrinism, relations to the four "normal" Pauline letters, and developments in apocalyptic thought.

388 Gruner, Stephan. "Besteht zwischen den 2. und 1. Briefe an die Gemeinde von Thessalonich eine literarische Abhängigkeit?" *Weidenauer Studien* 2 (1908) 419-464.

A number of scholars have pointed to literary dependence between 1 and 2 Thessalonians as an expected rather than surprising feature, and so use this fact as a powerful argument against the Pauline authorship of these letters. Such arguments go back to F. C. Baur, and were most forcefully clarified by William Wrede. A detailed examination of each of the parallels suggested by Wrede shows that the two letters are not, in fact, literarily dependent upon each other. Thus the main argument that literary dependence between 1 and 2 Thessalonians argues against the authenticity of these two letters is no longer a valid claim.

389 Harnack, Adolf von. "Das Problem des zweiten Thessalonicherbriefes," *Sitzungsbericht der Preussischen Akademie der Wissenschaft zu Berlin, philosophisch-historischen Classe* 31 (1910) 560-578.

The persistent problem that still remains in the investigation of 2 Thessalonians is determining which portions are dependent upon the actual letters and which are themselves authentic. Wrede's investigation of this topic has marshalled the greatest number of arguments against authenticity. In an attempt to solve the puzzle of 2 Thessalonians, thirteen propositions are advanced, distinguishing between the situation, audience, and background of 1 and 2 Thessalonians. 1 Thessalonians is addressed to the larger, pagan Christian community in Thessalonica, while 2 Thessalonians, also a genuine Pauline letter, has a stronger tone and is addressed to a small, factional Jewish-Christian church in the same city. This is consistent with what is known of the Thessalonian church from Acts 17:4.

390 Hilgenfeld, Adolf H. "Die beiden Briefe an die Thessalonicher, nach Inhalt und Ursprung," *Zeitschrift für wissenschaftliche Theologie* 5 (1862) 225-264.

Against F. C. Baur and others who have followed him, 1 Thessalonians can be recognized as an actual writing of Paul, but a writing which cannot be compared in thought and significance with his later, undisputed letters. The apostle has still not reached the high point of his writing. 2 Thessalonians, although it appears to represent the same circumstances of the first letter, was actually written at a much later time. Support for this is found in the rather catholic commendations of 2 Thess 2:13-3:5, the view of the Lord Jesus as God, and a changed perspective regarding the future.

391 Holland, Glenn Stanfield. "'A Letter Supposedly from Us.' A Contribution to the Discussion about the Authorship of 2 Thessalonians," *The Thessalonian Correspondence* (ed. Raymond F. Collins; Bibliotheca ephemeridum theologicarum lovaniensium 87; Leuven: Leuven University Press, 1990) 394-402.

The citation of a revered figure of the past as the authority for information about the events of the end of the world is a self-conscious tradition among apocalyptic writers, and one of which Paul shows himself to be aware in 1 Corinthians and 1 Thessalonians. In light of this fact, it is particularly striking that the apocalyptic scenarios of 2 Thess 1:7b-10 and 2:3-12 lack any such citation of a revered figure of the past as their authority for the very original ideas about the future which these passages contain. The omission of such a reference is problematic and thus suggests that Paul is not the author of 2 Thessalonians. If, however, this letter was written by someone other than Paul, then the problem disappears. For Paul himself is the revered figure of the past whose authority is the basis for the apocalyptic scenario presented by an author of a later generation.

392 Hollmann, Georg. "Die Unechtheit des zweiten Thessalonicherbriefs," *Zeitschrift für die neutestamentliche Wissenschaft* 5 (1904) 28-38.

Four reasons eliminate the Pauline authorship of 2 Thessalonians: its close relationship to 1 Thessalonians; the disagreements between 2 Thess 2:1-12 and 1 Thess 5:1-11; the lack of a personal voice in 2 Thessalonians; and the comparison of 2 Thess 2:2 with 2 Thess 3:17. Each of these four reasons works together but also stands on its own.

393 Holsten, C. "Zur Unechtheit des Ersten Briefes an die Thessalonicher und zur Abfassungszeit der Apocalypse," *Jahrbücher für Protestantische Theologie* 36 (1877) 731-732.

The inauthenticity of 1 Thessalonians can be proven from a single verse. A comparison of Rev 2:2 and 1 Cor 13:13 with 1 Thess 1:3 shows that the Pauline follower who wrote 1 Thessalonians combined together three fundamentals of Paul with three expressions of Jewish Christianity, showing that he had the letters of Revelation from the Ephesian Christian community before him. Thus the letter dates to the time after the death of the apostle and in the time of 1 Clement.

394 Holtzmann, Heinrich Julius. "Zum zweiten Thessalonicher Brief," *Zeitschrift für die neutestamentliche Wissenschaft* 2 (1901) 97-108.

Two points need to made with respect to recent studies of 2 Thessalonians and the inauthenticity of this letter. First, there is new material in this letter, for example, at 2:1-12 (vv 2-9, 11, 12). Second, this letter is a paraphrase and variation of 1 Thessalonians, as seen from the various repetitions at parallel places. The eschatological certainty of 1 Thessalonians is eliminated--a sign of the later composition of 2 Thessalonians.

395 Hurd, John C. "Concerning the Authenticity of 2 Thessalonians" (Unpublished Paper: Annual Meeting of SBL in Dallas, 1983) 1-21.

The following factors and evidence have the cumulative effect of supporting the Pauline authorship of 2 Thessalonians: (1) the external evidence classes 2 Thessalonians with the accepted letters, thus creating an initial presumption of genuineness; (2) the awkwardness of 2 Thessalonians placed soon after 1 Thessalonians should not be used as evidence against authenticity, since these arguments (and others) favor the reverse ordering of the letters; (3) a developmental view of Paul's theology provides a place for 2 Thessalonians as the earliest letter and does not reveal anachronisms in phraseology or concepts; (4) the apocalyptic eschatology is consistent with the eschatology of a stage in

Paul's thought prior to 1 Thessalonians and 1 Corinthians; (5) in genre 2 Thessalonians is not an "epistle" but a "letter" and there are no clear examples of pseudepigraphic letters, only epistles; (6) the letter structure (i.e., A-B-A') and style (i.e., chiasm) agree with Paul's known habits; (7) a historical occasion for the letter at an early point in Paul's career can be found, whereas its occasion and purpose as a later letter are much more difficult to see; and (8) the autographic subscription (3:17) makes good sense in a first letter to the community, but is incautious as the device of a later writer.

396 Klöpper, Albert. "Der zweite Brief an die Thessalonicher," *Theologische Studien und Skizze aus Ostpreussen* 8 (1889) 73-139.

Despite the claims of Friedrich Kern (1123) and others concerning the presence of the Nero *redivivus* myth in 2 Thessalonians, this letter comes from the hand of Paul. 2 Thessalonians contains no sign of the Nero myth, even if such signs can be found in Revelation. 2 Thessalonians belongs to the genre of apocalyptic literature which is pre-Neronian and thus within Paul's lifetime.

397 Laub, Franz. "Paulinische Autorität in nachpaulinischer Zeit (2 Thess)," *The Thessalonian Correspondence* (ed. Raymond F. Collins; Bibliotheca ephemeridum theologicarum lovaniensium 87; Leuven: Leuven University Press, 1990) 403-417.

On the basis of its dependence on 1 Thessalonians and its differing eschatology, 2 Thessalonians is indisputably inauthentic. 2 Thessalonians was written as if it did not know of the existence of 1 Thessalonians, although it literarily imitated it, but without directly imitating it. The result was a Pauline Thessalonian letter written to express the correct understanding of the expected parousia (2 Thess 2:1-12).

398 Lipsius, Richard Adelbert. "Über Zweck und Veranlassung des ersten Thessalonicherbriefs," *Theologische Studien und Kritiken* 27 (1854) 907-934.

Although F. C. Baur is generally correct in his historical reconstruction of the development of early Christianity, he is wrong in his rejection of the Pauline authorship of 1 Thessalonians. The authenticity of this letter is seen in the presence of a sufficient number of Pauline characteristics. These include a Pauline differentiation regarding the gospel, that it was received from God and not from men. This assertion is a direct response to an accusation made by the Jews against the apostle.

399 Littleton, Harold Elijah, Jr. "The Function of Apocalyptic in 2 Thessalonians as a Criterion for its Authorship" (Unpublished Ph.D. Dissertation; Nashville, TN: Vanderbilt University, 1973).

The functions of apocalyptic in Paul's letters include the following: providing the framework within which to understand the cross-resurrection event and history, setting the basis and authority for exhortation and history, setting the basis and authority for exhortation and paraenesis, understanding evil and suffering, establishing a framework of hope, setting the tone of an entire letter, validating the apostle's claim to authority, and providing the impetus to urgency in an expectation of imminent parousia. When 2 Thessalonians is read with a view to these functions, apocalyptic serves as a telling criterion in the issue of Pauline authorship. 2 Thessalonians is eschatologically oriented, but it uses apocalyptic language to create an indeterminate sense of the future, to prove that the end is not near, and to dissuade the readers from apocalyptic expectations. This letter does not reflect Paul's relationship between apocalyptic and soteriology; it uses neither the cross-resurrection event to interpret history nor the apocalyptic context to discuss life and death. The apocalyptic context of faith, hope, and love is absent as faith is redefined as the content of belief, hope ignored, and love seen without relation to God's apocalyptic act in the cross-resurrection event. There is no use of apocalyptic to lend urgency to paraenesis. The conclusion, therefore, is that Paul did not write 2 Thessalonians.

400 MacDougall, Daniel. "The Authenticity of II Thessalonians with Special Reference to its Use of Traditional Material" (Unpublished Ph.D. Dissertation; Aberdeen: University of Aberdeen, 1993).

The earliest external witness of 2 Thessalonians is Polycarp, whose letter shows that the terminus *ad quem* of this Pauline letter is about 90 CE. The "tradition" appealed to in the letter (2 Thess 2:15; 3:6) is not a post-Pauline development but a characteristic of the undisputed letters of Paul. An analysis of the terminology of tradition in the New Testament and Apostolic Fathers, and the traditions in 1 Corinthians, 1 Thessalonians, and 2 Thessalonians, reveals that 2 Thessalonians displays the same form, terminology, function, and volume of tradition as are found in the undisputed letters of Paul. The doctrinal content of the traditions, eschatology, and imitation is Pauline. The eschatology does not present a theology of delay, but rather the Thessalonians can know that the day of the Lord has not arrived because the Lord Jesus has not yet returned to gather his people (the κατέχων) and defeat Satan ("the lawless one"). Nor does the letter show a post-Pauline exaltation of the apostle, for the exemplary behavior of the missionaries is part of Paul's regular evangelistic practice. The christology and soteriology of the letter are entirely consistent with Paul's teaching. A literary analysis of the letter, especially of the traditions in the letter, shows that 2 Thessalonians is an actual letter and not literarily dependent on 1 Thessalonians. Thus the external attestation, the use of tradition, the theology, and the literary style, all show 2 Thessalonians to be an authentic letter from Paul.

401 Manen, Willem Christiaan van. *Onderzoek naar de Echtheid van Paulus' tweeden brief aan de Thessalonicenses* (Utrecht: L. E. Bosch & Zoon, 1865).

This study, explicity devoted to the authenticity of the Thessalonian correspondence, rejects the Pauline authorship of 2 Thessalonians.

402 Milligan, George. "The Authenticity of the Second Epistle to the Thessalonians," *The Expositor, 6th Series* 9 (1904) 430-450.

The external evidence clearly indicates that 2 Thessalonians was recognized as Pauline in the early church. The internal evidence, however, has caused many to question its authenticity. The principal objections to Pauline authorship fall into three categories: (1) the language and style of the letter; (2) its literary relationship to 1 Thessalonians; and (3) the character of its doctrinal contents. Although 2 Thessalonians admittedly possesses a number of unique features, there is not sufficient evidence to warrant the conclusion that it is not from the hand of Paul. Furthermore, the failure of those who reject this letter to present any adequate explanation of how it arose, or of the authority it undoubtedly possessed in the early church, is in itself strong presumptive evidence that the traditional view is correct and that we have here an authentic work of Paul.

403 Munro, Winsome. "The Later Stratum in 1 and 2 Thessalonians," *Authority in Paul and Peter: The Identification of a Pastoral Stratum in the Pauline Corpus and 1 Peter* (Society for New Testament Studies Monograph Series 45; Cambridge: Cambridge University, 1983) 82-93.

The "subjection material" of the New Testament--passages dealing with subjection to authority--does not belong with the more primitive eschatological stratum of tradition, but was introduced later in the first half of the second century as part of a later stratum extending across the Pauline corpus and 1 Peter. In 1 and 2 Thessalonians this later stratum appears in 1 Thess 1:5b, 6a, 7, 2:1-16, 4:1-12, 5:12-15, 21b, 22 and in 2 Thess 2:15, 3:4, 6-15. These passages deal in particular with ecclesiastical office and seek to eliminate the unauthorized activities of charismatics. While the former group is to be honored for their labor in the congregation, the latter group is to be cast out unless they desist and find self-supporting work elsewhere. The apostles serve as a model of physical work to the disorderly, and of diligent labor in teaching the word for recognized leaders.

404 Rauch, Christian. "Zum zweiten Thessalonicherbrief," *Zeitschrift für wissenschaftliche Theologie* 38 (1896) 451-465.

In response to the defense of Pauline authorship by Wilhelm Bornemann, the following two theses are forwarded in support of the inauthenticity of 2 Thessalonians. The first is that 2 Thessalonians was written after the Apocalypse of John but before the Epistle of Barnabas. The second is that 2 Thessalonians, written from a Jewish-Christian standpoint, attempted to put the Pauline eschatology in its proper place in terms of Jewish Christianity. As a result, the letter stands as a monument to the strength of early Christian eschatology at the beginning of the second century.

405 Reiche, Johann Georg. *Authentiae posterioris epistolae ad Thes. vindiciae* (Göttingen: Vandenhoeck & Ruprecht, 1829).

406 Rhijn, C. H. van. "De Jongste Literatuur over de Schriften des Nieuwen Verbonds: De Brieven aan de Thessalonikers," *Theologische Studiën* 4 (1886) 282-309.

As the earliest of Paul's letters, 1 and 2 Thessalonians are important for providing a picture of the apostle's earliest theology. These letters do not show a well-developed christology or soteriology, since law and grace are not explained in any substantive way nor is the doctrine of sin even discussed. The one teaching which is emphasized in both letters is that of eschatology. R. Steck's claim (449) that the apocalyptic picture of 1 Thess 4:15 draws its inspiration from 4 Ezra 5:42 is to be rejected. With respect to the perennial problem of the identity of the restrainer in 2 Thess 2:1-12, it is likely that here Paul has in view the emperor and the Roman state. Within a historical context in which the church has little political influence, it is the state which protects Paul and other believers by restraining the persecutions of the Jews until the one antichristian Jew arises. A brief overview of the historical and political situation of Thessalonica leads to a picture of the church there which is fairly consistent with that described in the letters.

407 Romaniuk, Kazimierz. "Problem Pawlowego autorstwa 2 Tes," *Roczniki Teologiczno-Kanoniczne* 21.1 (1974) 75-83.

A historical survey of how the problem of the authenticity of 2 Thessalonians has been treated shows that there is a contrast between Protestant exegetes, who typically reject the Pauline authorship of this letter, and Catholic exegetes, who generally have maintained its Pauline authorship. Most of the arguments which try to prove the inauthenticity of 2 Thessalonians are not convincing so that the traditional view should be affirmed. It may well be, however, that this letter was not written immediately after 1 Thessalonians but somewhat later, perhaps at the end of Paul's stay in Ephesus during the third missionary journey.

408 Rongy, H. "L'authenticité de la seconde aux Thessaloniciens," *Revue Ecclésiastique de Liège* 21 (1929) 69-79.

Two major objections have been raised against the authenticity of 2 Thessalonians. The first is an argument based on 2 Thess 2:1-2 and 3:17 which seem to imply that there was a letter circulating in Paul's name regarding the return of the Lord, but that it would have been too early for such a document to be found, if the letter were written around 50 CE. The second is the description of the Antichrist in 2 Thess 2:3-5. These objections do not recognize that, as 1 Thessalonians attests, Paul did not necessarily expect the imminent end of the world, and that the question of the identity of the Antichrist is obscure. An obscure passage does not constitute an argument against the authenticity of 2 Thessalonians.

409 Schmidt, Daryl D. "The Authenticity of 2 Thessalonians: Linguistic Arguments," *SBL 1983 Seminar Papers* (ed. Kent H. Richards; SBL Seminar Papers 22; Chico: Scholars Press, 1983) 289-296.

Contemporary linguistics, with its focus not simply on vocabulary and individual phrases but on sentence units and the syntactical relationships within a sentence, provide a more rigorous way to look at the linguistic evidence pertinent to literary questions such as authorship. A comparative study of the two Thessalonian letters with respect to their syntactical patterns and linguistic contact with the audience highlights clear differences. The syntactical style in 2 Thessalonians is closer to that found in Ephesians and Colossians, as it exhibits a more literary style with greater embedding complexity than the rhetorical style found in the unquestionably Pauline letters (1 Thessalonians, Romans, 1-2 Corinthians, Galatians).

410 ---. "The Syntactical Style of 2 Thessalonians: How Pauline Is It?" *The Thessalonian Correspondence* (ed. Raymond F. Collins; Bibliotheca ephemeridum theologicarum lovaniensium 87; Leuven: Leuven University Press, 1990) 383-393.

Contemporary linguistics help describe more precisely the syntactical features which characterize sentences. One important feature is complexity, which is related to the number and type of constituent clauses in a sentence and their relationship to the main clause. The syntactical style of 2 Thessalonians is in several ways closely related to that of Ephesians and Colossians and distinct from the rest of the unquestionably Pauline letters. Although the syntactical style of the letter is not the only factor to consider in evaluating the authenticity of 2 Thessalonians, it is sufficiently non-Pauline to justify the conclusion that this letter does not come from the hand of Paul.

411 Schmithals, Walter. "Zur Abfassung und ältesten Sammlung der Paulinischen Hauptbriefe," *Zeitschrift für die neutestamentliche Wissenschaft* 51 (1960) 225-245.

The fundamental recognition of F. C. Baur and his school for the exegesis of the main Pauline letters was that there was a single front which disrupted his mission, against which he fights in Galatians, 1 and 2 Corinthians, Philippians, and the Thessalonian letters, the last of which reflects church polemic. This has not been followed in past exegesis in its assessment of the Pauline polemic, instead allowing Paul to face different opponents in his different letters. This creates a difficulty in assessing Paul's third missionary journey, during which all of his seven main letters were written. A synoptic chart shows the parallels in these letters. 1 and 2 Thessalonians, the last of the letters written, except for Romans, were written at the time when Paul was coming to terms with the Corinthian erroneous teaching, giving evidence that the apostle was not dealing with an acute threat to the community in Thessalonica, but with an erroneous teaching which was spreading.

412 Soden, Hans von. "Der erste Thessalonicherbrief," *Theologische Studien und Kritiken* 58 (1885) 263-310.

The current state of discussion of 1 and 2 Thessalonians rejects their authenticity, which can be disputed, against the argument of the Baur school. First, the formal character of the letter must be discussed, including the linguistic arguments and the style of the letter. Then there must be a consideration of its theological content, and the historical dating of the letter. In none of these considerations is there an indication that the letter is non-Pauline. In all regards it is Pauline, and compares favorably with the four major Pauline letters.

413 Stepien, Jan. "Autentycznosc listow do Tessaloniczan," *Collectanea Theologica* 34 (1963) 91-182.

There has been much discussion concerning the authenticity of the Thessalonian letters, especially the second letter. Internal evidence supports the claim that both letters are from the hand of Paul. The similarities between both letters can be explained by the common theological perspective of the apostle, and the differences by the changed situation and objective.

414 ---. "Pawlowy charakter nauki dogmatycznej i moralnej listów do Thessaloniczan," *Ruch Biblijny i Liturgiczny* 13 (1960) 243-268.

The Pauline character of the dogmatic and moral teachings in 1 and 2 Thessalonians testifies to the authenticity of these disputed letters. In particular, the divine names and the eschatological teaching are decidedly Pauline. The catechetical style of the two letters goes back to the oral forms which Paul adopted and in his later letters modified considerably. Although the unique needs of the Thessalonian community gave rise to some distinctive emphases in these letters, the theological statements and ethical exhortations as a whole are thoroughly Pauline.

415 ---. "Problem wzajemnego stosunku literackiego listów do Tessaloniczan i próby jego rozwiazania," *Ruch Biblijny i Liturgiczny* 13 (1960) 414-435.

An examination of the problem of the literary relationship between 1 and 2 Thessalonians and the various solutions which have been proposed illustrates the weaknesses of those arguments which advocate the inauthenticity of these letters. Although not without problems, the simplest and most convincing argument recognizes both 1 and 2 Thessalonians as being written by Paul. The similarities between the two letters can be explained by a psychological reason: 1 Thessalonians is the fruit of the long and intensive labor of Paul's heart and mind; thus the ideas contained in it were easily recalled, when the occasion arose, in a form hardly different from that already used. The differences between the two letters are due to the different circumstances which occasioned them.

416 Trilling, Wolfgang. "Literarische Paulusimitation im 2. Thessalonicherbrief," *Paulus in den neutestamentlichen Spätschriften: Zur Paulusrezeption im Neuen Testament* (ed. Karl Kertelge and Gerhard Lohfink; Quaestiones disputatae 89; Freiburg: Herder, 1981) 146-156.

The non-Pauline authorship of 2 Thessalonians has only recently been widely acknowledged and mostly in German-speaking circles. The pseudepigraphal authorship of this letter can be seen first of all in its literary dependence on 1 Thessalonians. This involves a consideration of its literary predecessor and the kind of use it makes of the first letter. 2 Thess 1:1-2, for example, takes the prescript of 1 Thessalonians over almost directly. Second, there is the evidence of the theological alterations and developments. 2 Thessalonians reflects a later development when Jesus is spoken of with God language and several Pauline concepts have been altered. For example, the differences in the eschatology of 2 Thessalonians from that of the authentic Pauline letters are well known. Third, there is the theological development of the "apostle," in which Paul moves from being human to becoming the founder of the tradition.

417 ---. *Untersuchungen zum zweiten Thessalonicherbrief* (Leipzig: St. Benno, 1972).

2 Thessalonians is clearly deutero-Pauline. This conclusion is arrived at through the following four chapter discussion. First, there is a critical overview of the controversy over authenticity, showing this monograph to be conceptually a continuation of the work of William Wrede as well as selections from other earlier scholars. Turning away from arguments based on relations with a previous letter and eschatology, the case against the authenticity of 2 Thessalonians next considers matters of style (e.g., various kinds of phrases, expressions, and preferred words), including its tone (which lacks any personal references), form-critical considerations, and the theology of the letter. The discussion of the letter's style is a direct response to the arguments supporting the authenticity of 2 Thessalonians forwarded by Beda Rigaux (147). Third, a form-critical analysis of each passage of significance demonstrates that the letter was not by Paul but was a didactic letter sent not to any specific community. Finally, the characteristics of this pseudepigraphal writing are established on the basis of its theology, which, in its use of tradition and view of God and Christ, reflects a later period, with the author standing within the Pauline tradition.

418 Verhoef, Eduard. "The Relation between 1 Thessalonians and 2 Thessalonians and the Inauthenticity of 2 Thessalonians," *Hervormde Teologiese Studies* 53.1-2 (1997) 163-171.

Attempts to defend the authenticity of 2 Thessalonians by claiming either that 2 Thessalonians was written first (C. Wanamaker: 182) or that 1 Thessalonians was written by Silas while 2 Thessalonians was written by the apostle (C. Lecompte: 104, 105) are not convincing on grammatical grounds. The great similarities between the two letters are best explained by viewing 2 Thessalonians as a pseudepigraphal letter.

419 Widla, B. "Nowe spojrzenie na autentycznosc 2 Tes," *Studia Theologica Varsaviensia* 14.1 (1976) 227-232.

A reappraisal of the authenticity of 2 Thessalonians in light of the recent claims of Wolfgang Trilling, *Untersuchungen zum zweiten Thessalonicherbrief* (417).

420 Wrede, William. *Die Echtheit des zweiten Thessalonicherbriefs untersucht* (Texte und Untersuchungen zur Geschichte der altchristlichen Literatur 24.2; Leipzig: Henrichs, 1903).

2 Thess 2:4 requires a later dating of 2 Thessalonians. The hypothesis that this letter is not Pauline is confirmed by an analysis of its vocabulary, composition, contents, and theological orientation. The use of the temple indicates that it was probably written after 70 CE. Although it is impossible to ascertain who might have written this pseudepigraphal letter, its date in the early second century appears quite probable.

421 Wrzól, Josef. *Die Echtheit des zweiten Thessalonicherbriefs* (Biblische Studien 19.4; Freiburg: Herder, 1916).

In spite of the arguments of William Wrede (420) against the authenticity of 2 Thessalonians, there remains good evidence that Paul was the author of this letter. One can account for similarities in language and structure between 1 Thessalonians and 2 Thessalonians not on the basis of copying by a later pseudepigrapher but on the basis of Paul having kept a copy of the first letter, to which he referred when composing the second. The problems in Thessalonica had developed after the apostle had sent 1 Thessalonians and thus there was a need for him to clarify what had been inadequately stated in the first letter.

422 ---. "Sprechen II. Thess. 2,2, und 3,17 gegen den paulinischen Ursprung des Briefes?" *Weidenauer Studien* 1 (1906) 271-289.

2 Thess 2:2 and 3:17 have played a key role in discussions concerning the authenticity of 2 Thessalonians. If analyzed in their appropriate context, these two verses should be seen not as indicating forgery but as signs of authenticity.

Other Relevant Sources:

306, 317, 327, 424, 427, 428, 434, 435, 438, 439, 441, 447, 464, 465, 467, 492, 493, 496, 566, 768, 795, 815, 970, 1011, 1097, 1178, 1180.

E. The Unity of the Thessalonian Letters

423 Bohlen, Reinhold. "The Unity of 1 Thessalonians," *Theology Digest* 36.2 (1989) 132-134.

Originally published in German as "Die neue Diskussion um die Einheitlichkeit des 1. Thessalonicherbriefes: Eine Kurzinformation für die Verkünigungspraxis," *Trier theologische Zeitschrift* 96.4 (1987) 313-317.

After a mid-nineteenth century challenge, scholarship has almost unanimously agreed on the Pauline authorship of 1 Thessalonians because of content, vocabulary, and style. Yet questions persist about the letter's unity. Rudolf Pesche (430), for example, contends that 1 Thessalonians was redacted from two different Pauline letters to this Macedonian congregation. Pesche holds that the redactor wanted to impart greater importance in the composite letter than each alone had, and that Paul's formulaic epistolary structure allowed easy redaction of this letter. This partition hypothesis is not only plausible but also suggestive for additional redactive activity in Paul's other letters.

424 Bonsack, Bernhard. "Literarkritische Kapricen zu den Thessalonicherbriefen," *Theologische Kaprizen: Festschrift für Hans Friedrich Geisser zum 60. Geburtstag* (ed. Markus

Baumgartner and Hans Jürgen Luibl; Zürich: Univ. Theol. Fak. Inst. Hermeneutik, 1988) 180-190.

After an examination of a number of differing hypotheses, 1 Thessalonians still appears to be one Pauline letter, to which 2:9-12, 14-16, 3:3b-5 and 4:1-12 were later added. With respect to 2 Thessalonians, it appears that 2:1-12 not only could have been written by Paul but could have been written only by Paul and no one else. Thus in these two letters we have two authentic Pauline letters: 1 Thess 1:1-10, 2:13, 2:1-8, 2:17-3:3a, 3:6-13, 4:13-5:28, and 2 Thess 1:1-4, 2:1-3:3.

425 Carroll, Kenneth L. "The Expansion of the Pauline Corpus," *Journal of Biblical Literature* 72 (1953) 230-237.

It seems highly probable from the clues furnished by the Marcionite prologues, the seven-fold tradition reflected by the collections of Revelation and Ignatius, and the suggestion of 1 Clement, that the Corinthian and Thessalonian correspondence existed as two letters (both 1 and 2 Corinthians and 1 and 2 Thessalonians being united under one title for each pair) in the original edition of the Pauline Corpus rather than as four as we now have them. The editor and publisher of the Pauline corpus, located in Ephesus about 95 CE, did this so as to have seven letters--the number seven symbolizing the perfect completeness of the whole. The Pauline corpus was later expanded to include the Pastoral letters in an attempt to neutralize the effects of Marcion's canon. At this time both the Corinthian and Thessalonian correspondence each became two letters.

426 Collins, Raymond F. "Apropos the Integrity of 1 Thess," *Ephemerides theologicae lovanienses* 65 (1979) 67-106.
Republished in Raymond F. Collins, *Studies on the First Letter to the Thessalonians* (Bibliotheca ephemeridum theologicarum lovaniensium 66; Leuven: Leuven University Press, 1984) 96-135.

A number of twentieth-century scholars have called into question the integrity of 1 Thessalonians. These critics fall into two categories: (1) proponents of an interpolation theory (Rudolf Knopf, Maurice Goguel, Alfred Loisy, S. G. F. Brandon, Ernst Fuchs, Birger Pearson, Christoph Demke, Gerhard Friedrich, and Hendrikus Boers) and (2) proponents of a compilation theory (Robert Scott, Karl-Gottfried Eckart, Walter Schmithals, and Ebba Refshauge). An examination of the arguments against the unity of the letter reveals that they rest upon untenable presuppositions. The interpolation theories presuppose Pauline consistency in the articulation of thought and the use of language. The compilation theories assume that a certain epistolary form was normative for the composition of Paul's letters. In light of the untenable nature of these presuppositions and the weakness of the arguments advanced by the critics, as well as the unanimous witness of the manuscript tradition, the integrity of 1 Thessalonians ought to be maintained.

427 Demke, Christoph. "Theologie und Literarkritik im 1. Thessalonicherbrief: Ein Diskussionsbeitrag," *Festschrift für Ernst Fuchs* (ed. Gerhard Ebeling, Eberhard Jüngel, and Gerd Schunack; Tübingen: Mohr, 1973) 103-124.
Republished in English as "Theology and Literary Criticism in 1 Thessalonians," *Journal of Higher Criticism* 3.2 (1996) 194-214.

The difficulties in the structure of 1 Thessalonians and the tensions in its terminology and theology, which sometimes resemble the other Pauline letters and at other times the work of Luke, can be attributed to the fact that a post-apostolic author created this writing using parts of an authentic Pauline letter. In this process, he shaped above all the beginning (1:2-2:16), the middle (3:12-4:8), and the conclusion (5:23-27), thereby creating a two-part document that in the first part (1:2-3:13) presents the apostle, witnessed to by the church, as the true example and teacher for imitation by the faithful, and in the second part (4:1-5:28) provides guidance for faithful perseverance in holiness by raising up the apostolic tradition.

428 Eckart, Karl-Gottfried. "Der zweite echte Brief des Apostels Paulus an die Thessalonicher," *Zeitschrift für Theologie und Kirche* 58 (1961) 30-44.

There should no longer be any doubt that 2 Thessalonians was written not by Paul but by a pseudonymous writer at a later time. The authenticity of this letter has been questioned since Schmidt in 1801, even though it engendered significant debate. The Pauline authorship of 1 Thessalonians has also not remained beyond critical doubt since the time of Baur. This first letter offers a remarkable picture, combining both Pauline and non-Pauline elements. A form-critical analysis reveals that there are two authentic Pauline letters in 1 Thessalonians. The first established contact with the church and consists of 1:1-2:12, 2:17-3:4 and 3:11-13. Some four to six weeks later, in Athens, after Timothy returned, Paul wrote a second letter which consists of 3:6-10, 4:13-5:11, 4:9-10a and 5:23-26, 28. A comparison with other Pauline letters and the presence of certain liturgical features indicates that 4:1-8, 10b-12 and 5:12-22 are not authentic.

429 Kümmel, Werner Georg. "Das literarische und geschichtliche Problem des ersten Thessalonicherbriefes," *Neotestamentica et Patristica: Eine Freundesgabe Oscar Cullmann zum 60. Geburtstag* (ed. W. C. van Unnik; Novum Testamentum Supplements 6; Leiden: Brill, 1962) 213-222.
Republished in *Heilsgeschehen und Geschichte. Gesammelte Aufsätze 1933-1964* (ed. E. Grässer, O. Merk, and A. Fritz; Marburger theologische Studien 3; Marburg: N. G. Elwert, 1965) 406-416.

The question of the origin and unity of 1 Thessalonians is now being strongly called into question. K.-G. Eckart (428) has argued that 1 Thess 4:1-8, 10b-12 and 5:12-22 are non-Pauline paraenesis, indicating that the canonical 1 Thessalonians has been formed by combining two Pauline letters. These arguments can all be refuted and the unity of the letter ought to be recognized. The historical situation of 1 Thessalonians is that it was probably written in Corinth in 51 CE, after Paul's first visit to Athens.

430 Pesch, Rudolf. *Die Entdeckung des ältesten Paulus-Briefes. Paulus - neu gesehen: Die Briefe an die Gemeinde der Thessalonicher* (Herderbücherei; Freiburg: Herder, 1984).

Within 1 Thessalonians is found a still older Pauline letter, which was written by Paul from Athens to the Christian community in Thessalonica. This has been redacted together with a later letter written from Corinth to the same community. The basis for this reconstruction is a number of double features: thanksgiving, benediction, situation, epistolary closing and exhortation, among others. The first letter consisted of 2:13-16, 2:1-12, 2:17-3:5, 4:1-8, 3:11-18, and the second letter of 1:1, 1:2-10, 3:6-10, 4:9-12, 4:13-18, 5:1-11, 5:12-22, 5:23-28.

431 Refshauge, Ebba. "Literarerkritiske overvejelser: Til de to Thessalonikerbreve," *Dansk Teologisk Tidsskrift* 34.1 (1971) 1-19.

A literary and source-critical analysis of 1 and 2 Thessalonians indicates that these two letters have undergone major editorial changes. Both letters contain two openings (1 Thess 1:3-10 and 2:13; 2 Thess 1:3-12 and 2:13-14), in which the second and more compact opening seems to be the original one which was later developed. The same thing can be said about the two conclusions found in each letter (1 Thess 3:11-13 and 5:23-24; 2 Thess 2:16-17 and 3:16). Commencing from there, one could well take up again the convergent details which lead to reconstituting the two original letters by Paul: 2 Thess 2:13-14; 2:1-2; 3:11-15; 2:16-17; 3:17-18, and 1 Thess 2:13; 2:1-2; 1:6; 2:17-20; 3:5-10; 4:13-14; 5:1-5a; 5:9-11; 5:16-21 (22); 3:11-13; 5:25-28. One thus obtains two coherent letters which are well adapted to a concrete situation and of the same length as the indisputable Philemon.

432 Romaniuk, Kazimierz. "Czas powstania i jednos'c' literacka 1 Tes," *Verbum Crucis. Kardynalowi B. Kominkowi w holdzie* (Wroclaw, 1974) 150-160.

A literary analysis of 1 Thessalonians makes it difficult to accept the unity of the letter in its present form. Evidence of redactional activity appears in the eschatological material of 4:13-5:11.

433 Schmithals, Walter. "Die historiche Situation der Thessalonicherbriefe," *Paulus und die Gnostiker. Untersuchungen zu den kleinen Paulusbriefen* (Theologische Forschung 35; Hamburg-Bergstedt: Reich, 1965) 89-158.
Republished in English as "The Historical Situation of the Thessalonian Epistles," *Paul and the Gnostics* (trans. J. E. Steely; Nashville: Abingdon, 1972) 123-218.

A detailed study of 1 Thess 2:1-12 not only reaffirms the apologetic function of this passage but, along with other key passages in the letters, illumines the historical situation lying behind 1 and 2 Thessalonians. Four genuine letters of Paul to the Thessalonians have been combined to produce the two letters now found in the New Testament: Letter A (2 Thess 1:1-12 + 3:6-16), which was sent on first hearing news of disturbing happenings in the church; Letter B (1 Thess 1:1-2:12 + 4:2-5:28), which further attempts to help the church withstand the influence of Gnostic preachers; Letter C

(2 Thess 2:13-14 + 2:1-12 + 2:15-3:5 + 3:17-18), which is Paul's reply to news that a letter, falsely ascribed to him, has been circulated and has encouraged apocalyptic enthusiasm; and Letter D (1 Thess 2:13-4:1), which contains Paul's reactions after he has sent Timothy to clear up the problems in the church.

434 ---. "Die Thessalonicherbriefe als Briefkompositionen," *Zeit und Geschichte: Dankesgabe an Rudolf Bultmann zum 80. Geburtstag* (ed. Erich Dinkler; Tübingen: Mohr/Siebeck, 1964) 295-315.

A few scholars have rightly recognized that 1 Thessalonians consists of two actual Pauline letters. With respect to 2 Thessalonians, the Baur school has rejected this letter as inauthentic and a literary imitation of 1 Thessalonians. This, however, is not the most plausible explanation. The two proömiums of both 1 and 2 Thessalonians (the second being 2 Thess 2:13-14 and 1 Thess 2:13) and the two benedictions in each (2 Thess 2:16-3:5 combining both--the first ending at 1 Thess 4:2 and the second beginning at 5:23) indicate that 1 and 2 Thessalonians are made up of four authentic letters of Paul. Thess A = 2 Thess 1:1-12 + 3:6-16; Thess B = 1 Thess 1:1-2:12 + 4:3-5:28; Thess C = 2 Thess 2:13-14 + 2:1-12 + 2:15-3:5 + 3:17-18; Thess D = 1 Thess 2:13-4:2.

435 Sumney, Jerry L. "The Bearing of a Pauline Rhetorical Pattern on the Integrity of 2 Thessalonians," *Zeitschrift für die neutestamentliche Wissenschaft* 81.3-4 (1990) 192-204.

The parallels in the arrangement, themes, vocabulary, and movement of thought in 2 Thessalonians between 1:3-12 and 2:13-3:5 show that the A-B-A pattern or "sonata form" is present in this letter. This rhetorical pattern provides positive evidence for the integrity of 2 Thessalonians. There is no longer any need to appeal to theories of redaction to account for unique features of the letter's form. Since this rhetorical pattern is an authentically Pauline pattern found in 1 Thessalonians and 1 Corinthians, its presence in 2 Thessalonians also supports the authenticity of the letter. It seems less likely that a secondary author would have noticed this pattern and repeated it than that Paul himself used it again.

Other Relevant Sources:

598, 659, 863.

F. The Order of the Thessalonian Letters

436 Bristol, Lyle O. "Paul's Thessalonian Correspondence," *Expository Times* 40 (1944) 223.

The priority of 2 Thessalonians over 1 Thessalonians seems likely for the following reasons: (1) it is more probable that 1 Thessalonians is an elaboration of the same matters treated in 2 Thessalonians than the reverse scenario; (2) the death of some of the church's members (1 Thess 4:13-18) points to some time having elapsed between Paul's ministry there and the writing of 1 Thessalonians; and (3) the ecclesiastical organization presupposed in 1 Thess 5:12-13 suggests that this letter is of a later date.

437 Gregson, R. "A Solution to the Problems of the Thessalonian Epistles," *Evangelical Quarterly* 38.2 (1966) 76-80.

Problems related to the occasion and purpose of the Thessalonian correspondence can be resolved by inverting the canonical order of these two letters.

438 Hurd, John C. "The Jesus Whom Paul Preaches (Acts 19:13)," *From Jesus to Paul: Studies in Honour of Francis Wright Beare* (ed. Peter Richardson and John C. Hurd; Waterloo: Wilfrid Laurier University Press, 1984) 73-89.

2 Thessalonians is an authentic Pauline letter which was written immediately following the founding of the Thessalonian church. 1 Thessalonians is a later reply which responds to specific issues raised in a letter written to the apostle by the Thessalonians. A study of these two early letters, along with 1 Corinthians, with respect to such topics as the Lord's Supper, ethics, immoral men, missionary urgency, life in the kingdom, and the words of the Lord, demonstrates that Paul, at this stage of his life, is very conscious of the tradition he received from those who were in Christ before him and that his own first preaching was in direct continuity with theirs. Later events, however, caused Paul to modify and refine his early beliefs, and as a result, the specific dependency on Jesus' teaching no longer lies on the surface.

439 Manson, Thomas W. "St. Paul in Greece: The Letters to the Thessalonians," *Bulletin of the John Rylands University Library of Manchester* 35.2 (1953) 428-447.
Republished as Thomas W. Manson, "The Letters to the Thessalonians," *Studies in the Gospels and Epistles* (ed. Matthew Black; Manchester: Manchester University Press, 1962) 259-278.

Acts provides a historically accurate account of the events of Paul's missionary activities in Philippi, Thessalonica, Athens, and, finally, Corinth. A careful consideration of the two Thessalonian letters with respect to their authorship and interrelationship shows that both letters are genuine and that 2 Thessalonians was written first.

440 Neri, P. "2Ts: Ovverosia, prima lettera ai Tessalonicesi," *Bibbia e Oriente* 32.4 (1990) 230, 246.

The traditional ordering of the two Thessalonian letters should be reversed so that 2 Thessalonians is understood as Paul's first letter, written while he was still in Athens. This letter was written in response to what Paul had vaguely heard (2 Thess 3:11, "We hear that some among you are idle") whereas the later letter (1 Thessalonians) was based on the concrete report of his envoy, Timothy, the probable carrier of the earlier letter. The exhortation in 2 Thess 2:15 to "stand firm and hold to the teachings we passed on to you, whether by word of mouth or by letter" refers not to some previous letter but to 2 Thessalonians itself, the first letter sent by Paul to this congregation.

441 Rongy, H. "De Adjunctis et Scopo Scriptionis 2ae Ep. Ad Thessalonicenses," *Revue Ecclésiastique de Liège* 5 (1909) 97-100.

Although the canonical order is not necessarily the chronological one, it is wrong to date 2 Thessalonians before 1 Thessalonians, especially given the references to an earlier letter in 2 Thess 2:15 and 3:14. The mention of an alleged Pauline letter (2:2) does not disprove the authenticity of 2 Thessalonians. It was probably not a forgery, but a letter from another leading Christian which was mistakenly attributed to Paul.

442 Thompson, Edward. "The Sequence of the Two Epistles to the Thessalonians," *Expository Times* 56 (1945) 306-307.

Lyle Bristol's argument for the priority of 2 Thessalonians (436) fails to take account of four points of evidence: the early testimony of the Muratorion Fragment, the estimated period of the sojourns at Berea and Athens, the three classes of people within these Greek towns, and the persons addressed in the Thessalonian letters. These points of evidence provide additional evidence for the traditional ordering of the letters.

443 Thurston, Robert W. "The Relationship between the Thessalonian Epistles," *Expository Times* 85.2 (1973) 52-56.

The repetition of the triad "faith, hope, and love," both in the opening of 1 Thessalonians (1:3) and the closing of the letter body (5:8), suggests that this is the main outline of the letter as a whole: faith (1:2-3:11), love (3:12-4:12), and hope (4:13-5:22). A major objection to this outline is the presence of 2 Thessalonians in which Paul corrects the church whose faith he has very recently praised at great length in the preceding letter. One way to account for this seeming change in attitude between 1 and 2 Thessalonians is to reverse the order of the letters. T. W. Manson (439) has presented a number of compelling grounds for the priority of 2 Thessalonians. A reconsideration of these grounds, as well as a number of additional considerations, supports the conclusion that 2 Thessalonians was written first and delivered by Timothy on his return visit to Thessalonica.

444 Trudinger, Paul. "The Priority of 2 Thessalonians Revisited: Some Fresh Evidence," *Downside Review* 113 (1995) 31-35.

Although compelling evidence has been forwarded for the priority of 2 Thessalonians, comparatively little notice or credibility has been given to this view. In addition to the arguments of Johannes Weiss and, more recently, T. W. Manson (439), three other factors can be cited in support of reversing the order of the Thessalonian letters. The references in 1 Thessalonians to Paul's example as a hard worker (2:9), to sanctification (4:3-8), and to election (1:4-5), can all be seen as the apostle's explanation of these three topics which were first raised in 2 Thessalonians (3:7; 2:13).

445 West, J. C. "The Order of 1 and 2 Thessalonians," *Journal of Theological Studies* 15 (1914) 66-74.

A number of problems in the relationship between the two Thessalonian letters are solved if 2 Thessalonians is seen as having been written first. For example, the eschatology of 2 Thessalonians, with its marked Jewish coloring, is more naturally understood as earlier than that of 1 Thessalonians where Paul's thought is more advanced. Or again, the silence of 2 Thessalonians about any impending visit by Paul in contrast to 1 Thessalonians with its strong expectation of an immediate visit (2:17-18; 3:10) is easily explained if the order of the letters is reversed. Also, Timothy's mission fits better if it was subsequent to 2 Thessalonians and prior to 1 Thessalonians. Thus, 2 Thessalonians was the first letter Paul wrote to the Thessalonians, quite likely from Berea.

Other Relevant Sources:

307, 308, 378, 395, 447.

G. The Date of the Thessalonian Letters

446 Bosch, Jorge Sanchez. "La chronologie de la première aux Thessaloniciens et les relations de Paul avec d'autres églises," *New Testament Studies* 37 (1991) 336-347.

Two chronological questions need to be addressed: (1) Should 1 Thessalonians be considered as written prior to the rest of the Pauline letters? (2) Should the material in 1 Thessalonians be dated as posterior to that which is recounted in Gal 2:1-14, concerning Paul's relations with the Jerusalem community and the conflict in Antioch? On the basis of the available evidence, 1 Thessalonians is the oldest extant Pauline letter and indeed the earliest document of the New Testament (ca. 50-52 CE). Once this chronology is established, it is possible to examine the development of the relationships Paul had with other churches, including the later events at Jerusalem and the conflict at Antioch.

447 Grosheide, F. W. "De methode om de volgorde der Paulinische Brieven te bepalen, in het bijzonder in verband met de Brieven aan de Thessalonicensen onderzocht," *Gereformeered theologisch tijdschrift* (formerly *Wat zegt de Schrift?*) 20 (1919) 262-270, 305-319.

In recent times, attempts to establish a chronology for the Pauline letters have proceeded from assumptions based on external historical data and hypotheses related to doctrinal development. In such approaches, special revelation and internal evidence does not account for much. Typical of this approach is the work of W. Hadorn (317), who argues in favor of inverting the traditional sequencing of the Thessalonian letters and also concludes that both were written much later during Paul's third missionary journey. The parousia errors mentioned in both letters lead Hadorn to believe that an early writing was not possible, since much time would have been needed for these divergent errors to develop. Nevertheless, Hadorn's methods and conclusions are not convincing. The nature of the eschatological errors and the fact that they could not have occurred simultaneously require that 1 Thessalonians must have preceded 2 Thessalonians. Otherwise, Paul would have dealt with both errors in his first letter. Therefore, the traditional view that 1 Thessalonians was written at Corinth on the second missionary journey and that 2 Thessalonians was written a short time later is correct.

448 Schwank, Benedikt. "Der sogenannte Brief an Gallio und die Datierung des 1 Thess," *Biblische Zeitschrift* 15.2 (1971) 265-266.

Although Béda Rigaux believed that all had been said regarding the Delphi inscription regarding Gallio and the Pauline chronology (*Paulus und seine Briefe: Der Stand der Forschung* [Munich: Kösel-Verlag, 1964] 100), A. Plassart makes two observations regarding the fragmentary condition of the inscription and the difficulties of its interpretation ("L'inscription de Delphes mentionnant le Proconsul Gallion," *Revue des études grecques* 80 [1967] 372-78). As a result, the Pauline chronology seems to be that the emperor Claudius' letter was received in the Spring of 52-53, and Gallio was at the latest in his post in the Spring of 51-52. 1 Thessalonians was thus written at the latest at the end of 50, but more probably 49, and the Apostolic Council was more likely in 48.

449 Steck, R. "Das Herrenwort 1. Thess. 4, 15," *Jahrbücher für protestantische Theologie* 13 (1883) 509-524.

The eschatological section of 1 Thess 4:13-5:3 has the same viewpoint as 1 Corinthians 15, but it also has a few unique features, such as meeting Christ in the air. We have no previous source for the parousia for the living, which is grounded on an appeal to a word of the Lord (1 Thess 4:15). This word seems to be derived from 4 Ezra 5:42, which means that this letter must have been written after 4 Ezra. Thus 1 Thessalonians must date to the end of the first century and is the oldest example of the appropriation of Jewish apocalyptic by Christianity.

450 Suggs, M. Jack. "Concerning the Date of Paul's Macedonian Ministry," *Novum Testamentum* 4 (1960) 60-68.

Three statements in the letters of Paul (Phil 4:15-16; 1:5; 2 Thess 2:13) provide evidence that Macedonia was the apostle's first or very early missionary field. Conventional theories which, using the testimony of Acts, date Paul in Macedonia for the first time about 50 CE violate the plain language of the letters. If one chooses the expressed testimony of Paul over the witness of some late first-century "Luke," then the result is to date the apostle's presence in Macedonia to about 40 CE and the Thessalonian correspondence a short time later.

451 Uprichard, Robert Edward Henry. "An Examination of the Early Date Hypothesis for the Writing of 1 Thessalonians, with Particular Reference to Development in Paul's Theology" (Unpublished Th.D. Dissertation; Belfast: Queen's University of Belfast, 1976).

Other Relevant Sources:

313, 377.

H. The Form of the Thessalonian Letters

452 Baasland, Ernst. "Die περί-Formel und die Argumentation(ssituation) des Paulus," *Studia theologica* 42 (1988) 69-87.

A noticeable linguistic phenomenon in Paul is the eleven times that he uses the περί formula, three of them in 1 Thessalonians (4:9; 4:13; 5:1). This formula is largely overlooked or only briefly commented upon in the commentaries. An investigation of its usage in extra-biblical Greek literature, the papyri, and the church fathers indicates that the περί formula had, in the first instance, its location in the schoolroom in the disputation between students and teacher. In 1 Thessalonians, the usage is related to the theme of eschatology, and was probably used to further discussion by introducing the consequences of certain Christian teaching.

453 Barbaglio, Giuseppe. "Analisi formale e letteraria di 1 Tess. 1-3," *Testimonium Christi. Scritti in onore di Jacques Dupont* (ed. M. Agelini *et al.*; Brescia: Paideia, 1985) 35-56.

A formal and literary analysis of 1 Thessalonians 1-3 reveals the unity of this section of the letter as well as its constituent sections. The three references to the giving of thanks (1:2; 2:13; 3:9) should not be seen as three different thanksgivings but rather one prolonged and continuous thanksgiving. In this lengthy section Paul narrates the history of the "we-you" relationship between the missionaries and the Thessalonians. The text consists of the following sections: thanksgiving (1:2-10); apostolic apology, which takes up the motive of thanksgiving (2:1-12); repeated thanksgiving (2:13-16); and apostolic parousia with an apologetic intent (2:17-3:13).

454 Berger, Klaus. "Apostelbrief und apostolische Rede/Zum Formular frühchristlicher Briefe," *Zeitschrift für die neutestamentliche Wissenschaft* 65 (1974) 190-231.

This discussion of the form of early Christian letters compares them with Hellenistic letters, showing that the special letter formulae which Paul used were not only for theological reasons but for contextual and sociological reasons as well. The features worth considering include discussion of the "grace and peace" wish at the opening of letters. Their origin is not in epistolary literature of the time but in forms of Jewish mystical and revelatory literature (such as that of the Dead Sea Scrolls, the apocrypha, and pseudepigrapha). The thanksgiving also shows this influence, as opposed to that of Hellenistic letters, as is the case in the use of rhetoric, especially the diatribe. The result is a Christian letter with two clear parts: the theological argument and the paraenetic section.

455 Bjerkelund, Carl J. *Parakalô: Form, Funktion und Sinn der Parakalô-Sätze in den paulinschen Briefen* (Bibliotheca Theologica Norvegica 1; Oslo: Universitetsforlaget, 1967).

There are three kinds of παρακαλέω sentences: (1) those that use this verb and are the typical construction; (2) those that do not use this verb but still follow the typical construction; and (3) those that do not follow the typical construction but can be analyzed that way. Usually the παρακαλέω sentence is used for requests, with a number of synonyms also employed. It is not a technical term for paraenesis. Παρακαλέω sentences are found in the papyri (the primary material to use for the research of this topic), inscriptions, Greek authors, Jewish and Christian authors, as formulae used in various ways. The use of this formula in 1 and 2 Thessalonians is helpful in evaluating the claims of W. Schmithals (433, 434) concerning the integrity of these letters. Schmithals does not take into account in his argument the παρακαλέω sentences. This verb is used in the letter style, for example, in 4:1-2 to mark the end of the thanksgiving of chapters 1-3 and the beginning of the letter body in 4:1. Specific passages discussed are 1 Thess 4:10b-12, 5:14, 4:1, 5:12-13; 2 Thess 2:1-2 (pp 140-158).

456 Boers, Hendrikus. "The Form Critical Study of Paul's Letters. 1 Thessalonians as a Case Study," *New Testament Studies* 22.2 (1975/76) 140-158.

The form and function of the Pauline letter is clarified by focusing on 1 Thessalonians as a case study. 1 Thessalonians exhibits a completely normal letter form, with the exception of 2:13-16. If this passage is recognized as an anti-Jewish interpolation, the following form of the letter emerges: prescript (1:1); thanksgiving (1:2-10); apostolic apology (2:1-12); apostolic parousia (2:17-3:13); exhortation (4:1-5:22); and conclusion (5:23-28). 1 Thessalonians is a paraenetic letter with two characteristic main parts: philophronesis (chs 1-3) and exhortation (chs 4-5). The purpose of the letter is both to express Paul's joy and satisfaction with the Thessalonian believers and to spur them on to a way of life which is pleasing to God.

457 Callow, John. *A Semantic Structure Analysis of Second Thessalonians* (Dallas: Summer Institute of Linguistics, 1982).

A semantic structural analysis of 2 Thessalonians shows the letter to consist of the following major and minor units: 1:1-2; 1:3-12 (vv 3-4, 5-10, 11-12); 2:1-17 (vv 1-12 [1-3a, 3b-5, 6-8, 9-12], 13-14, 15, 16-17); 3:1-5 (vv 1-2, 3-5); 3:6-16a (vv 6-11, 12, 13, 14-15, 16a); and 3:16b-18.

458 Chapa, Juan. "Consolatory Patterns? 1 Thes 4,13-18; 5,11," *The Thessalonian Correspondence* (ed. Raymond F. Collins; Bibliotheca ephemeridum theologicarum lovaniensium 87; Leuven: Leuven University Press, 1990) 220-228.

1 Thess 4:13-5:11 is often considered part of a paraenetic letter influenced by a specific letter type: the "letter of consolation." This letter type had a very important place in the ancient world and fulfilled an important role in both philosophical and rhetorical traditions. But despite a number of formal and thematic similarities between 1 Thess 4:13-5:11 and the letter of consolation, this passage has greater affinities to the Jewish tradition.

459 ---. "Is First Thessalonians a Letter of Consolation?" *New Testament Studies* 40 (1994) 150-160.

The scattered consolatory topics in 1 Thessalonians are not in themselves sufficient evidence to classify the letter as thematically or literarily similar to the Greco-Roman letter of consolation. Nevertheless, 1 Thessalonians contains some rhetorical strategies current in literature of consolation. One is justified in calling it a consoling letter without intending to exclude other valid purposes.

460 Cornelius, E. "Die funksie van die 'danksegging(s)' in 1 Tessalonisense," *Hervormde Teologiese Studies* 49 (1993) 57-84.

The problem of multiple thanksgivings in 1 Thessalonians (1:2-10; 2:13-16; 3:9-13) is better approached with the help of an interactive model than from the traditional perspectives of form or content. This approach indicates that the term "thanksgiving" is a misnomer for these passages in 1 Thessalonians. Their function is rather to render the implied reader favorable toward the encoded author so that he/she can be receptive to the argumentation.

461 Crook, Zeba Antonin. "Paul's Riposte and Praise of the Thessalonians," *Biblical Theology Bulletin* 27.4 (1997) 153-163.

An honor and shame reading of 1 Thessalonians reveals that Paul wrote the letter as a riposte to a series of challenges that emanated from the young congregation. Paul defended his honor in this letter in several ways: by refuting the accusations of the Thessalonians directly and explicitly, by appealing to their memories of his conduct and his teaching, by correcting the erroneous views manifested in their own behavior and conduct, and, finally, by referring to his ascribed honor as one chosen by God and as an apostle of Christ. This letter also indicates that Paul considered it his business to keep the Thessalonians within the standard of behavior defined by God's "court of reputation." Therefore, while defending his honor, which he was culturally forced to do, Paul deliberately wrote praise (what others have identified as "warmth") into the letter, expressing pride in and love for the Thessalonians. This model also highlights how the praise of the letter in no way contradicts its defensiveness. Indeed, the praise in 1 Thessalonians functions as a central part of the rhetoric of Paul's riposte.

462 Faw, Chalmer E. "On the Writing of First Thessalonians," *Journal of Biblical Literature* 71 (1952) 217-225.

The chief weakness in the hypothesis of J. R. Harris (863), the first to propose that 1 Thessalonians is a response to a specific letter from Thessalonica, is his failure to see the stronger evidence for his position in chapters 4-5. For here one can find three converging lines of evidence in support of this theory: (1) the repeated use of the reply formula, περὶ δέ and its variants; (2) the abruptness of the transitions in 4:9, 4:13, 5:1 and 5:12; and (3) the seeming reluctance of Paul to discuss the subjects of brotherly love and the times and seasons of Christ's return. 1 Thessalonians, therefore, is Paul's reply based on both the letter from the church leaders in Thessalonica and the oral report from Timothy.

463 Hester, James D. "Inventional Strategies in Paul's First Letter to the Church in Thessalonica," *Rhetoric, Scripture and Theology: Essays from the 1994 Pretoria Conference* (ed. Stanley E. Porter and Thomas H. Olbricht; Journal for the Study of the New Testament Supplement Series 131; Sheffield: Sheffield Academic Press, 1996) 251-279.

In responding to the report from Timothy (1 Thess 3:6), Paul adapted the structure and topics of Athenian and Roman funeral orations, particularly those topics which dealt with the praise of ancestors, the honor of family traditions, and the exhortation for the living to imitate the virtues and the actions of the honored dead. Paul did this because those topics could be adapted to speak to the issue of the fate of those who had died in Christ and also to exhort the living members of the church to imitate the "heroes" of salvation history, including the missionary team who had first brought the gospel to Thessalonica, the Thessalonians themselves, and in fact all Christians who had suffered affliction "with joy"--the basic example of which were the churches of Judea. The complexities of the Thessalonian situation suggested to Paul the appropriateness of adapting the topics of a funeral oration in his written response to the congregation there.

464 Holland, Glenn Stanfield. *The Tradition that You Received from Us: 2 Thessalonians in the Pauline Tradition* (Hermeneutische Untersuchungen zur Theologie 24; Tübingen: Mohr/Siebeck, 1988).

A rhetorical analysis of 2 Thessalonians reveals the following outline for the letter: Epistolary prescript (1:1-2); Exordium (1:3-4); Narratio (1:5-12); Probatio (2:1-17); Exhortatio (3:1-13); Peroratio (3:14-16); and Epistolary postscript (3:17-18). This rhetorical structure reveals the function of the apocalyptic material which the letter contains: this material is the specific basis on which a battle between contending interpretations of the Pauline traditions was fought. The pseudepigraphal writer of 2 Thessalonians uses the letter as a kind of commentary on 1 Thessalonians, setting out the particular way in which the eschatology of that earlier letter ought to be understood. The author of 2 Thessalonians is concerned to show his readers where they stand in the eschatological sequence of events. The "beginning of the birth-pangs," culminating in the disaster of 70 CE, is now past and the readers exist in an intervening time prior to the day of the Lord. That day cannot come until the man of lawlessness is revealed. This evil figure is currently being restrained by the angel of God who is the agent of the divine will. The "mystery of lawlessness" already at work refers to the activity of the ἄτακτοι in the Thessalonian church.

465 Hughes, Frank Witt. *Early Christian Rhetoric and 2 Thessalonians* (Journal for the Study of the New Testament Supplement Series 30; Sheffield: JSOT Press, 1989).

2 Thessalonians is best understood as a deutero-Pauline or pseudo-Pauline letter. The emergence of the rhetoric of 2 Thessalonians is best explained by a theological conflict over end-time views among differing branches of Pauline Christianity after the apostle's death. 2 Thessalonians is a polemical response to other Paulinists who teach a fulfilled eschatology, which the author attacks by telling his readers that this heretical theology comes from a forged Pauline letter or letters. The theology which the author of 2 Thessalonians attacks is a theology underlying Colossians and Ephesians.

466 ---. "The Rhetoric of 1 Thessalonians," *The Thessalonian Correspondence* (ed. Raymond F. Collins; Bibliotheca ephemeridum theologicarum lovaniensium 87; Leuven: Leuven University Press, 1990) 94-116.

A comparison of 1 Thessalonians to several traditions within Greco-Roman rhetoric aids in the identification of the letter's rhetorical situation. This identification, in turn, serves as a useful matrix for exploring some of the historical questions connected with the letter. 1 Thessalonians is a fairly clear specimen of epideictic rhetoric and possesses the following structure: Exordium (1:1-10); Narratio (2:1-3:10); Partitio (3:11-13); Probatio (4:1-5:3); Peroratio (5:4-11); Exhortation (5:12-22); and Epistolary Conclusion (5:23-28). This use of epideictic rhetoric is completely consistent with an author's intent to strengthen a relatively good relationship which already exists.

467 ---. "The Social World of 2 Thessalonians," *Listening* 31.2 (1996) 105-116.

Rhetorical criticism helpfully bridges the gap between the analysis of the rhetorical situation and the social situation of 2 Thessalonians. This pseudonymous letter, which makes use of deliberative rhetoric, testifies to the struggle for power and control within the Pauline churches after the apostle's death. The opponents are fellow Pauline Christians with different views over end-time matters. This competing eschatology which is under attack by the writer of 2 Thessalonians is a theology also advocated in a couple of other pseudonymous letters: Colossians and Ephesians.

468 Hurd, John C. "Concerning the Structure of 1 Thessalonians" (Unpublished Paper: Annual Meeting of SBL in Los Angeles, 1972) 1-49.

A survey of the various formal elements found in 1 Thessalonians reveals that Paul had many forms and patterns available to him. Most of these forms and patterns become visible only through a comparative analysis with other letters of that day, whether by Paul or others. One pattern in 1 Thessalonians which conveniently organizes what Paul had to say in this particular letter is the triad of faith, love and hope--a triad found not only in the letter's opening (1:3) but near its close as well (5:8). The structure of 1 Thessalonians, therefore, may be roughly outlined as follows: Letter Opening (1:1-10); 1st Major Panel: Christian *Love* established in the Past (2:1-12); 2nd Major Panel: Christian *Faith*fulness in the present (2:17-3:8); 3rd Major Panel: Christian *Hope* for the Future (4:13-5:11); Letter Closing (5:12-28).

469 Jervis, L. Ann. *The Purpose of Romans. A Comparative Letter Structure Investigation* (Journal for the Study of the New Testament Supplement Series 55; Sheffield: JSOT Press, 1991).

The presupposition of this monograph is that by a comparative investigation of certain formal features of the letters of Paul, the function of any particular Pauline letter can be established. Although primarily concerned with determining the purpose of Romans, this epistolary analysis also examines the following sections of Paul's letters to the Thessalonians: the Letter Opening (1 Thess 1:1; 2 Thess 1:1-2): pp 70-72; the Thanksgiving (1 Thess 1:2-10; 2 Thess 1:3-12): pp 91-96; the Apostolic Parousia (1 Thess 2:17-3:13): pp 114-116; and the Letter Closing (1 Thess 5:23-28; 2 Thess 3:16-18): pp 140-142.

470 Johanson, Bruce Carl. *To All the Brethren: A Text-Linguistic and Rhetorical Approach to I Thessalonians* (Coniectanea Biblica; New Testament Series 16; Stockholm: Almqvist & Wiksell, 1987).

Communication models borrowed from text-linguistics, literary theory, and both modern and ancient rhetoric, helpfully serve to reconstruct the meaning of 1 Thessalonians as an act of communication. The persuasive strategies observed in the text-internal part-whole relations in relation to the accessible text-context features indicate that it is the rhetorical-persuasive function which dominates over other functions. In other words, the bulk of persuasive strategies are shown to be directed to solving the issues arising from the exigence reflected in 1 Thess 4:13-5:11. The integrity and unity of 1 Thessalonians are substantiated both in view of the overall rhetorical coherence of the text as a persuasive act and on the basis of intercorroborative criteria in the pragmatic, semantic and syntactic text-dimensions indicating a tightly woven, consistently symmetrical composition. At the same time, the text gives evidence of a rich, creative intertextuality of overlapping structures and functions common to ancient Greek letters and to rhetorical-persuasive discourse, as well as to Old Testament-Jewish exhortatory discourse appropriate to an anticipated worship-setting of reception. This complex intertextuality is seen as reflecting an intention to provide the text with appropriate features such that any simple generic classification of the text cannot be entirely adequate.

471 Kelcy, Raymond C. "A Grammatical and Syntactical Analysis of I Thessalonians" (Unpublished Ph.D. Dissertation; Fort Worth, TX: Southwestern Baptist Theological Seminary, 1963).

Grammar and syntax constitute the most vital factors in the exegesis of any passage of scripture, including 1 Thessalonians. Since God's revelation to humanity is found in human language, it seems reasonable to conclude that an understanding of words and their functions and of their mutual relations in sentences is necessary to an understanding of that revelation. It is true that other factors are necessary for a proper exegesis of scripture, namely, lexical, comparative, historical, and contextual considerations. Nevertheless, the grammatical factor is the most important of all.

472 Koester, Helmut. "I Thessalonians--Experiment in Christian Writing," *Continuity and Discontinuity in Church History: Essays Presented to George Huntston Williams on the Occasion of his 65th Birthday* (ed. F. Forrester Church and Timothy George; Studies in History of Christian Thought 19; Leiden: Brill, 1979) 33-44.

1 Thessalonians cannot be classified according to any of the known genres of ancient letters. This carefully composed document is actually an experiment in the composition of literature which signals the momentous entry of Christianity into the literary world of antiquity. With the creation of the Christian letter, Paul forged for himself a powerful political weapon in his struggle to organize and sustain the church he had founded. Since 1 Thessalonians is the first letter of its kind, Paul naturally could not rely on established Christian conventions. Instead he had to make use of non-Christian traditional materials such as the topos of the description of the "philosopher" in 2:1-12, the catalogue of vices derived from Hellenistic Judaism in 4:1-12, and the eschatological metaphors and cliches in 5:1-11.

473 Lambrecht, Jan. "Thanksgiving in 1 Thessalonians 1-3," *The Thessalonian Correspondence* (ed. Raymond F. Collins; Bibliotheca ephemeridum theologicarum lovaniensium 87; Leuven: Leuven University Press, 1990) 183-205.
Republished in Jan Lambrecht, *Pauline Studies: Collected Essays* (Bibliotheca ephemeridum theologicarum lovaniensium 115; Leuven: Leuven University Press/Peeters, 1994) 319-341.

A careful analysis of those genuine Pauline writings which contain one or more thanksgivings demonstrates that there are not two distinct types of thanksgiving as P. Schubert (484) proposed but one type containing three basic elements: (1) the stable "kernel" of the main clause (the present); (2) the reason for gratitude, i.e., the "memory" (the past); and (3) the "petition" (the future). This pattern is evident in 1 Thess 1-3 where each of the three elements (1:2-10; 2:13-16; 3:9-10) is separated from each other by a couple of seeming digressions which address issues of the relationship of Paul to the Thessalonian community (2:1-12: apology for Paul's past ministry in Thessalonica; 2:17-3:8: apology for Paul's present absence from Thessalonica). This structure provides a reliable insight into Paul's line of thought and particular aspects of his theology.

474 Lee, Robert, and Carolyn Lee. "An Analysis of the Larger Semantic Units of 1 Thessalonians," *Notes on Translation* 56 (1975) 28-42.

An analysis of the grammatical and lexical evidence found in the surface structure of the Greek text of 1 Thessalonians delineates the larger semantic units of the letter. 1 Thessalonians is a typical letter which is distinguished by (1) an introduction, which includes a greeting and a prayer (1:1-10); (2) a body, which contains the major portion of the letter (2:1-5:24); and (3) a conclusion, which ends the letter and includes some personal greetings and a prayer (5:25-28).

475 Lohmeyer, Ernst. "Probleme Paulinischer Theologie," *Zeitschrift für die neutestamentliche Wissenschaft* 26 (1927) 158-173.

The prescript of a Pauline letter has a double connection: one to the peculiarities of the situation between sender and receiver, and the other to the conventions of the letter form. The variations which Paul introduces in his epistolary prescript invite examination of their source and meaning. Here the "grace" and "peace" language, the references to God and Christ, and the use of "God our Father" are examined. 1 Thess 3:11 and 2 Thess 1:12 and 2:16 are examined in particular. It is noteworthy that in none of these instances is the name of God found without the article. This indicates that the usage predates Paul and is part of early Christian tradition.

476 Malbon, Elizabeth Struthers. "'No Need To Have Any One Write'? A Structural Exegesis of 1 Thessalonians," *SBL 1980 Seminar Papers* (ed. Paul J. Achtemeier; Chico, CA: Scholars Press, 1980) 301-335.
Revised and republished in *Semeia* 26 (1983) 57-83.

The application of Claude Lévi-Strauss' interpretive method, developed for the study of myth, to 1 Thessalonians elucidates the structure of this early Christian correspondence. An examination of the letter's syntagmatic structure (the chronological order of events, ideas, emotions, etc. presented in the text) and its paradigmatic structure suggests a parallel between the apostolic parousia and the parousia "of the Lord": both aim to re-establish a relationship, to fill an absence with a "presence." A typology of structural approaches to texts, based on a consideration of structuralist goals and textual foci, suggests both commonalities and distinctions among various structural approaches to texts, and outline a framework within which structural criticism might be said to operate.

477 Malherbe, Abraham J. "Exhortation in First Thessalonians," *Novum Testamentum* 25.3 (1983) 238-256.
Republished in Abraham J. Malherbe, *Paul and the Popular Philosophers* (Minneapolis: Fortress, 1989) 49-66.

Although the paraenetic character of 1 Thessalonians has long been recognized, often this letter is not carefully examined against the background of Greco-Roman traditions of moral exhortation so as to discern what would be striking to its Greek readers. In both halves of the letter (chs 1-3; 4-5), Paul makes generous use of the hortatory traditions current in his own day. At the same time, however, his use of this traditional hortatory material is marked by profound change as he reshapes it to express his experience of God working in him, or stresses the theological and religious dimensions of ethics, or uses traditional Christian material to address issues also of concern to pagan consolers.

478 ---. "Hellenistic Moralists and the New Testament," *Aufstieg und Niedergang der römischen Welt* 2.26.3 (ed. Wolfgang Haase; Berlin: de Gruyter, 1992) 267-333.

There is much affinity between Christian ethical teaching and that of the Hellenistic moralists. Given this recognized similarity of early Christian morality to its Hellenistic antecedents, the writings of the New Testament, especially the letters of Paul and James, can be expected to betray such influence. 1 Thessalonians, for example, exhibits the characteristics of a paraenetic letter. The description of the readers as "imitators," the theme of remembrance of what is already known, expressed by οἴδατε and μνημονεύετε, the description of Paul himself in an antithetical style, the theme of *philophronesis*, all contribute to this conclusion.

479 Menken, Maarten J. J. "The Structure of 2 Thessalonians," *The Thessalonian Correspondence* (ed. Raymond F. Collins; Bibliotheca ephemeridum theologicarum lovaniensium 87; Leuven: Leuven University Press, 1990) 373-382.

2 Thessalonians is a carefully constructed letter consisting of three major parts within an epistolary framework (1:1-2 and 3:17-18): 1:3-12; 2:1-17; 3:1-16. Each major part displays a concentric structure. The first section leads to the second by introducing the theme of the eschatological retribution for present suffering at the parousia of Christ. The third section draws the practical consequences from the warning against the supposition that the day of the Lord is here, especially as far as the undisciplined ones are concerned. The second section constitutes the most important part of the letter's message. An analysis of the structure of 2 Thessalonians aids the exegesis of the letter by highlighting the central points of each major part and of the letter as a whole, and by displaying correlations between corresponding elements.

480 Olbricht, Thomas H. "An Aristotelian Rhetorical Analysis of 1 Thessalonians," *Greeks, Romans, and Christians. Essays in Honor of Abraham J. Malherbe* (ed. David L. Balch, Everett Ferguson, and Wayne A. Meeks; Minneapolis: Fortress, 1990) 216-236.

Recent rhetorical studies have emphasized arrangement or structure, while paying relatively little attention to proofs (invention). A rhetorical analysis which is true to Aristotle, however, involves not just arrangement but proofs and style as well. Aristotle's *Rhetoric* is the only legitimate rhetorical handbook to use in studying Paul's letters, since the remaining extant handbooks are Roman and date to after the apostle's time. Modern scholars have applied the three Aristotelian genres too rigidly, none of which fit 1 Thessalonians. The new setting of the Christian assembly--a setting not envisioned by Aristotle--requires the creation of a new genre: "church rhetoric." It is based on the Christian vision in which the world is the arena where God, through his Son and the

Spirit, carries out his divine purposes among humans. Paul's purpose in 1 Thessalonians is to do precisely what he said he did during his original ministry there: "encouraging, comforting, and urging you to lead lives worthy of God" (2:12). Thus, the kind of church rhetoric found in 1 Thessalonians can be designated as "reconfirmational."

481 Patte, Daniel. "Method for a Structural Exegesis of Didactic Discourses: Analysis of 1 Thessalonians," *Semeia* 26 (1983) 85-136.

There exists a need to establish a method of structural exegesis aimed at elucidating the "system of convictions" (fundamental and "narrative" semantic systems) of didactic texts such as Paul's letters. To accomplish this goal, the characteristics of didactic discourses are considered, showing in the process their differences as compared with narrative texts. The results of this comparative analysis are a proposed methodology involving a series of specific analytical steps. The validity of this methodology is verified through an analysis of 1 Thessalonians. This analysis does not present the exegetical results aimed at by the method. Rather, this analysis merely shows how the fundamental and "narrative" semantics of the text is *organized* in this didactic text, i.e., *how* Paul's system of convictions is manifested in the letter.

482 Rivera, Luis Fernando. "Estructuras de la I y II epístola a los Tesalonicenses," *Revista Bíblica* 38 (1976) 67-68.

1 Thessalonians is to be outlined according to the following major divisions: greeting (1:1); the thanksgiving, which has the exhortation as its goal (1:2-3:13); the exhortations grounded in the gospel (4:1-5:24); final admonitions and greetings (5:25-28). The structure of 2 Thessalonians is as follows: introduction (1:1-2); the action of thanksgiving (1:3-12); the content of the exhortation: the parousia (2:1-12); the action of thanksgiving (2:13-17); final admonitions (3:1-15); benediction (3:16-18).

483 Schnider, Franz, and Werner Stenger. *Studien zum neutestamentlichen Briefformular* (New Testament Tools and Studies 11; Leiden: Brill, 1987).

An analysis of the various epistolary formulae in the New Testament letters involves a comparative study of these documents, with a particular focus on the opening, closing, and body sections. Both 1 and 2 Thessalonians open with the prescript, with the only distinctive features being the lack of titles attributed to the sender and co-senders and the way in which the recipients as a church are identified in relation to God and Jesus Christ. These distinctive features may be indicative of the early Pauline letter form. The issue of the thanksgiving in 1 and 2 Thessalonians is complex as they are the only letters with multiple thanksgivings (1 Thess 1:2-10; 2:13-16; 3:9-13; 2 Thess 1:3-12; 2:13-14). The opening convention of the "self-recommendation" in 1 Thess 2:1, 2:17 and 2 Thess 2:1 establishes the sender's authority over the recipients by giving the justification for writing. The formulae identified in the closing are the final exhortations (1 Thess 5:12-25; 2 Thess 3:1-16), the closing instructions (1 Thess 5:26-27), and the benediction (1 Thess 5:28; 2 Thess 3:17-18).

484 Schubert, Paul. *Form and Function of the Pauline Thanksgivings* (Beihefte für Zeitschrift für die neutestamentliche Wissenschaft 20; Berlin: Töpelmann, 1939).

Direct exegesis of the Pauline thanksgivings with reference to their respective letters reveals beyond any shadow of doubt their strictly epistolary form and function. A form-critical or comparative analysis of the Pauline thanksgivings reveals that they exhibit two structural types: the more elaborate thanksgivings (type Ia--Phlm, 1 Thess, Col, Phil), which characterize the more intimate and personal letters; and the simpler thanksgivings (type Ib--1 Cor, Rom, 2 Thess), which characterize the less intimate and less personal letters. The primary purpose of the Pauline thanksgiving, as also that of the epistolary thanksgiving in the papyrus letters, is to introduce the vital theme of the letter. An analysis of the Pauline thanksgiving in the light of the usages of εὐχαριστῶ, etc., throughout the writings of the Greco-Roman world leads to the conclusion that Paul was not just a Jew who was "exposed" to Hellenistic "influences," but that he was an indigenous Hellenist.

485 Simpson, John W., Jr. "Shaped by the Stories: Narrative in 1 Thessalonians," *Asbury Theological Journal* 53 (1998) forthcoming.

Reading 1 Thessalonians as rhetoric rather than report involves looking at the letter not for direct information about the addressees but for what the letter tells the addressees about themselves. Whatever the actual circumstances and background of their congregation's origin, Paul gives them a self-understanding which includes a background untouched by Judaism, a conversion under the preaching of the missionary-authors which brought them into the "salvation" side of the boundary running through humanity, a unity as a congregation, and a love for the missionaries. They are also told that they know all about this, which amounts to telling them "to remember it this way." Thus they are being shaped by the stories as the stories are alluded to in the letter. This structuring of the addressees' memory and self-understanding has the purpose of validating their experience, providing a basis for exhortation, validating the work of Paul and his associates, and providing the addressees with a congregational tradition.

486 Smith, Abraham. *Comfort One Another. Reconstructing the Rhetoric and Audience of 1 Thessalonians* (Literary Currents in Biblical Interpretation; Louisville: Westminster John Knox, 1995).

Paul consciously constructed 1 Thessalonians in the form of a Hellenistic letter of consolation and he exploited the rhetorical and social conventions of the consolatory tradition to both comfort and challenge believers in Thessalonica. This is evident from, among other things, the striking similarities between Paul's first letter to the Thessalonians and the Hellenistic consolatory tradition. Following the simplified *dispositio* of the consolatory letters, the structure of 1 Thessalonians consists of the exordium (1:1-5), consolatory arguments (1:6-2:16; 2:17-3:13; 4:1-5:22) and the peroratio (5:23-25).

487 Thieme, Karl. "Die Struktur des ersten Thessalonicherbriefes," *Abraham Unser Vater: Juden und Christen im Gespräch über die Bibel. Festschrift für Otto Michel zum 60. Geburtstag* (ed. Otto Betz, Martin Hengel, and Peter Schmidt; Arbeiten zur Geschichte des Spätjudentums und Urchristentums 5; Leiden: Brill, 1963) 450-458.

An analysis of 1 Thessalonians according to the repeated use of key words aids the interpretation of this letter. Such an analysis is especially helpful in identifying the boundaries of the major sections in the letter. 1 Thessalonians can thus be divided into the following five major units: 1:2-2:16; 2:17-3:10; 4:1-12; 4:13-5:11; 5:12-24.

488 Vanhoye, Albert. "La composition de 1 Thessaloniciens," *The Thessalonian Correspondence* (ed. Raymond F. Collins; Bibliotheca ephemeridum theologicarum lovaniensium 87; Leuven: Leuven University Press, 1990) 73-86.

A text-linguistic approach which is not bogged-down with sigla and meta-language is the best approach to try and understand the structure of 1 Thessalonians. It is interesting to note that there is already a high degree of agreement on the primary divisions of 1 Thessalonians, and even, surprisingly, on the secondary divisions. Unfortunately, the use of rhetorical criticism based on the ancient rhetorical manuals has obscured the significance of these divisions. It would be far better to take an approach which recognizes the epistolary nature and origin of 1 Thessalonians. Such an approach reveals a triangular relationship in the letter, affirmed on several occasions, between the Lord, Paul and his co-workers, and the Thessalonians. This is the most significant and specific trait of the letter as a whole.

489 Walton, Steve. "What has Aristotle to Do with Paul? Rhetorical Criticism and 1 Thessalonians," *Tyndale Bulletin* 46.2 (1995) 229-250.

A number of scholars have recently used insights from rhetorical criticism to understand 1 Thessalonians. Four main answers have been given to the question of the letter's rhetorical genre: deliberative, epideictic, paraenesis, and a letter *sui generis*. A key issue connected with this question is whether Paul faced opponents in the church at Thessalonica (1 Thess 2:1-12). The evidence favors a negative conclusion and this makes it unlikely that the letter should be classified as forensic rhetoric. Instead, the letter's focus on praise and blame suggests that its rhetorical genre is epideictic.

490 Werner, John R. "Discourse Analysis of the Greek New Testament," *The New Testament Student and His Field* (ed. John H. Skilton and Curtiss A. Ladley; Philadelphia: Presbyterian and Reformed Publishing, 1982) 213-233.

Careful attention to lexical unity, grammatical coherence, and boundary features provides more objective criteria by which to discern in a confident manner paragraph structures of the New Testament letters. When these linguistic criteria are applied to 2 Thessalonians, the following outline of the letter emerges: Letter Opening (1:1-2); Section 1 (1:3-12); Section 2 (2:1-12); Section 3 (2:13-17); Section 4 (3:1-5); Section 5 (3:6-15); Letter Closing (3:16-18).

491 Wuellner, Wilhelm. "The Argumentative Structure of 1 Thessalonians as Paradoxical Encomium," *The Thessalonian Correspondence* (ed. Raymond F. Collins; Bibliotheca ephemeridum theologicarum lovaniensium 87; Leuven: Leuven University Press, 1990) 117-136.

The concern for what kind of rhetoric Paul practices in his first letter to the Thessalonians must be focused not on rhetorical "schemes" *in* 1 Thessalonians but on the rhetorical structure *of* 1 Thessalonians. This letter is best understood as a *paradoxon enkomion*, a widely known and popular sub-genre of epideictic rhetoric. The rhetorical structure of 1 Thessalonians is as follows: Exordium (1:1-10); the "Main Argument" in the Letter (2:1-5:22); Peroration: Recapitulation and Final Appeal (5:23-28).

Other Relevant Sources:

352, 430, 443, 494, 496, 552, 647, 695, 696, 697, 757, 841.

I. The Purpose of the Thessalonian Letters

492 Aarde, Andries G. van. "The Second Letter to the Thessalonians Reread as Pseudepigraph," *Journal of Higher Criticism* 3.2 (1996) 237-266.

The traditional interpretation of 2 Thessalonians as an authentic letter of Paul in which the primary problem which he addressed was that of the delayed parousia can no longer be sustained. Once this letter is recognized as pseudepigraphal, it is possible to reread 2 Thessalonians as an anti-Sadducean polemic. The "lawless" figure who takes his seat in the temple and proclaims himself to be God symbolizes the Sadducean temple authorities. The Roman administration can thus be seen as the "restrainer" of this enemy. In addition, it was the Sadducean aristocracy who served as patrons, thereby resulting in the embarrassing situation of some Christians being still dependent on these unbelieving, well-to-do benefactors. The strongly Old Testament and Jewish character of the coming judgment exacted at Christ's return is also readily understood against the background of an anti-Sadducean polemic.

493 Day, Peter. "The Practical Purpose of Second Thessalonians," *Anglican Theological Review* 45.2 (1963) 203-206.

The pseudonymous writer of 2 Thessalonians has one thoroughly Pauline trait: the theological message does not stand alone, but is the ground for a practical course of action. Thus the eschatological discussion of 2:1-17 serves as the basis for the practical exhortations of 3:6-15. The writer of 2 Thessalonians significantly expands Paul's admonition in 1 Thess 4:11-12 concerning work in order to oppose the establishment of paid clergy.

494 Donfried, Karl Paul. "The Theology of 1 Thessalonians as a Reflection of its Purpose," *To Touch the Text: Biblical and Related Studies in Honor of Joseph A. Fitzmyer* (ed. Maurya P. Horgan and Paul J. Kobelski; New York: Crossroad, 1989) 243-260.

1 Thessalonians is about God who is present among his elect and suffering people and who is leading them to their promised salvation. The theological themes found in the letter are a response to situations created by persecution and martyrdom as well as to the problem of living the Christian life in the midst of a pagan culture. External evidence that the Thessalonian church was under attack is found in 2 Cor 8:1-2, the witness of Acts 17:1-9, and the close relationship between a Jewish theology of martyrdom with that found in 1 Thessalonians. A number of other passages either explicitly (1:6; 2:13-16; 3:3; 3:4) or implicitly (1:4; 1:7; 2:18; 3:5; 4:13) also point to a situation of persecution in the Thessalonian church. 1 Thessalonians, therefore, is not primarily a "paraenetic" letter but a "paracletic" letter--a *consolatio*. More precisely, this letter is a λόγος παραμυθητικός to a Christian congregation suffering the effects of persecution.

495 Giblin, Charles Homer. "The Heartening Apocalyptic of Second Thessalonians," *The Bible Today* 26 (1988) 350-354.

2 Thessalonians is a pseudepigraphal letter that contains sober yet heartening sets of warnings, encouragement, and prayer, written in the language of apocalyptic. The author deliberately, even humbly, submerged his own identity in order to maintain a more general, apostolic line of teaching as he felt he could recapitulate it for his own times and in view of new, ecclesial needs: persecutions or harassments from outside the community (1:3-12); confusion about events associated with the Day of the Lord (2:1-17); and problems from disorderly (not just "idle") Christians.

496 Peterson, Robert John. "The Structure and Purpose of Second Thessalonians" (Unpublished Ph.D. Dissertation; Cambridge, MA: Harvard University, 1967).

A comparison of the epistolary structure and outline of 2 Thessalonians with that of 1 Thessalonians, as well as the use of apocalyptic material in 2 Thessalonians, highlights both the structure and purpose of the second letter to the Thessalonians. The author of 2 Thessalonians, whether it be Paul or someone else, used two sources for this letter. From 1 Thessalonians, he took the epistolary outline, which was then fitted around material which came out of the common early Christian apocalyptic tradition. The purpose of the letter is to cool down apocalyptic enthusiasm rooted in the belief that the "Day of the Lord" is dawning. The writer wants to counter such a claim and get the community to return to more normal activities. This is accomplished by using an apocalyptic argument to counter an apocalyptic enthusiasm.

Other Relevant Sources:

1104.

J. The Theology of the Thessalonian Letters

497 Agouridis, Savas. "The Intense Expectation of the End Times: How It was Dealt with in 1 and 2 Thessalonians [in Greek]," *Deltio Biblikon Meleton* 17 (1988) 5-22.

Persecution and affliction not only focus attention on the end times but can also lead to the notion that they themselves are the immediate premonitions of the parousia, which is what happened in Thessalonica. Whether or not 2 Thessalonians was written by Paul, it completes the eschatological concerns of 1 Thessalonians with a new concentration on the signs and timetable of the end. The author presumably counters an eschatological scenario of a Thessalonian circle based on the words of an early Christian prophet or the interpretation of an Old Testament text or even a letter purporting to be from Paul.

498 Aletti, Jean-Noël. "L'apôtre Paul et la parousie de Jésus Christ. L'eschatologie paulinienne et ses enjeux," *Recherches de science religieuse* 84.1 (1996) 15-41.

The interpretation of Pauline eschatology is dominated by the question of its agreements with Jewish apocalypse. The common points cannot be contested, but should not hide the notable differences, which are based on the preeminence of Christ in the Pauline vision of the final events. Neither the expectation nor the delay of the parousia appears to have had, despite what is commonly asserted, a decisive influence on Paul's thinking. He was concerned more about reconciliation with God through the cross and the inauguration of a new humanity by the resurrection of Christ. The deutero-pauline letters do not fundamentally modify Paul's eschatology except insofar as they accentuate the dominance of christology in the vision of the endtime. It is always Paul's knowledge of the risen one, the second Adam, which directs his reflections and helps to decipher the final destiny of humankind in Christ.

499 Alsup, John E. "Eschatology and Ethics in Paul," *Austin Seminary Bulletin* 94 (1978) 40-52.

In 1 Thessalonians and Romans, Paul has presented eschatology primarily in kerygmatic-ethical terms. He did not speculate about the future with the excited imagination of an apocalypticist, but utilized eschatological affirmations for the present, particularly as they pertain to the questions of Christian conduct and behavior. 1 Thessalonians shows that Paul inherited the structure of ethical eschatology and that, even at this early date, he began to develop his own synthesis. Romans shows that he reflected further on the inherited structure and made the connections between eschatology and ethics more precise as he anticipated a ministry in Rome and beyond. Eschatology has been placed in the service of ethical discourse in a supportive role.

500 Arzt, Peter. *Bedrohtes Christsein. Zu Eigenart und Funktion eschatologisch bedrohlicher Propositionen in den echten Paulusbriefen* (Beiträge zur biblischen Exegese und Theologie 26; Frankfurt: Lang, 1992).

This revised thesis is an investigation of the form and function of the eschatologically threatening statements within the authentic Pauline letters. It uses dependency theory to identify these statements on the basis of grammar and the semantics of a human dimension and a divine dimension guaranteed by God himself. The function and image of God given by each statement is the center of analysis. The passages concern those being affected by eschatological threats and those making them. The eschatologically threatening propositions are aimed at Christian being and living, often contrasted by the addressees' environments. They are confronted with internal and external challenges to their Christian life, and in their relationship between them and Paul, the addressees are urged to live as real Christians. God's intention is their salvation. They are warned of ways of believing or living in contrast to their living as Christians. Passages in 1 Thessalonians which are discussed include the following: 2:1-4; 2:13-16; 3:5; 4:1-8; and 5:1-11 (pp 190-198).

501 Baird, William. "Pauline Eschatology in Hermeneutical Perspective," *New Testament Studies* 17 (1970/71) 314-327.

Paul's eschatological language has undergone change, but not a gradual development out of Jewish apocalyptic into Hellenistic forms as many have asserted. Instead, the changes in Paul's language and thinking about the end times are due in greater part to the diverse historical situations which he was addressing.

502 Bassler, Jouette M. "Paul's Theology: Whence and Whither? A Synthesis (of sorts) of the Theology of Philemon, 1 Thessalonians, Philippians, Galatians and 1 Corinthians," *SBL 1989 Seminar Papers* (ed. David J. Lull; Atlanta: Scholars Press, 1989) 412-423.

Although Paul was not a systematic theologian, there nevertheless seems to be a pattern or structure in his thinking. A helpful image for construing this underlying theology is that of the lens: the raw material of Paul's theology (the kerygma, scripture, traditions, etc.) passes through the lens of Paul's experience (his common Christian experience as well as his unique experience as one "set apart by God for the gospel") and generates a coherent (and characteristic) set of convictions. While it would be too much to claim this as the center of Paul's theology, the conviction of God's election, sealed by the empowering presence of the Spirit, is the basis for most of what the apostle writes.

503 ---. "Peace in All Ways. Theology in the Thessalonian Letters: A Response to R. Jewett, E. Krentz, and E. Richard," *Pauline Theology, 1: Thessalonians, Philippians, Galatians, Philemon* (ed. Jouette M. Bassler; Augsburg: Fortress, 1991) 71-85.

Differing presuppositions regarding the authorship of 2 Thessalonians have led Robert Jewett (547) and Edgar Krentz (558) to quite different assessments of the theology of this letter. It is better, therefore, to adopt a complementary approach which is primarily literary in nature and ignores the historical and social context. The opening and closing references to grace and peace (1:2; 3:16, 18) suggest that the main sections of the letter are concerned with peace and that peace in its eschatological, ecclesiological, and social dimensions is the theological goal of 2 Thessalonians. With regard to 1 Thessalonians, the presuppositions underlying Earl Richard's claims (598) about the theology of this letter are also suspect. The evidence suggests instead that the theme of peace, along with the concept of sanctification, is the distinctive feature of the theology of 1 Thessalonians.

504 Becker, Jürgen. "Die Erwählung der Völker durch das Evangelium. Theologiegeschichtliche Erwägungen zum 1 Thessalonikerbrief," *Studien zum Text und zur Ethik des Neuen Testaments. Festschrift zum 80. Geburtstag von Heinrich Greeven* (ed. Wolfgang Schrage; Beiheft zur Zeitschrift für die neutestamentliche Wissenschaft 47; Berlin/New York: de Gruyter, 1986) 82-101.

The traditional themes found in 1 Thessalonians, such as an early kind of missionary preaching to the Gentiles (1:9-10), the Christian hope for the resurrection (4:13-18), and the Pauline conflict with the Jews (2:14-16), are not sufficient to warrant its worth in the scope of Pauline theology. This is seen in the letter's development of the theme of election through the gospel. This theme is then further developed by Paul in other letters, such as Romans and 1 and 2 Corinthians.

505 ---. "Der I. Thess als Zeuge antiochenischer Missionstheologie," *Paulus. Der Apostel der Völker* (Tübingen: Mohr, 1989) 138-148.
Republished in English as "First Thessalonians as Testimony of Antiochene Mission Theology," *Paul, Apostle to the Gentiles* (Louisville: Westminster/John Knox, 1993) 130-140.

Paul wrote 1 Thessalonians so soon after his departure from Antioch that his statements in this letter can be considered still Antiochene and belonging to the first of the three prominent periods in the apostle's thought. Here Paul demonstrates the influence of both his background in Hellenistic Judaism and his earlier life and work in the church at Antioch. The apostle presents in this letter a theology of election--God's eschatological election of grace accomplished by the calling of the gospel. This theology of election provides the organizing coordinate system in which all other statements of 1 Thessalonians find their place.

506 Blake, Buchanan. "The Apocalyptic Setting of the Epistles to the Thessalonians," *The Expositor, 9th Series* 3 (1925) 126-139.

Apocalyptic appears in Paul's earliest letters, 1 and 2 Thessalonians, as a limiting and hindering factor--something to be laid aside when he reached a fuller comprehension of the essential teachings of Jesus in its spiritual fullness. The words of 1 Thess 1:10 ("to wait for his son from heaven...who delivers us from the wrath to come") introduce two themes that receive an apocalyptic interpretation in the letters: the second coming of Christ and the deliverance from the final judgment. The fundamental error of the apocalyptic attitude towards life was the way in which all importance was placed upon the future, so that the value of the present life was consequently depreciated.

507 Brandenburger, Egon. "Pistis und Soteria," *Zeitschrift für Theologie und Kirche* 85 (1988) 165-198.

In which conceptual and mental framework does the early Christian language of "to come to faith" (πιστεύειν in the aorist, along with the present and perfect forms) find its original situation? After a survey of previous research, one can recognize that the language of belief does not come from Hellenistic religious discourse, but it is missionary language. Old Testament and related Jewish texts show the role which the language of belief had. Four Pauline passages illustrate this usage in early Christianity: 1 Thess 1:8-10; 1 Cor 15:1ff; Rom 10:9; and Rom 9:30-10:21. 1 Thess 1:8-10 shows that a belief formula (v 10b) and christology (v 10c) had an early place at the beginning of the Gentile mission.

508 Brandon, T. S., Sr. "The Influence of Apocalyptic Concepts in the Thessalonian Epistles" (Unpublished Ph.D. Dissertation; Fort Worth, TX: Southwestern Baptist Theological Seminary, 1963).

509 Burkeen, W. Howard. "The Parousia of Christ in the Thessalonian Correspondence" (Unpublished Ph.D. Dissertation; Aberdeen: University of Aberdeen, 1979).

510 Calle, Francisco de la. "La pneumatología paulina (Rom; 1 y 2 Cor; Gal; Fil; 1 y 2 Tes)," *Estudios Teológicos* 9.1 (1975) 23-96.

511 Collins, Raymond F. "God in the First Letter to the Thessalonians: Paul's Earliest Written Appreciation of *ho theos*," *Louvain Studies* 16 (1991) 137-154.

The θεός to whom Paul refers so often (thirty-six times, more than any other noun) in 1 Thessalonians is the God of the biblical tradition. These references, along with other allusions to the Old Testament, cluster around the themes of the way of life appropriate to God's holy people and the eschatological wrath of God. But even though Paul has retained the traditional, Judeo-biblical, core meaning of ὁ θεός, some shift in the apostle's understanding of the one and only God has taken place. Paul's social world and personal identity were changed by his new appreciation of God, focused on the relationship between God-Father and Jesus-Son.

512 ---. "'The Lord Jesus Christ,'" *The Bible Today* 26 (1988) 338-343.

This brief article contains some theological reflections on Paul's faith in Jesus and his use of the titles "Son," "Lord," and "Christ" in 1 and 2 Thessalonians.

513 ---. "Paul's Early Christology," *Studies on the First Letter to the Thessalonians* (Bibliotheca ephemeridum theologicarum lovaniensium 66; Leuven: Leuven University Press, 1984) 253-284.

An examination of the three creedal formulas in 1 Thessalonians (1:10, 4:14; 5:9-10) and the Christological titles "Son," "Christ," and "Lord," shows that Paul is not so concerned with the nature of Jesus Christ as he is with the ultimate salvific significance of Jesus Christ. The christological titles manifest a functional christology. A certain priority can be given to the title "Son" which, though little used, is the first title to which specific attention is drawn by Paul. It indicates the close relationship between Jesus and the Father, and thus shows that Jesus is qualified to assume divine functions, particularly insofar as he is the mediator of salvation. The closeness of relationship between Jesus and the Father is manifest in the death and resurrection to which the title "Christ" draws attention. Yet, as Paul's choice of christological titles indicates, he has principally exploited the notion that Jesus is "Lord."

514 ---. "The Theology of Paul's First Letter to the Thessalonians," *Louvain Studies* 6 (1976/77) 315-337.
Republished in Raymond F. Collins, *Studies on the First Letter to the Thessalonians* (Bibliotheca ephemeridum theologicarum lovaniensium 66; Leuven: Leuven University Press, 1984) 230-252.

It is true that Paul was not a systematic theologian who speculated upon the divine essence in theoretical or abstract terms. Nevertheless, one would expect that a writer like Paul, who invokes the name of God no less than thirty-six times in his brief, first letter to the Thessalonians and whose religious experience was such that it included a theocentric dimension, would have reflected upon God to some extent. A study of 1 Thessalonians with respect to the titles and attributes of God, his relationship to humankind, and his divine activity in the final times illustrates the complexity of Paul's thought and demonstrates that his understanding of God is indeed a touchstone of his theology.

515 Conchas, Daniel de. "A Doutrina da Ressureiçâo em Sâo Paulo," *Revista de Cultura Bíblica* 3.13 (1959) 209-223.

A study of the three main passages where Paul speaks expressly about the resurrection of the dead (1 Thess 4:13-18; 1 Cor 15; Rom 8) reveals that the apostle's reasoning is the same in all three: if Christ rose, then we will also rise; if we do not rise, then Christ did not either, and our faith is vain. These passages also emphasize that God the Father is the efficient cause of our resurrection. Believers, however, can also cooperate through the grace given to them by the indwelling of the Holy Spirit. Christ is the model, and therefore the exemplary cause of our resurrection. Although Paul addresses directly only the subject of the resurrection of the righteous, he presupposes and teaches also the resurrection of the wicked (see Acts 24:15).

516 Cortés Fuentes, David. "El mensaje apocalíptico de Pablo en primera de Tesalonicenses como un medio de esperanza," *Apuntes* 13.3 (1993) 190-197.

Although an apocalyptic perspective and language have often been considered alienating and escapist, the opposite is true in Paul's use of such language and perspective in

1 Thessalonians. When one takes into account the social composition of the Christian community in that city, and the pressures under which it was operating, it is clear that in this case apocalyptic language serves as a counter-language, opposing a perspective which would lead to defeatism. Through apocalyptic language, Paul reminds his readers that their final destiny is not in the hands of the powers that now oppress them. This is a liberating word to a community which sees very little hope of immediate relief in the social order in which it lives. The way in which Paul uses apocalypticism, therefore, leads not to complacency or to escapism, but rather to hope and commitment. "Hoping against hope: that is the hope of those who have none."

517 Cranfield, C. E. B. "Thoughts on New Testament Eschatology," *Scottish Journal of Theology* 35 (1982) 497-512.
Republished in C. E. B. Cranfield, *The Bible and Christian Life: A Collection of Essays* (Edinburgh: T. & T. Clark, 1985) 105-126.

It is commonly claimed that the early church believed that the end of the world would certainly occur within a very short period of time and was thus forced to revise its eschatology by the inescapable logic of this world's unexpected continuance. This assertion, however, needs to be challenged. Despite the claim that the New Testament exhibits three different eschatologies sundered from each other by the intervention of two unexpected turn of events (first, the eschatology of Jesus; second, separated from it by the unexpected issue of Jesus' ministry in his death and resurrection and the continuing life of the disciples in this age, the eschatology of the primitive church; and third, separated from the second by the failure of the parousia to occur within the first generation of Christians, the eschatology which has been modified as a result of the delay of Christ's return), the evidence suggests an essential consistency of eschatological thought in the New Testament. This agreement stands out all the more impressively in view of the undoubted differences of idiom, emphasis and circumstance.

518 Custer, Stewart. "The Theology of 1 Thessalonians," *Biblical Viewpoint* 9.1 (1975) 46-50.

A brief theological analysis of the following five subjects in 1 Thessalonians: christology, God the Father, the Holy Spirit, salvation and eschatology.

519 Czerski, Janusz. "Eschatologia w listach do Tesaloniczan," *Chrystus i Kosciól. Wybrane teksty Nowego Testamentu* (ed. Feliks Gryglewicz; Lublin: Towarzystwo Naukowe Katolickiego Uniwersytetu, 1979) 111-117.

With his eschatological statements in the two Thessalonian letters, Paul answers actual questions and concrete needs of the church in Thessalonica. The apostle not only clears up the confusion which existed in the congregation about future events but also uses these eschatological comments to ground his ethical warnings.

520 Danker, Frederick, and Robert Jewett. "Jesus as the Apocalyptic Benefactor in Second Thessalonians," *The Thessalonian Correspondence* (ed. Raymond F. Collins; Bibliotheca ephemeridum theologicarum lovaniensium 87; Leuven: Leuven University Press, 1990) 486-498.

It is often claimed that 2 Thessalonians, with its distantly futuristic content, lacks a theology of grace. The language of this letter, however, shares many similarities with the benefactor system of the Greco-Roman period such that Jesus emerges as an apocalyptic benefactor. The extensive use of benefaction language not only points to a well developed theology of grace shared by the writer and his audience, but it also provides the basis for reconstructing a scenario of benefaction which underlies the christology of this letter. Grace and salvation already received through Christ are here brought into relation with anticipated benefactions when the Lord returns. This apocalyptic christology is as crucial for 2 Thessalonians as for 1 Thessalonians.

521 Davis, Richard Howard. "Remembering and Acting. A Study of the Moral Life in Light of 1 Thessalonians" (Unpublished Ph.D. Dissertation; New Haven, CT: Yale University, 1971).

Christian existence in 1 Thessalonians can be summarized by the phrase "remembering in action." This phrase calls attention to the central place which living memory holds both in Paul's life and work and in believers' behavior. A recurring feature of the apostle's exhortation in 1 Thessalonians is his use of "you know," embodying an appeal to his hearers' memory. Initially this appeal served to establish a basis of dialogue with his readers, providing both the prerequisite and content of his exhortation. In light of an examination of its uses, it is possible to characterize remembering formally as an event of total comprehension and, as such, a profoundly religious activity. For the Thessalonians, to remember is to participate in that world defined by the gospel of God and to grasp all events and relationships in light of that foundation. The notion of imitation (1 Thess 1:6; 2:14) plays an important role in remembering, since imitation is a form of remembering in action. Indeed, to focus on imitation shows the properly behavioral, performative nature of remembering.

522 Dewailly, Louis-Marie. "Une Communauté naissante: Thessalonique. I. Naissance en vie chrétienne," *La Vie spirituelle* 104 (1961) 359-376.

As the first books to be written of what would become the New Testament, the Thessalonian correspondence holds a special place in the history of Christian self-definition. In these letters, we see Paul trying to show the Thessalonians, in his absence, how to live as new Christians with a collective new life. The traits of this new life include holiness, being "in the Lord," and living a life "worthy of the Lord." Interior traits to be sought after by the individual are faith, love, and hope. Although the largest part of his teaching is positive, Paul also reinforces his previous teaching to the Thessalonians (when he was present with them) concerning sin.

523 ---. "Une Communauté naissante: Thessalonique. II. Saint Paul Apôtre," *La Vie spirituelle* 105 (1961) 254-269.

The Thessalonian letters are concerned not only with describing the Christian life for its readers (see 522) but also Paul's role as an apostle and the function he has in the mission to the Gentiles. The description of Paul as one who is divinely appointed to speak the word of God to pagans in order that they might be saved gives the picture of a person whose entire rational and emotional nature is uniquely devoted to his missionary task.

524 Didier, Georges. "Dans l'attente du Seigneur. Les Épitres aux Thessaloniciens," *Désintéressement du chrétien: La rétribution dans la morale de Saint Paul* (Théologie 32; Lyon: Aubier, 1955) 22-40.

The overarching theme of the two letters to the Thessalonians is properly understood as a movement between the opposing eschatological themes of punishment and recompense. Several motifs encapsulate these overarching themes, but discussions of fear and hope are the primary ways in which they are communicated. However, discussions of the *object* of the Thessalonians' hope and of Paul's own personal life also contribute. The second letter is more sober than the first, but is also more explicit concerning Paul's personal involvement and feelings (as seen, for example, in his renunciation of his rights as an apostle). In the end, when reading the Thessalonian correspondence, it is important not to lose sight of Paul's apostolic dynamism, born of his passion to serve, which was itself born of his passionate love for his converts.

525 Donfried, Karl P. "The Theology of 1 Thessalonians," *The Theology of the Shorter Pauline Letters* (Karl P. Donfried and I. Howard Marshall; Cambridge: Cambridge University Press, 1993) 1-79.

1 Thessalonians is an authentically Pauline letter in the ancient epideictic rhetorical genre, written from Corinth in the early forties to console a fledgling church suffering formal persecution. Christians have run afoul of the city authorities for refusing to participate in local religious and civic cults. Some have even been martyred for their faith and so Paul conveys a prophetic word of assurance to the survivors (4:13-18). The letter contains a fair amount of pre-Pauline material and it is this tradition and its transformation, rather than the late Paul represented in Galatians or Romans, which must serve as the starting point for understanding the evolution of Pauline theology. The phrase "in Christ" is an especially appropriate place to begin such a study of the development of Pauline thought. Although Luke places Paul within his larger theological portrayal of unity and consensus, the portrait of the apostle which he presents is more accurate than P. Vielhauer's classic study suggests.

526 ---. "The Theology of 2 Thessalonians," *The Theology of the Shorter Pauline Letters* (Karl P. Donfried and I. Howard Marshall; Cambridge: Cambridge University Press, 1993) 81-113.

2 Thessalonians is not, strictly speaking, a genuinely Pauline letter, though it was written shortly after 1 Thessalonians and to the same community. Rather, one of Paul's companions--either Timothy or Silas--wrote the letter in response to a new eschatological problem disturbing the church. By employing a deliberative form of rhetoric, together with an apocalyptic scenario reminiscent of the book of Revelation, the author of this letter seeks to demolish the views of a group of spirit-filled charismatics who claim that in some enigmatic way the day of the Lord has already arrived. They also claim that their special status entitles them to financial support. This letter refutes the first claim with a strictly future-oriented eschatological timetable and refutes the second with an appeal to the tradition of good order established by Paul's example of working for a living.

527 Dumais, Marcel. "Cartas a los Tesalonicenses," *Cartas de Pablo y Cartas católicas* (ed. M. Marrey, P. Dornier, and M. Trimaille; Introducción a la lectura de la Biblia 8; Madrid: Ediciones Cristiandad, 1985) 37-60.

The author begins by analyzing some introductory aspects of the Thessalonian letters such as the historical situation and their purpose, with a brief comment on the authenticity of 2 Thessalonians. Then, based on the key words, he argues in favor of the unity of 1 Thessalonians and suggests a structure for each letter. He also pays attention to the differences in tone between both letters and their simple style mixed with some difficult expressions for modern readers. Finally, he presents a summary of the theological content of both letters in which the prominent themes are the Christian life, missionary spirituality, the parousia and its precedent signs.

528 Fee, Gordon D. "The Thessalonian Correspondence," *God's Empowering Presence. The Holy Spirit in the Letters of Paul* (Peabody, MA: Hendrickson, 1994) 39-80.

A study of the references to the Holy Spirit in 1 and 2 Thessalonians (1 Thess 1:4-6; 2:15; 4:8; 5:16-18; 5:19-22; 5:23-24; 2 Thess 1:11; 2:1-2; 2:8; 2:9; 2:13) shows that Paul has a rather full-orbed understanding of the Spirit as lying at the heart of the Christian life. Here the Spirit possesses a variety of functions in the lives of believers: making effective the call to Christ through apostolic preaching; producing holiness and good works; causing joy and prayer and thanksgiving; and being visibly present in the form of prophetic utterances. Although Paul does not stress much of this himself, the very fact that the Spirit lies so close to the surface in his epistolary conversation with the Thessalonian believers reveals Paul's presuppositions about the fundamental role which the Spirit plays in the Christian life.

529 Feuillet, André. "Le 'ravissement' final des justes et la double perspective eschatologique (résurrection glorieuse et vie avec le Christ après la mort) dans la Première Epître aux Thessaloniciens," *Revue Thomiste* 72.4 (1972) 533-559.

There is a demonstrable development in Paul's thought concerning the participation of the believer in the resurrection of Christ. In 1 Thessalonians, it is clear that participation in this resurrection is not the object of the eschatological hope of believers, which changes by the time of Romans, and certainly by Colossians. Drawing a distinction between the Jewish biblical tradition and the influence of Hellenism, this article argues that the eschatology in 1 Thessalonians is profoundly Jewish, and only touched at the periphery by Hellenism, as Paul does not ascribe immortality to the soul but to the body. In both 1 Thessalonians and Philippians, the apostle believes both in the glorious transformation of the faithful at the second coming (1 Thess 4:17; Phil 1:6; 1:10-11; 2:16) and in the union of the believer with Christ immediately after death (1 Thess 5:10; Phil 1:23).

530 Floor, Lambertus. "Die verhouding tussen indikatief en paraklese in die Nuwe Testament, toegelig vanuit die eerste brief aan die Tessalonisense," *In die Skriflig* 24.2 (1990) 155-165.

The teaching on eschatology is of utmost importance in the first letter of Paul to the Thessalonians. Regarding the parousia of Christ, Paul presents a number of instructions concerning the process of sanctification. When the apostle deals with paraenetic material, he does not command but requests. Those who have been called to sanctification should not continue to live in impurity, for God has given the Holy Spirit, who is the Spirit of sanctification. The indicative of the parousia is linked with the paraclesis of sanctification through the Holy Spirit. God, who called the members of the church in sanctification, has given the Holy Spirit to fulfil all his obligations. The relation between the indicative and paraclesis in this letter, therefore, is of a pneumatological nature.

531 Fransen, Irénée. "Le Jour du Seigneur: 1-2 Thessaloniciens," *Bible et vie chrétienne* 8 (1954) 76-88.

The hope in the return of Christ was the cause of the changes which took place in Paul's thinking. Because of this, the Thessalonian letters are the essential starting-point for any comprehension of Pauline theology. Although his manner of hoping may have changed, the object of his hope did not. The message of the letters to the Thessalonians can be summed-up in the cry of hope and faith: "Come Lord Jesus!"

532 Fuerbringer, L. "Leading Thoughts on Eschatology in the Epistles to the Thessalonians," *Concordia Theological Monthly* 13 (1942) 183-192, 265-273, 321-329, 401-414, 511-518, 591-603, 641-654.

The central eschatological claims of the two Thessalonian letters may be summarized as follows. First, Jesus will return, and do so suddenly, as a thief in the night. Second, he will not do so, however, until the great Antichrist has been revealed. Third, Jesus will come to exact vengeance upon the unbelievers and to glorify the believers. Fourth, the return of Jesus will include various steps: (1) Jesus will appear in glory; (2) the dead in Christ will rise; (3) Christians still living, together with those called back to life, will be caught up in the clouds; and (4) both will be forever with the Lord. Fifth, the teaching of Jesus' return should strengthen believers' faith, motivate holy living, caution against error, give comfort in tribulation, and confirm hope. These key eschatological teachings are supported by a careful examination of four passages in the Thessalonian letters: 1 Thess 4:13-18; 5:1-11; 2 Thess 1:3-12; 2:1-12.

533 García-Moreno, Antonio. "La realeza y el señorío de Cristo en Tesalonicenses," *Estudios Bíblicos* 39.1-2 (1981) 63-82.

Although it is in the "captivity letters" that Paul's thought reveals a more developed christology, it is already possible to find in his earliest letters, 1 and 2 Thessalonians, a clear understanding of the royalty and lordship of Christ. This conclusion is supported by an extensive analysis of the frame and the body of both letters, in which, through his use of several words, particularly the term "Lord," Paul shows his indebtedness to the Old Testament. Moreover, the divinity of Christ is suggested in different ways throughout both letters. Further support comes from an analysis of the pericopes with eschatological content, in which both the parousia of the Lord and his work as judge serve to enhance the greatness and majesty of the messianic king.

534 Ghini, Emanuela. "La parusia del Cristo e dell'Anticristo nelle lettere ai Tessalonicesi," *Parola, Spirito e Vita* 8 (1983) 119-132.

535 Giesen, Heinz. "Naherwartung des Paulus in 1 Thess 4,13-18?" *Studien zum Neuen Testament und seiner Umwelt* (Linz, Austria: A. Fuchs, 1985) 123-150.

It is commonly claimed that the earliest Christians believed in the imminent end of the world at the parousia of Christ. This thesis, however, will not stand up to critical testing. In light of the context of 1 Thess 4:13-18 and a comparison with what is said in 1 Cor 15:51-54 regarding the transformation of all things at the parousia, Paul is providing a basis for the Thessalonians' hope in the death and resurrection of Jesus. If they have no hope for their dead, then they have not grasped what it is that distinguishes Christians. Paul helps them by clarifying that it is not an imminent parousia which they are expecting, but that they should be leading Christian lives in preparation for the eschaton.

536 Glasson, T. Francis. "Theophany and Parousia," *New Testament Studies* 34 (1988) 259-270.

The origin of the parousia doctrine (i.e., a visit by a messianic figure from heaven) cannot be traced to the apocalyptic literature of the intertestamental period as has so often been claimed. Neither does this belief originate from Jesus himself. Instead the parousia teaching was the early church's application to Jesus of the Old Testament teaching concerning the coming of the Lord. The Old Testament theophanies provide the key to the New Testament parousia.

537 Grayston, Kenneth. "The Pauline Writings (I)," *Dying, We Live: A New Enquiry into the Death of Christ in the New Testament* (London: Darton, Longman and Todd, 1990) 8-16.

A study of the passages in 1 Thessalonians which refer, directly or indirectly, to the death of Jesus (1 Thess 1:9-10; 2:14-16; 4:13-14; 5:1-11) shows that Christ's resurrection carries the main theological weight in this letter, not his death. Other than Paul's explanation that Christ died for believers so that he could be Lord of both dead and living Christians, the death of Christ has no positive theological function.

538 Guido, A. "La teologià della preghiera nelle lettere di Paolo ai Tessalonicesi" (Unpublished Th.D. Dissertation; Rome: S.T.D., 1981).

539 Günther, Hartmut. "'Das ist der Wille Gottes, eure Heilung' (1 Th 4,3): Bindung und Freiheit im Leben der Christen," *Luterische Theologie und Kirche* 10 (1986) 1-16.

The concept of "holiness" is important for New Testament ethics. It is the will of God, and is related to Christian obligation and freedom. 1 Thess 4:3-8 is in the midst of a paraenetic section. Holiness here is seen in terms of what it means to live in distinction from a world that has fled from God. Yet Paul does not speak of withdrawing completely from society or of having a disdain for the world.

540 Halamka, Ronald Frank. "I and II Thessalonians on Pastoral Care for Recent Converts" (Unpublished Ph.D. Dissertation; Chicago, IL: Concordia Seminary, 1975).

An analysis of 1 and 2 Thessalonians in terms of its historical and social context and its message leads to the discovery of several theological principles of pastoral care for recent converts. The function of this kind of pastoral care is to apply the gospel to recent converts for progress in working faith, laboring love, and enduring hope. In performing this function, pastoral care impresses on these new Christians God's goals for their own lives. It also equips and motivates recent converts to make a visible and verbal witness of the gospel to people in society and the world.

541 Hartman, Lars. "The Eschatology of 2 Thessalonians as Included in a Communication," *The Thessalonian Correspondence* (ed. Raymond F. Collins; Bibliotheca ephemeridum theologicarum lovaniensium 87; Leuven: Leuven University Press, 1990) 470-485.

The pseudepigraphal author of 2 Thessalonians is less a theologian who tries to come to grips with the theological problem of the delay of the parousia than he is a pastor who wants to strengthen the faithful in their afflictions. In the context of persecution where believers may be tempted to abandon the faith, the author felt that an authoritative word from Paul was needed. He used existing theological ideas, possibly partly known by his addressees, to show that the present tribulations are not the end but the beginning of the end. He thus hopes to strengthen his addressees in the face of opposition and to encourage them to remain faithful.

542 Haufe, Günter. "Individuelle eschatologie des Neuen Testaments," *Zeitschrift für Theologie und Kirche* 83.4 (1986) 436-463.

In the examination of individual eschatology, one must consider the question of its context, aim, and theological foundation. These are discussed in the Synoptic, Pauline and Johannine writings. Several of Paul's statements in 1 Thessalonians are in terms of the final judgment (1 Thess 1:10; 5:8-9). 1 Thess 4:13-18 discusses the extent of death and resurrection. The problem in Thessalonica was not death itself, but that death was happening before the expected parousia. This led to the fear that those Christians who had already died would be disadvantaged at the parousia. Paul calms such fears by conveying to his readers new information about events connected with the return of Christ. The resurrection of deceased believers and their full participation in the parousia is guaranteed because of Christ's resurrection from the dead.

543 Hays, Richard Bevan. "Crucified with Christ: A Synthesis of 1 and 2 Thessalonians, Philemon, Philippians, and Galatians," *SBL 1988 Seminar Papers* (ed. David A. Lull; SBL Seminar Papers 27; Atlanta: Scholars Press, 1988) 318-335.
Republished with minor changes in *Pauline Theology 1: Thessalonians, Philippians, Galatians, Philemon* (ed. Jouette M. Bassler; Minneapolis: Fortress, 1991) 227-246.

Paul's letters presuppose the foundational story of what God has done to bring salvation to his elect people. Nowhere within his letters does Paul narrate this foundational story in detail, but he constantly cites it in an allusive manner as a warrant for the claims and arguments he makes. There are three themes of this story which Paul highlights in his letters to the Thessalonians, Philemon, the Philippians and Galatians: the relation of Israel and Gentiles in God's election; Jesus as a representative figure who enacts the destiny of God's people; and the community's vocation to participate in the way of the cross.

544 Henneken, Bartholamäus. *Verkündigung und Prophetie im Ersten Thessalonicherbrief. Ein Beitrag zur Theologie des Wortes Gottes* (Stuttgarter Bibelstudien 29; Stuttgart: Katholisches Bibelwerk, 1969).

This study of texts with prophetic significance in 1 Thessalonians begins with passages concerning the self-identity of the apostle (1 Thess 2:3-6, 9, 10; 2:7, 8, 11; 3:2) and his proclamation of the word (1:5; 2:16). Next are those passages concerned with the reception of the word (1:6; 2:13; 4:8) and the proclamation of the word in the community (1:7, 8; 4:18; 5:11, 14). Last comes the discussion of passages dealing with the prophetic word itself, including the role of Paul as prophet (4:15-17; 2:1-4) and prophecy in the community (5:20).

545 Hodgson, Robert, Jr. "Gospel and Ethics in First Thessalonians," *Bible Today* 26 (1988) 344-349.

The gospel and ethics in 1 Thessalonians are a first and intrepid blend of faith and action. Paul believed that the gospel--the story of the person and pilgrimage of Jesus, culminating in his victory over death and ongoing presence in the church--impacted in a radical way human conduct in the area of sexual behavior (4:3-5), business (4:6), and politics (5:12-16).

546 Howell, Don N., Jr. "Confidence in the Spirit as the Governing Ethos of the Pauline Mission," *Trinity Journal* 17 (1996) 203-221.

An examination of the explicit references to the Spirit in the Thessalonian letters (1 Thess 1:5-6; 4:8; 5:16-24; 2 Thess 1:11; 2:1-2; 2:13) shows the depth of Paul's dependence and confidence in the work of the Holy Spirit as the essential cause of the church's growth and maintenance. The Spirit has been intimately involved on every level of the church-planting endeavor in Thessalonica: in the initial proclamation of the gospel by the missionaries (1 Thess 1:5-6), in the conversion of the Thessalonian believers (1 Thess 1:5-6), in the holy lives of the new Christians (1 Thess 4:8; 5:16-18), and in the exercise of spiritual gifts (1 Thess 5:19-22; 2 Thess 2:1-12). Thus, Paul is confident that, despite his forced and extended absence, the same Spirit will preserve, strengthen, and perfect this young church.

547 Jewett, Robert. "A Matrix of Grace: The Theology of 2 Thessalonians as a Pauline Letter," *Pauline Theology 1: Thessalonians, Philippians, Galatians, Philemon* (ed. Jouette M. Bassler; Minneapolis: Fortress, 1991) 63-70.

The central theme in the apocalyptic theology of 2 Thessalonians, reflecting the earliest stage of theological development in Paul's letters, is the tension between the "already" and "not yet." This theme in turn rests on assumptions which Paul shares with a congregation whose faith had been evoked in response to the gospel--the good news not only about a future apocalyptic triumph but also about salvation already achieved by Christ.

548 Kampling, Rainer. "Freude bei Paulus," *Trierer theologische Zeitschrift* 101 (1992) 69-79.

In 1 Thessalonians, the oldest letter of the apostle, the theme of joy is emphasized, and already here one finds the foundational aspects of the Pauline understanding of joy. In 1 Thess 1:6 Paul speaks of the joy of the Holy Spirit in the midst of affliction. In 1 Thess 2:19-20 he speaks of his joy with the community of believers in Thessalonica. In 1 Thess 3:9 he speaks of the joy which he has from and before God. In 1 Thess 5:16 he ends the letter with a group of closing exhortations, one of which is "rejoice always."

549 Kaye, Bruce N. "Eschatology and Ethics in 1 and 2 Thessalonians," *Novum Testamentum* 17.1 (1975) 47-57.

The view that the problem of the "disorderly" in Thessalonica was related to a false or one-sided eschatological teaching finds no support in 1 Thess 4:13-18, 5:1-11 and 2 Thess 2:1-12. These three eschatological passages do not provide anything which would suggest that either Paul's position, or those which he was discussing, implied any abandonment of ethical obligations. In fact, the two passages in 1 Thessalonians contain material which heightens and confirms a sense of ethical obligation. Furthermore, Paul treats the problem of the disorderly (2 Thess 3:6-13) in a pragmatic way, which hardly seems appropriate if the problem arose from an error in theological understanding. Finally, the notion that an imminent parousia teaching may lead to a diminution of moral effort, and, more specifically, to idleness is contradicted by Paul's insistence upon the continuity between the present situation and the post-parousia situation, and upon the ethical character of conversion and faith. The problem of the disorderly, therefore, was something that Paul anticipated when he was first in Thessalonica and it probably had local and perhaps social roots.

550 Keck, Leander E. "Images of Paul in the New Testament," *Interpretation* 43 (1989) 341-351.

The image of Paul reflected in his genuine letters, his non-genuine letters (2 Thessalonians, Ephesians, Pastorals), and Acts involves a collage of diverse pictures rather than a single portrait. This diversity can be seen in comparing Paul's last authentic letter (Romans) with his first (1 Thessalonians). In the former, Paul is the proud apostle who is able in a masterful fashion to weave into a sustained argument diverse ideas which he has adapted to his own ends. In the latter, Paul is the warm-hearted pastor who is passionately and personally involved in the lives of his young converts. These images of Paul, however, are distorted in such inauthentic passages as Rom 16:17-20 and 1 Thess 2:14-16, as well as in the later pseudepigraphal Pauline letters and Acts. These diverse images of Paul reflect an extended struggle in the church for the legacy of Paul. Alternative "Pauls" were promoted not only in second-century Christian Gnosticism but already in the first century as well.

551 Kegel, Günter. *Auferstehung Jesu - Auferstehung der Toten. Eine traditionsgeschichtliche Untersuchung zum Neuen Testament* (Gütersloh: Gerd Mohn, 1970).

Three passages in 1 Thessalonians (1:9-10; 4:14; 4:16) are part of the earliest Christian tradition regarding the resurrection of Jesus. All of them reflect traditional language. 1:9-10 provides a motivation for mission in 1 Thessalonians, while 4:14 and 4:16 reflect a knowledge of the Jesus tradition. These three texts probably reflect the first time that Paul wrote about the resurrection of the dead.

552 Kieffer, René. "L'eschatologie en 1 Thessaloniciens dans une perspective rhétorique," *The Thessalonian Correspondence* (ed. Raymond F. Collins; Bibliotheca ephemeridum theologicarum lovaniensium 87; Leuven: Leuven University Press, 1990) 206-219.

Following a method of interpretation based not only on the findings and patterns of classical philology, but also on pragmatism and modern rhetorical criticism (albeit critical of rhetorical approaches which rely solely on the ancient manuals), it is possible to gain a fresh perspective on Paul's eschatology as expressed in 1 Thess 4:13-18 and 5:1-11. Such analysis shows that, in this first letter written by the apostle, he wrestles with words and concepts to formulate a doctrine of eschatology which is able to respond to the real difficulties which he and his churches encountered. The apostle's rhetoric is marked much more by this need to express than by a desire to influence his readers.

553 Koester, Helmut. "Apostel und Gemeinde in den Briefen an die Thessalonicher," *Kirche: Festschrift für Günther Bornkamm zum 75. Geburtstag* (ed. Dieter Lührmann and George Strecker; Tübingen: Mohr/Siebeck, 1980) 287-298.

1 Thessalonians resists being defined in terms of questions concerning apostolic character. Paul does not here face an opposition who questions his apostolic qualifications. 1 Thessalonians, more so than the later letter to Thessalonica, shows life being endured in the light of the eschatological act of God, even in the face of tribulations. The experience of tribulations is a sign of the presence of the gospel. This differentiates 1 Thessalonians from 2 Thessalonians, in which the relationship between the apostle and his community is not one of unity, but it is written reflecting opposition between the leader and those subordinate to him. This entirely different view of the two letters with respect to the relationship of the apostle to his community raises questions concerning the authenticity of the second letter.

554 ---. "From Paul's Eschatology to the Apocalyptic Schemata of 2 Thessalonians," *The Thessalonian Correspondence* (ed. Raymond F. Collins; Bibliotheca ephemeridum theologicarum lovaniensium 87; Leuven: Leuven University Press, 1990) 441-458.

Both letters to the Thessalonians exclusively use traditional apocalyptic materials. There is no evidence whatsoever that the beliefs of the community in Thessalonica are in any way influenced by the pagan background of the converts or by millenarian propaganda and sentiments related to the specific cultural and social situation of the members of the community (contrary to the claims of Jewett, Donfried, etc.). Traditional apocalyptic sequences of events are known to Paul and are used in 1 Thessalonians to answer specific questions which the community faced (the fate of those who have died in 4:13-18; the "seasons and times" in 5:1-11). The author of 2 Thessalonians also makes use of traditional apocalyptic schemata but in a manner different than that found in the first letter.

555 Kreitzer, Larry Joseph. "The Parousia and the Final Judgment in Paul," *Jesus and God in Paul's Eschatology* (Journal for the Study of the New Testament Supplement Series 19; Sheffield: JSOT Press, 1987) 93-129.

The Old Testament concept of the Day of the Lord (Yahweh) becomes transposed within the Pauline letters into the Day of the Lord (Christ). There are a variety of expressions used by Paul to denote this eschatological event. There are also eleven Old Testament passages which have been christologically reinterpreted by the apostle in his letters and these Pauline texts can be classified as follows: (1) a referential shift of "Lord" from God to Christ (Rom 10:13; Phil 2:10-11; 1 Thess 3:13; 1 Thess 4:14; 2 Thess 1:7-10; 2 Thess 1:6-12; 2 Thess 1:9; 1 Thess 4:15-18); (2) a referential shift of pronouns from God to Christ (Rom 9:33); and (3) a referential shift of description of the Day of the Lord from God to Christ (Rom 11:26; 1 Thess 5:8).

556 Kremer, Jacob. "Auferstanden - auferweckt," *Biblische Zeitschrift* 23 (1979) 97-98.

The interpretation of ἠγέρθη as a theological passive stands in opposition to the oldest translations which take the verb in a middle sense. Where the verb is not bound with the idea of rising from the dead in Hellenistic Greek, it has a middle meaning, and, in contexts of a changed form of resurrection from the dead, the divine passive is not in view. Thus its synonym is ἀνέστη ("he stood up"). The earliest uses do not link this rising with the cross, as it is connected in later times. Thus expressions such as "God has raised him" (Rom 10:9; 1 Cor 6:14; see 1 Thess 1:10; Gal 1:1, etc.) are secondary, intended to explain the resurrection as an act of God.

557 ---. "Was heisst Parusie und Parusieerwartung heute? Überlegungen zu den Parusieaussagen von 1 Thess," *Bestellt zum Zeugnis. Festsgabe für Bischof Johannes Pohlschneider zur Vollendung d. 75. Lebensjahres* (ed. Karl Delahaye; Aachen: Einhard, 1974) 251-268.

The teaching of the parousia of Jesus and the parousia expectation was not an appendage of Christian proclamation but was tightly bound with the belief that God has raised Jesus from the dead. The parousia of Christ meant fulfillment and revelation of what Israel had hoped for, and, with the resurrection of Jesus, had its beginning.

558 Krentz, Edgar. "Through a Lens. Theology and Fidelity in 2 Thessalonians," *Pauline Theology 1: Thessalonians, Philippians, Galatians, Philemon* (ed. Jouette M. Bassler; Philadelphia: Fortress, 1991) 52-62.
An expanded version of this article was later published under the title "Traditions Held Fast: Theology and Fidelity in 2 Thessalonians," *The Thessalonian Correspondence* (ed. Raymond F. Collins; Bibliotheca ephemeridum theologicarum lovaniensium 87; Leuven: Leuven University Press, 1990) 505-515.

The theology which underlies 2 Thessalonians and gives this pseudepigraphal work its unity is the fundamental conviction that God is a God of justice who will vindicate his suffering church. All *theologoumena* in the letter are related to this central apocalyptic conviction, which functions as a lens to focus the letter's theology on the traumatic situation faced by those who remain faithful to God. Thus 2 Thessalonians is essentially a letter with one theme: faithful endurance under persecution. The writer ransacks the resources of apocalyptic thought so as to rouse his readers to steadfast waiting as the apocalyptic calendar unfolds.

559 ---. "Traditions Held Fast: Theology and Fidelity in 2 Thessalonians," *The Thessalonian Correspondence* (ed. Raymond F. Collins; Bibliotheca ephemeridum theologicarum lovaniensium 87; Leuven: Leuven University Press, 1990) 505-515.
This is an expanded version of an earlier article entitled "Through a Lens: Theology and

Fidelity in 2 Thessalonians," *Pauline Theology 1: Thessalonians, Philippians, Galatians, Philemon* (ed. Jouette M. Bassler; Minneapolis: Fortress, 1991) 52-62.
For annotation, see 558.

560 Lambrecht, Jan. "A Call to Witness by All: Evangelisation in 1 Thessalonians," *Teologie in Konteks. Opgedra aan A. B. du Toit* (ed. J. H. Roberts, W. S. Vorster, J. N. Vorster *et al.*; Pretoria: Orion, 1991) 321-343.
Originally published as "De apostolische Inzet van de eerste Christenen: Een actualiserende Lezing van 1 Tessalonicenzen," *Collationes* 18 (1988) 403-417. Republished in Jan Lambrecht, *Pauline Studies: Collected Essays* (Bibliotheca ephemeridum theologicarum lovaniensium 115; Leuven: Leuven University Press/Peeters, 1994) 343-361.
Five passages in 1 Thessalonians (1:6-8 and 2:13; 2:1-12; 2:17-3:13; 4:1-12; 5:12-14) show that evangelisation at Thessalonica occurred through the concerted actions of three factors: (1) the apostles and church leaders who proclaimed the gospel; (2) the word of the Lord which brought about a radical change deep within all Christians; and (3) the electing and loving activity of God.

561 Lamm, Wilbur Clayton. "The Apocalyptic Background and Elements in the Thessalonian Epistles" (Unpublished Ph.D. Dissertation; Louisville, KY: Southern Baptist Theological Seminary, 1948).

562 Laub, Franz. *Eschatologische Verkündigung und Lebensgestaltung nach Paulus: Eine Untersuchung zum Wirken des Apostels beim Aufbau der Gemeinde in Thessalonike* (Biblische Untersuchungen 10; Regensburg: Pustet, 1973).
Eschatology is an essential part of Christian existence, and hence was an important issue in the founding and building of the Christian community in Thessalonica. Major issues which needed to be confronted included the apparent failure to consider the place of death for its members, including a lack of Christian hope for the resurrection. Paul does not say when the parousia will actually occur. Eschatology also figures into considerations of the authenticity of the letters. On balance, in light of their differing eschatologies, 2 Thessalonians is inauthentic.

563 ---. "Paulus als Gemeindegründer (1 Thess)," *Kirche im Werden. Studien zum Thema Amt und Gemeinde im Neuen Testament* (ed. Josef Hainz; Paderborn: Schöningh, 1976) 17-38.
1 Thessalonians provides an excellent example of a concretization of Pauline theology in terms of seeing Paul as the founder of a community. 1 Thessalonians 1-3 is a revealing passage, since it reflects Paul's personal involvement with the founding of a community, and his struggle with various issues in the light of this, including authority versus service, and seeing himself as a model worthy of imitation.

564 Lewis, Gordon R. "Biblical Evidence for Pretribulationism," *Bibliotheca Sacra* 125 (1968) 216-226.

A pretribulational rapture of the church is consistent theologically and fits all the strands of biblical data: (1) The primary purpose of the tribulation, namely, the outpouring of divine wrath, is directed only to the ungodly, not to the church. (2) The Thessalonian letters teach deliverance from the coming day of vengeance by the rapture. The revelation of the man of sin precedes the day of wrath, and the rapture precedes the revelation of the Antichrist. (3) The Olivet Discourse does not treat the rapture of the church or the resurrection but Israel's role in the tribulation. Nothing here excludes an imminent rapture of the church. (4) The repeated emphasis of the whole New Testament on the preparedness for meeting Christ any time of any day most naturally is understood in terms of a pretribulational rapture of the church.

565 Lindars, Barnabas. "The Sound of the Trumpet: Paul and Eschatology," *Bulletin of the John Rylands University Library of Manchester* 67.2 (1985) 766-782.

A study of 1 Thess 4:13-5:11, 1 Cor 15, 2 Cor 5 and Rom 8:18-39 shows a consistent use of Jewish eschatological concepts, but with Christ as God's messianic agent in a day of judgment following a general resurrection. Paul contributed two major developments to his inherited apocalyptic eschatology: (1) his doctrine of justification by faith based on the past event of Christ's death as the divinely appointed means of atonement for human sins; and (2) his idea of the future life as a transformation from incorporation into Christ in this life to the intermediate state and then to the final glory. Paul handles the delay of the parousia without abandoning the eschatological framework of his message.

566 Lindemann, Andreas. "Zum Abfassungszweck des Zweiten Thessalonicherbriefes," *Zeitschrift für die neutestamentliche Wissenschaft* 68.1-2 (1977) 35-47.

The thesis of A. Hilgenfeld and H. J. Holtzmann that 2 Thessalonians corrected the false eschatology of 1 Thessalonians has been dismissed since the work of W. Wrede (420). This thesis, however, is more plausible than Wrede recognized. 2 Thess 2:2 shows that the author is correcting what was said in 1 Thess 4:13-18 and 5:1-11, and that 2 Thess 2:15 is an assertion of his own authority, reinforced by the reference to his own handwriting in 3:17. The pseudepigrapher is writing to correct the false eschatology regarding the near coming of the day of the Lord. The plausibility of this proposal is seen in the way the early church fathers understood apparent conflicts in the two letters.

567 Longenecker, Richard N. "The Nature of Paul's Early Eschatology," *New Testament Studies* 31 (1985) 85-95.

It is commonly argued that apocalyptic eschatology dominated Paul's outlook in his early days, while soteriology, christology, ecclesiology, and ethics came to assume importance only later. But while eschatology was a major factor in Paul's early thinking, a study of the Thessalonian letters highlights three significant matters that are frequently overlooked: (1) eschatology is not the major issue in 1 Thessalonians; (2) the basis of eschatological hope in these early letters is a functional Christology and not the reverse; and (3) Paul's purpose in raising eschatological themes is pastoral and not didactic. Thus the starting point for all of Paul's Christian theology is not apocalypticism but functional christology, namely, his commitment to the life, work, and resurrection of Jesus Christ.

568 Lubahn, Erich. "Hermeneutischer Ansatz für Eschatologie, mit beispielhafter Anwendung auf 2. Thessalonicher 2," *Zukunftserwartung in biblischer Sicht: Beiträge zur Eschatologie* (ed. Gerhard Maier; Monographien und Studienbücher 313; Wuppertal: Brockhaus, 1984) 114-123.

All of biblical eschatology has the resurrection of Jesus Christ as its pivotal point. The consequences for this are that a future apart from the resurrection of Christ leads to destruction and judgment, while a future through Christ's resurrection leads to holiness and an exalted God. The Thessalonian letters are two of the oldest in the New Testament (2 Thessalonians is authentic), with the second letter correcting a false understanding of the first. 2 Thess 2:1-17 is the high point of the letter and expresses the Pauline view of the apocalypse.

569 Lull, David J. "Salvation History. Theology in 1 Thessalonians, Philemon, Philippians, and Galatians: A Response to N. T. Wright, R. B. Hays, and R. Scroggs," *Pauline Theology 1: Thessalonians, Philippians, Galatians, Philemon* (ed. Jouette M. Bassler; Minneapolis: Fortress, 1991) 247-265.

The pattern of "salvation history"--the narrative "thought" pattern of Paul--in 1 Thessalonians, Philippians, and Galatians is as follows: (1) *before Christ*, the law was a disciplinarian while everything was in the grip of sin and while God's promise to Abraham awaited fulfillment; (2) *in the Christ-event*, Christ and the Spirit bring freedom and the fulfillment of the Abrahamic covenant; and (3) *in the life to come*, the work of Christ and the Spirit will be completed. This pattern of "salvation history" was constitutive of Paul's self-understanding as an apostle to the Gentiles. In this pattern, Jews and Gentiles are united in God's indivisible redemption of the world through faith in Jesus Christ.

570 Marshall, I. Howard. "Election and Calling to Salvation in 1 and 2 Thessalonians," *The Thessalonian Correspondence* (ed. Raymond F. Collins; Bibliotheca ephemeridum theologicarum lovaniensium 87; Leuven: Leuven University Press, 1990) 259-276.

A study of the "election" (1 Thess 1:4; 5:2; 2 Thess 2:13) and "calling" (1 Thess 2:12; 4:7; 5:23-24; 2 Thess 1:11; 2:14) language in 1 and 2 Thessalonians, as well as the prayers (1 Thess 3:10; 3:11-13; 5:23; 2 Thess 1:11-12; 2:16-17; 3:5; 3:16) and other relevant passages, leads to the following conclusions: (1) The theme of election is prominent in the theology of the letters. (2) The teaching of both letters on this subject is essentially the same. (3) Election language assures Gentile converts that they, along with Jews, belong to God's elect people. (4) On this basis Paul can use election language to encourage the readers in their struggle with persecution. (5) Election, therefore, is particularly related to perseverance. (6) Although the juxtaposition of the themes of election and the danger of falling away may appear to contemporary readers as a logical paradox, this problem did not manifestly trouble Paul. (7) There is no clear evidence to support the common contention that the elect are a body of specific individuals chosen before the foundation of the world to be effectually called and to attain to final salvation without any possibility of their falling away.

571 ---. "Pauline Theology in the Thessalonian Correspondence," *Paul and Paulinism: Essays in Honour of C. K. Barrett* (ed. Morna D. Hooker and S. G. Wilson; London: SPCK, 1982) 173-183.

Although 1 Thessalonians contains some interesting omissions, it nevertheless possesses the main features of Pauline theology. There is less of Paul's expected theology in 2 Thessalonians, but if this letter is regarded as a kind of explanatory appendix to 1 Thessalonians, this feature is understandable. It has become all the more apparent that the distinctiveness of the various Pauline letters is intimately related to the differing situations which the apostle was addressing. While his theology had a basic content, the actual expression of it could be quite varied, and what he wrote arose out of a creative encounter with congregations and the specific problems which they were facing.

572 Matera, Frank J. "An Ethic of Election. The Letters to the Thessalonians," *New Testament Ethics: The Legacies of Jesus and Paul* (Louisville: Westminster/John Knox, 1996) 123-137.

The Thessalonian correspondence provides an outstanding example of moral exhortation to a community of recent converts for whom the parousia is still a vibrant hope. In these letters Paul consistently reminds the community of its elected status. God has called the Thessalonians to a life of sanctification so that they can stand blameless before the Lord on the day of his parousia. To maintain their elected status, they must shun all immorality and uncleanness, and persevere in faith, love, and hope. In their daily lives they must work quietly as they wait for the Lord's return. Should they need an illustration of what it means to live in accordance with the gospel, they will find it in Paul.

573 Mearns, Christopher L. "Early Eschatological Development in Paul: The Evidence of I and II Thessalonians," *New Testament Studies* 27.2 (1980/81) 137-157.

Although many have postulated that development in Paul's thinking took place later in his life, an analysis of the Thessalonian letters suggests that the biggest change in the apostle's eschatology occurred at the beginning of his surviving correspondence. Paul's early move from a realized to a future eschatology was stimulated by four factors: (1) the impact of the increasing number of deaths among the earliest Christians; (2) the need to correct over-realized eschatological enthusiasm; (3) the necessity to emphasize a sequence of signs before the coming of the end; and (4) the re-animating of apocalyptic expectation by Caligula's attempt to impose living emperor worship in 40 CE.

574 ---. "Early Eschatological Development in Paul: The Evidence of 1 Corinthians," *Journal for the Study of the New Testament* 22 (1984) 19-35.

A radical change may be discerned in Paul's eschatology already before he wrote 1 Corinthians. By reconstructing the stages of the arguments which underlie and precede the existing text--a method which John Hurd calls "backward extrapolating"--it can be discerned that Paul's own earliest Christian eschatology was predominantly realized. His presentation of future apocalyptic teaching in 1 and 2 Thessalonians, in the "previous letter" to the Corinthians, and in 1 Corinthians, therefore, is evidence for a radical re-direction in his thinking and teaching.

575 Medley, E. "The Conception of Christ Suggested to a Heathen Inquirer by Paul's Earliest Extant Writing: A Study in 1 Thessalonians," *The Expositor, 5th Series* 4 (1896) 359-370.

A Gentile inquirer, whose interest in Christianity had been aroused by hearing Paul speak, would not find much explicit teaching about Christ in 1 Thessalonians. Yet this letter would implicitly teach him the following: Jesus Christ had lived on this earth, had died a violent death on behalf of his people, and had risen from the grave; wherever Jesus was now, he stood in such a relation to people in this world as is only possible to a living person; he exercises powers which are held to belong to the supreme God alone; he dominates all life, both in this world and in that unseen world into which the dead go; and one day he will come again in glory.

576 Mendoza Viray, Jaime. "La vocación cristiana en 1 y 2 Tesalonicenses" (Unpublished Ph.D. Dissertation; Pamplona, Spain: University of Navarra, 1990).

577 Menken, Maarten J. J. *Getransformeerde traditie: Christologie in 2 Tessalonicenzen* (Utrecht: Katholieke Theologische Universiteit, 1994).
Revised and republished in English as "Christology in 2 Thessalonians: A Transformation of Pauline Tradition," *Estudios Bíblicos* 4.54 (1996) 501-522.

The Christology of 2 Thessalonians should be understood in terms of a process, namely, "the transformation of tradition." Tradition here is understood as the aggregate of convictions, formulations, concepts, and thinking patterns which an author of a given scripture derives from his predecessors in the faith. Religious texts are "actualized traditions" written in response to new situations which require application of tradition and its reinterpretation within a framework of an accepted school of theology (e.g., Pauline, Petrine). The author of 2 Thessalonians knew and used three traditions: that found in 1 Thessalonians and other Pauline letters as well as early Jewish and Christian apocalyptic eschatology. The transformation of these three traditions can be seen in 2 Thessalonians in terms of: (1) the titles of Christ; (2) prayers and comparable expressions relative to the functions ascribed to God and Jesus; (3) the christological use of texts about God in the Old Testament; and (4) the eschatological role attributed by the author to Jesus.

578 Merk, Otto. *Handeln aus Glauben. Die Motivierungen der paulinischen Ethik* (Marburger Theologische Studien 5; Marburg: N. G. Elwert, 1968) 45-58.

A discussion of ethics and faith in Paul ought to begin with 1 Thessalonians, the oldest preserved Pauline letter. Chapters 4-5 form a unity which serves as the conclusion to chapters 1-3. 1 Thess 4:1-12 begins with 4:1-2, which forms a kind of heading for the following paraenesis. The section then states that the will of God is the holiness of Christians (v 3), developed in the following verses (vv 4-5). The Lord is the avenger concerning all these things, not being limited to a single thing (v 6), with the grounding of this provided in verse 7, which introduces a secondary motif. Then three examples of God's actions are provided (vv 6-8). Verses 9-12 constitute a new section on brotherly love. In 1 Thess 5:1-11, following a discussion of the parousia (4:13-18), Paul warns the Thessalonians in a second eschatological section not to worry about the end, since they know that the day is coming. In 1 Thess 5:12-18, the beginning of the letter is renewed. This is divided into two parts, under ethical (vv 14-18) and cultic (vv 19-22) points of view.

579 ---. "Zu Rudolf Bultmanns Auslegung des 1 Thessalonicherbriefes," *Glaube und Eschatologie: Festschrift für Werner Kümmel* (ed. Erich Gräser and Otto Merk; Tübingen: Mohr, 1985) 189-198.

A unpublished manuscript of Bultmann's lectures on 1 Thessalonians has several noteworthy points on the thanksgiving, the historical context (3:13 is especially important), the structure of the letter, faith, and eschatology.

580 ---. "Zur Christologie im Ersten Thessalonicherbrief," *Anfänge der Christologie. Festschrift für Ferdinand Hahn zum 65. Geburtstag* (ed. Cilliers Breytenbach and Henning Paulsen; Göttingen: Vandenhoeck & Ruprecht, 1991) 97-110.

Only in the last decade has the contribution of 1 Thessalonians to Pauline theology been recognized. In the area of christology, the following three areas are important: (1) God's electing acts, which provide the leading theological structure for the letter; (2) faith (πίστις/πιστεύειν), which is the entryway into christology; and (3) the parousia, in which creedal passages in the letter express the hope and expectation that the fundamental actions of God realized in Christ direct the future.

581 Míguez, Néstor O. "Lenguaje bíblico y lenguaje político," *Revista de Interpretacion biblica Latinoamericana* 4 (1989) 65-81.

The use of political language is one of the most contested elements of Liberation Theology. An analysis of 1 Thessalonians, however, reveals that Paul employs political language and political analogy in speaking about the Christian faith. This political language is one of confrontation and Paul gives it a counter-hegemonic sense. As a result he "de-ideologizes" political language and at the same time gives a political dimension to the experience of the Christian faith. The church thus now thinks of itself as a political entity. In fact, such words as "church," "Lord," "kingdom" and others are considered as religious terms today and in this sense they have lost their original function of providing an ideological critique. Faithfulness to Paul's thought requires the recovery of that language with its elements of confrontation and critique.

582 ---. "No como los otros, que no tienen esperanza. Ideología y estrategia del cristianismo paulino en la gentilidad. Lectura socio-política de la Primera Carta de Pablo a los Tesalonicenses" (Unpublished Ph.D. Dissertation; Buenos Aires: Instituto Superior Evangélico de Estudios Teológicos, 1988).

This thesis consists of three parts. The first is an explanation of the methodology employed--an eclectic approach involving such diverse fields as structural linguistics, socio-linguistics, and the social sciences. The second part is an analysis of the Greek world during the Roman empire, since it is that historical context which provides the social, economic, political, and cultural background against which 1 Thessalonians ought to be understood. The third and largest part is an analysis of 1 Thessalonians which demonstrates Paul's counter-cultural strategy in presenting a new ethical framework in the context of an imminent parousia.

583 ---. "Pablo y la revolución cristiana en el primer siglo," *Cuadernos de Teología* 10.1 (1989) 67-80.

Recent developments in comprehending the dynamics of society allow for a better understanding of Paul's strategy in forming and nurturing the emerging Gentile Christian community. As a strategist, Paul not only gave coherence to the Christian discourse but also transformed this discourse in a series of social, political, and moral practices. This can be clearly seen in 1 Thessalonians, which reveals that Paul's revolutionary strategy was formulated from the experience of oppression and lack of power. The apostle organized the church in the model of reciprocity rather than the prevailing model of his day, that of slavery. He also uses apocalyptic motifs to show the transitory nature of human power (the Roman empire) and to emphasize the certain victory of the people of God at Christ's return.

584 ---. "Para no quedar sin esperanza. La apocalíptica de Pablo en 1 Ts. como lenguaje de esperanza," *Revista de Interpretación Bíblica Latinoamericana* 7 (1990) 47-67.

Unlike those who do not see any sense in history, Christian communities, despite their oppression from the Roman empire and powerlessness, confront the oppressor with a symbol of hope. So the parousia in 1 Thess 4:13-18, filled with apocalyptic imagery, depicts the moment when power is overtaken and the kingdom of God is fully established. In 1 Thess 5:1-11, the Christian faith confronts the empire by showing the impossibility of proportioning the peace and golden age that if offers. Eschatology, however, is not only a factor which strengthens the hope for liberation, but it also claims in the present an ethic against the holders of power. In this way, the symbol of hope is used as a means to confront oppression.

585 Molina Palma, Mario A. "La provisionalidad responsable: el tiempo cristiano en perspectiva escatológica," *Estudios Bíblicos* 45.3-4 (1987) 337-346.

The prevalent opinion in biblical studies maintains an evolutionary theory of New Testament eschatology. Support for this hypothesis is claimed to exist in passages such as 2 Peter 3, where the central motif focuses on the delay of the parousia rather than its imminence. A careful reading of this passage, however, shows that the emphasis here is not on chronology (the timing of the parousia) but on moral responsibility (the consequence of the parousia). In other eschatological passages of the New Testament the main emphasis is similarly not on chronology but on either encouragement to endure or the challenge to conversion. This attitude in which the Christian lives in the present with eschatological hope can be labeled "responsible provisionality," and helps one understand the apparent tension in eschatological matters in the Thessalonian letters. These letters do not emphasize the imminence of the parousia (1 Thess 4:13-18) or its delay (2 Thess 2:1-12) but rather recognize an uncertainty over the time of Christ's return which prompts an invitation to a watchful attitude (1 Thess 5:1-11).

586 Montague, George T. "The Spirit in Paul's Early Letters: Thessalonians and Philippians," *The Holy Spirit. Growth of a Biblical Tradition* (New York: Paulist Press, 1976) 127-133.

The description of the Spirit in Paul's earliest letters to the Thessalonians (1 Thess 1:4-6; 4:1-8; 5:19-22; 5:23; 2 Thess 2:1-3; 2:11; 2:13) and the Philippians (1:19) evidences continuity and discontinuity with that of the Old Testament. As the Spirit of sanctification, the Holy Spirit does not appear here as greatly different from the spirit of judgment and salvation found in the ethical preaching of the prophets. The Holy Spirit plays an important role in confirming the apostolic preaching in the listeners, and prophecy takes place in the community in a comprehensive way which has no easy analogue in the Old Testament community. That it is the Spirit of Christ indicates that the Spirit experienced by Paul and his first communities is the pouring out of the Spirit promised in the Old Testament to rest upon the Messiah, who is Jesus.

587 Moore, Hamilton. "Paul and Apocalyptic," *Irish Biblical Studies* 9 (1987) 35-46.

Passages like 1 Thess 4:13-5:1-11, 2 Thess 2:1-12 and 1 Corinthians 15 show that Paul clearly was influenced by the apocalyptic beliefs of his day concerning the end time. But while apocalyptic is an important part of Paul's basic theological structure, it does not constitute the coherent center of his thought. Although in his later letters Paul does not always express himself in the apocalyptic terms of the Thessalonian correspondence, there is no radical change of viewpoint, and very much of the same perspective--an apocalyptic world-view informed by the Christ-event--can be seen.

588 Morris, Leon. *1, 2 Thessalonians* (Word Biblical Themes; Dallas: Word, 1989).

After a brief examination of introductory issues (audience, authorship, date, order of letters), the major theological themes found in 1 and 2 Thessalonians are examined under the following headings: "The Living and True God," "Jesus Christ Our Lord," "The Last Things," "The Defeat of Evil," "The Christian Family," and "The Christian Life."

589 ---. "The Wrath of God," *Expository Times* 63 (1952) 142-145.
It has been common in recent years to espouse the conclusion that wrath cannot be applied in any meaningful and personal sense to God. The biblical writers, however, persist in regarding wrath as a personal activity of God. Paul, for example, in his letters to the Thessalonians (1 Thess 1:10; 2:16; 5:9; 2 Thess 1:7-9) uses vigorous language to depict God's personal activity in dealing with sinners. The idea that God cannot be angry represents a pagan, not a Christian, view of God.

590 Müller, Ulrich B. *Prophetie und Predigt im Neuen Testament: Formgeschichtliche Untersuchungen zur urchristlichen Prophetie* (Studien zum Neuen Testament 10; Gütersloh: Gütersloh Verlagshaus, 1975) 148-157, 165-171.
Two passages in the Thessalonian letters are especially relevant for a discussion of prophecy and preaching. First, a form-critical analysis of 1 Thess 5:1-11 divides the passage into two sections: the indicative section (vv 2-3), which proclaims the unfathomableness of the day of the Lord; and the cohortative section (vv 6-8 and 9-10), a christologically grounded section marked by the second-person plural and cohortative first-person forms. Second, in 1 Thess 4:13-18 Paul probably grounds his words of comfort for the problems of the community in a holy oracle, similar to that in 1 Cor 15:51-52.

591 Mycielski, Ludwik. "Apokaliptyczna szata literacka opisów paruzji Chrystusa z listów do Tesaloniczan," *Analecta Cracoviensia* 4 (1972) 147-179.
This article examines the apocalyptic symbols used in 1 and 2 Thessalonians to describe the second coming of the Lord (e.g., "cry of command," "call of an archangel," "trumpet blast of God," "heavenly angels," "power of the Lord," "flaming fire," "breath of the mouth of the Lord"). The background of these symbols lies in the Old Testament and an understanding of this original context is essential in properly interpreting their use in 1 and 2 Thessalonians.

592 Myre, Andre. "L'expérience présente du salut futur," *L'expérience comme lieu théologique* (ed. Elizabeth J. Lacelle and Thomas R. Potvin; Collection héritage et projet; Foi chrétienne 26; Montreal: Fides, 1983) 157-165.
The Thessalonian correspondence contains many elements which refer to the future hope of the believer for salvation. The vocabulary which Paul uses to speak about this topic in these first two of his letters is diverse, but this very diversity introduces an element of uncertainty and vagueness concerning his meaning. As a result, it is not possible to reconstruct a systematic synthesis of Pauline theology, and so any discussion of salvation must be done on a letter-by-letter basis.

593 Neyrey, Jerome H. "Eschatology in 1 Thessalonians: The Theological Factor in 1:9-10; 2:4-5; 3:11-13; 4:6 and 4:13-18," *SBL 1980 Seminar Papers* (ed. Paul Achtemeier; SBL Seminar Papers 19; Chico, CA: Scholars Press, 1980) 219-231.

Using 1 Thess 4:13-18 and 5:1-11 as normative indicators of Pauline eschatology, commentators have primarily concentrated on its apocalyptic character and its christological focus. This emphasis, however, is unbalanced for a proper assessment of all the eschatological material in 1 Thessalonians. In addition to a synoptic-like apocalyptic stream of eschatological material (4:13-18; 5:1-11), the letter also contains a missionary-preaching tradition (1:9-10; 2:4-5; 3:11-13; 4:6) in which there is a strong, even dominant, theological emphasis that it is God, not Christ, who sees, hears, judges, and requites. In fact, this missionary-preaching tradition is the typical expression of eschatological material in Pauline letters.

594 Pax, Elpidius. "Beobachtungen zur Konvertitensprache im ersten Thessalonicherbrief," *Studium biblicum Franciscani liber annuus* 21 (1971) 220-262.

The *Sitz im Leben* of a work is established above all in its linguistic usage. The world of 1 Thessalonians offers different sources for its conversion language. This letter is part of a group of texts which reflect a climate of conversion. These texts help to illuminate several dimensions of conversion, including the actual act of conversion, the religious results of conversion, the crisis of conversion with its inner and outer difficulties, traces of pagan Hellenistic religiosity in conversion language, and differences that 1 Thessalonians has from the Jewish proselyte milieu, even though this is where it is most at home.

595 ---. "Konvertitenprobleme im ersten Thessalonicherbrief," *Bibel und Leben* 13.1 (1972) 24-37.

The historical situation of 1 Thessalonians as it is often described does not necessarily open up the *Sitz im Leben* of the letter. Hearers respond to words differently, and it is therefore legitimate to ask about the mental disposition of the addressees, especially since the letter is written to converts. There is a particular personality type of a convert which is different from that of a person hostile to God. There is the further question of why someone would become a believer, and what would be the motive for conversion. These motives differ. There are also problems and difficulties faced by converts such as a feeling of isolation and the experience of persecution.

596 Pfister, Willibald. "Geist und Heiligung," *Das Leben im Geist nach Paulus. Der Geist als Anfang und Vollendung des christlichen Lebens* (Studia Friburgensia 34; Freiburg: Schweiz Universitätsverlag, 1963) 5-28.

Life in the Spirit, according to Paul, is both the beginning and the ending point of the Christian life. Life in the Spirit can be discussed in terms of four categories: "Spirit and Holiness," "Spirit and Life," "Life in the Spirit," and "the Spirit and Sonship." 1 Thess 4:1-8 is one of the three important passages regarding the Spirit and holiness.

In this beautiful example of a paraenetic section, here exegeted verse by verse, the apostle exhorts the Thessalonians to a God-pleasing transformation (vv 1-2), described in terms of its content (vv 3-8).

597 Reumann, John. "The Theologies of 1 Thessalonians and Philippians: Contents, Comparison, and Composite," *SBL 1987 Seminar Papers* (ed. Kent H. Richards; SBL Seminar Papers 26; Atlanta: Scholars Press, 1987) 521-536.

A comparison of 1 Thessalonians and Philippians concerning their respective claims about God, Christ, the Holy Spirit, anthropology, eschatology, the church, preaching, ethics, and so on, yields many areas of agreement in thought. Yet the results of such a comparative study need to be refined by further analysis and discussion before the next step can properly be taken with confidence: combining them into a single picture of Paul's thought.

598 Richard, Earl J. "Early Pauline Thought: An Analysis of 1 Thessalonians," *Pauline Theology, 1: Thessalonians, Philippians, Galatians, Philemon* (ed. Jouette M. Bassler; Minneapolis: Fortress, 1991) 39-51.

1 Thessalonians is a composite document in which a short earlier missive (2:13-4:2) has been inserted into a later Thessalonian letter (1:1-2:12 + 4:3-5:28). In these two missives, Paul presumes a given understanding of God, Christ, and Christian reality which not only permeates his correspondence but is also taken for granted by his audience. The facts--that God chooses and is petitioned in prayer, that Jesus is God's Son and is the means of salvation, and that believers are called to lead a life worthy of God and to love one another and all--are all accepted by both writer and audience. Their function is subsidiary to the document's principal concerns. In the early missive, Paul's focus is on the community's faith and love and its reciprocal concern for the missionaries. In the later missive, the purpose is both to reassure the community and to respond to its deep concerns. Although 1 Thessalonians does not offer a summation of Pauline thought, this composite document does provide a fixed point for such a study.

599 Rigaux, Béda. *Dieu l'a ressucité: Exégèse et théologie biblique* (Studii Biblici Franciscani Analecta 4; Gembloux: Duculot, 1973).

1 Thess 1:9-10 (pp 114-117) is one of three long confessions in the Pauline letters regarding the resurrection (the others are 1 Corinthians 15 and Rom 1:1-5). It is introduced with a pre-Pauline formula and has pre-Pauline elements, especially revealing Semitic traits which go back to the Old Testament. In context, it has a high christology and represents primitive Christian belief, perhaps originating in Antioch. 1 Thess 4:13-5:11 (pp 404-405) is an affirmation of the death and resurrection of Jesus, seeing resurrection and life with Jesus for all. His return is not a peripheral phenomenon.

600 ---. "Evangelium im ersten Thessalonicherbrief," *Wissenschaft und Weisheit* 35 (1972) 1-12.

The word "gospel" occupies a place of unusual importance in the religious movement started by Jesus. Particularly important passages for establishing its meaning in 1 Thessalonians are 1:5, 2:4, 2:7-8, and 3:2. The exegesis of these passages can be refined through a consideration of the *Sitz im Leben* of the book, in which it is seen that Paul's apostleship and the gospel go together. Paul's gospel is grounded in the death and resurrection of Jesus. It does not originate with Paul but offers a goal. The reality of the gospel is that it is the work of God and describes Christian existence between the death and resurrection of Jesus and the glorified life with God.

601 ---. "Vocabulaire chrétien antérieure à la première épître aux Thessaloniciens," *Sacra Pagina II* (ed. J. Coppens, A.-L. Descamps, and E. Massaux; Bibliotheca ephemeridum theologicarum lovaniensium 12; Duculot: Gembloux, 1958) 380-389.

The language of 1 Thessalonians shows development in its forms of expression from the time of the death of Jesus, reflected in the Synoptic Gospels and Acts, and the first letter of Paul in its proclamation of salvation. The difference between what actually belongs to the apostle and the developing tradition of the community makes it possible to arrive at the earliest language of the church and to create a link between the historical Jesus and the Christ of faith. An example of this is found in the phrasing in 1 Thess 1:9-10. This section interrupts the flow of Paul's thought, indicating previous formulation, especially in its statement in verse 10 on the resurrection from the dead. 1 Thess 2:13-16 also reflects language which comes from Jewish apocalyptic and Hellenistic anti-Jewish polemic.

602 Rivera, Luis Fernando. "Cristianismo existencial y expresión eucarística de la religión: 1 y 2 Tesalonicenses," *Revista Bíblica* 41 (1979) 75-89.

The earliest Christian communities opposed the life-controlling and theoretical world of the suprastructures, and substituted for it a new religious attitude: thanksgiving. This new perspective is possible because the church lives the transcendent dynamism of the *paraklēsis*. This is obvious in the Thessalonian correspondence where both thanksgiving and *paraklēsis* serve as the thematic structure of the letters. Even though opposition to the world results in tribulation and persecution, the church overcomes through *paraklēsis* and is led to final victory at the "day of the Lord."

603 Roetzel, Calvin J. "Election/Calling in Certain Pauline Letters: An Experimental Construction," *SBL 1990 Seminar Papers* (ed. David J. Lull; SBL Seminar Papers 29; Atlanta: Scholars Press, 1990) 552-569.

In the nexus of his own experience, that of his addressees, and his inherited traditions, Paul forges his views on "election" and "calling." This language--not just the words κλῆσις and ἐκλογή but a network of words, metaphors, symbols, rituals and myths which are part of Paul's election theology--can refer to those who are divinely appointed to suffer (1 Thess), to a community of believing Jews and Gentiles (Gal), and to those chosen without any concern whatsoever for their rank in society (1 Cor). The cross or

Jesus' passion, belonging as it does to the network of election/calling language, may serve as a model for the persecuted (1 Thess), as a symbol of inclusion (Gal), or as a wrecking bar to dismantle the hierarchical models of the spiritual elitists (1 Cor).

604 ---. "The Grammar of Election in Four Pauline Letters," *Pauline Theology 2: 1 & 2 Corinthians* (ed. David M. Hay; Minneapolis: Fortress, 1993) 211-233.

The proposal of Jouette Bassler (502) that the concept of election serves as a thread which ties together Paul's theology is a good one, although one must allow for the dynamic aspect of that theology. A study of the "grammar" of election--the way Paul's language *shapes* rather than merely *expresses* his view of the world--in 1 Thessalonians, Philippians, Galatians, and 1 Corinthians reveals that the apostle uses the language of election to achieve very different results. He portrays the elect as those called to suffer with Christ (1 Thess), as a community of believing Jews and Gentiles (Gal), and as those chosen by God without regard for rank, position, or circumstance (1 Cor). Election, for Paul, is less a key propositional or foundational element in his theology than an emerging, dynamic element in his larger field of discourse.

605 Romaniuk, Casimiro. "La volontà di Dio come motivo parenetico nelle Lettere di S. Paolo," *Rivista Biblica* 20.4 (1972) 353-368.

In reminding believers of their moral responsibilities, Paul frequently appeals to the will of God. Sometimes this appeal is explicit ("the will of God"), while on other occasions he speaks more generally of the "call" or "election" of God. This motivation for the Christian life appears frequently in the Thessalonian letters (1 Thess 4:3; 4:7; 5:9, 18; 2 Thess 2:14) but is less common in the later letters which make use of christological grounds for moral conduct. The emphasis of the will of God as a paraenetical motivation might be explained by the fact that Paul was still under the influence of the Old Testament, which presents God as universal king and supreme legislator of human conduct.

606 Romaniuk, Kazimierz. "Der Begriff der Furcht in der Theologie des Paulus," *Bibel und Leben* 11.3 (1970) 168-175.

In light of the eschatological themes in the Thessalonian letters, it is surprising that the word "fear" does not appear. This can be accounted for, no doubt, because of the religious atmosphere in Thessalonica where, in a context where people expected the imminent parousia, there was much uncertainty and fear.

607 Sabbe, M. "De Paulinische beschrijving van de parousie," *Collationes Brugenses et Gandavenses* 7.1 (1961) 86-114.

Paul's description of the parousia is dependent not on Hellenistic sources but on the Old Testament and apocalyptic traditions. The word "parousia" is, indeed, a Hellenistic term referring to local citizens leaving their city to meet a returning king or emperor. Paul, however, infuses into this technical term the expectations of Old Testament Jews and New Testament Christians. An extensive study of relevant texts demonstrates that the concepts associated with the parousia are clearly anticipated in the Old Testament prophetic and Jewish apocalyptic writings, including those of the Qumran community. Drawn from these sources are: "staging motifs," such as the angel of God or the trumpet of God announcing a new event; the clouds of heaven as the place of God's presence; a sequence of eschatological events such as the resurrection of the dead and final judgment; accompanying signs and portends; the sudden and ultimate victory over all God's enemies and those of his saints. Other key ideas which also point to Old Testament and apocalyptic sources include the Lord coming with his holy ones (or angels) and the day of the Lord.

608 Sahlin, Harald. "Paulus och Danielsboken," *Svensk Exegetisk Årsbok* 46 (1981) 95-110.

Paul gives evidence in a number of ways in his letters that he has been influenced by the book of Daniel. For example, it is possible that he has understood the four beasts in Daniel 7 as representing different evil cosmic powers and that this is reflected in his reference to four such powers in Eph 1:21, 6:12 and Col 1:6. The greatest evidence that Paul is indebted to Daniel, however, can be seen in his apocalyptic conceptions, especially as they are found in 1 and 2 Thessalonians.

609 Sand, Alexander. "Zur Frage nach dem 'Sitz Im Leben' der Apokalyptischen Texte des Neuen Testaments," *New Testament Studies* 18 (1972) 167-177.

The explicit apocalyptic texts of the New Testament are 1 Thess 4:13-18, 5:1-11, 2 Thess 1:4-12, 2:1-12, Mark 13 and the Apocalypse of John. An analysis of these texts indicates that apocalyptic material occurs relatively seldom in the New Testament, with the earliest texts probably coming out of a catastrophe such as the fall of Jerusalem. Nevertheless, the New Testament writers took this apocalyptic material and theologically adapted it and "Christianized" it for integration into their writings, so that it was used for polemical and apologetic purposes.

610 Schade, Hans-Heinrich. *Apokalyptische Christologie bei Paulus. Studien zum Zusammenhang von Christologie und Eschatologie in den Paulusbriefen* (Göttinger Theologische Arbeiten 18; Göttingen: Vandenhoeck & Ruprecht, 1981).

A discussion of apocalyptic christology must begin with the expectation of the Day of the Lord and its linguistic expression. 1 Thess 1:9-10 (and 1 Cor 15:25-28) is predicated on the use of traditional language regarding the "Son." In 1 Thess 5:1-11 Paul speculates on the end of time by employing the image of the thief in the night--an apocalyptic image. The Day has a double meaning, as the Day of the Lord and in terms of daylight, referring to sons of light. In terms of apocalyptic christology, 1 Thessalonians was a test to Paul's early theology. 1 Thess 1:9-10 occurs in the context of the opening of the letter and in the context of missionary preaching. 2:1-3:13 refers to believers in the end time. An apocalyptic understanding of the end times means a near expectation of the end. It puts into context the missionary preaching, including the present aspect of eschatology and the reality of belief, but it also looks to the future. 1 Thess 4:1-12, 5:1-11 and 5:12-22 are the grounding of Paul's ethics. The apostle uses a paraenetic tradition, with Jewish dualism. Themes which are developed include the following: being "with Christ" and "in Christ," an understanding of baptism, holiness, judgment, the Holy Spirit, calling and electing, and the relationship of the indicative and the imperative.

611 Schimanowski, Gottfried. "'Abgrenzung und Identitätsfindung': Paulinische Paränese im 1. Thessalonicherbrief," *Die Heiden: Juden, Christen und das Problem des Fremden* (ed. Reinhard Feldmeier and Ulrich Heckel; Wissenschaftliche Untersuchungen zum Neuen Testament 70; Tübingen: Mohr/Siebeck, 1994) 297-316.

The ways to establish and recognize Christian identity are questions frequently asked in New Testament studies. The paraenetic material in 1 Thessalonians occupies a special place in establishing Pauline thought on this issue. There are several smaller units of paraenetic material in the letter, but the major block is in 1 Thess 4:1-12. This passage is divided into three major parts, an introduction (vv 1-2), middle (vv 3-7), and conclusion (vv 9-12), followed by the two eschatological sections (4:13-18 and 5:1-11).

612 Schmidt, Andreas. "Erwägungen zur Eschatologie des 2 Thessalonicher und des 2 Johannes," *New Testament Studies* 38 (1992) 477-480.

Two different eschatological conceptions were being disseminated in Christian communities in Ephesus around 96 CE and these divergent views are reflected in 2 Thessalonians and 2 John. 2 Thess 1:7-10 depicts the coming of Christ "in glory," whereas 2 John 7 speaks of Christ coming "in the flesh." 2 Thess 2:3 depicts the future coming of the "son of destruction," whereas 2 John 7 speaks of the Antichrist who is already present.

613 Schneider, Johannes. *Der kommende Tag. Eine Einführung in den ersten Brief an die Thessalonicher* (Die urchristliche Botschaft 13; Berlin: Furche-Verlag, 1932).

614 Schnelle, Udo. "Der erste Thessalonicherbrief und die Entstehung der paulinischen Anthropologie," *New Testament Studies* 32 (1986) 207-224.

1 Thessalonians occupies a special place in the Pauline corpus. It not only differentiates itself from the later Pauline letters in the areas of ethics, anthropology, and eschatology, but it also has a fundamental difference in its teaching on justification and in the relationship of the apostle to Israel. Rather than reflect the later letters, 1 Thessalonians has a concept of law and righteousness which reflects the pre-Galatian situation. Similarly 1 Thess 2:14-16 advances a traditional motif that the Jews have hindered the mission and so threatened their own salvation. Thus, 1 Thessalonians provides evidence of being best understood as reflecting early Pauline theology.

615 ---. "Die Ethik des 1. Thessalonicherbriefes," *The Thessalonian Correspondence* (ed. Raymond F. Collins; Bibliotheca ephemeridum theologicarum lovaniensium 87; Leuven: Leuven University Press, 1990) 295-305.

There has been an increasing recognition in the last decade that 1 Thessalonians constitutes an important source of Pauline theology, especially since it represents the earliest Pauline thought. The ethical thought of this letter is contained in three thematic complexes: (1) the gospel, baptism and the giving of the Spirit; (2) the expectation of the return of the Lord Jesus Christ; and (3) the grounding of its eschatological thought in apocalyptic concepts. The ethical material in 1 Thessalonians is different from that of later Pauline letters, reflecting the pre-Pauline Hellenistic church. The ethic in this letter is not in the sphere of a specific teaching on justification, and there is no flesh/spirit dualism. Unlike such passages as 1 Cor 15:17, 2 Cor 5:19-21, Gal 1:4, 2:17, 3:22 and Rom 6:8, sin in 1 Thessalonians still has an enslaving power over the human. There is no attempt in the letter to ground its ethical teaching in the Old Testament, and for Paul the divine act in humanity (indicative) and the resulting acts of humanity (imperative) are characteristic.

616 Schulz, Siegfried. "Der 1. Thessalonicherbrief als einziges Zeugnis der frühpaulinischen Ethik," *Neutestamentliche Ethik* (Zürcher Grundrisse zur Bibel; Zürich: Theologischer Verlag, 1987) 301-333, 610-613.

A discussion of New Testament ethics must recognize its problems and its various sources. These latter include Jesus and his approach to the Mosaic law and his ethical radicalism, the post-Easter Jesus, the Hellenistic church, and then the fight against gnosticism and libertinism. 1 Thessalonians provides a test for early Pauline ethics. This letter contains sharp moral commands for holiness and norms for life. The motives of the early Pauline ethic are the warning of the final judgment, the Lord Jesus, baptism, and the question of non-Christians. The indicative and imperative are evident in 1 Thessalonians. 1 Thessalonians is an ethical letter, and the gospel serves as an expectation of the end. 2 Thessalonians is a polemical tract in letter form. The final judgment is the reward.

617 Scroggs, Robin. "Salvation History: The Theological Structure of Paul's Thought (1 Thessalonians, Philippians, and Galatians)," *Pauline Theology 1: Thessalonians, Philippians, Galatians, Philemon* (ed. Jouette M. Bassler; Minneapolis: Fortress, 1991) 212-226.

Since the topics treated in Paul's letters are in large measure determined not by the apostle but by his congregations, it may well be impossible to determine the "central" message or theology of Paul. Nevertheless, an overwhelming quantity of statements in his letters fall into the often-maligned category of "salvation history." Paul knows himself to be part of a grand story, the past of which he reads out of the Torah, the present from his experience of the Christ-event and the church, and the future from his hope in the constancy of God. On the basis of 1 Thessalonians, Philippians, and Galatians alone, the character of Paul's structure of salvation history is as follows. On the one hand, it certainly includes the full picture of God's relationship with Israel, interpreted in terms of God's foreordained intention to include Gentiles as well as Jews within the ultimate aim of salvation. On the other hand, the Christ-event brings something radically new to human possibility, because only through that historical event do Jews and Gentiles have the possibility of living in a faithful relationship with God.

618 Sellin, Gerhard. "Die Auferstehung ist schon geschehen. Zur Spiritualisierung apokalyptischer Terminologie im Neuen Testament," *Novum Testamentum* 25.3 (1983) 220-237.

It is commonplace in New Testament studies to claim that the concept of Paul's resurrection to life from the dead was already in Hellenistic Christianity before Paul, probably through gnostic or mystery-religions influence. However, clarification of terminology and questions of religions-history, as well as an examination of the two central texts, Rom 6:1-14 and Col 2:11-13, show that Paul, under the influence of apocalyptic thought, developed a two-part eschatology. The past is the new life since baptism, and the future remains for the resurrection of Christians. In 2 Thess 2:2, as a result of further development of apocalyptic, the day of the Lord stands as the turning point. The pseudepigraphal author is responding to 1 Thessalonians, not Romans 6, in order to show that it is wrong to think of a coming parousia, but that believers should view themselves as already living spiritually in the day of the Lord.

619 Shillito, Edward. "Paul upon Prayer. A Study of Prayer in 1 Thessalonians," *The Expositor, 8th Series* 22 (1921) 438-444.

In the Pauline letters there is no systematic analysis of prayer and no apology for it. It is always related to the central truths of the gospel and to the whole Christian experience which responds to that truth and grace. The phrase "before" (e.g., "before our God and Father," "before our Lord Jesus") used several times in 1 Thessalonians (1:3; 2:19; 3:9, 13), shows that prayer for Paul was a response to a living and present person. His prayers involved both thanksgiving (1:2-3; 2:13; 3:9) and petition (2:17; 3:6, 8, 12-13), both for his readers and for himself (5:23). The supreme reward of prayer in Thessalonica is an assurance of the soul with respect to the future which overcomes the perils of the present.

620 Smalley, Stephen S. "The Delay of the Parousia," *Journal of Biblical Literature* 83 (1964) 41-54.

Instead of a radical departure from Paul's earlier view of the parousia, the delay of which gave rise to hasty revisions, we are confronted in the Pauline letters with a homogeneous eschatological outlook, in which Paul's own background and intellect, as well as the differing milieu and problems of his readers, cause more or less the same thing to be said in different ways. Although there may be a shift of emphasis, there is no generically different perspective.

621 Snyder, Graydon F. "Apocalyptic and Didactic Elements in 1 Thessalonians," *SBL 1972 Proceedings* (ed. L. C. McGaughy; 2 vols.; N.P.: Society of Biblical Literature, 1972) 1.233-244.

Four possibilities have been forwarded to explain Pauline ethics: (1) interim ethics: Paul's more radical demands are due to the imminence of the end; (2) ethics of Parousia-delay: since the end was not coming, Paul felt obliged to give his congregations practical ethical advice; (3) counter-parousiacal ethics: Paul attempts to counter a prematurely realized eschatology with some community norms; and (4) apocalyptic ethics: Paul's demands are rooted in his apocalyptic thought. The strength of this last possibility can be seen in 1 Thessalonians and the relationship in this letter between its apocalyptic (4:13-5:11) and didactic elements (4:1-12; 5:12-22).

622 ---. "Sayings on the Delay of the End," *Biblical Research* 20 (1975) 19-35.

Prior to the exile Old Testament passages involving the Day of the Lord referred to a coming day of judgment on a given people. During the exile and afterwards, the same Day of the Lord oracle could occur but more likely the prophet spoke of a delay during which repentance could occur. In apocalyptic passages the delay motif continues as a literary convention either to accommodate the end time of the oracle to the present day, to allow time for the purposes of God to be fulfilled, or for theodictic purposes. The vast majority of delay passages in the New Testament fall in the category observed in late apocalyptic: the end will come following certain attitudinal or behavioral changes and improvements. There are two types of paraenetic delay passages. One stresses "waiting" (1 Thess 1:9-10)--an attitude of expectancy with regard to ultimate justification. The other stresses "watching" (1 Thess 5:1-11)--an attitude of expectancy with regard to judgment.

623 Söding, Thomas. "Der Erste Thessalonicherbrief und die frühe paulinische Evangeliumsverkündigung. Zur Frage einer Entwicklung der paulinischen Theologie," *Biblische Zeitschrift* 35 (1991) 180-203.

1 Thessalonians is the earliest Pauline letter. Written in 50 CE, about the time of the Apostolic Council and the missionary work which Paul and Barnabas had begun, the proclamation of the gospel to the pagan Christians in Thessalonica introduces a very important theme and leads to two questions: "What did the apostle preach in his earliest proclamation of the gospel?" and, "What holds together the content of his preaching and its universal perspective?" There is also the issue of whether an early letter like 1 Thessalonians is representative of Paul's theology. Using 1 Thessalonians in comparison with the main letters, it can be determined that the fundamentals of early Pauline proclamation are found in 1 Thessalonians and consisted of the following: the futuristic eschatological perspective, the "gospel of God" (2:2, 8, 9), the "gospel of Christ" (3:2), soteriology, the universality of the gospel and the call of the heathen, and the proper response to the gospel: belief, love, hope, and freedom from the law.

624 ---. *Das Liebesgebot bei Paulus. Die Mahnung zur Agape im Rahmen der paulinischen Ethik* (Neutestamentliche Abhandlungen 26; Münster: Aschendorff, 1995) 68-100.

There are many texts in Paul's letters which are relevant for the command to love one's neighbor. In 1 Thessalonians, such texts include 1:3, 3:11-13, 4:9-12, 5:8 and 5:13. An analysis of these passages indicates that for Paul love is the authentic response of believers to the gospel in their relationships with other persons, and that it is inextricably bound to the theocentric soteriology of the gospel.

625 Spross, Daniel Brett. "Sanctification in the Thessalonian Epistles in a Canonical Context" (Unpublished Ph.D. Dissertation; Louisville, KY: Southern Baptist Theological Seminary, 1988).

The concept of sanctification in the Thessalonian letters (1 Thess 2:10-12; 3:9-13; 4:1-8; 5:23-24; 2 Thess 1:9-12; 2:13-15) in a canonical context is a paradigm for understanding the concept of sanctification in the canonical Pauline corpus and an essential foundation for a biblical theological understanding of the doctrine of sanctification within the Christian community. Paul's understanding of sanctification is basically in harmony with a Jewish understanding thereof, namely, a relationship with God. Sanctification typically relates to the practical implications of what the saving work of God means in the lives of those who believe, in both their new relationship to God and the implications of that relationship to the rest of humanity. The concept of sanctification found in the first letter to the Thessalonians is so compatible with that found in the second that it seems highly unlikely that anyone other than Paul wrote 2 Thessalonians.

626 Stanley, David Michael. "The Earliest Correspondence: First and Second Thessalonians," *Christ's Resurrection in Pauline Soteriology* (Analecta Biblica 13; Rome: Pontifical Biblical Institute, 1961) 81-93.

There are four texts in the Thessalonian letters which are especially relevant to Paul's conception of salvation: 1 Thess 1:9-10 ("The Pauline Kerygma to the Pagans"); 4:14 ("Eschatological Orientation of Christ's Resurrection"); 5:9-10 ("The Purpose of the Redemption"); and 2 Thess 2:13-14 ("Further Precision of Paul's Soteriology").

627 Stählin, Wilhelm. "Die Gestalt des Antichristen und das *KATECHON*," *Glaube und Geschichte. Festgabe für Joseph Lortz* (ed. I. Iserloh and P. Manns; Baden-Baden: Bruno Grimm, 1958) 2.1-12.

The figure of the Antichrist is presented in different ways in the New Testament, appearing in Revelation, 2 Thessalonians, and the Johannine Letters. What these descriptions do have in common is the idea of opposing order and that this threat will intensify.

628 Steele, E. Springs. "The Use of Jewish Scriptures in 1 Thessalonians," *Biblical Theology Bulletin* 14.1 (1984) 12-17.

A number of aspects of Paul's theology, psychology, and hermeneutic are suggested by his allusions to the Jewish scriptures in 1 Thessalonians (2:4; 2:16; 3;13; 4:5; 4:6;

4:8; 5:8). The theological presuppositions of the allusions represent almost entirely the theology of the letter as a whole (e.g., God is the God of the prophets, the God of wrath for the unconverted, the Father of Jesus, the one who elects). Psychologically, these allusions show that Paul viewed his apostleship in a distinctly prophetic manner and is also in many respects still Jewish in his view of history and unconverted Gentiles. The most distinctive feature of Paul's hermeneutic revealed in his allusions to the Jewish scriptures is the manifest discontinuity with the literal or historical sense of the text which it allows. This discontinuity is related to his conversion, which causes him to read the Hebrew Bible as a new book and thus to bring into existence a specifically Christian interpretation.

629 Stepien, Jan. "Czas paruzji w Listach sw. Pawla," *Ruch Biblijny i Liturgiczny* 14.6 (1961) 291-298.

Scholars have reached different conclusions over the question of whether Paul expected an imminent return of the Lord and thus felt deceived over its delay. The apostle, along with the rest of the early church, anticipated the speedy return of Christ but also recognized the possibility that the parousia might be delayed. Paul's preaching on the parousia, however, was concerned less with the timing of that future event than with leading the hearer into a relationship with Christ.

630 ---. "Eschatologia s'w. Pawla," *Studie Theologica Vrsaviensia* 1 (1963) 32-171.

An understanding of Paul's eschatology is best achieved through an analysis of 1 and 2 Thessalonians as well as 1 Corinthians. These three letters reveal that the source of Paul's eschatological views can be found in the teachings of Jesus, early Christian catechesis, the Old Testament, and Jewish writings from the intertestamental period.

631 Strecker, Georg. "Indicative and Imperative according to Paul," *Australian Bible Review* 35 (1987) 60-72.

1 Thessalonians should be understood as a witness to early Pauline theology. Already at this stage the two pre-Pauline lines of tradition have been united: (1) the absolute, pneumatic and enthusiastic indicative of salvation grounded in baptism and without an imperative consequence; and (2) the relative, Old Testament and Jewish indicative, which requires the ethical imperative as its complement.

632 Sumney, Jerry L. "Paul's 'Weakness': An Integral Part of His Conception of Apostleship," *Journal for the Study of the New Testament* 52 (1993) 71-91.

"Weakness" was integral to Paul's understanding of his apostleship much earlier than his controversy with opponents in Corinth. A survey of Hellenistic philosophers' discussions about an appropriate manner of life, Jewish reflections on the meaning of suffering, and the diverse types of early Christian missionaries shows that Paul saw weakness as an integral part of his self-understanding and as a reflection of the crucified Messiah from at least the beginning of his first mission to Europe. An examination of 1 Thessalonians reveals that, even though Paul did not use the term "weakness" to describe his manner of life, the major elements of the delineation of his weakness in 2 Corinthians were present in the first Thessalonian letter and were already important in his self-understanding.

633 Theobald, Michael. "'Prophetenworte verachtet nicht!' (1 Thess 5, 20). Paulinische Perspektiven gegen eine institutionelle Versuchung," *Theologische Quartalschrift* 171.1 (1991) 30-47.

The article first considers Paul's treatment of prophecy in 1 Corinthians 12-14, with particular attention to his efforts at preserving the charismatic dimension and avoiding its total regularization or institutionalization. Next it explores the relation between the kerygma and prophecy, first with reference to Paul's teachings about eschatology (1 Thess 4:15-17; 1 Cor 15:51-52; Rom 11:25-26), and then in the form of five theses. Finally, it reflects on the deutero-Pauline resolution of the tension and how the tension can be made fruitful in the church today.

634 Therrien, Gérard. "Première épître aux Thessaloniciens," *Le discernement dans les écrits pauliniens* (Études bibliques; Paris: Gabalda, 1973) 63-79.

This study of the word δοκιμάζω in Paul, and especially its moral implications, begins with an analysis of the use of the word/concept in the Greek and Jewish worlds, as well as the rest of the New Testament. Treatment of 1 Thessalonians takes place before turning to 1 and 2 Corinthians, Galatians, Romans, Philippians, Ephesians, the Pastorals, and concluding with a discussion of its moral and doctrinal implications. 1 Thess 2:3-4 is an example of a "biographical reminder," elucidating the negative and positive predicates regarding the apostle and his approval by humans, concluding that the apostle's vocation to preach the gospel, the authority of his doctrine and the exigence of a moral life are dependent upon divine approval. 1 Thess 5:19-22 concludes a larger passage which contains a series of exhortations, this one regarding spiritual discernment. This involves discerning the will of God, which means accepting that which is good and rejecting that which is bad. In this way, the authentic will of God is seen in each circumstance.

635 Ubieta, José Angel. *La Iglesia de Tesalónica: Una iglesia en proceso de evangelización* (Bilbao: Desclée de Brouwer, 1988).

636 Uprichard, Robert Edward Henry. "The Person and Work of Christ in 1 Thessalonians," *Irish Biblical Studies* 1 (1979) 12-29.
Revised and republished under the same title in *Evangelical Quarterly* 53.2 (1981) 108-114.

The paucity of references to the person and work of Christ in 1 Thessalonians has led some to conclude that this letter reflects the thinking of an early, immature Paul. The apparent meager christology of 1 Thessalonians, however, is dictated not so much by the lack of maturity in Paul as by the specific circumstances which the letter addresses. Furthermore, the same truths which animate all of Paul's letters are at least implicitly found here. The work of Christ includes not only the parousia but also his death "for us" and resurrection. The application of that work includes being "in Christ" and under his authority. The person of Christ is highlighted by his unique and close relationship to the Father, his exalted position and titles (Jesus, Son, Lord, Christ). The letter's christology, therefore, is not "stunted" and does not support the thesis of a radical development in Paul's thought during his letter-writing period.

637 Viard, André. "L'Évangile de Jésus Christ dans la première Épître aux Thessaloniciens," *Angelicum* 56.4 (1979) 413-427.

The particular advantage of studying the "gospel" in 1 Thessalonians is that in this letter Paul emphasizes the points which he had made while in their midst and which they had uniformly accepted, without his being encumbered in controversies which had taken place elsewhere, such as among the Corinthians, the Galatians, and the Romans. The gospel stresses the good news of salvation offered to humans by God through the death and resurrection of Christ, his Son, who has become the Lord and now shares the kingdom and glory of his Father. Those who accept the good news are called to possess these with him. To be united with Christ they must renounce the pagan world and live truly for God under the guidance of the Spirit and animated by faith and love in the service of the gospel.

638 Wegenast, Klaus. "Das Problem der Tradition im Galater- und im 1. Thessalonicherbrief," *Das Verständnis der Tradition bei Paulus und in den Deuteropaulinen* (Wissenschaftliche Monographien zum Alten und Neuen Testament 8; Neukirchen: Vluyn, 1962) 34-50.

A discussion of the problem of tradition in Galatians and 1 Thessalonians reveals that Paul in 1 Thess 2:13 uses language which indicates that he sees himself as passing down tradition in a fairly fixed form. This would refer to the tradition which Paul passed on to the Thessalonians during his stay there. An analysis of 1 Thess 4:1-12, 2 Thess 2:15, and 2 Thess 3:6 indicates the presence of tradition which does not stem from the paraenetic tradition of the historical Jesus but which has been created by Paul.

639 Wenham, David. "The Future Coming of the Lord," *Paul: Follower of Jesus or Founder of Christianity?* (Grand Rapids: Eerdmans, 1995) 289-337.

The expectations of Paul for the future are not merely *similar* to that of Jesus, they are *dependent* on the teachings and traditions of Jesus. The most important evidence for connections between Paul's eschatological teaching and the Jesus-tradition is found in 1 and 2 Thessalonians, specifically in the following items: "wrath" (1 Thess 2:16); "the word of the Lord" (1 Thess 4:15); the "thief in the night" (1 Thess 5:2); sleeping and staying awake (1 Thess 5:5-7); the suddenness of the Lord's coming (1 Thess 5:3); the call not to be shaken or misled (2 Thess 2:2-3); a terrible event which must precede the end (2 Thess 2:3-8); and misleading signs and wonders (2 Thess 2:9). Although some of these connections are more certain than others, they have the cumulative effect of demonstrating the dependency of Paul on the teaching and traditions of Jesus.

640 ---. "Paul and the Synoptic Apocalypse," *Gospel Perspectives II: Studies of History and Tradition in the Four Gospels* (ed. Richard T. France and David Wenham; Sheffield: JSOT Press, 1981) 345-375.

There is significant overlap between the eschatological traditions which Paul passed on to the Thessalonians (e.g., the thief [1 Thess 5:2-4], the coming of the Lord from heaven [1 Thess 1:10; 3:13; 4:14-17; 2 Thess 1:7-10; 2:1], the sacrilegious lawless one [2 Thess 2:1-12], persecution by the Jews [1 Thess 2:14-16]) and the eschatological traditions preserved in the Synoptics, especially Matthew. Although there are no grounds to conclude that Paul knew the traditions of Matthew 23 in the context of Matthew 24-25, there is some evidence for a pre-Pauline account of the coming of the abomination/lawless one followed by the victorious coming of the Son of Man--this being the core of the Synoptic discourse.

641 Wiederkehr, Dietrich. *Die Theologie der Berufung in den Paulusbriefen* (Studia Friburgensia 36; Freiburg: Universitätsverlag Freiburg, 1963) 36-75.

This analysis of the verb καλεῖν ("to call") and its cognates, as well as other words in individual contexts, discusses five passages in the Thessalonian letters: 1 Thess 2:12; 4:7; 5:24; 2 Thess 1:1; 2:13-14. These passages emphasize such features as the fact that the one who calls is God, not only at the beginning (i.e., at conversion) but continually. The instrument of his calling is the gospel and its proclamation. God calls in his holiness, through the Spirit, to advance holiness. The ones called are those who believe--sanctified Christians. God, who calls through his will, is able to achieve his aim at the return and appearance of the Lord Jesus Christ in glory.

642 Wiefel, Wolfgang. "Die Hauptrichtung des Wandels im eschatologischen Denken des Paulus," *Theologische Zeitschrift* 30.2 (1974) 65-81.

In discussions of eschatology the current tendency to discuss almost exclusively the cosmological dimensions without giving attention to the fate of the dead or corporate aspects apart from individual salvation is not biblically justifiable. A study of 1 Thess 4:13-18, 1 Cor 15:50-57, 2 Cor 5:1-10 and Philippians demonstrates that Paul's primary concern so far as eschatology is concerned lies at the level of the individual. "To be always with the Lord" (1 Thess 4:17) is the apostle's definition of the basic goal for the believer.

643 Willi, Thomas. "Das Erlöschen des Geistes," *Judaica* 28 (1972) 110-116.

Jesus and his followers were not the first ones to maintain the return of the Spirit in light of the reign of God (1 Thess 4:8).

644 Wischmeyer, Oda. "Das Gebot der Nächstenliebe bei Paulus. Eine traditionsgeschichtliche Untersuchung," *Biblische Zeitschrift* 30.2 (1986) 161-187.

Paul's comments on love form the first written and transmitted contribution of extant Christianity on this theme. The starting point for a tradition-historical investigation of verbs of love is Lev 19:18 in Rom 13:8-9. By the time the traditional material reached 1 Thess 4:9, Paul had formed an actual *agapē* ethic.

645 Wright, N. T. "Putting Paul Together Again: Toward a Synthesis of Pauline Theology (1 and 2 Thessalonians, Philippians, and Philemon)," *Pauline Theology 1: Thessalonians, Philippians, Galatians, Philemon* (ed. Jouette M. Bassler; Minneapolis: Fortress, 1991) 183-211.

Pauline theology is that integrated set of beliefs which informed and undergirded Paul's life, mission and writing, coming to expression in varied ways throughout all three. The content of this set of beliefs can be grouped under the twin heads of Jewish theology, namely, monotheism and election. A study of the letters of 1 and 2 Thessalonians, Philippians and Philemon shows how these two convictions were redefined in Paul's thinking by means of his christology.

Other Relevant Sources:

274, 313, 321, 330, 333, 348, 381, 413, 451, 475, 494, 650, 660, 667, 690, 692, 703, 736, 770, 837, 838, 894, 903, 925, 926, 934, 948, 1003, 1012, 1028, 1041, 1080, 1165.

III. Exegetical Treatments of 1 Thessalonians

A. 1 Thessalonians 1:1

646 Askwith, Edward Harrison. "'I' and 'We' in the Thessalonian Epistles," *The Expositor, 8th Series* 1 (1911) 149-159.

Paul uses the first person singular "I" five times in the Thessalonian letters (1 Thess 2:18; 3:5; 5:27; 2 Thess 2:5; 3:17). This raises the question whether the first person plural "we" in these letters should be interpreted as a real ("proper") or literary ("epistolary") plural. A brief survey of Paul's use of the singular and plural in his other letters demonstrates that "we" is used as a real plural. This is also the pattern found in the Thessalonian letters. The plural reflects Paul's willingness to include co-workers with himself and the five instances of the shift to the singular can all be easily explained by their respective contexts.

647 Binder, Hermann. "Paulus und die Thessalonicherbriefe," *The Thessalonian Correspondence* (ed. Raymond F. Collins; Bibliotheca ephemeridum theologicarum lovaniensium 87; Leuven: Leuven University Press, 1990) 87-93.

In the prescripts of both 1 Thessalonians (1:1) and 2 Thessalonians (1:1) three senders are listed. This could mean that Paul did not conceive of the letters himself, but that he, by way of dictation, also allowed his co-senders to express themselves. This thesis can be established by considering the character of the second missionary journey in Acts 15:22-18:23.

648 ---. "Silvanus: Ein Beitrag zur Theologiegeschichte des Urchristentums," *Theologische Versuche* (ed. Joachim Rogge and Gottfried Schille; Berlin: Evangelische Verlagsanstalt, 1983) 99-103.

Silvanus, who appears in the prescript to the Thessalonian letters and in 2 Cor 1:19, can be identified with Silas in Acts as accompanying Paul on his second missionary journey and perhaps also with the author of 1 Peter. Did this Silvanus play a larger role than the recounting of these facts for which he is usually given credit? Acts does not clarify the situation, but his placement in second position in the prescript of both Thessalonian letters indicates his probable role as co-author, as well as fellow visitor to the cities on Paul's missionary journey. Several commentators have noted the non-Pauline character of apocalyptic material in 1 and 2 Thessalonians and these sections were probably formulated by Silvanus.

649 Byrskog, Samuel. "Co-Senders, Co-Authors and Paul's Use of the First Person Plural," *Zeitschrift für neutestamentliche Wissenschaft* 87 (1996) 230-250.

The question of co-senders, co-authors and Paul's use of the first person plural is too complicated an issue to be treated collectively rather than individually. The inclusion of co-sender(s), an unusual and thus a likely intentional epistolographic feature, has two related functions: (1) to establish or maintain good relations between the correspondents; and, more importantly, (2) to ground the legitimacy of the letters in the collegiality of Paul's associates. There is, however, no self-evident connection between labels such as co-senders and co-authors. With respect to the use of the first person plural, there is not much evidence for the literary plural in the Pauline letters. The plurals are mostly real plurals. This is true, for example, of 1 Thessalonians, which appears to be a collective letter reflecting Paul's close relation to and equal standing with his associates.

650 Collins, Raymond F. "'The Church of the Thessalonians,'" *Louvain Studies* 5 (1974/75) 336-349.
Republished in Raymond F. Collins, *Studies on the First Letter to the Thessalonians* (Bibliotheca ephemeridum theologicarum lovaniensium 66; Leuven: Leuven University Press, 1984) 285-298.

In the opening salutation of 1 Thess 1:1 ("To the church of the Thessalonians in God the Father and the Lord Jesus Christ"), the term ἐκκλησία has lost none of its formal significance and each of the qualifying phrases is significant for an understanding of early Pauline ecclesiology. Therefore, even though this letter contains less explicit comments about church order than other Pauline correspondences, 1 Thessalonians ought not be passed over as a fruitful source of New Testament ecclesiology.

651 Goulder, Michael D. "Silas in Thessalonica," *Journal for the Study of the New Testament* 48 (1992) 87-106.

In 1 Thessalonians Paul frequently reminds his readers that he discussed the points in the letter while he was with them during his brief mission there: the need to keep working (4:11-12), the parousia in the near future (4:13-18), the desirability of marriage (4:1-8), and his own integrity (2:1-12). Parallels with 1 Corinthians suggest that all these points are related, via a counter-teaching that the kingdom of God had already begun. Hence converts gave up work and sex and were grief-stricken when a fellow Christian died. A similar situation seems to underlie 2 Thessalonians, where false doctrines appear to have made ground: that the day of the Lord has come (2:1-12), that one should cease working (3:6-15), and that more reminders are needed of what Paul said during his original mission. Where did these false teachings come from? How did they arise so quickly in the Thessalonian church, already manifesting themselves during Paul's original mission? The answer lies in the person of Silas: he was there; he was a trusted member of the Jerusalem church; he had opportunity to write to the Thessalonians, claiming to represent the teachings of Paul; and he rather suddenly vanished from the scene in Paul's writings and Acts. The Thessalonian letters are our first evidence of the profound cleft between the Pauline and the Jerusalem missions--in this case a personal cleft between the two missionaries, Paul and Silas.

652 Laurent, J. C. M. "Der Pluralis maiestaticus in den Thessalonicherbriefen," *Theologische Studien und Kritiken* 41 (1868) 159-166.

In the Thessalonian letters, Paul always uses the plural to refer to himself when he is referring to himself as an apostle, and speaks in the sense of an authority figure. When Paul does not want to speak in that way, or wishes to speak more personally or privately, he uses the singular. Exegesis of the following significant passages bears this out: 1 Thess 1:3; 2:9, 17, 18; 3:2, 6; 2 Thess 1:2; 3:1, 8.

653 Lieu, Judith M. "'Grace to You and Peace': The Apostolic Greeting," *Bulletin of the John Rylands University Library of Manchester* 68 (1985) 161-178.

A survey of the opening greetings in other New Testament and early Christian letters demonstrates that the canonical letters contain many of the proper conventions of the letter form but also exhibit distinct features. Paul took the Semitic formula and combined "peace" with his own distinctive "grace" to emphasize the religious content and give the greeting more than merely conventional force. Furthermore, the distinctive Christian "grace" speaks both of the "apostolic" authority of the sender and of the divine gifts given to the recipient. Paul initiated the epistolary use of the greeting formula or, at least, gave it an unmistakable apostolic stamp.

654 Lofthouse, W. F. "'I' and 'We' in the Pauline Letters," *The Bible Translator* 6.2 (1955) 72-80.

Paul's use of the singular and plural is neither caprice nor careless but there is always a discernible reason for his choice, even though the apostle himself may not have been conscious of it. When Paul wrote "I," he was thinking of himself as distinct from his companions, his hearers, and the church in general, and of experiences which others could not share. When Paul wrote "we," he was thinking of himself as one of a number, either the little band of his companions, his readers, or the whole company of believers. Thus the first person singular stands for distinctness and the first person plural for some measure of identification.

655 Pereyra, Roberto. "Paul's Earliest Statement Concerning the Christian Church: A Review and Evaluation of Research into Paul's Association of the Term ἐκκλησία to ἐν Χριστῷ in 1 Thessalonians" (Unpublished Ph.D. Dissertation; Berrien Springs, IN: Andrews University, 1995).

Paul is defining the term ἐκκλησία by a theological and christological hermeneutic. From a theological perspective, the Christian church at Thessalonica is a gathering of those who were loved (1:4), chosen (1:4; 5:9), and called by God to sanctification (2:12; 4:7; 5:23-24). Her existence, reality, and meaning are centered in the historical initiative and intervention of θεῷ πατρί (1:1). From a christological perspective, this New Testament community was constituted in "the Lord Jesus Christ." The use of the preposition ἐν in connection with the expressions (ἐν) κυρίῳ Ἰησοῦ Χριστῷ—ἐν Χριστῷ Ἰησοῦ (1:1; 2:14) may have more than a locative or descriptive connotation. This Pauline construction might point out the Messiah of the Old Testament as the *instrument-agent* by whom a different ἐκκλησία would be established in Thessalonica. The phrase "(in) the Lord Jesus Christ/in Christ Jesus" does not seem to be an expression of mystical or individual piety, nor just a statement to designate any Christian community, to express ownership and spiritual union with Christ, to differentiate the Christian assemblies from other ones, or to emphasize the unity of Christians everywhere. Rather, it is an ecclesiological formula that confirms God's saving work through Jesus and recognizes the significance of Jesus' messiahship as the Christ of the Old Testament predictions.

656 Ramsay, William Mitchell. "Dr. Milligan's Edition of the Epistles to the Thessalonians," *The Expositor, 7th Series* 7 (1909) 1-17.

The commentary of George Milligan on the Thessalonian letters (126) marks in several important respects a distinct progress in method beyond the customary style of commentary on the Pauline letters. Much has been learned through recent discoveries about the ancient customs and practices of letter writing, and this knowledge is helpfully used by Milligan to illumine Paul's letters to the Thessalonians. His commentary is also significant for its treatment of key words such as the adjective ἄτακτος and its derivatives, the phrase "brothers loved of God," στέφανος, παρουσία and ἐπιφάνεια, to mention just a few. Milligan also rightly sees Paul as the actual author of the two letters, despite the use of the first person plural throughout the documents. This issue, illustrated not only in the Thessalonian letters but in Galatians as well, shows how much importance must be attached to the superscription of the Pauline letters by those who would fully comprehend their practical power.

657 Schlier, Heinrich. *Der Apostel und seine Gemeinde. Auslegung des ersten Briefes an die Thessalonicher* (Freiburg: Herder, 1972).

Republished in Spanish as *El apóstol y su comunidad* (Madrid: Ediciones Fax, 1974).

Essentially a reprint of his six articles on 1 Thessalonians published in 1962-1963 (658, 756, 829, 883, 968, 1029).

658 ---. "Auslegung des 1. Thessalonicherbriefes (1,1-10)," *Bibel und Leben* 3.1-2 (1962) 16-25.

Despite the uncertainty concerning the date and provenance of 1 Thessalonians, this letter was probably written during the first part of Paul's stay in Corinth at the end of his second missionary journey. With thanks to God and a heart-felt concern for his church Paul writes to the believers in Thessalonica. The opening section of the letter includes the prescript but more importantly the thanks of the apostle to God for the past belief of the church in Thessalonica and his thankful remembrance of their election.

659 Scott, Robert. "1 and 2 Thessalonians," *The Pauline Epistles. A Critical Study* (The Literature of the New Testament; Edinburgh: T. & T. Clark, 1909) 215-233.

1 Thessalonians is divided by a prayer at 3:11-13 which clearly separates the letter into two parts. The style of the letter prior to 3:11 differs from that of chapters 4 and 5. Since the greeting of 1:1 cites the names of Silvanus and Timothy in addition to that of

Paul, it is likely that these companions of Paul had something to do with the composition of the letter. It appears, then, that 1 Thessalonians 1-3 (and 2 Thessalonians 3) was composed by Timothy who depended largely on Philippians and slightly on 2 Corinthians. Silvanus is responsible for 1 Thessalonians 4-5 (and 2 Thessalonians 1-2), which shows contact with Ephesians and other writings of the second Christian generation. The compilation of the two documents into one was accomplished by Timothy between 70-80 CE.

Other Relevant Sources:

308, 327, 389, 820, 821, 1038.

B. 1 Thessalonians 1:2-10

660 Beaudean, John William, Jr. "Gospel, Word of God, and Community: Theology of Preaching in First Thessalonians," *Paul's Theology of Preaching* (National Association of Baptist Professors of Religion Dissertation Series 6; Macon, GA: Mercer University Press, 1988) 29-58.

1 Thessalonians contributes substantially to our understanding of Paul's theology of preaching. The frequent references to his preaching in 1:2-2:14 are surrounded by important key terms which provide a first glimpse of Paul's understanding of the theological origin, function, and expected results of preaching in his ministry. Preaching is the mediating term between the word of God and the gospel, which is both a message and a saving environment. Paul understands preaching as the direct, vocal activity of the creative word of God in time and space. Preaching is always the preaching of the gospel: it is oral and cumulative in nature.

661 Benson, G. P. "Note on 1 Thessalonians 1:6," *Expository Times* 107 (1996) 143-144.

Paul's statement in 1 Thess 1:6 seems to echo Jesus' words in the explanation of the parable of the sower. The apostle recalls how in the midst of persecution the Thessalonians "received the word (δεξάμενοι τὸν λόγον) in much affliction, with joy (μετὰ χαρᾶς) inspired by the Holy Spirit." Jesus' explanation of the parable of the sower, Luke 8:13, somewhat similarly reads: "And the ones on the rock are those who, when they hear the word, receive it (δέχονται τὸν λόγον) with joy (μετὰ χαρᾶς)." If this allusion is deliberate, then Paul in 1:6 refers not only to the Lord as an example of holding on to the gospel with joy in the face of persecution ("You became imitators of us and of the Lord") but also to the teaching of the Lord which tells believers to do this.

662 Boyce, James L. "Graceful Imitation: 'Imitators of Us and the Lord' (1 Thessalonians 1:6)," *All Things New: Essays in Honor of Roy A. Harrisville* (ed. Arland J. Hultgren,

Donald H. Juel, and Jack D. Kingsbury; Word & World Supplement Series 1; St. Paul, MN: Word & World, 1992) 139-146.

1 Thessalonians, particularly 1 Thess 1:6, provides a much broader perspective for the understanding of the notion of "imitation" than has been offered in previous studies, which have restricted their focus to notions of example, authority, and obedience. To be an imitator of Paul is to be called into a relation of mutual support in which authority and obedience, mentoring and modeling all have their place, but in which, above all, leader and follower alike know themselves to be created, sustained, and supported by the power of God. It is a "grace-ful imitation," because it is always empowered by the grace and mercy of God.

663 Brant, Jo-Ann A. "The Place of *mimēsis* in Paul's thought," *Studies in Religion/Sciences religieuses* 22.3 (1993) 285-300.

An examination of the classical understanding of μίμησις and an exegetical analysis of the texts in which Paul presents himself as one to be imitated (1 Thess 1:6-7; 2:14; 1 Cor 4:16-17; 11:1; Phil 3:17) are two essential steps in reaching a proper understanding of the place of "imitation" in Paul's thought. The authority of Paul's example lies in the fact that he concretely manifests the ethic inherent to a life in Christ. Just as an object of art can teach one about beauty, Paul's example teaches others about life in Christ.

664 Bussman, Claus. *Themen der paulinischen Missionspredigt auf dem Hintergrund der spätjüdisch-hellenistischen Missionsliteratur* (Europäische Hochschulschriften; Reihe 23; Theologie 3; Bern: Lang, 1971) 38-56.

1 Thess 1:9-10 takes up a formula rooted in missionary practice. The formula probably stems from the Hellenistic-Jewish missionary tradition, especially if "whom he raised from the dead, Jesus" is an addition. The insertion is pre-Pauline, since it has linguistic features which are traditions-history related. The missionary preaching reflected here has as its central point the proclamation of God. The secondary point is the proclamation of judgment, which the resurrection of Jesus fundamentally transforms. The Hellenistic-Jewish concepts stand out in these transformations. The nearness to the Jewish missionary proclamation allows this proclamation not to be overplayed.

665 Canipe, John Clifton. "The Holy Spirit and Power in Evangelism as Demonstrated in Selected Pauline Texts in 1 Thessalonians and 1 Corinthians" (Unpublished Ph.D. Dissertation; Fort Worth, TX: Southwestern Baptist Theological Seminary, 1997).

A detailed, exegetical analysis of 1 Thess 1:2-7 and 1 Cor 2:1-5 demonstrates the importance of the Spirit and power in evangelism. These two passages show that the biblical model for evangelism rests upon the functional role of the Spirit and power. Evangelism characterized by the activity of the Spirit and the presence of divine power is the most biblical expression of the gospel message as well as the most effective. In order to meet the challenges, and even obstacles, to the gospel in the twenty-first century, Christians must embrace a fully biblical model for evangelism which has as its foundation the Spirit and power.

666 Castelli, Elizabeth Anne. *Imitating Paul: A Discourse of Power* (Literary Currents in Biblical Interpretation; Louisville, KY: Westminster/John Knox, 1991).

Imitation functions in four Pauline letters (1 Thess 1:6; 2:14; Phil 3:17; 1 Cor 4:16; 11:1; Gal 4:12) as an artifice of power. That is, by rationalizing his own superordinate status as natural and true, and by calling on his addressees to imitate this model, Paul inevitably was involved in a power relationship. Denied the physical powers of the dominant culture, early Christianity and Paul in particular used ideological power instead to secure unity and to suppress deviancy. This hegemony of the identical suppressed dissident voices and enforced a totalizing, closed system. Imitation, then, became a part of Paul's strategy of social control.

667 Collins, Raymond F. "The Faith of the Thessalonians," *Louvain Studies* 7 (1979) 249-269.
Republished in Raymond F. Collins, *Studies on the First Letter to the Thessalonians* (Bibliotheca ephemeridum theologicarum lovaniensium 66; Leuven: Leuven University Press, 1984) 209-229.

An examination of Paul's use of the language of faith in thirteen passages in 1 Thessalonians (1:3; 1:7; 1:8; 2:4; 2:10; 2:13; 3:2; 3:5; 3:6; 3:7; 3:10; 4:14; 5:8) shows that there is a difference of nuance and emphasis between faith in his first letter and that in his later correspondence. Paul's preference for the plural participle form and his use of the formula "your faith" indicates a communitarian dimension of faith in 1 Thessalonians which does not receive similar emphasis in his later letters. The high concentration of faith language in 1 Thessalonians (as well as in Romans and Galatians) indicates how important this theme is in the letter. Crucial to Paul's notion of faith is the realization that faith, along with love and hope, characterizes the mode of existence of the new person.

668 ---. "The Growth of Resurrection Faith," *Emmanuel* 86 (1980) 277-282.
Republished in Raymond F. Collins, *Studies on the First Letter to the Thessalonians* (Bibliotheca ephemeridum theologicarum lovaniensium 66; Leuven: Leuven University Press, 1984) 339-345.

1 Thessalonians contains two statements about the resurrection of Jesus which belonged to the church's tradition: 1:10 and 4:14. Paul uses this traditional or confessional material about the resurrection to emphasize that, by raising Jesus from the dead, God had done something quite different from anything he had done before. In the mighty act of raising Jesus from the dead God has grounded the salvation of each one who believes.

669 ---. "Paul at Prayer," *Emmanuel* 88 (1982) 412-419.
Republished in Raymond F. Collins, *Studies on the First Letter to the Thessalonians* (Bibliotheca ephemeridum theologicarum lovaniensium 66; Leuven: Leuven University Press, 1984) 356-364.

1 Thessalonians contains two prayers of thanksgiving (1:2-5; 2:13), two prayers of petition (3:11-13; 5:23), a prayer report (3:9-10), and two exhortations on prayer (5:17-18; 5:25). An examination of these passages reveals that Paul was a man of intense and frequent prayer, and that his prayer effected a ministerial quality.

670 ---. "Paul's First Reflections on Love," *Emmanuel* 87 (1981) 107-113.
Republished in Raymond F. Collins, *Studies on the First Letter to the Thessalonians* (Bibliotheca ephemeridum theologicarum lovaniensium 66; Leuven: Leuven University Press, 1984) 346-355.

Although studies of Paul's ideas on love typically look to such passages as 1 Corinthians 13, Rom 5:5, and Gal 5:22, there is much on this subject in his earliest letter, 1 Thessalonians. Here Paul employs the noun ἀγάπη ("love") five times (1:3; 3:6; 3:12; 5:8; 5:13), the verb ἀγαπᾶν ("to love") twice (1:4; 4:9), and the adjective ἀγαπητός ("beloved") once (2:8). An analysis of these texts witnesses to the preeminent place given to love by Paul in his preaching and letter writing.

671 Corriveau, Raymond. "The Thessalonian Correspondence," *The Liturgy of Life. A Study of the Ethical Thought of St. Paul in His Letters to the Early Christian Communities* (Studia: Travaux de recherche 25; Brusseles: Desclée de Brouwer, 1970) 25-35.

1 Thess 1:9 is a significant text for the idea of the Christian life as worship. Whether it is considered as part of a primitive baptismal hymn or as a repetition of primitive formulae of the apostolic kerygma, the importance of this verse is that it clearly shows the Christian life to be cultic in nature. Conversion means a turning away from idols, a "turning towards" and a "coming back" to God, in view of giving him a total service of one's life. Christianity is a complete consecration involving belonging, obedience, and brotherly love--in short, total service and adoration of the living and true God.

672 Costello, C. J. "Problems in Bible Revision. Saint Paul's Epistles to the Thessalonians," *Catholic Biblical Quarterly* 1 (1939) 256-263.

There are a number of important instances in the Thessalonian letters (1 Thess 1:3; 4:1; 4:3-8; 4:10b-11; 5:14; 2 Thess 3:6, 7, 11; 3:12) in which the revised translation of the Rheims-Douay version differs from the wording of the original. Although the sense of the biblical text in some cases is obscured or not correctly rendered by a too faithful adherence to the Latin Vulgate, the revised translation as a whole is very good.

673 Crofts, Marjorie. "Metaphors in the Five Ts," *Notes on Translation* 8.4 (1994) 35-52.

After noting problems which can occur when translating metaphors and possible "adjustments" which can be made, the article presents an analysis of metaphors in

1-2 Thessalonians, 1-2 Timothy, and Titus. For each item the metaphor is given, its parts are identified (image, topic, point of similarity), and a statement of the comparison is usually given in full.

674 DeBoer, Willis Peter. "The Imitation of Paul: Exegetical Studies," *The Imitation of Paul* (Kampen: Kok, 1962) 92-139.

Paul's references to the imitation of himself derive from the spiritual father/child relationship between himself and his readers. The child brings to expression the way of life which he has seen in his father and which he has learned from him. The two passages in the Thessalonian letters which deal with the imitation of Paul (1 Thess 1:6; 2 Thess 3:7-9) reflect the differing moods of the two letters. 1 Thessalonians is a letter of joy--Paul's profound relief at the news that his Thessalonian converts were remaining faithful to their commitment to Christ in spite of Paul's abrupt departure, his continued suffering, and the persecution which they themselves were enduring. They had accepted this suffering with joy and thus had become imitators of Paul and of the Lord. The mood in 2 Thessalonians, however, is changed as the problems addressed in the first letter are more serious than previously thought. Now imitation is no longer an accomplished fact but, at least for a segment of the congregation, a missing essential. Imitation of Paul's work habits and his self-sufficiency is a basic and essential response to the gospel.

675 Delay, Emile. "ΑΔΙΑΛΕΙΠΤΩΣ," *Revue de Théologie et de Philosophie* 33 (1950) 66-74.

The adverb ἀδιαλείπτως ("unceasingly") in Paul's letters is always connected to the concept of prayer. There are two options usually taken by exegetes for understanding its sense: (1) qualitatively, meaning that the prayer is an attitude of life which is perpetual; or (2) quantitatively, meaning that the prayer actually never ceases. The better option, however, is a combination of these two ideas, as they are co-dependent. The one notion enriches the other.

676 Denton, D. R. "Hope and Perseverance," *Scottish Journal of Theology* 34 (1981) 313-320.

The virtues of hope (ἐλπίς) and perseverance (ὑπομονή) are closely related. 1 Thess 1:3, Rom 8:25, and Rom 12:12 stress that perseverance arises from hope. Yet Rom 5:4 and 15:4 indicate that perseverance gives rise to hope. 1 Cor 13:7 presents the two virtues as correlative with neither derived from the other. This combination of hope and perseverance in Paul's writings is equivalent to the Old Testament concept of "waiting."

677 Easley, Kendell H. "The Pauline Usage of *PNEUMATI* as a Reference to the Spirit of God," *Journal of the Evangelical Theological Society* 27 (1984) 299-313.

The thirty-five instances where Paul employs the dative πνεύματι, when this means the divine (as opposed to human) Spirit, are studied (there is only one occurrence in 1 Thessalonians: 1:5). The purpose is to uncover whether this expression is a set term, paralleling ἐν Χριστῷ. The evidence shows that Paul uses πνεύματι neither as a set formula nor as a technical term. It refers generally to that effective agent of God's power whereby certain Christian experiences come to pass and whereby believers are enabled to fulfill certain expectations.

678 Elias, Jacob W. "'Jesus Who Delivers Us from the Wrath to Come' (1 Thess 1:10): Apocalyptic and Peace in the Thessalonian Correspondence," *SBL 1992 Seminar Papers* (ed. Eugene H. Lovering; SBL Seminar Papers 31; Atlanta: Scholars Press, 1992) 121-132.

Although apocalyptic writings with their vivid military imagery have often provided justification for the support of war, apocalyptic can also be connected with the theme of peace. In the Thessalonian correspondence, the theme of deliverance from wrath (1 Thess 1:10; 2 Thess 3:1-3) and the experience of suffering both for Paul and his co-workers (1 Thess 1:6; 2:2) as well as for the Thessalonian church (1 Thess 1:6; 2:14-16; 3:4; 2 Thess 1:4-8) function to undergird the theme of love in the paraenetic material (1 Thess 3:12; 5:8; 5:15; 2 Thess 3:15) and the theme of peace in the wish-prayers (1 Thess 5:23-24; 2 Thess 3:16). Paul's apocalyptic theological perspective leads him to advocate neither ethical passivity nor synergistic activism in the face of evil but rather revolutionary trust in God, who in Christ both historically and eschatologically delivers and will yet deliver the faithful from wrath.

679 Friedrich, Gerhard. "Ein Tauflied hellenistischer Judenchristen (1. Thess. 1,9f)," *Theologische Zeitschrift* 21 (1965) 502-516.
Republished in *Auf das Wort kommt es an. Aufsätze zum 70. Geburtstag* (ed. Johannes H. Friedrich; Göttingen: Vandenhoeck & Ruprecht, 1978) 236-250.

The thesis of A. Seeberg that 1 Thess 1:9-10 reflects a belief formula which Paul has taken up can be further strengthened, albeit by modifying slightly his proposal. Three points can be made. First, the language of this passage is not typically Pauline, substituting language of the cross for early Christian apocalyptic language. Second, there is a two-part strophic structure to these verses. The first part deals with the Gentile Christians--their past conversion, their present service of God, and their expectation in the future coming of the Son. The same triple time reference is found in the second part: Christ rose from the dead, rescues believers now, and will save them from the coming judgment. Third, a tradition-historical comparison shows that the material is not Hellenistic but Jewish-Christian. The reference to "idols," the description of God as "living and true," the use of the verb "to serve," suggest Jewish thinking. There is no mention of the Redeemer's pre-existence and glorification as in Hellenistic Christian hymns.

680 Getty, Mary Ann. "The Imitation of Paul in the Letters to the Thessalonians," *The Thessalonian Correspondence* (ed. Raymond F. Collins; Bibliotheca ephemeridum theologicarum lovaniensium 87; Leuven: Leuven University Press, 1990) 277-283.

There emerges already in 1 Thessalonians a pattern in the use of imitation which will be developed more fully in other Pauline writings. This pattern involves admonishment to joyful acceptance of suffering and to self-support while preaching the gospel in imitation of Paul, whose authority is rooted in his own imitation of Christ. Thus the theme of imitation in Paul is more important than has often been recognized. In Thessalonica, Paul exhibited three characteristics which he exhorts his readers to imitate: cooperation with grace in work, suffering for the sake of the gospel, and developing community.

681 Havener, Ivan. "The Pre-Pauline Christological Credal Formulae of 1 Thessalonians," *SBL 1981 Seminar Papers* (ed. Kent H. Richards; SBL Seminar Papers 20; Chico, CA: Scholars Press, 1981) 105-128.

Three pre-Pauline Christological creedal formulae can be found in 1 Thessalonians (1:9c-10; 4:14a; 5:10a). A study of the formulaic character of these formulae, what they say in themselves, and how they are used in their immediate context, shows that Christ could be perceived in different ways already in this earliest extant Christian writing. The three formulae represent three different portrayals of Christ which are not necessarily contradictory. Paul, at least, seems to accept these different portrayals without being disturbed at their differences. He uses each formula for his own particular purpose and does not try to harmonize them.

682 Holtz, Traugott. "'Euer Glaube an Gott': Zu Form und Inhalt von 1 Thess 1,9f," *Die Kirche des Anfangs. Festschrift für Heinz Schürmann* (ed. Rudolf Schnackenburg, Josef Ernst, and Joachim Wanke; Freiburg: Herder, 1978) 459-488.

1 Thess 1:9-10 contains a striking sentence in which Paul recapitulates the events of conversion with regard to the Christian community at Thessalonica. The statement contains a pre-Pauline formula with non-Pauline language. Thus, the form and content of this statement indicate that it is a short summary of the first missionary proclamation as it was made to the Christian community, that is, the first tradition handed down was that of repentant Christians (see Heb 6:1; Acts 14:15-17; 17:22-31).

683 ---. "Traditionen im 1. Thessalonicherbrief," *Die Mitte des Neuen Testaments: Einheit und Vielfalt neutestamentlicher Theologie. Festschrift für Eduard Schweizer zum siebzigsten Geburtstag* (ed. Ulrich Luz and Hans Weder; Göttingen: Vandenhoeck & Ruprecht, 1983) 55-78.

Throughout 1 Thessalonians Paul draws on tradition. Sometimes he uses traditional missionary phrasing, especially when describing the conversion of the Thessalonians. This language is also similar to the kind of language used in Jewish missionary propaganda (1 Thess 2:13-16). In other places, such as 1 Thess 5:1-11, Paul has apparently incorporated much traditional apocalyptic material, which he draws together with 1 Thess 4:13-17, which has probably also incorporated traditional material. The word ἤπιοι should be retained in 1 Thess 2:7.

684 Hutter, A. "Note sur la traduction de 1 Thessaloniciens 1:5 dans la TOB," *Ephemerides theologicae lovanienses* 60.2 (1985) 259-260.

By playing too freely with the vocabulary, grammar, and syntax of 1 Thess 1:5, the Traduction Oecumenique de la Bible (TOB) has distorted the sense of the Greek text. Specifically, this translation has rendered the complementary relationship of *non seulement-mais aussi* by the elimination of *aussi* and the addition of the word *montrer*, thus altering the sense of the text, even if the theology is not wrong.

685 Jonge, Marinus de. "Some remarks in Connection with a Translator's Handbook on Paul's Letters to the Thessalonians," *The Bible Translator* 30 (1979) 127-134.

The first part of this article comments on *A Translator's Handbook on Paul's Letters to the Thessalonians* by Paul Ellingworth and Eugene Nida (52) and how this work illustrates important aspects of discourse analysis. The second part of this article examines 1 Thess 1:6-10 and 2:14-16 to substantiate the thesis that discourse analysis should be combined with form-critical analysis. The article concludes with a brief response by Ellingworth and Nida.

686 Kemmler, Dieter Werner. "1 Th 1,5," *Faith and Human Reason: A Study of Paul's Method of Preaching as Illustrated by 1-2 Thessalonians and Acts 17,2-4* (Novum Testamentum Supplements 40; Leiden: Brill, 1975) 149-168.

1 Thess 1:5 ("our gospel was among you not in word alone but also in power ...") has often been interpreted in a way that contrasts "word" and "power" and in which the former term refers to the dead and empty eloquence of humans. This interpretation, however, is not only unjustified but it also betrays the crucial importance of a straightforward narration of the gospel message.

687 Krentz, Edgar. "Evangelism and Spirit: 1 Thessalonians 1," *Currents in Theology and Mission* 14.1 (1987) 22-30.

1 Thess 1:6-10 presents a number of significant items which help clarify Paul's mode of evangelism: a summary of Paul's initial proclamation (vv 9-10); a reference to the Thessalonian believers' "imitation" of him that suggests a consideration of Paul's "life-style" as proclaimer (v 6; 2:1, 12); the powerful acts which accompanied his gospel (v 5); and the effects of Paul's proclamation on the Thessalonians. Paul's gospel was about salvation from the threat of coming judgment and it produced a certainty which expressed itself as joy in the midst of persecution. The Christian life to which Paul invited people was based on faith, supported by love for other Christians, and directed to the eschatological future. The Spirit ratified the proclamation by producing effects or fruits in believers' lives.

688 Kuhn, Heinz-Wolfgang. "Die Bedeutung der Qumrantexte für Vertändnis des Ersten Thessalonicherbriefes Vorstellung des Münchener Projekts: Qumran und das Neue Testament," *The Madrid Qumran Congress. Proceedings of the International Congress*

on the Dead Sea Scrolls, Madrid 18-21 March, 1991 (ed. Julio Trebolle Barrera and Luis Vegas Montaner; 2 vols.; Leiden: Brill, 1992) 1.339-353.

The Qumran texts are helpful for elucidating six passages in 1 Thessalonians: (1) 1:5, which refers to the power of God and his Holy Spirit (see 1QH 7:6-7); (2) 2:7-8, 11, which juxtaposes the image of a nurse and a father, both showing the relationship of a community leader and the community (see 1QH 7:20-22); (3) 2:16, which describes God's destroying rage against those who do not belong to the community (see 1QM 3:9); (4) 3:5, which identifies Satan as one who tempts the pious ones to fall (see 1QS 3:20-25); (5) 5:4-9, which makes use of the expression "children of light" and a military metaphor (see 1QS 3:13-15, 20-21; 4:18-19, 22-23); and (6) 5:15, which exhorts believers to repay no one evil for evil but only goodness (see 1QS 10:17-18). How Paul came into (apparently indirect) contact with specific Qumran statements (especially 5:4-9) can no longer be ascertained.

689 Langevin, Paul-Émile. "Jésus, qui nous délivre de la colère qui vient (1 Th 1,9-10)," *Jésus Seigneur et l'eschatologie. Exégèse de textes prépauliniens* (Studia: Travaux de Recherche 21; Bruges/Paris: Desclée/de Brouwer, 1967) 43-106.

A form-critical analysis of 1 Thess 1:10 and 5:2 places these passages in their historical and epistolary contexts. 1 Thess 1:9-10 is introduced by "the word of the Lord" (v 8) and consists of stereotyped phrases which emphasize repentance and wrath. The style of this passage shows itself to be pre-Pauline. The Christology of this passage--with Jesus as the Son of God--is suited to Paul's purpose. 1 Thess 5:2 relies heavily on an Old Testament background and is based on the equating of the day of the Lord Jesus with the day of the Lord Yahweh, which has strong eschatological overtones.

690 ---. "Le Seigneur Jésus selon un texte prépaulinien, 1 Thess 1,9-10," *Sciences ecclésiastiques* 17.2-3 (1965) 263-282, 473-512.

On the basis of a careful analysis of 1 Thess 1:9-10, it is possible to determine that the material in these verses is pre-Pauline. Contextual, literary, and theological elements of these verses all point to this conclusion. 1:9-10 forms a part of the kerygmatic proclamation with which Paul had first evangelized the Thessalonians and now serves as a resumption of that process--a recitation. As a result, the christology of these verses is a witness to the christology of the primitive church from which Paul had received his tradition. The principal characteristics of this christology are: (1) Jesus is the natural Son of God, and he will perform divine functions; (2) Jesus rose from the dead on Easter, and he is the eschatological Savior expected on the Day of the Lord (1 Thess 5:2); and (3) Jesus is the κύριος Ἰησοῦς of the pre-Pauline tradition (Phil 2:9-11; Rom 10:9; 1 Cor 16:22; etc.).

691 Lohfink, Gerhard. *Die Himmelfahrt Jesu: Untersuchungen zu den Himmelfahrts- und Erhöhungstexten bei Lukas* (Studien zum Alten und Neuen Testament 26; Munich: Kösel, 1971) 81-89.

Ascent to heaven is found in Greek and Roman sources, and in the Old Testament and Judaism, including apocalyptic and pseudepigraphal literature. Ascent to heaven is also found in the writings of the early church, including Paul. 1 Thess 1:9-10 switches from a concrete description to formulaic, traditional language before returning to the concrete situation of the Thessalonians' conversion. For Paul, the resurrection of Jesus is the presupposition of the ascent to heaven ("whom he raised from the dead" is formulaic).

692 Merk, Otto. "Nachahmung Christi. Zu ethischen Perspektiven in der paulinischen Theologie," *Neues Testament und Ethik. Festschrift für R. Schnackenburg* (ed. Helmut Merklein; Freiburg: Herder, 1989) 172-206.

The "imitation of Christ" for Paul lies in the midst of a complex of questions, which include Pauline ethics and the area of the Jesus-Paul debate. In 1 Thess 1:6 it is not an imitation of the earthly Jesus but of the risen Lord which has taken place through God in death. 1 Thess 2:14 is different from the other "example" passages, since it speaks of the imitation of the church rather than of Paul and/or Christ.

693 Munck, Johannes. "I Thess. I.9-10 and the Missionary Preaching of Paul. Textual Exegesis and Hermeneutic Reflections," *New Testament Studies* 9.2 (1963) 95-110.

The widely held view that 1 Thess 1:9-10 contains a summary of typical missionary preaching represents an over-emphasis of the otherwise valid contention that Paul possessed a mass of ready-made formulae of Christian kerygma and theology. Actual exegesis and hermeneutical reflection on these verses, however, show that it is the particular historical situation of the Thessalonian congregation and not traditional formulations which supplies the key for interpreting the text. 1 Thess 1:9-10 anticipates later passages in the letter such that these introductory words can be said to state the essential message of this document.

694 Murillo, L. "Annotationes homileticae (1 Thessal. 1, 1-10)," *Verbum Domini* 3 (1923) 328-332.

"Homiletical notes" on 1 Thess 1:1-10 are given under the following headings: "Introduction to the epistle," "The apostle comforts the believers after sending Timothy and then writing the epistle (1 Thess)," "The exercise of the theological virtues (faith, love, hope) among the new believers," "The exercise of the virtues is a clear demonstration of their election unto life," "The desire to imitate their teachers and Christ," and "The Thessalonian believers are an example to other congregations."

695 O'Brien, Peter T. *Introductory Thanksgivings in the Letters of Paul* (Novum Testamentum Supplements 49; Leiden: Brill, 1977).

The introductory thanksgivings of Paul's letters constitute a distinct epistolary unit, exhibiting two basic structures: one formally simple, the other complex. These thanksgivings have a varied function: epistolary, didactic, and paraenetic, and they provide evidence of his pastoral and/or apostolic concern for his readers. Paul's introductory thanksgivings were not meaningless literary devices but were integral parts of their respective letters, setting the tone and introducing the themes that were to follow (1 Thess 1:3-3:13: pp 141-166; 2 Thess 1:3-12 and 2:13-17: pp 167-196).

696 ---. "Thanksgiving and the Gospel in Paul," *New Testament Studies* 21.1 (1974) 144-155.
Although the structure of Paul's introductory thanksgivings may well have been Hellenistic, the contents show that other influences have been at work. The language has its roots in diverse sources such as the Old Testament and Judaism, early Christian worship, and early missionary preaching. But whatever the source from which Paul draws, he uses the terms and phrases with a remarkable degree of flexibility, adapting and applying them to the specific situation of the addressees. A striking feature of the thanksgivings is the frequent use of "gospel" and its synonyms. It is regularly found in the prayers of thanksgivings where the grounds for thanksgiving are spelled out. Paul often stresses the dynamic, almost personal activity of the gospel and on three occasions (1 Thess 1:5; Col 1:5-6; 1 Cor 1:4-8) applies verbs to the recipients of the gospel themselves. Thus Paul's prayers of thanksgiving are directed to God in gratitude for what he has done through the gospel. The apostle now looks with confidence to a similar dynamic activity in the lives of believers themselves.

697 ---. "Thanksgiving within the Structure of Pauline Theology," *Pauline Studies: Essays Presented to F. F. Bruce* (ed. Donald A. Hagner and Murray J. Harris; Grand Rapids: Eerdmans, 1980) 50-66.
Paul mentions the subject of thanksgiving more often per page than any other Hellenistic author, pagan or Christian. He also exhibits a greater degree of flexibility in using the terms for thanksgiving than other New Testament writers, employing them in various types of material. The number of occurrences and, more importantly, their place within the various contexts show that the theme of thanksgiving was of some importance for the apostle. Thanksgiving in Paul is never *prima actio* but *reactio*--a response to God's saving activity through Christ in creation and redemption.

698 Patte, Daniel. "Reading Paul so as to Hear his Gospel Anew," *Chicago Studies* 24 (1985) 339-356.
The interpretive method of structural exegesis or "semiotics" results in a reading of Paul so as to hear his gospel anew. This method, illustrated in a study of 1 Thess 1:1-10, involves four distinct types of readings of the text. The first reading examines the relationship between the author and readers. The second reading takes note of all that appears odd, illogical, strange, or repetitious, since such tensions in the logical unfolding of an argument signal that the author is struggling to express his/her convictions in terms which the readers will understand. The third reading examines the argument and its warrants, and so reveals what the author views as particularly important. The fourth reading studies the opposition of actions (i.e., antitheses) in the text, since these show

what the author considers to be the most important point(s) of all (see 1:5, "for our gospel came to you not only in word but also in power and in the Holy Spirit and with full conviction").

699 Pesce, Mauro. "Ricostruzione del kerygma ai tessalonicesi sulla base di 1 Ts 1,9-10," *Annali di Storia dell'Esegesi* [Bologna] 2 (1985) 23-47.

An analysis of 1 Thess 1:9-10, along with information gleaned from other early, authentic, Pauline letters, allows one to reconstruct the form and content of the gospel or kerygma as preached by Paul and his fellow missionaries.

700 Reinhartz, Adele. "On the Meaning of the Pauline Exhortation: '*mimmētai mou ginesthe* -- become imitators of me,'" *Studies in Religion/Sciences religieuses* 16.4 (1987) 393-403.

A study of the relevant "imitation" passages in Paul (1 Cor 4:16; 11:1; Phil 3:17; 1 Thess 1:6) shows that there are three features which they all share. Two of these are the points which form the consensus of scholarly opinion about Paul's exhortations to imitation, namely, that it reflects both Paul's perception of his apostolic authority as based in Christ and the nature of his apostolic relationship to the churches which he founded. The third and new feature is that, in all cases, Paul's call to imitation is to be found in the context of a defense of his own apostleship. The exhortation to imitation conveys to his churches his *right* to exhort them in this manner, even in the face of opinions to the contrary within the churches themselves.

701 Roberts, J. H. "The Eschatological Transitions to the Pauline Letter Body," *Neotestamentica* 20 (1986) 29-35.

One of the transitional techniques marking the beginning of the letter body is the "eschatological climax," i.e., those eschatological references at the end of the thanksgiving sections which by their nature give the impression that a climax has been reached. The four clearest examples of an eschatological climax are 1 Cor 1:7-8, Phil 1:10 (but see also 1:6), 1 Thess 1:10 and 2 Thess 1:6-10. A study of these passages demonstrates the significant function which these eschatological climaxes have in foreshadowing important eschatological pronouncements in the body of their respective letters.

702 Romaniuk, Kazimierz. "Z teorri i praktyki chrzescijanstwa w oparciu o 1 Tes 1,5," *Ruch Biblijny i Liturgiczny* 34.3 (1981) 155-162.

703 Roosen, Antoon. "Das Zeugnis des Glaubens in 1 Thessalonicher 1,6-10," *In libertatem vocati estis (Gal 5,13). Festschrift für Bernhard Häring* (ed. Henre Boelaars and Réal Tremblay; Studia Moralia 15; Rome: Academia Alfonsiana, 1977) 359-383.

Paul's concept of the apostolate is worldwide. His mentioning of Macedonia and Achaia in 1 Thess 1:6-10 is not in the first place a political formula but a theological or missionary topos, borrowed from Paul's theological self-understanding and missionary strategy. The apostle did not think of himself in terms of a single city or place, but in terms of functioning over areas as large as provinces and regions. Similarly, he sees the character of the Thessalonians' faith in terms of not a place but the entire area of the Greek lands. The faith of the Thessalonians is attested and active in an evangelistic manner in the entire world. 1 Thess 1:6-10 thus illustrates well the reason why Paul visited major centers in his missionary strategy.

704 Rossano, Piero. "La parola e lo spirito. Riflessioni su 1 Tess 1,5 e 1 Cor 2,4-5," *Mélanges Bibliques en Hommage au R. P. Béda Rigaux* (ed. Albert-Louis Descamps and André de Halleux; Gembloux: Duculot, 1970) 437-444.

705 Schneider, Gerhard. "Urchristliche Gottesverkündigung in Hellenistischer Umwelt," *Biblische Zeitschrift* 13 (1969) 59-75.

As with Acts 17:31 and Heb 6:1-2, 1 Thess 1:9-10 contains what Harnack called "the missionary preaching to the heathen in nuce." We have here not only in its kerygmatic scheme a christology structured around the proclamation of God, but also the kerygma of Jesus having been raised up by God to the position of Savior. Paul calls for belief by the Thessalonians. This structure of monotheistic proclamation of God by the early church has its basis in Jewish missionary preaching and proselytization, joined with the proclamation of Christ in the context of the last things. This joining together of theology and christology reflected the kerygma of the early church, and was not influenced by polytheistic folk religion or Stoic belief.

706 Snyder, Graydon F. "A Summary of Faith in an Epistolary Context: 1 Thess. 1:9,10," *SBL 1972 Proceedings* (ed. L. C. McGaughy; 2 vols.; N.P.: Society of Biblical Literature, 1972) 2.355-356.

1 Thess 1:9-10 serves as a confirmation of the success of the apostolic preaching at Thessalonica. As such it describes progressively the shift from pagan to Christian: first, welcoming the apostolic messenger; second, turning from idols to serve the living God; third, waiting for his Son from heaven. That same progression serves as the basis for the structure of the letter: the presence of the apostle at Thessalonica (2:1-3:13); serving God by living a holy life (4:1-12); and waiting for the return of Christ (4:13-5:11).

707 Stanley, David Michael. "'Become Imitators of Me': The Pauline Conception of Apostolic Tradition," *Studia Biblica et Orientalia Analecta Biblica* (Analecta biblica 10-11; Rome: Pontifical Biblical Institute, 1959) 291-309.
Republished under the slightly modified title "'Become Imitators of Me': Apostolic Tradition in Paul," *The Apostolic Church in the New Testament* (Westminster, MD: Newman, 1965) 371-389.

A study of the scattered references in Paul's letters where the apostle calls upon his readers to imitate him leads to the following conclusions. First, Paul urges the imitation of himself only to those congregations which he has founded. Second, this imitation is the necessary result of having accepted "his" gospel, which creates a special relationship between himself and the churches he founded. While Paul insists that his kerygma is essentially the same as that preached by other apostles, he is also aware that, as his personal testimony to Christ, his preaching and way of life have their own characteristic modalities, determined chiefly by his conviction that he carries on the role of Christ as the Suffering Servant of God. Third, the *imitatio Christi*, which Paul proposes to his communities, is thus a mediated imitation. It springs both from Paul's apostolic authority as an authentic representative of Christian tradition, and from the recognized need of those he has fathered in the faith to have an objective, concrete norm against which they can "test" the influence of the Spirit.

708 ---. "Imitation in Paul's Letters: Its Significance for His Relationship to Jesus and to His Own Christian Foundations," *From Jesus to Paul. Studies in Honour of Francis Wright Beare* (ed. Peter Richardson and John C. Hurd; Waterloo, ON: Wilfrid Laurier University Press, 1984) 127-141.

An examination of the Pauline texts in which imitation and example appear makes it clear that they are employed in a sense only analogous to ordinary usage. They are intended to point to a reality transcending merely human exemplarity, moral influence, or external simulation. Nor can Pauline imitation be reduced to obedience to the apostle's authority. Paul's singular use of imitation and example is the result of his radical insight into the gospel as the communication of God's saving power in Christ and his total awareness of human impotence vis-à-vis that divine power. In urging the imitation of himself upon his own Christian converts, Paul endeavors to lead them to share his own experience of humankind's need to rely with full confidence on the divine power graciously offered through "his gospel."

709 Szymanek, Edward. "Wiara jako Przedmiot nauczania wg sw. Pawla," *Ruch Biblijny i Liturgiczny* 36 (1983) 214-223.

An analysis of faith as an object of teaching in the following passages from Paul's letters: 1 Thess 1:9-10; 4:14-17; 1 Cor 15:1-8; Rom 4:25; 10:9.

710 Trevijano Etcheverria, Ramón. "La misión en Tesalónica (I Tes 1,1-2,16)," *Salmanticensis* 32.3 (1985) 263-291.

1 Thessalonians, the first letter of the apostle, is a valuable testimony of the constant relationship between Paul, the missionary, and a church founded by him. After vain attempts at revisiting the church of Thessalonica, he resorts to this means whereby he wants to make his apostolic presence felt, something that is particularly clear in 1:1-2:16. Although the church has proven to be faithful in the midst of trials, Paul feels the need to encourage it because the expectation of an imminent parousia, along with the newness of their Christian life, provides a context for disappointment (1:1-10). Paul recounts in 2:1-13 his ministry to the Thessalonians in language which resembles a person attacked as a sophist, and at the same time reveals his selfless commitment to the gospel, which

was the foundation for the ethical exhortation of his preaching. Finally, the allusion to their persecution in 2:14-16 reveals that the Thessalonians are experientially related not only to Paul but to the entire church, in both a solidary and an exemplary way.

711 Wallace, Daniel B. "A Textual Problem in 1 Thessalonians 1:10: Ἐκ τῆς Ὀργῆς vs. Ἀπὸ τῆς Ὀργῆς," *Bibliotheca Sacra* 147 (1990) 470-479.

1 Thess 1:10 contains a textual variant which involves the interchange of prepositions. Although the external evidence favors ἐκ (supported by better, earlier witnesses), it is scanty (no papyri, discounted versions, late and few fathers). The internal evidence seems so strong in favor of ἀπό that it must override the more tentative external preference. This reading *might* offer some support for a pre-tribulational rapture.

712 Ware, James. "The Thessalonians as a Missionary Congregation: 1 Thessalonians 1,5-8," *Zeitschrift für die neutestamentliche Wissenschaft* 83 (1992) 126-131.

In light of 1 Thess 1:5-8 it is significant that nowhere in his letters does Paul command his congregations to preach the gospel. Such a command would not have been consistent with Paul's conviction that preaching the gospel had been entrusted to him as a result of his apostolic activity. Yet Paul was confident that his congregations would continue his missionary activity, as God's power at work in his preaching of the gospel continued to be active in those who had believed the message (see 1 Thess 2:13). Through this power the gospel with which he had been entrusted had come to the Thessalonians and had in turn sounded forth from them.

713 Watt, J. G. van der. "The Use of ζάω in 1 Thessalonians: A Comparison with ζάω/ζωή in the Gospel of John," *The Thessalonian Correspondence* (ed. Raymond F. Collins; Bibliotheca ephemeridum theologicarum lovaniensium 87; Leuven: Leuven University Press, 1990) 356-369.

There are similarities and differences in the way ζάω and ζωή are used by Paul in 1 Thessalonians (1:9; 3:8; 4:15, 17; 5:10) and John in his gospel, and to explain both is no easy task. It is interesting, however, that the uses of ζάω in 1 Thessalonians, which in some degree correspond with the uses in John, occur in 1:9-10 and 5:10--both passages where Paul makes use of traditional material. It is possible, then, that the similarities between 1 Thessalonians and John represent a general pre-Pauline and thus very early way of thinking by Christians. Although there may not have been a common written source, Paul and John were somehow exposed to similar teachings about the living God who gives life to believers through Christ, which inspired them both to incorporate this powerful message into their theologies, although differently.

714 Weir, T. H. "1 Thessalonians i. 3," *Expository Times* 34 (1922/23) 525.

The difficulty of 1 Thess 1:3 is knowing whether the three genitives (faith, love, hope) express origin, possession or accompaniment. The simplest explanation is that they are adjectival genitives, so common in Hebrew and the New Testament, which should be rendered as follows: "your faithful (or loyal) work, your loving labor, and your hopeful patience." The dependence of the last genitive ("of the Lord") is not on "hope" but "patience." Patience here means "waiting," from the Hebrew *qavah*, and refers to the "hopeful waiting for the Lord."

715 ---. "Notes on 1 & 2 Thessalonians," *Expository Times* 35 (1924) 140.
The genitives in 1 Thess 1:3, 2:13, 19, 4:5, 16, 2 Thess 1:7, 8, 11, and 2:10, 19 should all be taken as equivalent to adjectives in English: e.g., "your faithful work, your loving labor, and your hopeful waiting" (1 Thess 1:3); "an audible word" (1 Thess 2:13); "a glorious crown" (1 Thess 2:19).

716 Weiss, Wolfgang. "Glaube--Liebe--Hoffnung. Zu der Trias bei Paulus," *Zeitschrift für die neutestamentliche Wissenschaft* 84.3 (1993) 196-217.
Paul closes 1 Cor 13:13 with the well-known triad: faith, hope and love. This same triad is found in 1 Thess 1:3 and 5:8. In 1:3 the triad of faith, love, and hope (note the change in order) outlines Paul's comments about the Thessalonian Christians' belief, linked to words which are typically Pauline, creating a triad which is not typical. In 5:8 the triad is used by Paul to introduce traditional motives for the paraenetic judgment. These triads serve to enclose the body of the Thessalonian letter, with one following the prescript and the other closing the paraenesis. There is one further triad in 1 Thessalonians at 3:6 and the three themes of faith, love and hope are also seen in the paraenesis of 4:1-8. These triads probably originate in the two Pauline dyads of faith and love and faith and hope.

717 Wengst, Klaus. *Christologische Formeln und Lieder des Urchristentums* (Studien zum Neuen Testament 7; Gütersloh: Mohn, 1972).
This thorough study of christological formulae and hymnic passages in early Christianity discusses several of the major Pauline passages (e.g., Phil 2:6-11; Col 1:15-20), with some attention to the use of such phrasing in the Thessalonian letters, especially 1 Thess 1:9-10, 4:14 and 5:10, which are all creedal statements in part or whole. For example, 1 Thess 5:10 uses the phrase "the one who died for us," a traditional Christological formula, probably reflecting the earliest stages of Christian thinking (see also Rom 5:6; 8:3; 14:15; 1 Cor 15:3).

718 Wenham, David. "The Paulinism of Acts Again: Two Historical Clues in 1 Thessalonians," *Themelios* 13 (1988) 53-55.
Two texts from 1 Thessalonians throw light on the historical plausibility of Acts: 1:9-10 and 5:12-13. The first passage contains a summary of Paul's preaching to the Thessalonians, which is remarkably similar to his Areopagus speech or sermon (Acts 17:16-31). The second passage shows that Paul established in Thessalonica some sort of eldership, thereby agreeing with the claim in Acts 14:23 that the apostle appointed elders in his newly founded churches.

719 Wilckens, Ulrich. "1. Thess 1,9,10 und Hebr 5,11-6,2," *Die Missionsreden der Apostelgeschichte: Form- und traditionsgeschichtliche Untersuchungen* (Wissenschaftliche Monographien zum Alten und Neuen Testament 5; Neukirchen-Vluyn: Neukirchener, 1961) 81-86.

A fundamental question is whether there is an early Christian testimony in which one certain kind of preaching scheme is visible. That is found in two places: 1 Thess 1:9-10 and Heb 5:11-6:2. There are four parts to 1 Thess 1:9-10: (1) "How you turned to God from idols to serve a living and true God, (2) and to wait for his Son from heaven, (3) whom he raised from the dead, (4) Jesus, the one who delivers us from the wrath to come." This statement points to the future and the expectation of the Son coming from heaven. It uses non-Pauline language which is formulaic, including the words for "turn," "wait," and "save."

720 Wynne, G. R. "The Problem of the Epistles to the Thessalonians," *The Expositor, 7th Series* 4 (1907) 364-372.

The problem of the Thessalonian letters is that the lofty praise given in 1 Thess 1:8 and the maturity of the church's faith in the face of persecution seem incredible given the very brief time of Paul's ministry in Thessalonica and the short interval between his departure and the writing of the first letter. The problem is mitigated somewhat by the fact that Paul's converts were largely Gentile proselytes from the Jewish synagogue who had already been drawn out of their pagan background and thus were prepared for purer teaching by Jewish influence. The best explanation, however, lies in the miraculous work of the Holy Spirit among the believers at Thessalonica.

Other Relevant Sources:

359, 363, 460, 473, 484, 507, 513, 599, 603, 604, 658, 660, 747, 820, 1072.

C. 1 Thessalonians 2:1-12

721 Abraham, M. V. "Diakonia in the Early Letters of Paul," *Indian Journal of Theology* 32 (1983) 61-67.

A study of the concept of diakonia, defined rather narrowly as referring to the ministry of Paul and his co-workers, in 1 Thessalonians, Galatians, 1 and 2 Corinthians, reveals the following. First, there is a close relationship between Paul and his message in which the gospel has priority over the preacher. Second, there is a close relationship between Paul's ministry and suffering: although it is the lot of all Christians to endure suffering, the apostle stands in the vanguard of the battle and bears the brunt of the attack. Finally, Paul is frequently forced to give an apologetic defence of his ministry (1 Thess 2:1-12; 1 Cor 1-4, 9; 2 Cor 2:14-7:4; 10-13).

722 Baumert, Norbert. "Ὀμειρόμενοι in 1 Thess 2,8," *Biblica* 68 (1987) 552-563.
On the basis of different readings in Job 3:21 (LXX), Ps 63:2 (Symmachus), and a fourth-century epigram from Iconium, the meaning of the enigmatic term ὁμειρόμενοι in 1 Thess 2:8 most likely is "loving disposition or yearning" (Bauer). The term itself derives from the verb μείρεσθαι with a prothetic omicron, is semantically in line with "divide, separate," and should be taken in the passive sense "having been separated."

723 Beyer, A. "Zeugnisse des ersten Briefes an die Thessalonicher über das Alte Testament," *Nach dem Gesetz und Zeugnis* 29 (1929) 495-496.
The Old Testament is informative for understanding the following passages from 1 Thessalonians: 2:1-12; 4:6; and 4:13-5:11.

724 Collins, Raymond F. "Paul, as Seen through his Own Eyes. A Reflection on the First Letter to the Thessalonians," *Louvain Studies* 8.4 (1980/81) 348-381.
Republished in Raymond F. Collins, *Studies on the First Letter to the Thessalonians* (Bibliotheca ephemeridum theologicarum lovaniensium 66; Leuven: Leuven University Press, 1984) 175-208.
A number of passages and expressions in 1 Thessalonians reveal Paul's early self-understanding. The title "apostles of Christ" (2:7) draws attention to the idea that Paul and his companions were emissaries of Jesus Christ. His "autobiographical confession" (2:1-12) sets apostleship in the context of contemporary expectations about philosophers, statesmen, and prophets. The chief characteristics of an apostle, according to Paul, were eschatological consciousness, integrity, gentleness in exercising authority, and prayerfulness. Paul's prayer (3:11-13; 5:23-24) is marked by joy, thanksgiving, and intercession. His relationship with the Thessalonians is rooted in faith.

725 Cranfield, C. E. B. "A Study of 1 Thessalonians 2," *Irish Biblical Studies* 1 (1979) 215-226.
Republished in C. E. B. Cranfield, *The Bible and Christian Life: A Collection of Essays* (Edinburgh: T. & T. Clark, 1985) 19-33.
This brief examination of 1 Thessalonians 2 comments on the text in a verse-by-verse fashion and offers homiletical insights as to how the text applies to our contemporary situation.

726 Crawford, Charles. "The 'Tiny' Problem of 1 Thessalonians 2,7: The Case of the Curious Vocative," *Biblica* 54.1 (1973) 69-72.
A survey of how the textual problem in 1 Thess 2:7 between the readings νήπιοι ("babes") and ἤπιοι ("gentle") has been handled by Christian commentators from the church fathers through the twentieth century shows that the best solution was first forwarded in 1727 by Daniel Whitby: νήπιοι should be read not as a nominative but as a vocative. 1 Thess 2:7 should thus be rendered: "But we, O Children, were among you as a nurse nourishes her own children."

727 Delobel, Joël. "One Letter Too Many in Paul's First Letter? A Study of (ν)ήπιοι in 1 Thess 2:7," *Louvain Studies* 20 (1995) 126-133.

On the basis of both transcriptional and intrinsic probability, ἤπιοι ("gentle") is the most likely reading of 1 Thess 2:7, despite the impressive manuscript attestation in favor of the alternate reading of νήπιοι ("babes"). Rather than using the weight of their apostleship, Paul and his companions have been "gentle" with the young Christian community at Thessalonica, like a nurse who takes care of her children.

728 Denis, Albert-Marie. "L'Apôtre Paul, prophète 'messianique' des Gentils. Étude thématique de 1. Thess II,1-6," *Ephemerides theologicae lovanienses* 33.2 (1957) 245-318.

Paul deliberately uses terms chosen from the Old Testament to describe his apostleship. The use of imagery from the "servant songs" of Isaiah cannot be underestimated, and it is very plausible to see Paul using this imagery, as well as other material drawn from the Old Testament, to present himself as a continuation of the prophetic line. The apostle, however, also uses imagery foreign to the Old Testament, which recalls the language of imperial declarations. Paul sees the promise of the Old Testament prophets fulfilled in his mission to the Gentiles and encapsulated in the gospel of Christ.

729 Donfried, Karl Paul. "The Kingdom of God in Paul," *The Kingdom of God in 20th-Century Interpretation* (ed. Wendell Lee Willis; Peabody, MA: Hendrickson, 1987) 175-190.

Paul uses "kingdom/kingdom of God" language in seven passages: 1 Thess 2:10-12; Gal 5:21; 1 Cor 4:20; 6:9-10; 15:24; 15:50; Rom 14:17 (also 2 Thess 1:5 which is not considered to be Pauline in the strict sense). Paul understands that the kingdom of God is consummated in the future but that it has already achieved anticipatory reality in the present through the resurrection and reign of Christ. Paul's statement in 1 Thess 2:12 that he did speak to the Thessalonians about the kingdom during his original ministry with them supports the accuracy of the Acts 17 account, not only with regard to Paul's use of king/kingdom language but also with regard to the fact that this language may well have served as the catalyst for the animosity which he and his co-workers aroused in Thessalonica.

730 Fowl, Stephen. "A Metaphor in Distress: A Reading of ΝΗΠΙΟΙ in 1 Thessalonians 2.7," *New Testament Studies* 36 (1990) 469-473.

On both text-critical and contextual grounds the reading of νήπιοι ("babes") is to be preferred to that of ἤπιοι ("gentle"). Paul uses the metaphor of "babes" to contrast the innocence of infants with his rights as an apostle of Christ to make demands. The problem, however, is that infants are not only innocent but also dependent and demanding, especially with respect to food and lodging. Paul's metaphor is thus "in distress"--in danger of making the exact opposite point which he wishes to make. Paul thus rescues the metaphor by following it with another. The subsequent metaphor of a nurse constrains the initial metaphor in order to provide the right contrast between his own behavior and that of a demanding apostle. Paul's emphasis on the scrupulous motives behind his preaching to the Thessalonians is maintained and the general logical flow of the argument is preserved.

731 Gaventa, Beverly Roberts. "Apostles as Babes and Nurses in 1 Thessalonians 2:7," *Faith and History: Essays in Honor of Paul W. Meyer* (ed. John T. Carroll, Charles H. Cosgrove, and E. Elizabeth Johnson; Atlanta: Scholars Press, 1991) 193-207.

The best textual evidence supports the reading of νήπιοι in 1 Thess 2:7 so that Paul here uses two metaphors to describe himself and his fellow missionaries: that of "babes" and "nurses" (τροφός). The second metaphor does not derive from the topos of the philosopher and his gentleness but the well-known figure of a nurse and her continued affection for her charges well into adulthood. Thus Paul juxtaposes two mixed metaphors so as to explain the preceding reference to "apostles of Christ": on the one hand, an apostle is childlike in contrast to the charlatan, who constantly tries to secure personal benefit from his audience; on the other hand, an apostle is a responsible adult, a nurse who approaches her charges with care and affection.

732 Geréb, Z. "A Thesszalonikabeliekhez irott elsö levél magyarázata--2,1-13," *Református Szemle* 70 (1977) 133-139.

A brief exegetical analysis of 1 Thess 2:1-13.

733 Gibbins, H. J. "1 Thessalonians ii. 6," *Expository Times* 14 (1902/03) 527.

The prepositional phrase ἐν βάρει in 1 Thess 2:7 refers to the right of Paul as an apostle either to receive financial support or to receive glory from others. Although the former view is strongly supported by the use of the cognate ἐπιβαρῆσαι later in 2:9, it suffers from the fact that there appears to be no real antithesis between the clause in which these words appear and the clause which immediately precedes it (2:6). A possible solution, however, lies in a change of punctuation: putting a full stop at the end of 2:6 and beginning a new sentence at 2:7. The resulting paraphrase would be: "Though we had the right as apostles to become a charge to you, yet we did not make use of our right."

734 Gillman, John. "Paul's Εἴσοδος: The Proclaimed and the Proclaimer (1 Thess 2,8)," *The Thessalonian Correspondence* (ed. Raymond F. Collins; Bibliotheca ephemeridum theologicarum lovaniensium 87; Leuven: Leuven University Press, 1990) 62-70.

What function does the expression "to share the gospel of God and our very selves" (2:8) have in the larger context of 1 Thess 2:1-12? Although 2:1-12 has some paraenetic function, its more pressing concern is apologetic. Paul is concerned to call forth from the memory of the community the kind of person he was when he was present with them during his founding visit (εἴσοδος). By reestablishing the character of his ethos among the community, Paul preserves both the truth of the gospel and the integrity of his own person in which the gospel is lived out.

735 Gribomont, Jean. "Facti sumus parvuli: La charge apostolique (1 Th 2,1-12)," *Paul de Tarse: Apôtre de notre temps* (ed. A.-L. Descamps, L. de Lorenzi, and G. Benelli; Série monographique de 'Benedictina'; Section paulinienne 1; Rome: Abbaye de S. Paolo, 1979) 311-338.

There are two major issues with regard to 1 Thess 2:1-12: (1) the reasons for the image which Paul draws of his apostleship; and (2) the variant reading in 2:7 of either νήπιοι ("babes") or ἤπιοι ("gentle"). An examination of the witnesses to this passage among the church fathers up to the patristic age makes it clear that there remains some ambivalence on this reading throughout the early life of the Church. The better manuscripts, however, together with Paul's usual pattern of metaphorical inversion, argue for the reading of νήπιοι.

736 Gutierrez, Pedro. *La paternité spirituelle selon Saint Paul* (Études bibliques; Paris: Gabalda, 1968) 87-117.

The metaphor of paternity was frequent and widespread in the ancient world, occurring in the Old Testament, Qumran, rabbinic literature, and Hellenism. 1 Thess 2:7-8, 10-11 has two images used in its context: that of the nourisher and that of the father. The image of the father is qualified in several ways as "holy," "just," and "blameless." The relationship is founded on the transmission of the Christian faith ("to you who believe"). The pedagogical activity is also described.

737 Haufe, Günter. "Reich Gottes bei Paulus und in der Jesustradition," *New Testament Studies* 31 (1985) 467-472.

A form-critical comparison of the "kingdom of God" statements in Paul and in the Jesus tradition shows that they have significant parallels. 1 Thess 2:12 speaks of a successful calling through God into his kingdom and glory. This calling to repentance constitutes the positive tenor of the baptism exhortation. This form is continued in a related Hellenistic form by Paul.

738 Hock, Ronald F. "Paul's Tentmaking and the Problem of his Social Class," *Journal of Biblical Literature* 97.4 (1978) 555-564.

The social class to which Paul belonged is hinted at in his citizenship, his occupation (1 Thess 2:9; 1 Cor 4:12; see also 2 Thess 3:6-10), and his language about his work. In both 1 Cor 9:19 and 2 Cor 11:7, Paul's choice of language in referring to his work reflects not the attitude of the typical artisan (so A. Deissmann) or of the working rabbi who was taught to love labor (so many scholars), but rather the snobbish and scornful attitude so typical of upper class Greeks and Romans. By working at a slavish and demeaning trade, Paul sensed a considerable loss of status--a loss which makes sense only if he were from a relatively high social status.

739 ---. "Paul's Life as an Artisan-Missionary," *The Social Context of Paul's Ministry. Tentmaking and Apostleship* (Philadelphia: Fortress, 1980) 26-49.

A study of Paul's life as an "Artisan-Missionary"--his travels, lodging, and work--leads to the following conclusions. First, Paul used the workshop as a social setting for his preaching and missionary efforts. Second, Paul's tentmaking labor served a paradigmatic function for his paraenesis on work (his commands on work in 1 Thess 4:11-12 do not respond to an actual problem of idleness but reflect his familiarity with the moral traditions of the Greco-Roman philosophers). Third, Paul in 1 Thess 2:1-12 was not reacting to any accusations directed against himself but rather was dissociating himself, as any serious minded philosopher had to do, from the many frauds who tried to pass themselves off as philosophers.

740 ---. "The Workshop as a Social Setting for Paul's Missionary Preaching," *Catholic Biblical Quarterly* 41 (1979) 438-450.

There are several reasons to suppose that Paul used the workshop as one of the various social settings (in addition to the synagogue, house, lecture hall, and city gate) for his missionary activity. The workshop was a recognized social setting in Paul's day for intellectual discourse, a setting recognized as such by many (e.g., Plutarch) but used only by certain Cynics. Evidence from the Cynics' discussions--the number of people involved, the activities pursued, the subjects raised, the kinds of people present--helps to reconstruct with more detail and confidence a picture of Paul in his workshop, busy making tents while preaching the gospel.

741 Holloway, Joseph O. *Peripateô as a Thematic Marker for Pauline Ethics* (San Francisco: Mellen, 1992).

Although the "walking" metaphor in the ancient Near East was a common one, it was normally expressed by the verb πορεύομαι and only rarely by περιπατέω. This suggests that Paul's use of the unexpected term had a significantly greater impact in those passages where the metaphor is employed than if the customary term had been used. A study of the twenty-three passages in which Paul uses περιπατέω with reference to the lives of Christians (1 Thess 2:12; 4:1, 12; 2 Thess 3:6, 11 = pp 29-58) shows that the apostle employed this verb to introduce themes which he considered to be fundamental.

742 Holtz, Traugott. "Der Apostel des Christus: Die paulinische 'Apologie' 1. Thess. 2,1-12," *Als Boten des gekreuzigten Herrn. Festgabe für Werner Krusche zum 65. Geburtstag* (ed. Heino Falcke, Martin Onnasch, and Harald Schultz; Berlin: Evangelische Verlagsanstalt, 1982) 101-116.

Paul makes much use in 1 Thess 2:1-12 of language and argumentation typical of popular philosophy. Nevertheless, because Paul is so emotionally involved in this passage, 1 Thess 2:1-12 appears to be an apology which has an actual or concrete situation. Paul was being equated--possibly by the Jews of the city--with the wandering preachers common in his day who were widely seen to be dishonest and motivated only by self-interest and financial gain. Paul distinguishes himself sharply from these wandering preachers, thereby ensuring not only the integrity of himself as a Christian preacher but also of the gospel which he proclaimed.

743 Horbury, William. "I Thessalonians ii.3 as Rebutting the Charge of False Prophecy," *Journal of Theological Studies* 33.2 (1982) 492-508.

It is commonly thought that the charges rejected in the defense of Paul's preaching in 1 Thess 2:3-4 recall those levelled at Greco-Roman wandering philosophers. It is better, however, to interpret the verse within the biblically-rooted discussion of false prophecy. Paul is concerned with contemporary charges of false prophecy. This is especially borne out by the vocabulary employed in the passage (παράκλησις, πλάνη, ἀκαθαρσία, δόλος) but is also supported by a passage of Justin's *Dialogue* and agrees with certain other features of 1 Thessalonians. 1 Thess 2:3 may thus be rendered periphrastically: "Our prophetic exhortation arises not from seduction to apostasy, nor from the spiritual uncleanness which possesses the false prophet; it is not preached with the guileful insincerity which would cover falsehood."

744 Kemmler, Dieter Werner. "1 Th 2,2f," *Faith and Human Reason: A Study of Paul's Method of Preaching as Illustrated by 1-2 Thessalonians and Acts 17,2-4* (Novum Testamentum Supplements 40; Leiden: Brill, 1975) 168-177.

The juxtaposition of τὸ εὐαγγέλιον and ἡ παράκλησις in 1 Thess 2:2-3 has been explained in a variety of ways which affect the issue of the relation of faith and human reason in Paul's preaching. A careful analysis of these words in their context indicates that ἡ παράκλησις here is not (1) the third step of ethical exhortation which follows after preaching and teaching, (2) the manner of preaching the gospel, (3) a technical term for a particular kind of gospel preaching, or (4) an exhortatory address directed only toward "feelings" and the "will" as opposed to the "intellect" and "understanding." This term in 1 Thess 2:3, as in 4:18, 5:11 and 2 Thess 2:16, is directed just as much to the emotions as to the intellect. "Consolation" can only come about when the "feeling" of grief is removed through the knowledge which replaces "ignorance." This is what παράκλησις was meant to achieve then and is meant to achieve again and again in the two Thessalonian letters.

745 Knoch, Otto B. "'Ihr sollt niemand auf Erden euren Vater nennen!' (Mt 23,9): Biblische Überlegungen zu Eigenart und rechtem Vollzug des Bischofs- und Priesteramtes," *'Diener in Eurer Mitte': Festschrift für Dr. Antonius Hofmann, Bischof von Passau zum 75. Geburtstag* (ed. Rainer Beer, A. Leidl *et al.*; Schriften der Universität Passau; Reihe Katholische Theologie 5; Passau: Passavia Universitätsverlag, 1984) 46-63.

In keeping with Jewish tradition Paul calls himself a "father," not as a title, but as a spiritual father figure through his teaching and preaching. This is why he also calls the members of the Christian community his "children."

746 Lyons, George Leroy. "Modeling the Holiness Ethos: A Study Based on First Thessalonians," *Wesleyan Theological Journal* 30.1 (1995) 187-211.

The high density of explicit holiness terminology in 1 Thessalonians demonstrates that this theme is of central importance in the letter. The autobiographical material of chapters 1-3 and, in particular, 2:1-12, function to present Paul as a model of living a holy life. This exemplary behavior of the apostle, which indirectly challenges the Thessalonians to holiness in the first half of the letter, is echoed in the second half of the letter (chs 4-5) where the believers in Thessalonica are confronted with explicit commands to holiness in various areas of life.

747 ---. *Pauline Autobiography: Toward a New Understanding* (SBL Dissertation Series 73; Atlanta: Scholars Press, 1985).

An examination of the autobiographical statements of Paul in Galatians and 1 Thessalonians refutes the widely-held assumption that the apostle writes in the autobiographical mode only reluctantly and almost always apologetically. In order to avoid the offensiveness of boasting and self-praise, Paul employs the conventional "antidotes" of ancient autobiographers, particularly the frequent utilization of antithetical constructions. This feature of Paul's autobiographical remarks, along with the faulty interpretive technique of "mirror reading," has been largely responsible for modern scholarship's mistaken assumption that these remarks are almost uniformly apologetic in function. Paul's autobiographical remarks, however, function not to defend his person or authority but to establish his *ethos* as an "incarnation" of the gospel of Jesus Christ. Paul is concerned that, by imitating him, his readers too should incarnate the gospel. His autobiographical remarks rarely supplement the major concerns of a letter but rather support it by means of a flesh-and-blood illustration.

748 Malherbe, Abraham J. "'Gentle as a Nurse': The Cynic Background to 1 Thess. ii," *Novum Testamentum* 12.2 (1970) 203-217.
Republished in Abraham J. Malherbe, *Paul and the Popular Philosophers* (Minneapolis: Fortress, 1989) 35-48.

The Cynic background to 1 Thess 2:1-12, first posited by Martin Dibelius, has important consequences for how one interprets the function of this Pauline passage. There are striking similarities between 1 Thess 2:1-12 and the picture of the Cynic philosopher sketched by Dio Chrysostom. These parallels suggest that, as Dio was not responding to specific charges raised against him personally, so also Paul was not defending himself against criticisms made by some in Thessalonica.

749 Milligan, George. "A Rare New Testament Verb," *The Expositor, 9th Series* 2 (1924) 226-228.

The verb ὁμείρομαι in 1 Thess 2:8 is a *hapax legomenon* in the New Testament, occurring elsewhere in scripture only in Job 3:21 and in Symmachus's rendering of Psalm 62(63):2. Confirmation of its form and meaning are supplied by a sepulchral inscription from Lycaonia where the grieving parents are said to be "greatly desiring their child" (ὀμειρόμενο[ι] περὶ παιδός).

750 Okeke, George E. "The Context and Function of I Thess. 2:1-12 and Its Significance for African Christianity," *African Journal of Biblical Studies* 2 (1987) 77-88.

Paul was probably not being apologetic in 1 Thess 2:1-12 due to being accused of the vices associated with quack apostles or self-interested Cynic philosophers. Rather the suggestion of J. R. Harris (863) that, behind the canonical 1 Thessalonians, stands the letter of the Thessalonian church to Paul seems a strong clue to the understanding of the seeming apology of the apostle. This passage has an important message for the African church today, namely, that its church leaders should carry out their ministry in words, deeds, and manner of personal life in a defensible way to the glory of Christ whom they represent.

751 Okorie, A. M. "The Pauline Work Ethic in 1 and 2 Thessalonians [in Greek]," *Deltio Biblikon Meleton* 24.1 (1995) 55-64.

The many passages in 1 and 2 Thessalonians which refer to work reveal three aspects of the Pauline work ethic: theological, demonological, and anthropological. The Pauline work ethic is predicated not on the "works of the law" but rather on the "work of faith" and "labor of love," which are energized by being "in Christ."

752 Palmer, Darryl W. "Thanksgiving, Self-Defense, and Exhortation in 1 Thessalonians 1-3," *Colloquium or The Australian and New Zeeland Theological Review* 14 (1981) 23-31.

Paul's ostensible self-defence in 1 Thess 2:1-12 shares a significant number of items with the standard self-defence of Cynic philosophers and orators. Just as these philosophers were not necessarily defending themselves against specific charges, neither was Paul. The apostle does not, however, use every item of Cynic self-defence but relates his choice of themes specifically to the Thessalonian situation. Moreover, he defends himself on issues which he elsewhere either praises or exhorts the Thessalonians. Both connections (self-defense and praise, self-defense and exhortation) are aided by the motif of imitation. In other cases he both gives thanks for and exhorts the Thessalonians on the same matters. The result is that, in this letter, both thanksgiving and ostensible self-defense serve in a thoroughgoing way the purposes of exhortation.

753 Rensburg, Fika J. Janse van. "An Argument for Reading νήπιοι in 1 Thessalonians 2:7," *A South African Perspective on the New Testament: Essays by South African New Testament Scholars Presented to Bruce M. Metzger* (ed. J. H. Petzer and Patrick J. Hartin; Leiden: Brill, 1986) 252-259.

Although the reading νήπιοι (1 Thess 2:7) has stronger external attestation, it is commonly rejected on internal grounds, namely, the reading "babes" does not make sense in the context. The logical thought structure of the passage, however, shows that νήπιοι must be the original reading. 1 Thess 2:1-12 consists of three pairs of positive-negative statements: vv 1-2; vv 3-4; vv 5-12 (vv 5-7a: negative; vv 7b-12: positive). If the reading ἤπιοι ("gentle") were to be adopted, then verse 7b would no longer be a positive counterpart to verses 6-7a's negative demarcation about Paul's original exhortation, and the structural pattern so clearly witnessed in verses 3-12 would be broken. Thus there are, in fact, internal probabilities for adopting the stronger attested reading of "babes."

754 ---. "Hallmarks of a Genuine Minister of the Word of God. An Interpretation and Application of 1 Thessalonians 2:1-12," *Koers* 53.3 (1988) 406-425.

Syntactic and semantic considerations make it clear that 1 Thess 2:1-12 constitutes an independent pericope. The text of this passage should include the more strongly attested νήπιοι ("babes") in verse 7, as well as a major punctuation break after "among you" in verse 7a. The passage exhibits a clear structure, consisting of three pairs of positive-negative statements: vv 1-2 (theme), vv 3-4 (grounds for the theme), vv 5-12 (vv 5-7a: negative grounds; vv 7b-12: positive grounds). The traditional view of the historical context is that Paul is responding to malicious gossip about his motives and character. It has been argued more recently, however, that the antithetical pattern of the passage is typical of the rhetorical style of that day and that Paul is not reacting to specific accusations against him. Whatever Paul's motives were in 1 Thess 2:1-12, here he is placing his total ministry of the gospel in Thessalonica under a magnifying glass on behalf of the believers there. This passage has important implications for those engaged in the ministry today: true ministry does not spring from either error or impure motives and does not try to deceive.

755 Rossano, Piero. "Preliminari all'esegesi di 1 Tess. 2,1-12," *Bibbia e Oriente* 7.3 (1965) 117-121.

1 Thess 2:1-12 belongs to the literary genre of autobiographical confession which was rather rare in the ancient world but can be found in Jeremiah and Epictetus. The structure of this passage involves a heavy use of antithesis, which is frequent in Greek writing. Yet it also manifests a distinctive Semitic trait, namely, the circular (wave or spiral) development in which a fundamental idea is repeated with additions. The central theme in 2:1-12 is that Paul preaches the gospel of God with unselfish love, and this theme is repeated several times (vv 1-2, 3-4, 5-8, 9-12).

756 Schlier, Heinrich. "Auslegung des 1. Thessalonicherbriefes (2,1-16)," *Bibel und Leben* 3 (1962) 89-97.

1 Thess 2:1-16 develops the summary statement of 1:4 regarding the election of the Thessalonians to faith. 2:1-12 reviews Paul's previous stay with the believers in Thessalonica and 2:13-16 reviews their reception of the word of God.

757 Schoon-Janssen, Johannes. *Umstrittene "Apologien" in den Paulusbriefen: Studien zur rhetorischen Situation des 1. Thessalonicherbriefes, des Galaterbriefes und des Philipperbriefes* (Göttinger Theologische Arbeiten 45; Göttingen: Vandenhoeck & Ruprecht, 1991).

This volume seeks with the help of form-critical criteria to illumine the content of Paul's "potential apologies" and to clarify their life-settings in Paul's relations with his communities. After definitions and methodological clarifications (on Paul's uses of ancient epistolography, Greco-Roman rhetoric, diatribe style, and Old Testament quotations), it concentrates on three potential apologies and their stylistic contexts: 1 Thess 2:1-12; Gal 1:1-2:21; and Phil 3:4-6; 4:17. It compares the backgrounds of the passages and stresses the significance of their differences for an exact historical-critical exegesis, and concludes with observations on Paul's conflicts with his opponents and his rhetoric in them for the development of his theology. With respect to 1 Thess 2:1-12, it is concluded that Paul had no organized opposition in Thessalonica so that this passage is in no real sense a defense.

758 Stählin, G. "Zum Gebrauch von Beteuerungsformeln im Neuen Testament," *Novum Testamentum* 5.2/3 (1962) 115-143.

In the fourth antithesis of the Sermon on the Mount (Matt 5:34-37), Jesus prohibits swearing oaths. Nevertheless, Jesus himself seems to deviate from his own prohibition (see Mark 8:12; Matt 26:63-64; Luke 22:16, 18; the use of "truly I say to you," and related phrases). Although Paul seems to know the words of Jesus about swearing oaths, the apostle also seems to do this very thing in 2 Cor 1:18, 23, 1 Thess 2:4, 10, Rom 1:9, Phil 1:8, Gal 1:20 and 2 Cor 11:10-11. Paul never swears for the sake of personal interest but swears only "before God," and, like Jesus, swears in the light of truth from God. The explanation for this practice lies in Jesus' consciousness of his unique relation to the Father and, correspondingly, in Paul's sense of divine calling as an apostle.

759 Stegemann, Wolfgang. "Anlass und Hintergrund der Abfassung von 1 Th 2,1-12," *Theologische Brosamen für Lothar Steiger* (ed. Gerhard Freund and Ekkehard Stegemann; Diehlheimer Blätter zum Alten Testament und seiner Rezeption in der Alten Kirche 5; Heidelberg: Esprint, 1985) 397-416.

In 1 Thess 2:1-12, Paul does not rely on a standard rhetorical convention or topos in writing to the persecuted Thessalonian church. Paul is here writing to a church of former pagans who were the first Christian community to experience persecution. He instead refers to imitation of suffering which he has experienced as a way of coming to terms with this experience.

760 Strelan, John G. "Burden-Bearing and the Law of Christ: A Re-examination of Galatians 6:2," *Journal of Biblical Literature* 94 (1975) 266-276.

βάρος and its cognates are used in the extant Greek literature in the sense of "financial burden." In at least fifty percent of the Pauline uses of the βάρος word-family a financial sense is intended. Understanding τὰ βάρη of Gal 6:2a as "financial burdens" makes good sense in the context provided by Gal 6:1-10. Elsewhere in the Pauline letters references to a financial burden occur in contexts concerning the material support of the apostles (1 Thess 2:7, 9; 2 Thess 3:8; 1 Cor 9; 2 Cor 12:16; Phil 4:15-17; 1 Tim 5:16-18). Also involved are such matters as "sharing" in the gospel and the apostle's right to expect maintenance. The cumulative effect of this evidence is to support the hypothesis that the phrase "bear one another's burdens" (Gal 6:2a) is an exhortation to each Christian to shoulder his share of a common financial obligation.

761 Taylor, Richard A. "A Model of the Ministry," *Biblical Viewpoint* 9.1 (1975) 19-27.
Paul defends the character of the apostolic witness in Thessalonica (2:1-12), a defense occasioned by vicious slander from the Jewish community which had been directed against the missionaries. After this, the apostle expresses his great thanksgiving for his readers' reception of the gospel when it was preached to them (2:13-16). Finally, Paul explains why he has not revisited Thessalonica and also enlarges upon the delight that these stalwart converts have given to him.

762 Vanderhaegen, Jean. "Quand l'amour de Dieu vous atteignait. 1 Th 2,7b-9.13," *Assemblées du Seigneur* 62 (1970) 13-20.
There are two distinct parts to 1 Thess 2:1-16. The first section, 2:1-12, concerns the significance of the arrival of the apostles at Thessalonica, and the second, 2:13-16, treats the reception of the gospel message by the believers. Within this context, it is possible to see an important interchange between a second person plural and first person plural party throughout the passage, with the verb γίνομαι functioning as the operative connection between them. Paul focuses on the love which he and his co-workers have for the Thessalonians, and on the faith which is theirs. Paul uses this double focus so that the Thessalonians might understand the origin of this love (God) and that their faith shows this love to be theirs as well.

763 Weima, Jeffrey A. D. "An Apology for the Apologetic Function of 1 Thessalonians 2:1-12," *Journal for the Study of the New Testament* 68.4 (1997) 73-99.
Modern interpreters have too quickly abandoned the long-held view that Paul in 1 Thess 2:1-12 is in some real sense defending himself. Despite the widespread claims of recent exegetes that this passage functions only as implicit paraenesis in which Paul presents himself as a model for the Thessalonians to imitate, evidence from the thanksgiving section (1:2-10), the apostolic parousia (2:17-3:10), the antithetical statements of 2:1-12, and the repeated appeals in this passage to the Thessalonians' first-hand knowledge about Paul's original ministry in their city strongly suggests that the primary function of 2:1-12 is defensive or apologetic. This apologetic function can be more fully appreciated in light of a reconstruction of the passage's historical context.

764 Winter, Bruce W. "The Entries and Ethics of Orators and Paul (1 Thessalonians 2:1-12)," *Tyndale Bulletin* 44.1 (1993) 55-74.

Paul recounted his original coming (εἴσοδος: 1:9; 2:1) to Thessalonica (1 Thess 2:1-12) in terms which are clearly intended to show his deliberate renunciation of entry conventions and the ethics of orators. Writing from Corinth, where believers expected him to adopt an approach similar to that of professional orators, Paul wanted to ensure that the same erroneous thinking did not become a problem among the believers in Thessalonica. There is no need, therefore, to posit a Pauline "apology" against criticisms of Jewish, Gnostic, or Gentile Christian teachers or to understand Paul as cloaking himself in the guise of the ideal philosopher.

765 ---. "Is Paul among the Sophists?" *Reformed Theological Review* 53.1 (1994) 28-38.

A study of 1 and 2 Corinthians, as well as 1 Thessalonians, reveals Paul's antipathy toward the use of rhetoric. He renounced the use of oratory in preaching as inappropriate, for it was designed to draw attention to the messenger and his rhetorical abilities, and not the content of the message. In 1 Thess 2:1-12, Paul engages in a defence of his original "entry" to Thessalonica and reminds the believers there of his ethical conduct, thereby making it clear that he did not operate like the public orators in their city.

766 Zimmer, Friedrich. "I Thess. 2,3-8 erklärt," *Theologische Studien Herrn ... Professor D. Bernard Weiss zu seinem 70. Geburtstag dargebracht* (Göttingen: Vandenhoeck & Ruprecht, 1897) 248-273.

767 Zsolt, Geréb. "A Thesszalonikabeliekhez írott elsö levél 2. Része 1-13. Verseinek Magyarázata," *Református Szemle* 70 (1977) 133-139.

A verse-by-verse exposition of 1 Thess 2:1-13.

Other Relevant Sources:

433, 489, 710.

D. 1 Thessalonians 2:13-16

768 Baarda, Tjitze. "'Maar de toorn is over hen gekomen' (1 Thess. 2:16c)," *Paulus en de andere Joden: exegetische bijdragen en discussie* (ed. H. Jansen, S. J. Noorda, and J. S. Vos; Delft: Meinema, 1984) 15-74.

The Old Testament and the Qumran literature are very helpful in illumining the meaning of the problematic text of 1 Thess 2:13-16. Suffering, as the "red thread of redemptive history," continues with the Thessalonian Christians, for they suffer at the hands of their countrymen just as the Jewish Christians suffer at the hands of non-believing Jews. In the midst of such persecution, God shows his kindness by speedily avenging those who persecute his true people, whether they be Gentile or Jew. In 1 Thess 2:13-16, then, Paul is speaking of the "Anti-Israel" within Israel who are not obedient to the Lord. The past tense of the key word "has come" suggests that God's judgment has come upon these persecutors now, as in the past. There is here, therefore, no reference to Israel as a race nor a call for future persecution of the Jewish people in general. It is simply a confirmation that the Thessalonian Christians are chosen, just as the Jewish Christians are, and so stand in a long line of those who suffer for their faith--a sure sign of their salvation.

769 Bacon, B. W. "Wrath 'unto the uttermost,'" *The Expositor, 8th Series* 22 (1922) 356-376.

The context of both the verse itself and current events as they are reflected in Christian writings suggest that the usual and literal sense of the aorist ἔφθασεν ("has overtaken") in 1 Thess 2:16 is to be preferred over any "proleptic" understanding of the past tense as a figurative reference to the final judgment. Events experienced by Jews during the years 40-50 CE (e.g., rebellion against Rome led by Theudas, famine, reduced religious freedoms, expulsion from the imperial city) were such that Paul could justly look back at the past decade and say that God's wrath had come upon the Jews "unto the uttermost."

770 Bammel, Ernst. "Judenverfolgung und Naherwartung: Zur Eschatologie des ersten Thessalonicherbriefes," *Zeitschrift für Theologie und Kirche* 56.3 (1959) 294-315.

1 Thess 2:15-16 is a known interpretive crux. It has become an arena for the fight over the authenticity of the letter and the place where various interpolation hypotheses play themselves out. This passage, as the high point of the letter to the Thessalonians, may be variously interpreted, but must have been clear to its original readers. Jewish apocalyptic expectation in light of Roman domination forms its background. Although this passage seems to have the end times in view, certain other passages in Paul's letters argue against an imminent expectation of the end. Thus, the near expectation of the end in 1 Thessalonians is not an expression of an integral part of Paul's theological scheme.

771 Baumbach, Günther. "Antijudaismus im Neuen Testament--Fragestellung und Lösungsmöglichkeit," *Kairos* 25 (1983) 68-85.

The concept of "antijudaism" has been misunderstood, including a failure to define the criteria by which one determines the presence of antijudaism. Four passages in the Pauline letters have bearing on this discussion: 1 Thess 2:15-16; Galatians 3-4; Phil 3:4-11; and 2 Corinthians 3. 1 Thess 2:15-16 is the earliest reference to the "Jews" in the Pauline letters. The claim that this reference to the Jews is a later, post-apostolic, redactional addition, reflecting anti-Semitic early Catholicism, must be rejected. Instead, the passage probably reflects the apostle's self-understanding of a historical situation.

772 Beck, Norman A. "Anti-Jewish Polemic in the Epistles of Paul," *Mature Christianity: The Recognition and Repudiation of the Anti-Jewish Polemic in the New Testament* (London: Associated University Press, 1985) 39-50.

Form-critical and theological considerations make it almost certain that a redactor, from a theological and political position similar to that expressed in Luke-Acts or the Matthean tradition, inserted 2:13-16 into 1 Thessalonians. Christian interpreters, during centuries of reading Paul and understanding his work within the framework provided later in the book of Acts, have accepted 1 Thess 2:13-16 as Paul's own composition and permitted this redactional excursus to color their perception of Paul. Modern translations should consider a variety of options (e.g., render "the Jews" of verse 14 as "their political leaders," put parentheses or brackets around vv 13-16, relegate the verses to a footnote, or delete the verses entirely) to lessen the embarrassment these four verses are for Christians who consider the bible to be authoritative for faith and life.

773 Broer, Ingo. "'Antisemitismus' und Judenpolemik im Neuen Testament: Ein Beitrag zum besseren Verständnis von 1 Thess 2:14-16," *Biblische Notizen: Beitraege zur exegetischen Diskussion* 20 (1983) 59-91.

1 Thess 2:14-16 reflects a polemic of a Christianity which has not yet separated from Judaism--a polemic against Jews who are rejecting its message. The passage can be adequately understood only against the background of this polemical situation with the Jews (and perhaps early Christianity), and cannot now be transferred to Christianity after its separation from Judaism, without a serious displacement of the sense of the passage taking place.

774 ---. "'Der ganze Zorn ist schon über sie gekommen': Bemerkungen zur Interpolationshypothese und zur Interpretation von 1 Thess 2.14-16," *The Thessalonian Correspondence* (ed. Raymond F. Collins; Bibliotheca ephemeridum theologicarum lovaniensium 87; Leuven: Leuven University Press, 1990) 137-169.

Theories regarding 1 Thess 2:14-16 being an interpolation ought to be rejected on methodological grounds, especially as several key questions remain unsolved by such proposals. Instead, Paul introduces in 1 Thessalonians the deuteronomistic prophetic statements in their sharpest form in order to bring his brothers in the flesh to repentance and to recognition of Christ. 1 Thess 2:14-16, with its definite wrath of God over the Jews, is thus an expression of Paul's struggles concerning Israel.

775 Coppens, Joseph. "Une diatribe antijuive dans I Thess. II, 13-16," *Ephemerides theologicae lovanienses* 51 (1975) 90-95.

Birger Pearson's view (794) that 1 Thess 2:13-16 is a later interpolation into the letter is subject to critique, especially his argument that the passage reflects a condemnation of all Jews, the only possible basis for arguing against the authenticity of this passage. Paul's use here of direct language of wrath (which could refer to natural disasters), especially with reference to false Jews, is also found in 2 Cor 11:24, Gal 2:13, Rom

2:28 and Phil 3:2, where Paul also expresses hope that the Jews will be converted. Thus the integrity of the letter can be maintained.

776 Davies, W. D. "Paul and the People of Israel," *New Testament Studies* 24 (1977/78) 4-39.

What is Paul's attitude to his own people in the perspective of his interpretation of the gospel as a whole? A study of 1 Thessalonians, Galatians, 2 Corinthians, and Romans shows how the apostle redefined the law in terms of Jesus the Messiah. For Paul, the Jews' rejection of the gospel was both Pyrrhic and temporary. The charge of anti-Semitism against Paul cannot be sustained, for his criticism of the law and Judaism are not uniformly negative and they are intramural, not from without. On the contrary, Paul allows the Jews a historical priority in the history of salvation, though not a national or ethnic superiority.

777 Donfried, Karl Paul. "Paul and Judaism: I Thessalonians 2:13-16 as a Test Case," *Interpretation* 38 (1984) 242-253.

J. Christiaan Beker's provocative treatment of Pauline theology in his *Paul the Apostle* (Philadelphia: Fortress, 1980) helps to understand the apocalyptic context of the apostle with greater precision and therefore sheds new light on the controversial passage of 1 Thess 2:13-16. There is no need to postulate that all or even part of this passage is a later interpolation. An awareness of Paul's apocalyptic orientation allows the interpreter to bring together several traditions which make plausible the view that 1 Thess 2:13-16 expresses Paul's attitude toward Judaism and is thus not a later interpolation. Beker's analysis, therefore, is helpful in re-evaluating the function of 1 Thess 2:13-16, both with regard to the coherent structure of Paul's theology in general and with regard to the contingent interpretation necessary to deal with the particular situation faced by Paul in Thessalonica.

778 Geiger, Georg. "1 Thess 2,13-16: Der Initiationstext des christlichen Antisemitismus?" *Bibel und Liturgie* 59.3 (1986) 154-160.

Is the charge of anti-Semitism a just one for the apostle's words in 1 Thess 2:13-16? Anti-Semitism as racial discrimination must be distinguished from anti-Judaism as a theological concept. 1 Thess 2:13-16 is not a Pauline call to hatred of the Jews, but is very similar to the kind of "anti-Judaism" which is found in the Qumran writings (e.g., 1QM 1:1-2, 5, 22b-24; 2:15-16; CD 20:25-26).

779 Gilliard, Frank D. "Paul and the Killing of the Prophets in 1 Thess. 2:15," *Novum Testamentum* 36.3 (1994) 259-270.

It has been common to understand the words of 1 Thess 2:15 as a diatribe against "the Jews, who killed both the Lord Jesus and their prophets." There are two problems, however, with this interpretation. First, the text only refers to "*the* prophets," not "*their* prophets." Thus there is the possibility, indeed probability, that Paul has in view not

Jewish prophets but Christian prophets who were martyred (e.g., John the Baptist, Stephen, James the son of Zebedee). Second, there is compelling evidence that Ἰησοῦν ("Jesus"), unexpectedly separated from τὸν κύριον ("the Lord"), is a parenthetical appositive to which Paul emotionally adds for emphasis καὶ τοὺς προφήτας ("and the prophets"). Paul added this parenthetical phrase to avoid the pagan cultic connotations of κύριος. The sentence thus should read: "the Jews who killed the Lord--Jesus and his prophets--and drove us out." Paul is not referring to all Jews but only to those who had killed Jesus and some Christian prophets.

780 ---. "The Problem of the Antisemitic Comma between 1 Thessalonians 2.14 and 15," *New Testament Studies* 35 (1989) 481-502.

The comma between 1 Thess 2:14 and 2:15 ("the Jews, who killed both the Lord Jesus and the prophets, and drove us out"), found in most English and Romance-language translations, has led commentators to take the articular participle in verse 15 as a non-restrictive clause (i.e., it describes all Jews, not just a restricted group of Jews). As a result, this passage takes on a strongly anti-semitic flavor. There is compelling evidence, however, that the comma should be omitted and the clause taken as restrictive: Paul is referring only to those Jews who killed the Lord Jesus and the prophets.

781 Haacker, Klaus. "Elemente des heidnischen Antijudaismus im Neuen Testament," *Evangelische Theologie* 48.5 (1988) 404-418.

Three Pauline texts are important for trying to understand the relationship between polemical New Testament passages and anti-Jewish language of pagan antiquity: 1 Thess 2:14-16; Gal 4:21-31; and Gal 5:12. 1 Thess 2:14-16 reflects Old Testament, early Jewish and early Christian traditions, although it calls to mind the polemic against the Jews found in the pagan world of ancient Judaism. Although this tradition can be seen in texts from a number of ancient authors, this is not the meaning intended by Paul. The statements that the apostle makes regarding the Jews seem to mean that the Jews, through their hindering of the mission to the Gentiles, conform in certain ways to the widespread prejudice of the non-Jewish world. It is something akin to the language of the misanthropy of the Jews, which brings to mind the Gentile hatred of the Jews, even if it is on a different level.

782 Holtz, Traugott. "The Judgement on the Jews and the Salvation of All Israel: 1 Thes 2,15-16 and Rom 11,25-26," *The Thessalonian Correspondence* (ed. Raymond F. Collins; Bibliotheca ephemeridum theologicarum lovaniensium 87; Leuven: Leuven University Press, 1990) 284-294.

The severe attack of Paul against the Jews in 1 Thess 2:15-16 has commonly been seen to contradict his expectation of the eschatological salvation of Israel in Rom 11:25-26. Nevertheless, these passages--to the extent that they deal with the same topic--really concur with one another and with Paul's thinking elsewhere. For example, the sharp attack against the Jews in 1 Thess 2:15-16, reaching its climax in the statement of judgment on the Jews, agrees with Paul's opinion about the "Jews" in Romans 1-3 after his theological reflection on the revelation of the gospel. Or again, not just 1 Thess 2:16 but also Romans 9-11 shows not the slightest doubt that members of the synagogue who reject the gospel of Jesus Christ have fallen into judgment. The situation of the Jews is really no different from that of the Gentiles: they may be hopeless in their present state of judgment but they are not incapable of reaching salvation.

783 Hurd, John C. "Paul ahead of His Time: 1 Thess. 2:13-16," *Anti-Judaism in Early Christianity*. I. *Paul and the Gospels* (ed. Peter Richardson and David Granskou; Studies in Christianity and Judaism 2; Waterloo, ON: Wilfrid Laurier University Press, 1986) 21-36.

1 Thess 2:13-16 appears to be anomalous and out of place if taken as an utterance of Paul, but it fits well with the post-70 CE attitude of the church. Thus some have argued for either the non-authenticity of the letter as a whole (F. C. Baur) or, more commonly, of just 2:13-16 (W. Eckart, B. Pearson). Nevertheless, this passage does fit the A-B-A or "sonata" pattern typical of Paul and therefore is by no means anomalous. Furthermore, one must analyze this passage within its hermeneutical unit, namely, 1 Thessalonians rather than other Pauline letters. And within the apocalyptic framework of the letter as a whole, 1 Thess 2:13-16 makes eminently good sense. This passage shows that there was a time in Paul's career when, under the influence of an apocalyptic perspective, he was ahead of his time in expressing a historical-theological anti-Judaism.

784 Hyldahl, Niels. "Jesus og joderne ifolge 1 Tess 2,14-16," *Svensk Exegetisk Årsbok* 37/38 (1972/73) 238-254.

1 Thess 2:14-16, though not "anti-Semitic," is anti-Jewish and marks Paul's break with the Jews, or rather their break with him. 1 Thess 2:16 is not necessarily in conflict with Romans 11, in that the latter passage teaches that only a miracle can save Israel. 1 Thess 2:14-16 attests to an ethnic division: the Gentile-Christian congregation in Thessalonica is being persecuted by fellow Gentiles, as the congregations in Judea--and Paul himself, as well as his Jewish-born co-workers--are being persecuted by Jews. If questions have been raised about his sincerity (indicated by the apology in 2:1-12), Paul's answer is that the sufferings of the Thessalonians have brought them in line with the Judean Christians and Paul himself, and that is the proof of the authenticity of his message.

785 Johnson, Sherman E. "Notes and Comments (I Thess 2:16)," *Anglican Theological Review* 23 (1941) 173-176.

B. W. Bacon (769) has argued convincingly that Paul in 1 Thess 2:16 was not speaking proleptically about the future judgment of the Jews but rather looking back on a series of disasters that befell the Jews. Paul, however, may have had still other miseries in mind than those cited by Bacon: (1) a riot in Jerusalem at Passover in which Josephus claims that twenty thousand people--undoubtedly an exaggerated number--were killed;

(2) a famine in Rome sometime in 49-51 and a famine in Greece in 48 or 49; and (3) the terror which infected the Roman world in the later days of Claudius' reign and the various omens which were believed to announce the coming wrath of the gods.

786 Kampling, Rainer. "Eine auslegungsgeschichtliche Skizze zu 1 Thess 2,14-16," *Begegnungen zwischen Christentum und Judentum in Antike und Mittelalter. Festscrift für Heinz Schreckenberg* (ed. Dietrich-Alex Koch, Herman Lichtenberger *et al.*; Schriften des Institutum Judaicum Delitzschianum 1; Göttingen: Vandenhoeck & Ruprecht, 1993) 183-213.

The situation is decisive for a historically-based understanding of 1 Thess 2:14-16. In the Christian conflict with the Jews the concept of the violent fate of the prophets became an established topos with its christological fulfillment. It is not necessary to discover the direct dependence of 1 Thess 2:14-16 on this tradition, but a number of different traditions have played a part in its growth.

787 Légasse, Simon. "Paul et les Juifs d'après 1 Thessaloniciens 2,13-16," *Revue Biblique* 104.4 (1997) 572-591.

Paul re-uses in 1 Thess 2:13-16 the topos incriminating the infidelity of Israel in order to condemn Jewish blocking of the apostolic preaching and to declare eschatological punishment on the culprits. In Romans 9-11, under the influence of a different state of mind and under the pressure of circumstances from the community, Paul's polemic leaves room for the future salvation of Israel.

788 Lüdemann, Gerd. "1 Thessalonicherbrief," *Paulus und das Judentum* (Theologische Existenz heute 215; Munich: Chr. Kaiser, 1983) 22-27.

1 Thess 2:13-16, an authentic part of Paul's letter, provides a comparison of redaction and tradition (see Mark 12:1-9, with reference to killing the prophets, killing Jesus, and wrath on the Jews). The apostle sees the Jews as subject to judgment since they hindered the conversion of the Gentiles. Paul may have the Claudius incident in mind. 1 Thess 4:13-18 offers a future picture of the Lord coming from heaven. The picture is positive in that the Church comes from both Jews and Gentiles.

789 Macky, Peter W. "Paul on the Present Wrath of God. Its Connection with Satan and the Powers," *Proceedings of the Eastern Great Lakes and Midwest Biblical Societies* 14 (1994) 151-168.

When Paul said in 1 Thess 2:16, "the wrath has now come upon them at last," he was speaking in his most direct and least symbolic manner, meaning: "Their deserved punishment has at last fallen on them." At other times, to other audiences, he might have described the very same events by saying symbolically, "God has unleashed Satan on them," or "the rulers of this present age have wielded God's sword over them." Those were his two other (more symbolic) ways of speaking about the divine punishment which comes upon sinners in the present. Here, however, by speaking simply of "the wrath,"

Paul seems to have been emphasizing that this is God's own judicial response to their activity which had "displeased God" (2:15).

790 Michel, Otto. "Fragen zu 1 Thessalonicher 2,14-16. Antijüdische Polemik bei Paulus," *Antijüdäismus im Neuen Testament? Exegetische und systematische Beiträge* (ed. Willehad P. Eckert, Nathan P. Levison, and Martin Stöhr; Abhandlung zum christlich-jüdischen Dialog 2; Munich: Chr. Kaiser, 1967) 50-59.
Republished in *Dienst am Wort: Gesammelte Aufsätze* (ed. Klaas Haacker; Neukirchen-Vluyn: Neukirchener, 1986) 202-210.

In 1 Thess 2:14-16 Paul has adopted a polemical style which usually sprang from Israel being against Israel in order to maintain the claim to being the people of God. Instead, Paul stands in the midst of an argument between Jew and Gentile, with Gentle Christians still opposed to Jews. The material upon which Paul draws is based on both tradition-historical material regarding the death of Jesus and his own material in the light of his own missionary situation. The latter is placed in eschatological categories regarding the destiny of humanity.

791 Murrell, N. Samuel. "The Human Paul of the New Testament: Anti-Judaism in I Thess 2:14-16," *Proceedings of the Eastern Great Lakes and Midwest Biblical Societies* 14 (1994) 169-186.

The desire to free the apostle from charges of anti-Semitism has wrongly driven many to deny the Pauline authorship of 1 Thess 2:14-16. Paul's concern in this passage, however, is not race or ethnicity but theology. Given his commitment to the new burgeoning theology still being developed through his ministry and writing, and the persistent attempt by some orthodox Jews to derail it, Paul gave a spontaneous and visceral response to what he saw as a persistent problem by lashing out against "Jewish theology" and its traditional ways of thinking. The words of 1 Thess 2:14-16, therefore, are anti-Judaism but not anti-Semitic.

792 Müller, Paul-Gerhard. "Judenbeschimpfung und Selbstverfluchung bei Paulus," *Bibel und Kirche* 44 (1989) 58-65.

Paul's comments about the "Jews" in 1 Thess 2:14-16 must be interpreted in light of his desire to remain a Jew even as a Christian and out of his continued love for the Jewish people. The apostle used motifs from Old Testament and pagan anti-Jewish polemics to deal with what was historically a conflict within Judaism. His statements need to be interpreted in light of their historical intent and not in the sense of anti-Jewish or anti-Semitic comments.

793 Okeke, George E. "I Thessalonians 2.13-16: The Fate of the Unbelieving Jews," *New Testament Studies* 27.1 (1980) 127-136.

1 Thess 2:13-16 and Romans 9-11 are two distinct Pauline approaches to the question of the fate of humankind in the *Heilsgeschichte*. In 1 Thessalonians the sense of the

nearness of the parousia is the context for his harsh statement about the Jews and all persecutors of the church. In Romans where the parousia is delayed, Paul deals with the problem of Jewish unbelief and he has the conviction that ultimately they will accept the mercy of God in Christ. The purpose of God remains constant but Paul's view of that salvific purpose, relative to the Jews, is different in 1 Thessalonians and Romans. The difference does not make 1 Thess 2:13-16 non-Pauline.

794 Pearson, Birger A. "1 Thessalonians 2:13-16: A Deutero-Pauline Interpolation," *Harvard Theological Review* 64 (1971) 79-94.

There are compelling historical, theological, and form-critical reasons for believing that 1 Thess 2:13-16 is a deutero-Pauline interpolation. The aorist ἔφθασεν, which must refer to a past event, and the phrase εἰς τέλος, which underscores the finality of the "wrath" which has occurred, can only refer to the destruction of Jerusalem in 70 CE. The charge against the Jews of "killing the Lord Jesus" is incompatible with what Paul wrote elsewhere and similarly suggests a time after 70 CE. Finally, the distinctive use of the "imitation" theme in 2:14 and the presence of an extra thanksgiving in 2:13 support the conclusion that 2:13-16 does not belong to Paul's original letter but represents a later interpolation into the text. These verses were added to encourage the readers with reference to the embattled Christians in Palestine and to underscore now in a post-70 situation the "united front" of all Christians against the Jews who have at last suffered in the destruction of their city and temple the ultimate rejection and judgment from God.

795 Prins, J. J. "De eerste brief van paulus aan de Thessalonikers," *Theologische tijdschrift* 19 (1885) 263-310.

Schmidt is correct in affirming the Pauline authorship of 1 Thessalonians over against the claims of Baur and Holsten whose methods of reflection are questionable. Schmidt argues that 1 Thess 2:16 is not a proof of a post-Pauline date. This verse does not refer to the destruction of Jerusalem (so Baur) but likely to the Edict of Claudius (52/53 CE) which, for Paul, signaled the beginning of the end for the Jewish nation. Schmidt favors the view that the opponents mentioned in 1 Thess 2:15-16 are not Gentiles (so Lipsius and von Soden) but Jews--not Judaizers but Jews who were sympathetic to Gentile culture and practices. With regard to the authenticity of 2 Thessalonians, however, Schmidt argues against Pauline authorship on the grounds that the eschatology of 1 Thess 4:13-5:11 is irreconcilable with that of 2 Thess 2:1-12.

796 Reicke, Bo. "Judaeo-Christianity and the Jewish Establishment, A.D. 33-66," *Jesus and the Politics of his Day* (ed. Ernst Bammel and C. F. D. Moule; Cambridge: Cambridge University Press, 1984) 145-152.

The years 50 to 52 CE brought about violent quarrels between legalistic Jews and their neighbors in Rome, Alexandria, and Palestine. This revival of Jewish patriotism and zealotism was the background of the Jewish abuse of Christians in Judea, about which Paul complained in his first letter to the Thessalonians (2:14-16).

797 Richardson, Peter. "Eschatological Hindering in Thessalonica," *Israel in the Apostolic Church* (London: Cambridge University Press, 1969) 102-111.

Paul speaks negatively of unbelieving Israel in two places in his Thessalonian letters. The first is 1 Thess 2:14-16, where Paul's experience of almost unrelieved opposition by the synagogues in Thessalonica, Berea, and Corinth occasioned words of harsh criticism. The second is 2 Thess 2:3b-12, where the "apostasy" likely refers to the general Jewish failure to receive the gospel. In other words, the refusal of Israel becomes a form of relinquishing faith in what God is doing in Jesus Christ and so technically can be identified as an apostasy. Despite Paul's denunciation of unbelieving Israel in 1 and 2 Thessalonians, there is no trace of the idea that their rejection of the gospel has caused God to abandon his covenant people and to make the Gentiles heirs of salvation in their place.

798 Schippers, R. "The Pre-Synoptic Tradition in 1 Thessalonians II 13-16," *Novum Testamentum* 8.2-4 (1966) 223-234.

In 1 Thess 2:13-16, ἀκοή in verse 13 should be understood as "tradition" (rather than a reference to the preaching of the gospel) and Paul in verses 14-16 is creatively handling a pre-synoptic tradition. The apostle tells the Thessalonians how the churches in Judea are working with their sufferings at the hands of their countrymen and how they search for the solution to the problem of why they must endure so much from their countrymen by means of a tradition concerning sayings of the Lord. The answer is that they live at a decisive moment in the completion of the drama of the history of salvation. This movement contains a very alarming element for those who are causing that suffering. They are on the way to the climax, the outbreak of the wrath of God.

799 Schlueter, Carol J. *Filling up the Measure. Polemical Hyperbole in 1 Thessalonians 2.14-16* (Journal for the Study of the New Testament Supplement Series 98; Sheffield: JSOT Press, 1994).

Although Paul's abrasive statements about the Jews in 1 Thess 2:14-16 have long posed a problem for commentators, there is no need to resort to theories of inauthenticity or interpolation for this passage. Rather Paul, a skilled debater, used polemical hyperbole to polarize issues and to move his readers to his side while casting his opponents (in this case, the Jews) completely on the wrong side. The same rhetorical practice can be seen in other letters where, in the context of addressing opponents, Paul frequently amplified his main points through the use of hyperbole, exhibiting various levels of polemical intensity against his adversaries. A comparison of these letters also reveals that his polemic against other Christians is at least as strong as--if not stronger than--that against the Jews in 1 Thess 2:14-16.

800 Schmidt, Daryl D. "1 Thess 2:13-16: Linguistic Evidence for an Interpolation," *Journal of Biblical Literature* 102.2 (1983) 269-279.

The content of 1 Thess 2:13-16 does not fit well into the rest of the letter, nor into Pauline thought in general. With respect to its form, this section intrudes into the overall structure of the whole letter. Furthermore, the linguistic evidence suggests that it did not come from the same author as the rest of the letter, but is rather built around a conflation of Pauline expressions. Therefore, the interpolation hypothesis seems to be the best explanation for all three of these matters, especially since a very plausible setting for such an interpolation can be proposed.

801 Simpson, John W., Jr. "The Future of Non-Christian Jews: 1 Thessalonians 2:15-16 and Romans 9-11" (Unpublished Ph.D. Dissertation; Pasadena, CA: Fuller Theological Seminary, 1988).

Despite the form-critical, historical, theological, and linguistic difficulties of 1 Thess 2:13-16, these verses are most likely an original part of Paul's letter. Fundamental to Jewish apocalyptic eschatology was the belief in Israel's eschatological salvation. Verses 15-16, however, depart from this fundamental belief: the apostle holds out no hope for "the Jews," whose course will soon be consummated by God's wrath in the final judgment. In Romans 9-11, Paul responds to tendencies among some Gentile Christians and to his own perception of the existence of non-Christian Jews as that which calls into question the faithfulness of God. The heart of his response is his understanding of God's mercy as working by a principle of reversal. Paul believes that this principle will finally become effective for non-Christian Jews, leading to their salvation. This is not a simple return to the belief in Israel's salvation; it is only by speaking of Israel's destruction in Romans that Paul is able to speak there of its salvation. The basis of the differences between 1 Thess 2:13-16 and Romans 9-11 is not an accommodation to the "non-fulfillment of the parousia" so much as an expansion of Paul's understanding of his own mission--and of the present as the time of the Gentiles' salvation--and a lessening need for him to place distance between himself and the community from which he had come.

802 ---. "The Problems Posed by 1 Thessalonians 2:15-16 and a Solution," *Horizons in Biblical Theology* 12.1 (1990) 42-72.

At least four different approaches have been forwarded to explain the problems faced by 1 Thess 2:15-16, but none of these are completely convincing. The best solution begins by accepting that Paul here does speak harshly about "the Jews," but then focuses on development in the apostle's thinking and manner of expression in the time between the composition of 1 Thessalonians and that of Romans. This development was the result of Paul's effort to resolve the cognitive dissonance arising from his own break with his past.

803 Smiga, George M. "A Response to the Papers of N. Sam Murrell and Peter W. Macky in the Paul Working Group," *Proceedings of the Eastern Great Lakes and Midwest Biblical Societies* 14 (1994) 187-193.

Sam Murrell (791) rightly warns against the tendency of many modern commentators to conform their reading of Paul to the politically correct Paul they want to find. Thus one should not too easily conclude that 1 Thess 2:13-16 is a later interpolation simply because the apostle's words here do not match current fashions. Murrell is also likely correct in his claim that Paul's visceral outburst in this passage about God's wrath overtaking the Jews results from his personal experience with some of them in Thessalonica. Paul's anger at the Jews, however, was not simply that they opposed his "understanding" of the work of God but that they interfered with his mission activity. Peter Macky (789) is less convincing in his attempt to specify further the type of present wrath which Paul may have had in mind in 1 Thess 2:16.

804 Verhoef, Eduard. "Die Bedeutung des Artikels τῶν in 1 Thess 2,15," *Biblische Notizen* 80 (1995) 41-46.

The grammatical function of the article τῶν in 1 Thess 2:15 has important consequences for the interpretation of 1 Thess 2:13-16. Despite the negative implications of this view, it must nevertheless be concluded that the article functions in an amplifying, attributive sense. Paul directed his accusation literally against all Jews, although he knew that not all Jews were thus to be understood. Paul was carried away by his emotions--a regrettable but undeniable fact.

805 Weatherly, Jon Allen. "The Authenticity of 1 Thessalonians 2.13-16: Additional Evidence," *Journal for the Study of the New Testament* 42 (1991) 79-98.

Various points of evidence corroborate the hypothesis that 1 Thess 2:13-16 is authentic. Careful syntactical analysis demonstrates the text's formal consistency with its context. Several details indicate that the expression "the Jews" refers only to the persecutors of the Judean church and that the judgment of verse 16 is imminent, not realized. Consequently, the alleged theological contradiction with Rom 11:25-32 is ameliorated. Further examination of alleged linguistic inconsistencies between the text and the rest of 1 Thessalonians reveals that the text is entirely consistent with the style of the other, undisputed Pauline texts. The balance of the evidence thus favors the text's authenticity, especially in light of its universal external attestation.

806 ---. "Responsibility for the Death of Jesus in Paul: 1 Thessalonians 2.14-16," *Jewish Responsibility for the Death of Jesus in Luke-Acts* (Journal for the Study of the New Testament Supplement Series 106; Sheffield: Sheffield Academic Press, 1994) 176-194.

1 Thess 2:14-16 is authentic and thus this passage, along with the tradition underlying it, indicates that Jewish responsibility for the death of Jesus was a part of the preaching or teaching of at least some Christians before 50 CE. Since Christians in this period were almost certainly predominantly Jewish, it is likely that the assertion of Jewish responsibility for Jesus' death arose among Jewish Christians, probably in response to persecution and not as a Gentile-Christian anti-Jewish polemic. Paul's use of this motif in 1 Thess 2:14-16 asserts that only a portion of the Jewish people are responsible for the death of Jesus. The assertion is limited to Judea and is further limited to a faction who reject Jesus and oppose the gospel in contrast to Jewish Christians in Palestine, who continue to suffer persecution from their compatriots.

807 Wick, Peter. "Ist I Thess 2,13-16 antijüdisch? Der rhetorische Gesamtzusammenhang des Briefes als Interpretationshilfe für eine einzelne Perikope," *Theologische Zeitschrift* 50 (1994) 9-23.

Paul's comments about Jews in Judea in 1 Thess 2:13-16 must be understood as part of his effort to encourage the Thessalonian Christians in their faith (see 1:9b) in the midst of their sufferings at the hands of pagan compatriots. It is also important to recognize the clear parallels between 2:13-16 and 4:2-8. Just as in 2:15 Paul adopted pagan reproaches about the Jews, so in 4:2-8 (especially verse 5) he used Jewish polemics about the pagans. The apostle's criticism of the Jews was harsher, since it was a case of a Jew criticizing fellow Jews--a critique from the inside.

808 Wilson, William E. "I Thessalonians ii. 16," *Expository Times* 35 (1923/24) 43-44.

Paul thought of wrath being manifested in two ways: either as eschatological wrath or as the natural degeneration of humans as a consequence of sin. The latter understanding is evident in Rom 1:18-33 where Paul depicts the manifestation of God's wrath as the inability to judge correctly. 1 Thess 2:16 shows that Paul considered the Jews to have reached that terrible stage of judgment by which they no longer were capable of right judgment. ἡ ὀργὴ εἰς τέλος in 1 Thess 2:16 is thus equivalent to ἀδόκιμον νοῦν ("a mind incapable of right judgment") of Rom 1:28 or πώρωσις ("hardening") of Rom 11:25.

809 Wortham, Robert A. "The Problem of Anti-Judaism in 1 Thess 2:14-16 and Related Pauline Texts," *Biblical Theology Bulletin* 25.1 (1995) 37-44.

Analytical concepts developed in the fields of social psychology and symbolic anthropology provide new insights into the problem of Pauline anti-Judaism in 1 Thess 2:14-15 and other related texts by or about Paul. The evidence suggests that Paul may have been a prejudiced person and that he could well have written this disputed passage. First, the experiences of continued opposition from Jews throughout his ministry could have prompted Paul to employ anti-Jewish statements in responding to this continued opposition. Second, the data indicate that, at times, Paul appears to have been driven by strong feelings of inadequacy. Thus Christian, Gentile, or Jewish opposition to his message could have prompted him to characterize his opponents in an offensive manner throughout his letters. Paul's prejudice, however, was of a religious, not a racial nature.

Other Relevant Sources:

360, 550, 640, 662, 663, 666, 674, 692, 707, 708, 710, 725, 747, 756, 762, 834, 973, 1091, 1144.

E. 1 Thessalonians 2:17-3:10

810 Bammel, Ernst. "Preparation for the perils of the last days: 1 Thessalonians 3:3," *Suffering and Martyrdom in the New Testament: Studies Presented to G. M. Styler by the Cambridge New Testament Seminar* (ed. William Horbury and Brian McNeil; Cambridge: Cambridge University Press, 1981) 91-100.

The precise meaning of the verb σαίνεσθαι in 1 Thess 3:3 is difficult to ascertain. The best proposal is that it describes the reaction of people who are faced with an extreme situation. There are striking similarities between the language of 1 Thess 3:2-3 and that found in Jewish apocalyptic texts describing the traumatic events associated with the end times. This suggests that σαίνεσθαι here is best understood within the eschatological perspective of the whole letter and that Paul was worried about the possibility that the Thessalonian believers would be "disturbed" or "shaken" by the tribulations preceding the return of Christ--the so-called "messianic woes" of Jewish apocalyptic writings.

811 Baumert, Norbert. "Brüche im paulinischen Satzbau?" *Filología Neotestamentaria* 4 (1991) 3-20.

An analysis of 1 Cor 7:26, 1 Cor 7:2, 1 Thess 4:6, 2 Cor 10:2 and 1 Thess 3.3--all but 1 Cor 7:2 containing the dependent infinitive in the accusative with the neuter article τό--highlights a number of syntactic and semantic problems. New semantic conclusions allow for a resolution of the syntactic problems faced in 2 Cor 10:2 and 1 Thess 3:2, which in turn clarify the content and confirm the interpretations of 1 Cor 7:26 and 1 Thess 4:6. The construction δεόμενοι εἰς in 1 Thess 3:10 does not mean "to beseech" but rather "to long to." The construction κείμεθα εἰς in 1 Thess 3:3 does not mean "to be destined (to suffer)" but rather "to find oneself in/have come to this situation." In 1 Thess 4:6 the dependent infinitive is one of consequence or finality, and the same construction in 1 Thess 3:3 is an accusative of respect which functions like a noun.

812 ---. "'Wir lassen uns nicht beirren.' Semantische Fragen in 1 Thess 3,2f," *Filología Neotestamentaria* 5 (1992) 45-60.

The verb σαίνεσθαι in 1 Thess 3:3 does not have the sense "to hesitate, be troubled," but that of "to be deceived, seduced." σαίνειν is not related to σείειν. Its various meanings are illustrated in a range of Greek literature from Homer to the Hellenistic period. A consideration of the context of 1 Thess 3:2-3 and its use in the church fathers (Chrysostom, Theodoret, Theophilact, Oecumenius) confirms this sense.

813 Chadwick, Henry. "1 Thess. 3:3: σαίνεσθαι," *Journal of Theological Studies* 1 (1950) 156-158.

A recently discovered papyrus text contains a discussion between Origen and a Bishop Heraclides whose orthodoxy had been questioned by some in the Christian community. At the end of this discussion Origen states: "All the questions of faith that disturbed us have been examined." The quotation provides further evidence that the verb σαίνω used in 1 Thess 3:3 can have the sense of "to disturb, agitate, shake mentally."

814 Donfried, Karl Paul. "War Timotheus in Athen? Exegetische Überlegungen zu 1 Thess 3,1-3," *Die Freude an Gott - unsere Kraft. Festschrift für Otto Bernhard Knoch zum 65. Geburtstag* (ed. Johannes Joachim Degenhardt; Stuttgart: Katholisches Bibelwerk, 1991) 189-196.

Commentaries find it difficult to reconcile Acts 17:14-15 and 18:5 with 1 Thess 3:1-3. A consideration of the meaning of "we" and μόνοι ("alone") leads to the conclusion that "we sent" in 1 Thess 3:2 is a literary plural used in conjunction with μόνοι. Paul came to Athens alone, without Silas and Timothy. Thus the material in Acts 17:14-15 is essentially correct.

815 Ellis, E. Earle. "Paul and His Co-Workers," *New Testament Studies* 17 (1971) 437-452.

The picture which emerges from Paul's own letters and Acts is that of a missionary with a large number of associates. Strikingly, none of these associates are called prophet, teacher, pastor, elder, or bishop. The most used designations are, in descending frequency, συνεργός, ἀδελφός, διάκονος, and ἀπόστολος. Although the term "brothers" may at first glance appear to refer to Christians generally, there is evidence that it also carries a more restricted meaning. Indeed, it is probable that, when used in the plural with an article, "the brothers" in Pauline literature fairly consistently refers to a relatively limited group of workers, some of whom have the Christian mission and/or ministry as their primary occupation. This meaning suggests a new possibility about the recipients of 2 Thessalonians. It appears that this letter is, in fact, a Pauline letter but one that is written to Paul's Thessalonian co-workers, "the brothers," and not to the whole church.

816 Funk, Robert Walter. "The Apostolic *Parousia*: Form and Significance," *Christian History and Interpretation: Studies Presented to John Knox* (ed. William R. Farmer, John Knox, Charles F. D. Moule, *et al.*; Cambridge: Cambridge University Press, 1967) 249-268.

Republished with slight modifications as Robert W. Funk,"The Apostolic Presence: Paul," *Parables and Presence. Forms of the New Testament Tradition* (Philadelphia: Fortress, 1982) 81-102.

Paul's letters often contain a section where he is particularly concerned to make his presence--his *parousia*--felt, either by means of the letter itself, reference to an emissary, or mention of a future visit (see Rom 15:14-33; Phlm 21-22; 1 Cor 4:14-21; 1 Thess 2:17-3:13; Phil 2:19-24 and Gal 4:12-20). These apostolic parousia sections exhibit some degree of formal consistency. The function of these sections is not merely to inform readers about Paul's travel plans or other activities of his life. Rather, the apostolic parousia is an effective literary device by which Paul can exert his apostolic authority and power over his letter recipients.

817 Geréb, Z. "A Thesszalonikabeliekhez irott elsö levél magyarázata - 3:6-13," *Református Szemle* 71 (1978) 67-71.

A brief exegetical analysis of 1 Thess 3:6-13.

818 Heikel, J. A. "1. Thess. 3,2," *Theologische Studien und Kritiken* 106 (1935) 316.

The verb σαίνεσθαι, which usually means "to flatter," does not have this meaning in 1 Thess 3:3. Here it means "to allow oneself to be deluded." σαλεύεσθαι must also be given a passive sense in 2 Thess 2:1.

819 Knox, A. D. "Τὸ μηδένα σαίνεσθαι ἐν ταῖς θλίψεσιν ταύταις (I Thess. iii,3)," *Journal of Theological Studies* 25 (1924) 290-291.

Since it is impossible in 1 Thess 3:3 to find any suitable meaning for the reading σαίνεσθαι, the text should instead be read as παθαίνεσθαι ("to be filled with emotion"). The resulting translation would be: "that no one *break down* in these afflictions."

820 Lecompte, Cesar. "De korporatieve lezing," *Gereformeerd Theologisch Tijdschrift* 82 (1982) 147-160.

This article summarizes the author's unpublished Th.D. dissertation, "De Korporative Lezing: een nieuwe methode van tekstbenadering toegepast op 1 Thessalonicenzen" (Brussels: Universitaire Protestantse Theologische Faculteit, 1981).

The weaknesses of current methods of biblical interpretation require a new way of approaching the text. This new method involves three main elements: (1) the narrative reading or de-coding of the actual information in the text by means of proper language analysis; (2) the discursive reading of the text whereby the deciphered elements are to be understood in their cohesiveness; and (3) comparison with other methods, particularly the historical-critical method, in order to understand the praxis and thought of the text in the historical and cultural context in which it was written. When 1 Thess 3:1-5 is diagrammed to illustrate the first step of de-coding the actual information in the text, it becomes clear that the theme of "oppression" is the kernel of the passage's structure. A study of the pattern "we," "I," and "you" in 1 Thessalonians as a whole strongly suggests that the letter itself was a third attempt to deal with issues at Thessalonica, following Paul's inability to return and Timothy's later failure to reach the church in person.

821 Manus, Chris Ukachukwu. "1 Thessalonians 2:17-20, A Reflection on Paul's Use of the Plural Number and its Significance for Ministry in the African Churches," *African Theological Journal* 12 (1983) 76-87.

The use of the plural form of speech ("we") in 1 Thessalonians, especially 2:17-20, reveals an aspect of Paul's ministry hitherto unknown in African ecclesiastical structures. The text shows, among other things, that Paul's missionary service with his co-workers was a team-ministry: one with and for others. The singular "I" in 2:18 is merely a literary device to emphasize the pain of Paul's separation from the Thessalonians; the apostle is not drawing a contrast between himself and his co-workers. Paul's use of the plural designation suggests a collegial mode of ministry which sets the paradigm for developing a sound theology of ministry in contemporary African churches where, due to unavoidable constraints, acute shortages of personnel militate against the progress of evangelization in the vast continent of Africa.

822 Mitchell, Margaret M. "New Testament Envoys in the Context of Greco-Roman Diplomatic and Epistolary Conventions: The Example of Timothy and Titus," *Journal of Biblical Literature* 111.4 (1992) 641-662.

In 1 Thess 3:6-10 and 2 Cor 7:5-16 Paul works within some established conventions about envoys and their role in maintaining and reaffirming relationships between separated partners. The two social principles about envoys are: (1) that the envoy should have a reception proper to the one who sent him; and (2) that the envoy represents the one who sent him. The relationships between Paul and the two churches are thus affirmed (1 Thess) and reconfirmed (2 Cor) through the actions of the envoys and the retrospective narrative Paul composes as his response. This epistolary retrospective narrative, which mirrors formulas for responding to envoys in Hellenistic diplomatic correspondence, establishes the reciprocity of feeling of the two separated parties as attested by their treatment of the envoys on both ends of the transaction. The role of the envoy in these two instances clearly entails an important diplomatic service which helps to affirm and maintain Paul's relationships with his churches from a distance. Hardly mere substitutes for the universally preferable Pauline presence, these envoys were consciously sent by Paul to play a complex and crucial intermediary role which he could not play, even if present himself.

823 Morris, Leon. "ΚΑΙ ΑΠΑΞ ΚΑΙ ΔΙΣ," *Novum Testamentum* 1.3 (1956) 205-208.

The expression καὶ ἅπαξ καὶ δίς, which occurs only twice in the New Testament (1 Thess 2:18; Phil 4:16), does not appear to be classical or a Latinism (for the very common phrase *semel iterumque*). The fact that it occurs in the Septuagint without the initial καί suggests that the idiomatic expression consisted only of the words ἅπαξ καὶ δίς. On the basis of its occurrence in the Septuagint, it appears that this idiomatic expression is indefinite and does not mean "twice." It is simply a way of denoting a plurality of occasions (two or more), with no attempt at exact specification. If the initial καί in 1 Thess 2:18 is ascensive, then the meaning of this verse is: "because we wished to come to you, I, Paul, and that more than once."

824 Nestle, Eberhard. "Ein neues Wort für das Wörterbuch des Neuen Testaments," *Zeitschrift für die neutestamentliche Wissenschaft* 7 (1906) 361-362.
Republished in English as "I Thess. iii. 3," *Expository Times* 18 (1907) 479.

It has long been a puzzle how to translate the phrase τὸ μηδένα σαίνεσθαι in 1 Thess 3:3. The problem can be easily solved, however, by following the reading of F and G: σιαίνεσθαι ("to get disheartened, disgusted, unnerved"). This reading fits well the context of the passage.

825 Parry, St. John R. "σαίνεσθαι, I Thess. iii 3," *Journal of Theological Studies* 25 (1923/24) 405.

A handwritten note which F. J. A. Hort made in the margin of his copy of Wetstein suggests that he would have liked to emend the text of 1 Thess 3:3 to read σιαίνεσθαι ("to get disheartened, disgusted, unnerved").

826 Pelser, Gert M. M. "Geloofsgroei by Paulus?" *Hervormde Teologiese Studies* 41.2 (1985) 260-271.

Does Paul view faith as essentially an entity which can either grow or increase within the believer or as something given by God in different degrees to different people? An investigation of 1 Thess 3:10, Rom 12:3, 14:1, 2 Cor 10:15 and Phil 1:25 indicates that the answer to this question is negative. It seems that Paul views faith as simply being faith, nothing less or nothing more. In so far, however, as there is mention in Paul of growth connected with faith, this concerns the believer's answer to the imperative in the indicative by living up daily (and increasingly) to his faith. Essentially, faith cannot be weak or mediocre. If this should be the case, it ceases any longer to be faith.

827 Perdelwitz, R. "Zu σαίνεσθαι ἐν ταῖς θλίψεσιν ταύταις, 1 Thess. 3,3," *Theologische Studien und Kritiken* 86 (1913) 613-615.

There is much confusion over the meaning of the phrase found in 1 Thess 3:3. A consideration of several options shows that the difficulty of this verse can be overcome by conjecturing that the text should instead read as follows: τὸ μὴ δειλαίνεσθαι ἐν ταῖς θλίψεσιν ταύταις ("not to be cowardly in their tribulations").

828 Riggins, Walter. "The Parousia: Getting our Terms Right," *Themelios* 21.1 (1995) 14-16.

Several terms in the New Testament are used in association with the return of Jesus. (1) "Day of the Lord": this phrase and its many variations (e.g., "that day," "the day of wrath," "the day of Christ") highlight the double notion of punishment and vindication, final death and resurrected life, fear and joy. (2) "Maranatha": this Aramaic expression, found only once in the New Testament, means: "Come, our Lord!" (3) "Epiphaneia": this word is predominantly used to refer to the powerful and glorious nature of Christ's return. (4) "Apokalypsis": the verbal root of this term has to do with significant or intimate revelations, and so refers to the comfort and vindication of believers which will be revealed at the second coming of Christ. (5) "Parousia": this most frequently used term for Christ's return (e.g., 1 Thess 2:19; 3:13; 4:15; 5:23; 2 Thess 2:1, 8-9) often functioned in that day as a technical term for the "coming" of a visiting dignitary.

829 Schlier, Heinrich. "Auslegung des 1. Thessalonicherbriefes (2,17-3,13)," *Bibel und Leben* 3 (1962) 174-184.

The theme of Paul's thankfulness for both the Thessalonians' reception of the gospel of Christ and their perseverance in the faith during his absence unites this third section

(2:17-3:13) with the first two sections of the letter. Paul develops that theme here, especially in terms of the plans of the devil, which has resulted in his sending Timothy to Thessalonica in his place. Other characteristic traits of the apostle observed in this passage include his love of, and joy in, the church, as well as his insistence upon faith as constituting the true Christian life and as a complete surrender to God.

830 Spicq, Ceslaus. "Ἐπιποθεῖν, Désirer ou chérir?" *Revue Biblique* 64.2 (1957) 184-195.
The verb ἐπιποθεῖν, together with its cognates, is a specifically biblical word. The issue of whether it should be translated as "to desire" or "to cherish," although not very important theologically, is nevertheless an issue which requires resolution. An analysis of this word's occurrence in 1 Thess 3:6 shows that here the meaning of "desire" must be at work and it is clear that this desire is a result of the fidelity and attachment which the Thessalonians have for Paul. 1 Thess 2:7-8, however, provides the best example of the idea of tenderness associated with this word. Indulgent and gentle, Paul acts in a maternal manner toward the Thessalonians.

831 Wainwright, Allan. "Where did Silas Go? (And What Was his Connection with *Galatians*?)," *Journal for the Study of the New Testament* 8 (1980) 66-70.
Acts 17:14-16 and 1 Thess 3:1-2 indicate that Paul had been forced to leave Berea and move on to Athens, where he was later joined by Silas and Timothy. Timothy was then sent back to Thessalonica and Silas too was presumably sent somewhere, since Paul was left in Athens alone until his two fellow missionaries rejoined him in Corinth. Although the biblical text does not make it clear where Silas went, it is possible that he went to the churches in Galatia. This would explain why, among other things, the older and more mature Silas was not sent to the persecuted church in Thessalonica. Instead he was needed for an even more urgent mission to Galatia, a mission which perhaps only he could perform.

832 Wratislaw, A. H. "I Thess. III.3," *Journal of Philology* 2 (1869) 154.
While the later manuscripts have the articular infinitive construction of 1 Thess 3:3 in the dative case (τῷ μὴ σαίνεσθαι), the earlier reading of the neuter (τὸ μὴ σαίνεσθαι) is undoubtedly correct. There is exactly the same variation of case in an articular infinitive construction in Thucydides 2.102.5.

833 Zsolt, Geréb. "A Thesszalonikabeliekhez Irott elsö levél magyarázata 3,6-13," *Református Szemle* 71.1 (1978) 67-71.
A verse-by-verse exposition of 1 Thess 3:6-13.

Other Relevant Sources:

747, 1007.

F. 1 Thessalonians 3:11-13

834 Cerfaux, Lucien. "Les Saints de Jérusalem," *Ephemerides theologicae lovanienses* 2 (1925) 510-529.

The term "saints" can mean one of three things: (1) Christian believers, which is by far its most common meaning; (2) angels, which is rare; and (3) the particular group of Christians in Jerusalem, the holy city. 1 Thess 3:13 and 2 Thess 1:10 are the only places where the second meaning is apparent, and these reflect the language of apocalyptic literature. 1 Thess 2:14 falls into the last category.

835 Hewett, James A. "1 Thessalonians 3.11," *Expository Times* 87.2 (1975) 54-55.

Although numerous commentators have interpreted the use of a plural subject with a singular verb in 1 Thess 3:11 as an assertion of the deity of Jesus or the unity of Jesus and God the Father, this view cannot be substantiated on the basis of grammar alone. In view of Paul's beliefs as expressed in his other letters and the demands of the grammatical construction in 1 Thess 3:11, it may be suggested that the apostle employed the unusual syntax of a double subject, in which the distinct nature of each subject is maintained by the repeated definite article ("the God...and the Lord Jesus"), with a singular verb which maintains the intimacy of the two subjects, in order to avoid either a complete separation or a complete merging of the two subjects to whom he prayed: his God and his Lord.

836 Jewett, Robert. "The Form and Function of the Homiletic Benediction," *Anglican Theological Review* 51 (1969) 18-34.

A form critical analysis of the various benedictions found in the New Testament (1 Thess 3:11; 3:11-12; 5:23; 2 Thess 2:16-17; 3:5; 3:16; Rom 15:5-6; 15:13; Heb 13:20-21) shows that they exhibit a relatively high degree of formal similarity. These benedictions typically function in bringing a major section of the letter to conclusion and summarizing its major concerns and themes. The form and function of the benedictions point to their use in homiletical contexts.

837 Jovino, Paolo. "L'Église communauté des saints dans les Actes des Apôtres et dans les Épîtres aux Thessaloniciens," *Rivista biblica* 16 (1968) 495-526.

An examination of the use of the concept of "saints" in the Old Testament, the Qumran literature, Acts, and the Thessalonian letters shows that the concept is eschatological and apocalyptic in nature. Paul has taken over this use of the concept in his writings and, through a detailed exegesis of several passages in the Thessalonian correspondence, it is patently obvious that both the Old Testament and intertestamental eschatological sense is retained.

838 McCown, Wayne. "'God's Will For You': Sanctification in the Thessalonian Epistles," *Wesleyan Theological Journal* 12 (1977) 26-33.

An exegetical analysis of three passages in 1 Thessalonians (3:12-13, 4:3-8, and 5:23-24) shows how important the theme of sanctification is in this letter. Paul describes sanctification as experiential, ethical and encompassing a believer's whole life.

839 Montague, George T. "The Gift of Progress: Paul's Prayers," *Growth in Christ. A Study in Paul's Theology of Progress* (Kirkwood: Maryhurst Press, 1961) 3-36.
A simplified version of this monograph was later published under the title *Maturing in Christ. St. Paul's Program for Christian Growth* (Milwaukee: Bruce Publishers, 1964).

Four prayers in 1 and 2 Thessalonians show that, even though Paul found his readers' faith already worthy of praise and thanksgiving, he nevertheless envisions for them further spiritual growth: 1 Thess 3:10-13 ("Christ Makes Christians Grow through Charity unto Perfect Sanctity"); 1 Thess 5:23-24 ("God Progressively Sanctifies Christians"); 2 Thess 1:11-12 ("God Makes Christians Worthy of His Call and Completes the Work Begun"); and 2 Thess 2:16-17 ("The Father and the Son Console and Strengthen Hearts").

840 Ross, J. M. "1 Thessalonians 3.13," *The Bible Translator* 26.4 (1975) 444.

The allusion in 1 Thess 3:13 is to the current Jewish belief, based on Zech 14:5, that at the end of the age the Messiah would come to earth accompanied by a host of angels (see also 2 Thess 1:7; Matt 8:38; 25:31; Jude 14). Thus the "holy ones" of 3:13 are beings of a different order from the believers mentioned in 4:14-17.

841 Wiles, Gordon P. "Function of the Wish-Prayers in I Thessalonians," *Paul's Intercessory Prayers. The Significance of the Intercessory Prayer Passages in the Letters of St. Paul* (Society for New Testament Studies Monograph Series 24; Cambridge: Cambridge University Press, 1974) 45-71.

The wish-prayers in 1 Thessalonians (3:11, 12-13; 5:23) function in a variety of strategic ways. First, they possess a summarizing function: Paul adapts the conventional elements of the prayers such that they summarize and place the spotlight on the central message of the letter. Second, they have a paraenetic function: by mentioning the needs of the readers in prayer which they themselves will read together during worship, the apostle is encouraging them before God to fulfill the detailed exhortations found in the letter and the wish-prayers which sum them up. Third, the prayers have an instructional and perhaps catechetical function: Paul's own prayers, when written to be read by others, would be composed partly as pattern prayers upon which readers could model their own prayers. Finally, there may have been a liturgical purpose to the prayers as they were intended to form a part of the corporate worship of the readers.

Other Relevant Sources:

829, 955, 1069.

G. 1 Thessalonians 4:1-12

842 Adinolfi, Marco. "Etica "commerciale" e motivi parenetici in 1 Tess 4,1-8," *Bibbia e Oriente* 19 (1977) 9-20.

Paul expresses in 1 Thess 4:3-6a the divine requirements with respect to sexual matters. There is no notion, here, of "commercial ethics." The Thessalonians should diligently follow the norms which Paul has passed on to them not only out of fear of divine punishment but, more positively, because holiness in sexual conduct is part of God's salvific will and his gift of the Holy Spirit. Other motivations include the authority of Christ and of the apostle, the desire to please God, the fear of harming one's neighbor and of relapsing into old pagan vices. The accusation of "contractual morality" does not apply to Christianity as preached by Paul. For the apostle, justification and the Holy Spirit are gratuitous gifts of God which enable a person to act so as to please the Lord, and one receives gratuitously the eschatological gifts which culminate in being eternally with God in loving union.

843 ---. "Le frodi di 1 Tess. 4, 6a e l'epiclerato," *Bibbia e Oriente* 18 (1976) 29-38.

The verb πλεονεκτεῖν in 1 Thess 4:6 is particularly difficult to translate. Although some commentators have understood this word to be a prohibition against exploiting another in the area of commerce or business, the context clearly deals with sexual offenses. Heinrich Baltensweiler (848, 849) has argued that Paul here is addressing a Greek inheritance custom. In this legal custom, when there was no son, the daughter would become the sole heir to her father's property. In order that goods might not pass to another house, the law gave the nearest of kin the right to her hand. The results were frequent marriages among close relatives, especially between uncles and nieces, a multiplicity of divorces and law suits, and violent seizure of property. Thus, the verb πλεονεκτεῖν might refer to sexual sin, forbidding adultery and other illicit actions, or it might refer to the problems connected with certain inheritance customs.

844 ---. "La santita' del matrimonio in 1 Thes 4,1-8," *Rivista Biblica (Italiana)* 24.2 (1976) 165-184.

Republished with minor changes under the same title in Marco Adinolfi, *Il Femminismo della Bibbia* (Spicilegium Pontificii Athenaei Antoniani 22; Rome, 1981) 205-227.

Paul presents marriage in 1 Thess 4:1-8 as a positive institution which is integral to the divine plan of sanctification. A study of several key terms in the passage shows that the apostle views matrimony as not merely a remedy for concupiscence (see 1 Cor 7) but a desired act of God. The reasons why believers should live in marriage are that this state is part of God's saving will, his call to sanctification, his gift of the Holy Spirit, and it wards against the danger of falling back into the vices of paganism.

845 Argyle, A. W. "Parallels between the Pauline Epistles and Q," *Expository Times* 60 (1948/49) 318-320.

Parallels between passages in the Pauline letters (1 Cor 1:18-19; 9:13-14; 10:27; 1 Thess 4:8; Rom 2:1-3; 2:13; 2:19-21; 12:14) and sections from Matthew and Luke which can confidently be assigned to Q are sufficiently striking to justify the conclusion that Paul's mind was steeped in the oral tradition of Jesus' ethical sayings, grouped together as we find them in Luke and as we may infer they stood in Q.

846 Avotri, Solomon Kwami. "Possessing One's Vessel in 1 Thessalonians 4:4: Marital or Martial Metaphor?" (Unpublished Ph.D. Dissertation; Denver: Iliff School of Theology and University of Denver, 1991).

The issue in the use of σκεῦος in 1 Thess 4:4 is whether this is a "marital metaphor," which gives instruction about marriage, or a "martial metaphor," which gives instruction about Christian warfare. The issue depends, to a great extent, on how one translates the noun σκεῦος and the infinitive κτᾶσθαι in the sentence. When σκεῦος occurs in a sexual context, it is possible to interpret it as a euphemistic expression for the male organ--an interpretation which is supported by the sexual language of 4:3-5. There does not seem to be any fixed connotation for κτάομαι, but its meaning is imputed to it by its context. In light of the dominance of the theme of eschatology in 1 Thessalonians, it is best to conclude that σκεῦος is a marital metaphor which Paul employs, not to instruct on how to take a wife, but on how to keep away from marrying in order to consecrate oneself for the impending parousia. The possibility of this interpretation is supported by Paul's propensity toward celibacy as the mode of eschatological existence (1 Cor 7:25-38). It is also supported by the ascetic attitude of the gospel tradition concerning the parousia (Matt 24:37-39 = Luke 17:26-27, Luke 14:26; 20:34-35).

847 Bahnsen, Wilhelm. "Zum Vertändnis von 1. Thess. 4, 1-12," *Zeitschrift für wissenschaftliche Theologie* 47 (1904) 332-358.

A detailed exegesis of 1 Thess 4:1-12 reveals what the author (whether it is Paul or not cannot be settled) means for his readers to be holy.

848 Baltensweiler, Heinrich. *Die Ehe im Neuen Testament. Exegetische Untersuchungen über Ehe, Ehelosigheit und Ehescheidung* (Abhandlungen zur Theologie des Alten und Neuen Testaments 52; Zürich: Zwingli Verlag, 1967) 135-149.

This study of marriage and divorce in the New Testament first discusses the Old Testament, the world of the New Testament, and then the Gospels, before turning to particular passages in the letters. 1 Thess 4:3-8 is not making assertions about marriage, but is apparently addressing a quite specific problem that the Thessalonians were having. This passage touches upon the issue of marriage but is more specifically addressed to issues of holiness and unchastity, and the Greek institution of a woman's inheritance.

849 ---. "Erwägungen zu 1 Thess 4,3-8," *Theologische Zeitschrift* 19.1 (1963) 1-13.

Recent exegesis of 1 Thess 4:3-8 has understood Paul's exhortations here to be only of a general nature and not to reflect any actual problems in the Thessalonian church.

Against such a view, it needs to be recognized that this passage addresses a concrete situation of the Thessalonian community: it answers certain questions that the Thessalonians had raised in relation to a distinctive Greek custom, the right of a daughter who inherited her father's property when no sons survived. In that case the next of kin had the first claim to her hand. As a result the parties involved frequently obtained divorces so that they might enter into this new union, and marriages between close relatives resulted, that of an uncle and a niece being especially common. Moreover, the daughter's right to the inheritance was often challenged in court, and some of the contestants for the sake of strengthening their claims resorted to violence and took possession of some of the property. Paul's answer to the question raised by the Thessalonian Christians about this widespread Greek custom is clear: such marriages are forbidden.

850 Bassler, Jouette M. "Σκεῦος: A Modest Proposal for Illuminating Paul's Use of Metaphor in 1 Thessalonians 4:4," *The Social World of the First Christians: Essays in Honor of Wayne A. Meeks* (ed. L. Michael White and O. Larry Yarbrough; Minneapolis: Fortress, 1995) 53-66.

1 Cor 7:36-38 (a passage which likely speaks of spiritual marriages--a practice which Paul himself probably introduced), not 1 Cor 7:1-7, is the closest parallel to 1 Thess 4:4. As a result of his earlier teaching on the topic, Paul and the Thessalonians understood the word σκεῦος in 1 Thess 4:4 as a metaphorical reference to virgin partners--those who enter into "spiritual marriages" where both partners remain celibate. His advice to the members of this church was that, to achieve the goal of pleasing God, each of them should know the benefits of acquiring a virgin partner.

851 Baumert, Norbert. "Brautwerbung--Das einheitliche Thema von 1 Thess 4,3-8," *The Thessalonian Correspondence* (ed. Raymond F. Collins; Bibliotheca ephemeridum theologicarum lovaniensium 87; Leuven: Leuven University Press, 1990) 316-339.

A word- and text-semantic based investigation of the phrase σκεῦος κτᾶσθαι in 1 Thess 4:4 indicates that these words have the sense of "to obtain a wife." The surrounding verses (4:3-8) do not deal with two or three different themes but rather refer to a single concrete situation in the Thessalonian community. Holiness is meant to have a present sense, and is not meant to represent a number of different moral acts. The relations of husband and wife are supposed to be "holy" and one should not allow them to be damaged by sexual mistakes.

852 Beauvery, Robert. "πλεονεκτεῖν in 1 Thess. 4,6a," *Verbum domini* 33 (1955) 78-85.

The verb πλεονεκτεῖν in 1 Thess 4:6 has a commercial rather than a sexual reference. This conclusion is based on the normal meaning of πλεονεκτεῖν and its cognates, on the fact that Paul elsewhere distinguishes πλεονεξία from sexual immorality, and on the situation of Thessalonica as a thriving commercial center. It also fits with the broader context, and with the preceding verb ὑπερβαίνειν, which refers to any offence against the social order. Furthermore, the following words ἐν τῷ πράγματι can be translated "in any commercial affair." The objections that the surrounding context speaks exclusively of sexual impurity and that πρᾶγμα, when it has a commercial sense, is normally in the plural, are not persuasive. The former mistakenly assumes that the "impurity" of verse 7 has an exclusively sexual reference, and the latter fails to note that the singular πρᾶγμα, while it does occasionally have a commercial sense, *never* has a sexual one.

853 Bruston, C. "Deux articles de loi du christianisme primitif. D'après la première épître aux Thessaloniciens," *Revue de Théologie et des Questions Religieuses* 14 (1905) 160-162, 369-377.

It is impossible that 1 Thess 4:3-6 refers to a single commandment. Instead, it is better to understand these verses, along with verse 7, as two separate commands: one a positive command concerning the proper way to act toward others, the other a negative command concerning the way that affairs should be conducted in the brotherhood of the church. This is most likely a brief reference to a whole list of commands which Paul had previously given to the Thessalonians.

854 Carras, George P. "Jewish Ethics and Gentile Converts: Remarks on 1 Thes 4,3-8," *The Thessalonian Correspondence* (ed. Raymond F. Collins; Bibliotheca ephemeridum theologicarum lovaniensium 87; Leuven: Leuven University Press, 1990) 306-315.

Paul in 1 Thess 4:3-8 imposes on his Gentile converts a common Jewish ideal concerning sexuality. The Jewish character of the exhortations here can be seen in a number of ways: e.g., the verb παραλαμβάνω (vv 1-2) reflects a Hebrew term used technically in rabbinic schools for the transmission of tradition; the verb περιπατέω (vv 1 [2x], 12) echoes the rabbinic use of the word "to walk" as a term denoting moral conduct. This application of Jewish ethics to Gentile converts served a social function. It helped to distinguish these converts from the morals of their non-Christian contemporaries in a similar way that Jewish ethics marked out Jews from pagans.

855 Collins, Raymond F. "'This is the Will of God: Your Sanctification' (1 Thess 4:3)," *Laval théologique et philosophique* 39 (1983) 27-53.
Republished in Raymond F. Collins, *Studies on the First Letter to the Thessalonians* (Bibliotheca ephemeridum theologicarum lovaniensium 66; Leuven: Leuven University Press, 1984) 299-325.

The paraenetic section of 1 Thess 4:1-8 consists of three clearly distinct sections: introduction (vv 1-2), a triple exhortation (vv 3-5), and a triple motivation (vv 6-8). The introduction contains a pastoral parenthesis which recognizes the good work of the Thessalonians as well as a request that they "do so more and more." The triple exhortation is filled with exegetical difficulties. The problematic σκεῦος and κτᾶσθαι of verse 4 refer to "knowing how to live with one's wife in holiness and honor." The third exhortation does not introduce a new topic of injustice in business matters but continues to address the topic of sexuality, specifically warning against adultery. The triple motivation for fulfilling the preceding exhortations is found in the final judgment, the call to holiness, and the gift of the Holy Spirit. The passage was evidently not a direct response to a specific problem existing in the Thessalonian community. Rather, Paul was presenting Jewish ethical traditions in the light of Christian faith.

856 ---. "The Unity of Paul's Paraenesis in 1 Thess. 4:3-8: 1 Cor. 7:1-7, A Significant Parallel," *New Testament Studies* 29 (1983) 420-429.
Republished in Raymond F. Collins, *Studies on the First Letter to the Thessalonians* (Bibliotheca ephemeridum theologicarum lovaniensium 66; Leuven: Leuven University Press, 1984) 326-335.

There exists much debate whether 1 Thess 4:3-8 deals with only one issue (chastity) or two (chastity and justice). A faulty interpretation of 1 Cor 7:1-7 as an exhortation to an ascetic ideal of celibacy has somewhat clouded the interpretation of the Thessalonian passage. In fact, 1 Cor 7:1-7 encourages the readership to a sexually active marriage. This more accurate interpretation of the Corinthian passage inclines the expositor of 1 Thessalonians to interpret σκεῦος in the sense of "wife" and the entire verse as an exhortation to marriage as the normal and rightful place within which sexual activity takes place. That this is indeed the correct interpretation of 1 Thess 4:4 is supported by a number of Jewish parallels. In 1 Thess 4:6 Paul does not introduce a new topic of injustice in business practices but rather enjoins the Christian not to violate the marriage of others. Therefore, 1 Thess 4:3-8 deals with a single matter: chastity. Paul first exhorts his readership to chastity within marriage and then urges them to avoid adultery.

857 Deidun, Thomas J. "The Self-Understanding of the Communities Reflected in Paul's *Paraklêsis*," *New Covenant Morality in Paul* (Analecta Biblica 18; Rome: Biblical Institute Press, 1981) 15-28.

An examination of 1 Thess 4:1-12, the earliest extant passage of Paul's παράκλησις, reveals elements and motifs which demonstrate that Paul shares with his readers the presupposition that Christians form the holy "people of God," with characteristics analogous to the people of old. God's holy people are (1) separated from the "gentiles" and set over against them (2) to belong by virtue of the covenant to God, who thus (3) by his presence sanctifies its members and demands that they be holy (4) as a cult-community, holy and united, (5) pleasing to God and subject to his dominion, so that (6) he may be God in his people and before the nations.

858 Doignon, Jean. "L'exégèse latine ancienne de I Thessaloniciens 4,4-5 sur la possession de notre *uas*: schémas classiques et éclairages chrétiens," *Bulletin de littérature ecclésiastique* 83 (1982) 163-177.

The Latin church fathers' exegesis of 1 Thess 4:4-5 from the third to the fifth centuries reveals a division over the interpretation of *uas* (Greek: σκεῦος ["vessel"]). Although it only really started with Jerome, the abandonment of the interpretation of *uas* as an image of the human body did not throw the lines of interpretation of this verse into confusion. This interpretation had its roots in the Roman tradition, especially in the discussion of the ethics of marriage, which had been devalued or abandoned by the eastern tradition in favor of underlining its role as an antidote to sexual license, or its procreative role. This exegetical move, however, gave support to those who held a view of perfection which united chastity and marriage, and so both Jerome and Augustine were forced to qualify their positions.

859 Eddy, Paul R. "Christian and Hellenistic Moral Exhortation: A Literary Comparison Based on 1 Thessalonians 4," *Directions in New Testament Methods* (ed. Martin C. Albl, Paul R. Eddy, and Renée Mirkes; Marquette Studies in Theology 2; Milwaukee: Marquette University Press, 1993) 45-51.

A comparison of the moral exhortations found in 1 Thessalonians 4 with those found in Hellenism reveals both important similarities and differences. The similarities involve literary styles and conventions, and commonalities in moral codes. The most prominent differences involve the Christian motivation (regard for God and his call to holiness) and means (the transformative power of the Holy Spirit) for living the ethical life. Finally, the eschatological hope serves as the distinctive Christian foundation for present consolation and future glory.

860 Elgvin, Torleif. "'To Master His Own Vessel'. 1 Thess 4.4 in Light of New Qumran Evidence," *New Testament Studies* 43 (1997) 604-619.

A Qumran composition (Sapiential Work A, which is preserved in seven fragmentary copies: 1Q26; 4Q415/416/417/418a/418b/423) from the second century BCE, which still was in use and copied anew in Judea in the time of Paul, uses כלי חיקכה ("the vessel of your bosom") as a euphemism for the male organ. כלי is used twice in 1 Sam 21:6 for the sexual organ, and is used in a similar way in mishnaic and amoraic times. Greek sources, one of them contemporary with Paul, testify to the same meaning for σκεῦος. These references make it probable that 1 Thess 4:4 should be translated "that each of you learn to master his own (sexual) organ in holiness and honor." This expression probably has a comprehensive meaning: to behave and dress with decency (as is the meaning in Sapiential Work A), and, whether one is married or single, to master one's sexual drives with respect (τιμή) for others as well as for one's own body. The meaning "sexual organ" makes the precept in question a clear parallel to the preceding one "that you should avoid sexual immorality." The following precept "that in this matter no one should wrong his brother or take advantage of him" must also relate to sexual relations, either homosexual acts or adultery.

861 Geréb, Z. "A Thesszalonikabeliekhez irott elsö levél 4,1-8. Verseinek magyarázata," *Református Szemle* 71 (1978) 171-176.

A brief exegetical analysis of 1 Thess 4:1-8.

862 Grill, Severin M. "In das Gewerbe seines Nächsten eingreifen 1 Thess 4,6," *Biblische Zeitschrift* 11 (1967) 118.

There has been much debate whether the verb πλεονεκτεῖν in 1 Thess 4:6 continues to address the matter of sexual conduct or introduces the new subject of business practices. A consideration of the early versions and the interpretation of the church fathers demonstrates that the issue of marriage and proper sexual conduct continues to be in view.

863 Harris, J. Rendel. "A Study in Letter-Writing," *The Expositor, 5th Series* 4 (1898) 185-204.

The expressions used by Paul in 1 Thess 3:6 where he describes the good report brought by Timothy show that this communication was not oral but in the form of a letter and that Paul had this letter from the Thessalonians before him when he wrote 1 Thessalonians. The content of this letter from the Thessalonians can be largely reconstructed by a careful reading of chapters 1-3. In addition one can also discern behind the canonical first letter to the Thessalonians another and earlier letter of Paul--the real first letter to the Thessalonians--which Timothy carried with him to Thessalonica. Thus the canonical 1 Thessalonians is like a double palimpsest in which appears very faintly not only Paul's earlier letter to the Thessalonians but also the church's written response to his inquiries.

864 Hodgson, Robert, Jr. "1 Thess 4:1-12 and the Holiness Tradition (HT)," *SBL 1982 Seminar Papers* (ed. Keith H. Richards; SBL Seminar Papers 21; Chico, CA: Scholars Press, 1982) 199-215.

A comparison of 1 Thess 4:1-12 with 1 Peter 1:13-2:3, 11-12, as well as certain unique features of the former passage, shows that Paul here is making use of a tradition of ethical exposition of the Holiness Code in Leviticus 17-26. This holiness tradition was known in Hellenistic and Palestinian Judaism prior to its appearance in the New Testament. Paul may well have had access to this tradition in the form of a testimony or *florilegium*. If Paul intended 1 Thess 4:1-12 to be read and understood as Old Testament-Jewish exhortation, this suggests that some of the Thessalonians may have been sufficiently steeped in this tradition for such exhortations not to have been lost on them. Although it is not possible to determine whether these people were Diaspora Jews, God-fearers, or proselytes, it does not appear to be the case that the believers in Thessalonica were exclusively Gentile Christians.

865 ---. "The Testimony Hypothesis," *Journal of Biblical Literature* 98.3 (1979) 361-378.

The testimony tradition refers to the nascent church's practice of collecting, combining, and tailoring Old Testament excerpts in order to sanction and elaborate its evangelism, catechesis, liturgy, polemics, and paraenesis. The existence of such testimonies is suggested first by the presence of various extrabiblical anthologies (e.g., Pseudo-Phocylides, 4QTestim; 4QFlor). Further internal evidence for the presence of testimonies used by the church is provided by the following five features of certain New Testament texts: texts with peculiar readings, recurring sequences of testimonies, cases of false ascription, editors' prefaces, and apologetic organizational principles. A comparison of the paraenesis of 1 Thess 4:1-12 with 1 Pet 1:13-2:3, 11-12 provides a good test case to demonstrate the existence of a testimony and to show Paul's and Peter's use of traditional material in these passages.

866 Jensen, Joseph. "Does *Porneia* Mean Fornication? A Critique of Bruce Malina," *Novum Testamentum* 20.3 (1978) 161-184.

Bruce Malina ("Does *Porneia* Mean Fornication," *Novum Testamentum* 14 [1972] 10-17) has argued that the New Testament use of πορνεία does not mean "pre-betrothal, pre-marital, heterosexual intercourse of a non-cultic or noncommercial nature, i.e., what we call 'fornication' today" (p 17). A review, however, of Malina's use of the Old Testament, Qumran, and rabbinic literature does not support his conclusion. If the Old Testament considered fornication reprehensible, if the distinction between harlotry and fornication is not always clearly drawn, and if the Septuagint could use πορνεία to designate wanton sexual behavior, there is no basis for denying that the New Testament could use this word to designate simple fornication.

867 Joubert, H. "Die Christelike huwelikslewe volgens 1 Thessalonisense 4:3-6," *Die Studiekring* 2 (1952) 9-13.

868 Klassen, William. "Foundations for Pauline Sexual Ethics as Seen in I Thess. 4:1-8," *SBL 1978 Seminar Papers* (ed. Paul J. Achtemeier; SBL Seminar Papers 17; Atlanta: Scholars Press, 1978) 159-181.

An exegetical analysis of 1 Thess 4:1-8, as well as a comparison of Paul's treatment of πορνεία with that of Jewish (Josephus, Testaments of the Twelve Patriarchs) and Stoic (Zeno, Antipater of Tarsus, Musonius Rufus, Epictetus) writers of his day, reveals the distinctive features of the apostle's teaching on sexual ethics. Paul rejects both the concerns of ritual purity of his Jewish background and the concerns of morality as expressed among the Stoics. Instead, the foundation for Paul's teaching of sexual matters rests upon an affirmation of the Lordship of Jesus under which the will of God is defined as the process of making holy, accomplished through the gift and work of the Holy Spirit. It is the degree of specificity in Paul's ethics which is striking, and not the general principles which he develops.

869 Kloppenborg, John S. "ΦΙΛΑΔΕΛΦΙΑ, ΘΕΟΔΙΔΑΚΤΟΣ and the Dioscuri: Rhetorical Engagement in 1 Thessalonians 4.9-12," *New Testament Studies* 39 (1993) 265-289.

The expression περὶ δέ in 1 Thess 4:9 is best regarded as an epistolary shorthand introducing a matter of common concern. Given the context provided by 4:10-12, it is likely that the Thessalonians had expressed some puzzlement about how φιλαδελφία should be expressed, and particularly about the limits and possible abuses of quasi-familial solidarity. φιλαδελφία was best known as the near-proverbial virtue of the Dioscuri (the divine twins, Castor and Polydeuces). Paul presupposes his readers' acquaintance with the traditions connected with the Dioscuri and treats them, as did others in his day, as paradigms of φιλαδελφία. Given the broad popular appeal of the divine brothers as well as their special place among the civic cults of Thessalonica, the deliberate coinage of "god-taught," coupled with the use of φιλαδελφία, would naturally evoke the Dioscuri as a pattern for imitation. Paul's response to the Thessalonians' puzzlement, therefore, involved both specific exhortations to quiet living and a more general appeal based on the widely-known story of the divine brothers who exemplify familial affection and self-sacrificing love.

870 Kock, E. L. de. "Die taalkundige probleem van 1 Thess 4,3-7," *Die Studiekring* 4 (1964) 1-14.

871 Linder, J. R. "1 Thess. 4,3-5," *Theologische Studien und Kritiken* 40 (1867) 516-521.

De Wette proposed that σκεῦος ("vessel") in 1 Thess 4:4 refers to possessing one's own body in holiness and honor. However, the use of the noun σκεῦος, the verb κτᾶσθαι, and the reflexive pronoun ἑαυτοῦ here argues against De Wette's interpretation. Parallels in the other Pauline letters, as well as extra-biblical texts, leads to the conclusion that the sense of σκεῦος is "wife." The phrase in 4:4 should be rendered "win back your wife once and always."

872 Martin, Leonard M. "Moral Sexual Missionária de Paulo (Subsidios para uma moral do matrimônio no Brasil)," *Revista Eclesiástica Brasileira* 50 (1990) 515-536.

1 Thess 4:1-8 is treated within the larger context of an interpretation of Paul's teachings about sex and marriage in his early letters. The aim of this exegetical analysis is to apply these teachings to the new missionary situation of the Brazilian Roman Catholic Church. To that end a combination of the hermeneutics of Carlos Mesters and Clodovis Boff is employed. The two motivations behind Paul's general exhortations on sex and marriage in 1 Thess 4:1-8 are the believer's election to holiness and the proximity of the Day of the Lord. These two factors require Christians (1) to respect their bodies, both their own and their spouse's; (2) to recognize marriage as a positive institution; (3) to avoid sexual immorality; (4) to control their passions; and (5) to avoid harming their neighbor.

873 Maurer, Christian. "σκεῦος," *Theological Dictionary of the New Testament* (ed. Gerhard Friedrich; 10 vols.; Grand Rapids: Eerdmans, 1971) 7.358-367.

In the Pauline letters, especially under Old Testament influence, σκεῦος is used as a metaphor or similitude to denote certain aspects of humanity. The meaning of this term in 1 Thess 4:4 has been debated from the time of the church fathers to be either "body" or "wife." The solution to this issue lies in not examining the word σκεῦος individually but to consider its occurrence with another key word in the verse, the verb κτᾶσθαι. The meaning "wife" is supported by the figurative use in rabbinic writings of the Hebrew כְּלִי (which corresponds to the Greek σκεῦος) of women and euphemistically of sexual intercourse with a woman with verbs like "use" and "make."

874 McGehee, Michael. "A Rejoinder to Two Recent Studies Dealing with 1 Thess 4:4," *Catholic Biblical Quarterly* 51.1 (1989) 82-89.

The debate in 1 Thess 4:4 centers on the proper translation of the verb κτάομαι, which usually means "to acquire" or "to possess," and σκεῦος, which, used here metaphorically, means either "body" or "wife." Larry Yarbrough (892) has recently argued that this verse should be translated as, "Let each man know how *to obtain* his own *wife* in holiness and honor," while Raymond Collins (855) has advocated the rendering: "Each one of you know how *to live* with his *wife* in holiness and honor." The verse in question, however, is more correctly translated as: "Keep your *body* in holiness and honor." The interpretations of both Yarbrough and Collins are unlikely because: (1) it inadequately reflects the social situation of the early church; (2) it fails to fit the usual pattern Paul follows in paraenesis; and (3) it appears to conflict with what Paul says elsewhere about sex and marriage.

875 Míguez, Néstor O. "La ética Cristiana: Una opción contrahegemónica," *Cuadernos de Teología* 10 (1989) 15-25.

Although there are some elements of continuity between Christianity and its environment, Christian ethics represent basically a rupture with the dominant imperial ideology of pagan society. This is clearly seen in 1 Thess 4:1-12 where Paul, making use of a chiastic structure, presents the basic ideas which support his thesis. Here the life of faith is depicted in a dynamic fashion in the context of eschatological vocation and, in that sense, gives a specific identity to the people of God. As a result, the process of sanctification is also presented as a distinguishing mark of the people of God. This can be seen in the specific areas of sexuality and business where Christian relationships, in contrast to pagan practices allowed by the Roman empire, are characterized by respect for the other person. Yet it is ultimately the fact that the believer's relationship to God shapes all other relationships, which illustrates the key element of discontinuity between Christianity and the pagan world.

876 Nieder, Lorenz. *Die Motive der religiös-sittlichen Paränese in den paulinischen Gemeindebriefen: Ein Beitrag zur Paulinischen Ethik* (Münchener Theologische Studien: Historische Abteilung 12; Munich: Karl Zink, 1956) 4-14, 27-31.

1 Thess 4:1-8 and 5:1-10 are major paraenetic texts for establishing the foundational motivation of Pauline morality. 1 Thess 4:1-8 provides three subjects for the paraenesis: the concept of the "will of God"; the notion of separation from the Gentiles; and the depiction of the Lord as the "avenger" of all things. 1 Thess 5:1-10 is grounded in the use of imagery which is later explained such as night and day. The key idea here is that, if believers already belong to the "day," they will want to live appropriately. This call

to holiness is grounded in Jesus Christ, who, through his death and resurrection "for us," is established as the mediator of holiness for believers. 2 Thess 2:13-15 is a brief paraenetic section on election by God.

877 Ogara, Florentinus. "'Haec est ... voluntas Dei, sanctificatio vestra': In epistolam (1 Thess. 4,1-7)," *Verbum Domini* 18 (1938) 65-72.

The use of patristic sources, especially Chrysostom, in interpreting 1 Thess 4:1-7 leads to the following conclusions: (1) this passage must be seen in its historical and literary context; (2) patristic commentaries are especially helpful in explaining the vocabulary of verse 1; (3) "sanctification" in verse 3 refers primarily to sexual purity; (4) the enigmatic phrase σκεῦος κτᾶσθαι in verse 4 does not refer to getting married but to controlling one's body; and (5) the vocabulary of verse 6a refers to adultery rather than to greed.

878 Rickards, Raymond R. "1 Thessalonians 4,4-6," *The Bible Translator* 29.2 (1978) 245-247.

A survey of how six well-known translations (Revised Standard Version, New English Bible, Jerusalem Bible, Good News Bible, Phillips, Living Bible) render 1 Thess 4:4-6 illustrates the grammatical and exegetical problems faced in these verses. Most translate the phrase ἐν τῷ πράγματι (v 6) as "in this matter," supplying the word "this" for the Greek definite article on the assumption that Paul is still speaking about sexual immorality (rather than switching to a new topic of business malpractice). The majority of translations interpret σκεῦος (v 4) as "body" instead of "wife," although it is not clear how a believer cheats a Christian brother by treating his own body improperly and using it for selfish sexual gratification.

879 Roetzel, Calvin J. "Theodidaktoi and Handwork in Philo and I Thessalonians," *L'Apôtre Paul: Personalité, style, et conception du ministère* (ed. Albert Vanhoye; Bibliotheca ephemeridum theologicarum lovaniensium 73; Leuven: Leuven University Press, 1986) 324-331.

A Hellenistic Jewish piety similar to Philo's explains better the unusual combination of language and issues in 1 Thess 4:9-11 than does Hellenistic philosophy. As citizens of the kingdom of God waiting for the imminent arrival of the Son of the Man, the Thessalonians would be in an unusually strong position to claim a wisdom direct from God which needs no human teacher (5:12), which is immediate and timeless, and which already enjoys the eschatological release from work (4:11; 5:14). Paul's coinage and use of the term θεοδίδακτοι would appear then to be not a mild polemic against Epicurean views, but an attempt to make explicit what was already implicit in the term αὐτοδίδακτος known in Hellenistic Jewish circles. Paul radically recasts the traditional meaning of αὐτοδίδακτος to emphasize the social responsibilities of the "God-taught" in the church and to restore a future dimension to the eschatological perspective of the Thessalonians.

880 Rosner, Brian S. "Seven Questions for Paul's Ethics: 1 Thessalonians 4:1-12 as a Case Study," *Understanding Paul's Ethics* (Grand Rapids: Eerdmans, 1995) 351-360.

The seven questions which ought to be asked in understanding Paul's ethics deal with origin, context, social dimension, shape, logic, foundation, and relevance. When these questions are applied to 1 Thess 4:1-12, we discover that Paul's ethics here: (1) arise from a biblical/Jewish milieu; (2) are distinctly more theocentric than Greco-Roman ethics; (3) reflect a strong social dimension in which Paul continues to shape and nurture the community; (4) are adapted from both biblical/Jewish and early Christian moral teaching; (5) stress the separation of Christians from their pagan neighbors as the grounds for the exhortation to holiness; (6) are motivated christologically (believers are exhorted "in the Lord" [v 1]), ecclesiologically (love for fellow believers [vv 9-10]), and eschatologically (the coming judgment [v 6]); and (7) have general and abiding validity because they reflect the will of God (v 3) and originate not from Paul but from God himself (v 8).

881 Salleron, Louis. "1 Thess 4,4 - 'prendre femme'?" *La Pensée Catholic* 155 (1975) 61-69.

The phrase εἰδέναι ἕκαστον ὑμῶν τὸ ἑαυτοῦ σκεῦος κτᾶσθαι ἐν ἁγιασμῷ καὶ τιμῇ in 1 Thess 4:4 is translated in the Traduction Oecumenique de la Bible (TOB) as "that each one of you learn to take a wife so as to live in sanctity and honour." This translation is not defensible, as the text does not justify such an interpretative reading. The effect of such a translation puts the question of chastity solely in the province of marriage, and privileges this against a life of chastity not lived in the context of marriage. Much better is the translation, "That each of you learn to control the vessel (of flesh), which is his own, in sanctity and honour."

882 Sánchez, Benjamín Martín. "El capitulo cuarto de la primera Epistola a los Tesalonicenses," *Cultura Bíblica* 17 (1960) 351-354.

A brief exposition of three passages in 1 Thessalonians 4 (vv 1-8, 9-12, 13-18).

883 Schlier, Heinrich. "Auslegung des 1. Thessalonicherbriefes (4,1-12)," *Bibel und Leben* 3 (1962) 240-249.

The second half of the letter begins at 1 Thess 4:1. Whereas the word for exhortation was the keyword of the first half, this word, along with the word for request, are the key words for the second half. Thus Paul is addressing the way of life of the Thessalonian Christians and giving them paraenetic exhortation. The "vessel" of 4:4 refers to the obtaining of a wife.

884 Snyder, Graydon F. "The Literalization of the Apocalyptic Form in the New Testament Church," *Biblical Research* 14 (1969) 5-18.

The heart of biblical apocalyptic theology is a "radically disjunctive eschatology"--the affirmation of the absolute validity of God's promise to humankind through Israel and of the historical locus of its fulfillment, along with the denial that present history or current institutions of humankind can lead to that fulfillment. Paul's preaching of this kind of apocalyptic message was, in a Hellenistic world, understandably misunderstood. In some instances it was literalized dualistically so that a struggle between flesh and spirit resulted. In other instances it was literalized chronologically so that an actual end of time was expected. The former misunderstanding resulted in raproachment with gnostic spiritualization and eventually allowed for an alliance with spatially oriented philosophies. The latter resulted in a problem regarding the delay of the parousia. Examples of the literalization of the apocalyptic form in the Pauline church can be seen in Corinth (1 Cor 6:12-20; 7:1-40) and Thessalonica (1 Thess 4:9-12).

885 Spicq, Ceslaus. "La Charité fraternelle selon 1 Th. 4,9," *Mélanges bibliques rédigés en l'honneur de André Robert* (Travaux de l'Institut Catholique de Paris 4; Paris: Bloud et Gay, 1956) 507-511.

1 Thess 4:9 is the first time that Paul commands his churches to love. Far from this challenge being a doctrine simply according to Paul, the apostle makes it clear that it is a part of the gospel and the tradition of the Church. Paul only makes a vague reference to the idea of love without any explanation, because the Thessalonians know that all moral living rests on love, and they practice this love freely. ἀγάπη and φιλαδελφία formed the basis of the nascent Christian communities.

886 Tambyah, T. Isaac. "Θεοδίδακτοι. A Suggestion of an Implication of the Deity of Christ," *Expository Times* 44 (1933) 527-528.

Most understand 1 Thess 4:9 ("For you yourselves have been God-taught [θεο-δίδακτοι] to love one another") to point not so much to divine communication as to a divine relationship between believers and God inducing love. Paul, however, refers to a *direct* divine teaching given to believers. The unusual term θεοδίδακτοι refers to the teaching of Jesus in John 13:34 and 15:12, and *Jesus* is the "God" who is the author of the teaching of loving one another.

887 Ulonska, Herbert. "Christen und Heiden: Die paulinische Paränese in I Thess 4,3-8," *Theologische Zeitschrift* 43.1/2 (1987) 210-218.

1 Thess 4:3-8 belongs to what is probably the first and oldest letter of Paul to one of the Christian communities which he founded. In this correspondence the apostle says that the will of God is their holiness. By this Paul apparently means that they are to reject the sexual practices of the cult of Aphrodite, and that each person is to know his own wife. The concept of rejecting impurity and adopting holiness functioned as a belief which bound together the diverse members of the community. For Paul, the idea of brotherly love in the context of cult-practices of the surrounding world means rejecting the sexual element of lust between man and woman.

888 Vogel, Willy. "Εἰδέναι τὸ ἑαυτοῦ σκεῦος κτᾶσθαι. Zur Deutung von I Thess 4,3ff. im Zusammenhang der paulinischen Eheauffassung," *Theologische Blätter* 13 (1934) 83-85.

1 Thess 4:3-8 has proven difficult to interpret. The two major proposals are that "to acquire one's own vessel" means either "to take one's wife" (i.e., "to marry") or "to possess one's own wife in holiness and honor." These two proposals are subject to criticism, and point to a solution in light of 1 Cor 7:2-7. Paul expresses a reciprocal relationship of the husband being committed to the wife, and the wife remaining faithful to the husband, both under the authority of God.

889 Weima, Jeffrey A. D. "'How You Must Walk to Please God': Holiness and Discipleship in 1 Thessalonians 4:1-12," *Patterns of Discipleship in the New Testament* (ed. Richard N. Longenecker; McMaster New Testament Studies 1; Grand Rapids: Eerdmans, 1996) 98-119.

Although the theme of holiness is prominent throughout 1 Thessalonians, it especially comes to the fore in 4:1-12 where Paul deals with two specific problems threatening the Thessalonian church: sexual immorality and idleness. An examination of 1 Thess 4:1-12 in terms of its historical and social context, as well as the apostle's treatment of these two problems, demonstrates: (1) that Paul's exhortations here are grounded in his conviction that the predominantly Gentile believers at Thessalonica, as part of the renewed Israel or the eschatological people of God, already possess the gift of holiness, which was one of the anticipated blessings of the "new" or "everlasting" covenant in the Messianic Age, and (2) that in this passage Paul teaches that the distinguishing sign or boundary marker of authentic Christian existence, which separates believers in Christ from those of the world, is holiness.

890 Whitton, J. "A Neglected Meaning for *SKEUOS* in 1 Thessalonians 4.4," *New Testament Studies* 28.1 (1982) 142-143.

On the basis of a parallel Hebrew expression it is possible to translate 1 Thess 4:4 in the sense of "mastering one's (own) body," or, in this specific context, "controlling one's sexual urge," or "mastering one's self" in a sexual sense.

891 Wolniewicz, Marian. "'Ut sciat unusquisque vestrum vas suum possidere ...' (1 Thess 4,4)," *Roczniki Teologiczno-Kanoniczne* 10.2 (1963) 111-118.

The translator faces a definite challenge in attempting to render the intended sense of σκεῦος κτᾶσθαι in 1 Thess 4:4. Paul is not referring here to the believer's "wife" but rather to his "body" and the need for the Christian to have control over his body in the area of sexual conduct. This sense is confirmed by the parallelism between 1 Thess 4:3-8 and 1 Cor 6:12-20.

892 Yarbrough, O. Larry. "The Precepts on Marriage and Sexual Morality in 1 Thess 4:3-8," *Not Like the Gentiles: Marriage Rules in the Letters of Paul* (Society of Biblical Literature Dissertation Series 80; Atlanta: Scholars Press, 1986) 65-87.

The three precepts of 1 Thess 4:3-8 can best be translated as: "Abstain from sexual immorality; let each man know how to obtain his own wife; and let no man transgress against his brother by defrauding him in the matter of sexual relations." It is not these precepts themselves, however, but the claims about them which provide the real clues for understanding why Paul discusses marriage when writing to the Thessalonians. Paul reminds them of these precepts not because they had resorted to immoral practices or were in danger of doing so. Nor is he responding to questions on this subject matter brought by the returning Timothy. Paul is also not addressing these issues simply because they were standard topics in the Greco-Roman moral tradition. Instead, Paul refers to marriage and sexual morality because the traditional formulation of the precepts he knew distinguished believers from non-believers, and citing them would call attention to the special character of the community and their need to continue to lead a life which is pleasing to God.

893 Zsolt, Geréb. "A Thesszalonikabeliekhez írott elsö levél 4,1-8. Verseinek Magyarázata," *Református Szemle* 71.2 (1978) 171-176.

A verse-by-verse exposition of 1 Thess 4:1-8.

Other Relevant Sources:

332, 365, 438, 462, 499, 539, 549, 578, 596, 611, 643, 644, 739, 741, 1022, 1182, 1183, 1184, 1185, 1187, 1188, 1194, 1197, 1199.

H. 1 Thessalonians 4:13-18

894 Ahn Young-Sik, Joseph. "The Parousia in Paul's Letters to the Thessalonians, the Corinthians, and the Romans, in Relation to its Old Testament-Judaic Background" (Unpublished Ph.D. Dissertation; Pasadena, CA: Fuller Seminary, 1989).

Although the term is Hellenistic, Paul describes the parousia in theophanic language of the Old Testament. The parousia expectation is rooted in the Old Testament hope of the coming of God to his people in his final and glorious theophany. Moreover, to designate the parousia Paul uses the Day of Yahweh concept, which the prophets used to designate the intervention of God in various momentous historical events of the past, future, and imminent time. Furthermore, the coming of Christ at the end of the age is deeply related to the transcendental agent of God, in the apocalyptic writings, who descends from heaven in glory. Paul's teaching about the parousia functions differently depending on the historical context. The parousia is used to comfort and encourage the persecuted Christians at Thessalonica, to correct the overrealized eschatology at Corinth, and to support Paul's worldwide mission plan in his letter to the Romans. It is clear that the parousia is not just a peripheral but central theme of Paul's thought. With the Christ-event of the past (the "already"), the parousia of the future (the "not yet") stands as one of the two foci of his gospel.

895 Allison, Dale C., Jr. "The Pauline Epistles and the Synoptic Gospels: The Pattern of the Parallels," *New Testament Studies* 28 (1982) 1-32.

An examination of the explicit quotations and allusions to the Jesus tradition in Paul's letters leads to the conclusion that there is a pattern to the parallels. Most of the Pauline texts involved are not scattered evenly throughout the letters. The great majority are from just a handful of distinct portions of the correspondence: Romans 12-14, 1 Thessalonians 4-5, Colossians 3-4 and 1 Corinthians. In a similar fashion, the relevant synoptic texts are not randomly scattered throughout the gospels but belong for the most part to a few clearly distinct synoptic segments. This suggests that Paul knew and passed on to his churches at least three collections of logia: the sources which stand behind Mark 9:33-50, Luke 6:27-38, and the synoptic missionary discourses. It is also likely that Paul was familiar with a passion narrative, a collection of conflict stories, and several isolated sayings.

896 Allo, E. Bernard. "Saint Paul et la 'double résurrection' corporelle," *Revue Biblique* 41 (1932) 188-209.

Although millenarianism and discussions of a double resurrection exist in the writings both of the New Testament and of the church fathers, it is not possible to force these ideas on Paul. None of the Pauline passages which are applicable to the discussion of the parousia (1 Cor 15:22-26; 15:50-55; 1 Thess 4:13-18) speak of anything but an instantaneous, single resurrection.

897 Arróniz, José Manuel. "La parusía y su hermenéutica (1 Tes. 4,13-18)," *Lumen* 32.3 (1983) 193-213.

The apocalyptic background of 1 Thess 4:13-18 is manifested by the appearance of certain specific aspects: the paraenesis, the expectation of a near end of the times, the depiction of the eschatological events, and the participation of believers in the parousia. The imminence of the end, however, was not an essential element of Paul's faith, and a better understanding of the history of salvation and assurance of the presence of eschatological salvation allowed the apostle to come to terms with the delay of the parousia. It is for the same reasons that Paul later renounced the apocalyptic imagery of the passage while maintaining what was the central element of his hope, that is, being with Christ forever.

898 Askwith, Edward Harrison. "The Eschatological Section of 1 Thessalonians," *The Expositor, 8th Series* 1 (1911) 59-67.

A consideration of some grammatical and exegetical issues arising from 1 Thess 4:13-18 leads to the following conclusions. First, the prepositional phrase "through Jesus" in 4:14b should be taken with the earlier words "the ones who have fallen asleep" and not the following phrase "he will bring with him." The phrase "the ones who have fallen asleep through Jesus" means that these individuals were in a certain relationship with the risen and living Jesus when they died. Second, "the word of the Lord" in 4:15a refers to actual words from Jesus during his earthly ministry. Paul's deduction from these words is given in 4:15b, while the words themselves are found in 4:16. Third, the error of the Thessalonians who were grieving without hope for their dead arose from a misunderstanding of the future kingdom which they regarded as being of the earth. Paul corrects this wrong idea and highlights the supramundane character of the future resurrected life by teaching them that Christians will be taken up from the earth.

899 Baumgarten, Jörg. *Paulus und die Apokalyptik. Die Auslegung apokalyptischer Überlieferungen in den echten Paulusbriefen* (Wissenschaftliche Monographien zum Alten und Neuen Testament 44; Neukirchen-Vluyn: Neukirchener, 1975) 91-98.

1 Thess 4:13-18, which should be considered alongside 1 Cor 15:20-28, offers numerous problems of interpretation. Paul makes six related statements, including a christological creed regarding Jesus dying and rising, a promise regarding God raising those who sleep, an early Christian prophetic saying of Jesus, a depiction of an eschatological coming of Christ, an order to these events, and then a concluding statement that believers will be with the Lord. Paul does not address the origin of the question concerning those who are "asleep." His statements in this passage are designed to provide comfort for the community.

900 Becker, Jürgen. *Auferstehung der Toten im Urchristentum* (Stuttgarter Bibelstudien 82; Stuttgart: Katholisches Bibelwerk, 1976) 32-54.

1 Thess 4:13-18 shows, demonstrably for the first time in the history of early Christianity, how an actual problem over the death of Christians was worked out in the context of a Christian community. The traditional expectation of the parousia was expanded by Paul. The resurrection of the few dead Christians, whose death was seen as an exception in light of the general expectation of the imminent coming of the Lord, was expected on the basis of the analogy of what God had done for the dead Jesus in raising him up. On the basis of that expectation, all Christians will be together with the Lord.

901 ---. "Die Frage nach den entschlafenen Christen in 1 Thess 4,13-18," *Im Lichte der Reformation. Jahrbuch des Evangelischen Bundes* 23 (1980) 45-60.

In 1 Thess 4:13-18 Paul offers his view of Christian hope for those who die. He later revises this position, however, in 1 Corinthians 15 and Romans 8, after a consideration of the final destiny of Christians and the creation.

902 Bockmuehl, Markus N. A. "'The Trumpet Shall Sound': *Shofar* Symbolism and its Reception in Early Christianity," *Templum Amicitiae: Essays on the Second Temple Presented to Ernst Bammel* (ed. William Horbury; Journal for the Study of the New Testament Supplement Series 48; Sheffield: JSOT Press, 1991) 199-225.

Early Christian trumpet symbolism is characterized by the complete lack of any liturgical function for the instrument. Patristic thought, motivated by apologetic concerns and the contemporary philosophical critique of pagan ritual, developed into a considered opposition to all instrumental music. The remaining trumpet symbolism in the early fathers, therefore, tends to be reduced to pure allegory, so that the respective biblical passages come to mean anything *but* real trumpets. Instrumental music now belongs to the Old Testament past, but also to the worship of heaven and thus to the future. Thus, aside from their *ad hoc*, metaphorical use to denote the preaching of the gospel or the Christian life of worship, trumpets retain their original symbolic force in regard to only one area: the hope of the resurrection and the world to come.

903 Büttner, F. "Über die Entrückung der Gläubigen (1 Thess. 4,17)," *Neue kirchliche Zeitschrift* (also known as *Luthertum*) 9 (1898) 707-721.

The rapture of believers is an idea taught not only in 1 Thess 4:17 but elsewhere in scripture as well.

904 Cavallin, Hans C. "Parusi och uppståndelse: 1 Th. 4:13-18 som kombination av två slags eskatologi," *Svensk Teologisk Kvartalskrift* 59.2 (1983) 54-63.

A number of problems found in 1 Thess 4:13-18 (the reason for desperate mourning among the addressees, the asymmetry of the hypothetical construction, the relation of the phrase "through Jesus" to the verbs of verse 14, the meaning and contents of the "word of the Lord" of verse 15) may be explained by the assumption that Paul here introduces for the first time the Pharisaic Jewish belief in the resurrection of the dead into the primitive Christian expectation of the parousia. Paul appeals to the kerygma concerning Jesus' death and resurrection instead of the rabbinical arguments based on the Torah for the resurrection of the dead. The pericope may be described as a *consolatio mortis*, though very different from the Hellenistic and Roman philosophical ones found, for example, in Crantor and Cicero.

905 Cerfaux, Lucien. "The Second Coming," *Christ in the Theology of St. Paul* (trans. Geoffrey Webb and Adrian Walker; New York: Herder & Herder, 1959) 31-68. Originally published in French as *Le Christ dans la théologie de Saint Paul* (Lectio Divina 6; Paris: Cerf, 1954).

Although Paul uses a number of terms to describe the second coming of Christ ("apocalypse," "epiphany," "day of the Lord"), the term "parousia" is the most common. The scenario of the parousia is most clearly described in three passages: 1 Thess 4:13-18; 2 Thess 1:7-12; 2:3-12; and 1 Cor 15:20-28, 51-57. The description of the second coming in 1 Thessalonians shows quite clearly that Paul saw the parousia of Christ after the manner of a triumphal entrance in the Greco-Roman world. In light of this influence on Paul's thought, it can be seen that the apostle depicts Christians going out to meet the Lord so that they may come back with him in a procession to the earth where judgment will take place.

906 Collins, Raymond F. "From Good Friday to Easter: A Call for Metanoia," *Emmanuel* 98 (1992) 125-129, 147.

When Paul wrote about Jesus' resurrection "from the dead" (ἐκ τῶν νεκρῶν), it was always within the context of human solidarity. Because Paul considered Jesus' resurrection to have resulted from God's activity, he could write that, what God had done for Jesus, he will do for those who belong to Jesus (1 Thess 4:14-18; 1 Corinthians 15).

907 ---. "Tradition, Redaction, and Exhortation in 1 Thess 4,13-5,11," *L'apocalypse johannique et l'apocalyptique dans le Nouveau Testament* (ed. Jan Lambrecht; Bibliotheca ephemeridum theologicarum lovaniensium 53; Gembloux: Duculot, 1980) 325-343.

Republished in Ramond F. Collins, *Studies on the First Letter to the Thessalonians* (Bibliotheca ephemeridum theologicarum lovaniensium 66; Leuven: Leuven University Press, 1984) 154-172.

1 Thess 4:13-5:11 is a Pauline creation. The apostle has freely made use of traditional material, including not a few apocalyptic motifs, in order to supply what was lacking in the faith of the Thessalonians and to encourage them to live in accordance with their eschatological conditions. The use of apocalyptic motifs provides an explanation for Paul's assertion that the living will have no precedence over those who have died when it is a matter of salvation upon which one is focusing. Apocalyptic motifs intensify the challenge of the new mode of existence of the Thessalonian Christians. Throughout his exposition, whether focusing upon those who have died or those who are still alive, Paul proclaims the saving act of God and proclaims that Jesus is Lord. The time of the parousia matters little for both groups of believers. What is important is that Jesus is the ground of salvation for all who believe.

908 Cosby, Michael R. "Hellenistic Formal Receptions and Paul's Use of ΑΠΑΝΤΗΣΙΣ in 1 Thessalonians 4:17," *Bulletin for Biblical Research* 4 (1994) 15-34.

Erik Peterson's 1930 article (957) provided quotations from ancient papyri, inscriptions, and literature to demonstrate that behind Paul's words in 1 Thess 4:17 stands the custom of the Hellenistic formal reception of a dignitary. This viewpoint, widely held among biblical scholars, states that Paul presupposed that his readers in Thessalonica would understand his description of the parousia in light of such receptions. Thus the formal elements of these welcoming celebrations are unstated parts of the text because of Paul's use of the technical term ἀπάντησις. A re-examination of the relevant texts, however, reveals that ἀπάντησις was not a technical term and that all of the main elements of Hellenistic receptions are missing from 1 Thess 4:15-17. An analysis of the ancient descriptions of these receptions shows that most of their usual elements are actually the opposite of what one finds in Paul's description of the parousia. Instead of being a cipher for understanding what Paul meant, they function more as a foil--a loose pattern to play against when describing the coming of the heavenly king.

909 Custer, Stewart. "Prophetic Revelation," *Biblical Viewpoint* 9.1 (1975) 41-45.
A brief analysis of 1 Thess 4:13-18 ("The Reality of the Rapture") and 1 Thess 5:1-11 ("The Time of the Tribulation").

910 Delobel, Joël. "The Fate of the Dead according to 1 Thes 4 and 1 Cor 15," *The Thessalonian Correspondence* (ed. Raymond F. Collins; Bibliotheca ephemeridum theologicarum lovaniensium 87; Leuven: Leuven University Press, 1990) 340-347.
In Thessalonica, as well as in Corinth, Paul was faced with the issue of the fate of deceased Christians. In both cases, his answer is based on his fundamental conviction of Christ's resurrection and the future sharing in that resurrection by Christians. 1 Thess 4:15-17 and 1 Cor 15:51-52, in particular, exhibit significant parallels. From a methodological point of view, however, one must not underestimate the basic differences in the *Sitz im Leben* to which Paul's letters react, and not "over-extend" the data into an artificial harmonization. There exists between these passages basic differences which make any attempt to reconstruct a common source questionable.

911 Doignon, Jean. "La Lecture de I Thessalonians: 4:17 en occident de Tertullien à Augustin," *Jenseitsvorstellungen in Antike und Christentum. Gedenkschrift für Alfred Stuiber* (ed. T. Klauser and E. Dassmann; Jahrbuch für antike und Christentum 9; Münster: Aschendorff, 1982) 98-106.
Exegetes of 1 Thess 4:17 have debated whether this verse reflects Hellenistic or Jewish apocalypticism. Ancient exegetes from Tertullian to Augustine have tended to respond to this question in various ways: Tertullian evaluated the passage in terms of Stoicism; Hillary of Poitiers saw it as establishing the truthfulness of God; Ambrose saw it as paraenetic material on death; and Augustine read it as providing theological material concerning death.

912 Dupont, Jacques. "'Avec le Seigneur' a la Parousie," **ΣΥΝ ΧΡΙΣΤΩΙ**. *L'union avec le Christ suivant Saint Paul* (Paris: Desclée de Brouwer, 1952) 39-79.
The language of "meeting" in 1 Thess 4:17 has often been interpreted in terms of technical Hellenistic language. According to this imagery, when a visitor of importance came to a city, a group of citizens would go out to meet him and accompany him back to the city. This language, however, must be dismissed in light of the use of the language of meeting in the Septuagint. For example, the language of meeting in Exod 19:10-18, with its clouds, trumpets and the coming of the Lord, can account for Paul's use of similar language in 1 Thessalonians. This does not mean, however, that other language in the passage such as "appearance" is not Hellenistic.

913 Egelkraut, Helmuth. "Die Bedeutung von 1 Thess 4,13ff für eine Umschreibung christlicher Zukunftserwartung," *Zukunftserwartung in biblischer Sicht: Beiträge zur Eschatologie* (ed. Gerhard Maier; Monographien und Studienbücher 313; Wuppertal/Giessen: R. Brockhaus/Brunnen, 1984) 86-97.

1 Thess 4:13-18, despite its relative brevity, is central to Paul's view of this age, his missionary preaching, and especially the character of this letter. Paul states the thesis that believers have hope, and that this hope is grounded in faith, which is explicated by a "word of the Lord." Even though Christians have died, they have a hope grounded in what God has done and what he will do. This is expressed in a creedal formula, which links believers in a living relation with the death and life of Christ.

914 Ellingworth, Paul. "Which Way Are We Going? A Verb of Movement, especially in 1 Thess 4:14b," *The Bible Translator* 25 (1974) 426-431.

The translation of the verb ἄγω as "bring" in 1 Thess 4:14b implies that at some time in the future God, Jesus, and Christians who have died are coming down together from heaven to earth. This, however, is almost certainly not what Paul meant. The apostle's point of reference is on earth and he envisions Christians who have died as not coming down with Jesus from heaven but as being raised up by God to be with Jesus. One possible way to express this meaning is to translate 1 Thess 4:14b as: "so we believe that God will *take to himself*, with Jesus, those who have died believing in him."

915 Evans, Craig A. "Ascending and Descending with a Shout: Psalm 47.6 and 1 Thessalonians 4.16," *Paul and the Scriptures of Israel* (ed. Craig A. Evans and James A. Sanders; Journal for the Study of the New Testament Supplement Series 83; Studies in Scripture in Early Judaism and Christianity 1; Sheffield: JSOT Press, 1993) 238-253.

Although a number of Old Testament passages have been cited as the possible background of Paul's apocalyptic picture of Jesus' return in 1 Thess 4:16, no one (with the exception of a passing comment by Charles F. D. Moule) has seen a possible connection with Psalm 47:6. In addition to the verbal parallels between the Septagint of Psalm 46:6 and 1 Thess 4:16, both patristic and Jewish exegesis of this Old Testament passage confirms this possibility.

916 Fuchs, Ernst. "Hermeneutik?" *Theologia Viatorum* 7 (1960) 44-60.

1 Thess 4:13-18 and 5:1-11 have hermeneutical significance in answering questions concerning the end of the age, the timing of the parousia, and how this event will come about. Paul discusses these matters in connection with Jesus' death on the cross. The apostle's perspective, however, does not remain fixed on the cross but is strongly focused on the life of Jesus in our existence. With this established in our existence, we not only have hope during our lifetimes, but also have hope for the future fulfillment of God.

917 García del Moral, Antonio. "'Nosotros los vivos': ¿Convicción personal de Pablo o reinterpretación de un Salmo? (I Tes 4,13-5,11)," *Communio* 20.1 (1987) 3-56.

The content of "the word of the Lord" in 1 Thess 4:15 is more likely a reinterpretation of Psalm 115:18 (LXX) than Paul's personal inclusion among the living during the parousia. From that perspective, Paul would be defending the Christian teaching from Jewish attacks (mostly Sadducees), in which a better eschatological condition was argued for those who would be alive at the end of the times. Two aspects are highlighted in that defense. First, the souls of those who are dying in the Lord are brought immediately into the presence of the Lord (v 14). Second, the remnant--those who will be alive at the moment of the parousia--will not enjoy any advantage over the resurrected Christians (vv 15-17a). Paul ends with the exhortation contained in 4:17b-5:11, which, in a concentric fashion, highlights the theme of vigilance.

918 Gewalt, Dietfried. "1 Thess 4,15-17; 1 Kor 15,51 und Mk 9,1 - Zur Abgrenzung eines 'Herrenwortes,'" *Linguistica Biblica* 51 (1982) 105-113.

By comparing the texts of 1 Thess 4:15-17, 1 Cor 15:51 and Mark 9:1, a common "base-structure" containing some thirteen elements can be constructed. This base-structure is realized in three different paraphrastic "performances" which have specific syntactic, semantic, and pragmatic functions in their contexts. The semantic content of this base-structure is given in a metalinguistic description of "topics" which is not translated into an original Aramaic wording because this wording would only be another paraphrasis of the base-structure. The search for "words of the Lord" in Pauline letters is not useless, so that the hermeneutically negative function of 2 Cor 5:16 (according to Bultmann) is corrected.

919 Gillman, John. "Transformation and 1 Thess 4:13-18," "Transformation into the Future Life. A Study of 1 Cor 15:50-53, Its Context and Related Passages" (Unpublished Ph.D. Dissertation; Louvain: Catholic University of Louvain, 1980) 819-904.
Revised and republished as "Signals of Transformation in 1 Thessalonians 4:13-18," *Catholic Biblical Quarterly* 47.2 (1985) 263-281.

The relationship between the "assumption of the living and the dead" in 1 Thess 4:17 and the "transformation of the living and the dead" in 1 Cor 15:51-52 has long been a subject of controversy. There is no need or justification for resorting to developmental theories. Striking parallels of structure, themes, and vocabulary between these passages suggest that the theme of transformation, explicitly found in 1 Cor 15:51-52, is implicitly present in 1 Thess 4:15-17. This is confirmed by an analysis of the rapture and cloud imagery in 1 Thess 4:17. A survey of other future life passages (e.g., Phil 3:20-21; 2 Cor 5:1-10) confirms that transformation is a central motif in Paul's eschatological outlook.

920 Grässer, Erich. "1 Thess 4,13-18," *Bibelarbeiten, gehalten auf der rheinischen Landessynode 1967 in Bad-Godesberg* (Mühlheim, 1967) 10-20.

The problem with those dying in Thessalonica was probably not a major issue so long as the number of those dying was not large. When the numbers increased, however, the question was asked, not of what would happen to those who died, but of who would have the priority at the parousia: the ones who had died or those who were still living.

921 Green, E. M. B. "A Note on 1 Thessalonians iv. 15, 17," *Expository Times* 69 (1957) 285-286.

It is commonly held that Paul in 1 Thess 4:15, 17 expresses his belief that he will be among those who remain alive until the parousia, whereas in 2 Corinthians 5 he has given up this expectation. A closer examination of the context of the Thessalonian passage, however, suggests that Paul is not making a naive assertion about his personal expectations of survival, which he later had to revise. Rather, the apostle is directing a highly polemical thrust at those who did make such an assertion in Thessalonica, and drew from it the erroneous conclusion that they would gain an advantage over those who had predeceased them.

922 Gundry, Robert H. "A Brief Note on 'Hellenistic Formal Receptions and Paul's Use of ΑΠΑΝΤΗΣΙΣ in 1 Thessalonians 4:17,'" *Bulletin for Biblical Research* 6 (1996) 39-41.

Paul's description of the parousia in 1 Thess 4:15-17 comes closer to what we know of Hellenistic formal receptions than Michael Cosby (908) allows. Admittedly, ἀπάντησις does not by itself denote a reception of that kind. But the Thessalonian context, the αὐτός which calls special attention to Jesus' dignity as Lord or Emperor ("the Lord himself"--1 Thess 4:15), the remarkable fact that only here in the New Testament are Christians said to be "caught [up]...to meet the Lord in the air" (1 Thess 4:17, but see Matt 25:1, 6), and the appearance of elements of Hellenistic formal receptions also in other Pauline references to the parousia all combine to favor such a connotation for ἀπάντησις.

923 ---. "Comfort in 1 Thessalonians 4:13-5:11," *The Church and the Tribulation* (Grand Rapids: Zondervan, 1973) 100-111.

The theological and exegetical grounds for pretribulationism rest on insufficient evidence, *non sequitur* reasoning, and faulty exegesis. A careful analysis of 1 Thess 4:13-5:11 with respect to its historical context and key teachings (e.g., the "word of the Lord" in 4:15, the public nature of Christ's return in 4:16, the proper meaning of "to meet [εἰς ἀπάντησιν] the Lord in the air," the close relationship between 4:13-18 and 5:1-11, the reason why the Thessalonians needed to be instructed "concerning the times and seasons" in 5:1-11) provide positive evidence in support of a posttribulational understanding of Christ's return.

924 ---. "The Hellenization of Dominical Tradition and Christianization of Jewish Tradition in the Eschatology of 1-2 Thessalonians," *New Testament Studies* 33.2 (1987) 161-178.

In both 1 and 2 Thessalonians, earlier traditions--dominical and Jewish--are modified and used to correct certain misconceptions. Paul hellenizes dominical tradition in 1 Thess 2:19-20, 3:13 and 4:15-17 by portraying Christ's return as a festive imperial visit in which deceased as well as living Christians will participate. The hellenization has the purpose of correcting a wrong belief that the return will not involve the deceased. Paul then Christianizes Jewish tradition (e.g., 1 Thess 5:1-11: "the day of the Lord," "sons of day," image of birth pangs; 2 Thess 2:1-12: "the apostasy," "man of lawlessness") in order to heighten readiness for Christ's return--a readiness which he feared might be suffering from disappointment caused by the supposed non-participation of the deceased. The apostle also Christianizes Jewish tradition in order to cool down an overheated belief in the immediacy of Christ's return. The wish for quick release from persecution had fathered the thought of such release.

925 Guntermann, Friedrich. *Die Eschatologie des Hl. Paulus* (Münster: Aschendorff, 1932).
The grief experienced by the Thessalonians over "those who have fallen asleep" (1 Thess 4:13-18) stems from their failure to believe in the teaching regarding the resurrection of the dead. This lack of belief probably stems from the fact that Paul had not preached on the resurrection and is not due to any gnostic influence. The assertion that the day of the Lord is already here (2 Thess 2:2) is best clarified through gnostic influence. Regarding the falling away of believers, there is the difficulty of 2 Thess 2:3. The political meaning of the passage is to be rejected, as is the religious one of a Gentile and a Jewish apostasy. Instead, a Christian apostasy is likely, indicated already by antinomian and libertine tendencies from gnostic circles. The Antichrist (2 Thess 2:3-12) is not a moral force but a person. He is not Satan or a Jewish false messiah, but a superhuman, demonic being who already exists. Although identification of him with a certain temporal personality cannot be done, Paul or his source would have been able to link him with historical personages. The hindrance for the appearance of the Antichrist also cannot be identified with certainty, although it is probably a good force and not the Antichrist. The source of this tradition is uncertain, although mythological echoes are worth noting.

926 Haack, Ernst. "Eine exegetisch-dogmatische Studie zur Eschatologie über I Thessalonicher 4:13-18," *Zeitschrift für systematische Theologie* 15 (1938) 544-569.
Paul turns at 1 Thess 4:1 to admonition, including in 4:13-18 dogmatic teaching with the purpose of clarifying the comfort spoken of in verse 18 so that the Thessalonian believers might no longer grieve. Their pain appears to be due to the fact that some members of the community have died. Paul clarifies and comforts his readers by explaining that the death of these Christians is not permanent, using the euphemistic language of "sleep."

927 Harnisch, Wolfgang. *Eschatologische Existenz. Ein exegetischer Beitrag zum Sachanliegen von 1 Thessalonicher 4,13-5,11* (Forschungen zur Religion und Literatur des Alten und Neuen Testaments 110; Göttingen: Vandenhoeck & Ruprecht, 1973).
1 Thess 4:13-5:11 is a teaching section of Paul's letters where in a rather unique way almost all the central themes of his theology are allowed to ring out. 1 Thess 4:13-18 concerns hope for the dead and 5:1-11 deals with the eschatological existence of the believers. In the latter passage, there is a contrast between the past in verses 1-3 and the Pauline gospel with its apocalyptic orientation in verses 4-10, with the christological grounding in verses 9-10. These two sections nevertheless have a unity. The negative and positive in a Pauline antithesis are not merely ornamental.

928 Hartman, Lars. "The Eschatological Discourse and the Letters to the Thessalonians," *Prophecy Interpreted: The Formation of Some Jewish Apocalyptic Texts and of the Eschatological Discourse, Mark 13 Par* (Coniectanea Biblica, New Testament Series 1; Lund: Gleerup, 1966) 178-205.

The striking parallels between Paul's letters to the Thessalonians (1 Thess 4:13-18; 5:1-11; 2 Thess 1:1-12) and the eschatological discourse of Mark 13 (and its parallel synoptic passages) show that the apostle was familiar with the Old Testament texts which underlie that discourse. Paul bases his eschatological teaching to the Thessalonians on an earlier form of Mark 13 which he regards as an authoritative "tradition" originating from Jesus. That Paul is aware of the "midrashic" basis of this Jesus tradition can be seen in the fact that he supplements it with more Old Testament material (e.g., Dan 12:2 on the resurrection; Ezekiel 28 on the blasphemies of the lawless one; perhaps also the "restraining" force/person).

929 Haufe, Günter. "Funktion und Interpretation Urchristlicher Bekenntnissätze," *Theologische Literaturzeitung* 110.11 (1985) 785-794.

On the basis of form-critical and literary grounds, one can identify a number of confessional statements throughout the New Testament. Such statements are made to serve a number of different theological functions. These include succinct commentaries on Christian proclamation and belief (Rom 10:9), signs of kerygmatic-church unity (1 Cor 15:3b-5), foundations of theological argumentation (1 Thess 4:14), foundations of paraenetic argumentation (1 Cor 6:14), criticism opposing erroneous beliefs (1 Cor 12:3), and high points of Christian history (Phil 2:6-11).

930 Hayes, D. A. "A Study of a Pauline Apocalypse. I Thess. 4:13-18," *Biblical World* 37 (1911) 163-175.

1 Thess 4:13-18, along with 2 Thess 2:1-12 and 1 Cor 15:35-58, shows that Paul's eschatological conceptions were largely clothed in imagery typical of Jewish apocalyptic. Just as in the parables of Jesus one should look for the central truth of the story and ignore its minor details, so the same hermeneutical approach should be followed also in the apocalyptic passages of Paul. The central truth of 1 Thess 4:13-18 is that neither death nor life can separate the Christian from the Lord. There are great dangers associated with the attempt to interpret apocalyptic symbols literally and to deduce doctrines from the details of apocalyptic imagery. These dangers are well illustrated by the "Millerite" movement of 1843 and the "Doomsealer" excitement of 1890.

931 Herman, Zvonimir Izidor. "Il significato della morte e della rísurrezione di Gesù nel contesto escatologico di 1 TS 4,13 - 5,11," *Antonianum* 55.3 (1980) 327-351.

The eschatological section of 1 Thessalonians (4:13-5:11) opens and closes with two explicit references to Jesus' death and resurrection (4:14; 5:9-10). A study of this soteriological event in the context of 4:13-5:11 leads to the following conclusions. First, the fact that this pericope presupposes a present experience of salvation which is grounded in the death of Jesus and guaranteed at his return shows that Paul's theology possesses a well-defined form already very early in his writing ministry. Second, instead of dividing the pericope into the two parts of 4:13-18 and 5:1-11, as is typically done, a better division would be that of 4:13-5:3 and 5:4-11. Third, the principal argumentation which Paul uses to alleviate the grief of the Thessalonian believers is the present experience of salvation--an experience which is grounded in the death of Christ.

932 Hoffmann, Paul. "Die Bedeutung von 1 Thess 4,13-5,11 für die Vorstellung des Paulus vom 'Zwischenzustand,'" *Die Toten in Christus. Eine religionsgeschichtliche und exegetische Untersuchung zur paulinischen Eschatologie* (Neutestamentliche Abhandlungen 2; Münster: Aschendorff, 1966) 207-238.

1 Thess 4:13-5:11 reveals Paul's thinking on the time between the two comings of Christ. The theme of this passage is established through the concrete situation at Thessalonica in which Paul has heard that some have died, even though the imminent future return of Christ has not occurred. Paul's understanding of the place of death for Christians in the time between their death and resurrection (i.e., the intermediate state) is not addressed here. The emphasis is on life between the two comings of Christ.

933 Howard, Tracy L. "The Literary Unity of 1 Thessalonians 4:13-5:11," *Grace Theological Journal* 9.2 (1988) 163-190.

There are several compelling reasons for taking 1 Thess 4:13-5:11 as one literary unit and not as two distinct units separated by the περὶ δέ formula of 5:1. First, Paul's purpose is the same in both sections, namely, paraenetic. Paul points out the different effects which the parousia/Day of the Lord will have for believers and nonbelievers. Second, Paul appears to be describing a single aoristic event from two perspectives. For the believer this event will be a time of blessing and thus Paul uses the word "parousia" (4:13-18), whereas for the unbeliever it will be a time of judgment and thus Paul shifts his terminology to the "Day of Lord" (5:1-11). The third and fourth reasons are the most significant. The parallels exhibited with the Olivet Discourse, along with the inclusio between 4:13-14 and 5:9-10, support the claim that the entire passage is a single literary unit. Thus there is no reason to regard 5:1-11 either as a non-Pauline interpolation or as a reference to a different situation and event than that found in 4:13-18.

934 Hunzinger, Claus H. "Die Hoffnung angesichts des Todes im Wandel der Paulinischen Aussagen," *Leben angesichts des Todes. Beiträge zum theologischen Problem des Todes. Helmut Thielicke zum 60. Geburtstag* (ed. M. L. Henry *et al.*; Tübingen: Mohr/Siebeck, 1968) 69-88.

From the beginning, in so far as his oldest letter bears witness, the hope which Paul had was the knowledge of Christ in the face of death. The apostle always clearly announces this certainty, even though it is controversial regarding the concrete shape which this hope takes in Paul's presentation of it. Three passages are especially relevant to this subject: 1 Thess 4:13-18, 1 Corinthians 15 and Phil 1:21-26. In 1 Thessalonians,

Paul was unprepared for the death of a few members of the Christian community, since there was the expectation that all believers would live until the parousia. Paul himself had the expectation that the parousia would come before his death (1 Thess 4:15, 17). 1 Thess 4:13-18 is the oldest testimony regarding this problem. Here the hope for the dead is founded on both the resurrection of Jesus Christ and the word of the Lord, which is dependent upon an early Christian apocalyptic tradition. The goal of these apocalyptic events is that all believers end up being with the Lord--those who are alive at the parousia as well as those who have fallen asleep.

935 Hyldahl, Niels. "Auferstehung Christi--Auferstehung der Toten (1 Thess 4,13-18)," *Die paulinische Literatur und Theologie: Anlässlich der 50. jährigen Grüdungs-Feier der Universität von Ärhus* (ed. Sigfred Pedersen; Teologiske Studien 7; Göttingen: Vandenhoeck & Ruprecht, 1980) 119-135.

Most discussions of 1 Thess 4:13-18 handle the "resurrection of Christ" as a theme of New Testament theology and the "resurrection of the dead" as reflecting Jewish eschatological and apocalyptic thought. Rarely does New Testament exegesis try to relate the one to the other. This passage probably reflects Paul's adaptation of the resurrection of Christ to the unforeseen problem of Christian dying. The bringing of these Christians to life is seen as a form of resurrection but one which does not have anything to do with the general resurrection of the dead mentioned in 1 Cor 15:23.

936 Jackson, Paul Norman. *An Investigation of* κοιμάομαι *in the New Testament: The Concept of Eschatological Sleep* (Lewiston, NY: Mellen, 1996).

A diachronic and synchronic investigation of the concept of the "sleep of death" metaphor in pagan and biblical literature sheds light on the meaning of κοιμάομαι in the New Testament. Some of the principal conclusions reached are as follows. First, while the biblical tradition verbally assimilated the pagan notion of the "sleep of death," it conceptually departed from it with respect to its ontological model. Second, the "wholistic dualism" model is compatible with biblical anthropology, thanatology, and eschatology. Monism, therefore, is not the only ontological option for the postmortem state. Third, κοιμάομαι, in a predominant sense, theologically and functionally situates each deceased Christian in the pre-parousia disposition of the intermediate state in an intimate, conscious relationship with Christ.

937 Jones, Kenneth Lynn. "A Study of 1 Thessalonians 4:13-5:11 in the Light of Various Millennial Theories" (Unpublished Ph.D. Dissertation; Fort Worth, TX: Southwestern Baptist Theological Seminary, 1981).

An exegetical analysis of 1 Thess 4:13-5:11, along with a survey of various millennial theories, leads to the following conclusions. The most extensive treatment of the passage has been done by pretribulation-rapture premillennialists. This is because they see the passage as one of the basic statements of the pretribulation rapture of the church. The other millennial theories have treated the passage primarily in opposition to the pretribulation-rapture view. Each millennial theory has its own particular assets and liabilities. No absolutely final answers as to the validity or invalidity of any single millennial theory can be forthcoming from this passage. This conclusion is the most damaging to the pretribulation-rapture theory which relies most heavily upon this passage to establish its position. In 1 Thess 4:13-5:11 Paul was dealing with specific questions faced by the Thessalonian church and not giving a discourse on eschatology in general or on the millennium in particular.

938 Jurgensen, Hubert. "Awaiting the Return of Christ: A Re-Examination of 1 Thessalonians 4:13-5:11 from a Pentecostal Perspective," *Journal of Pentecostal Theology* 4 (1994) 81-113.

A synchronic (context, delimitation, structure, philology, grammar, rhetoric) and diachronic (use of traditional materials) analysis of the two parts of 1 Thess 4:13-5:11 makes clear not only the intentions of Paul and the situation of the Thessalonian church but also the significance that this passage has for Pentecostal theology today. The enthusiastic expectation of the return of Christ has frequently led into unhealthy speculation about dates and details. But while Pentecostal theology should continue to take seriously the hope of the parousia of Christ and hold to an "eschatology of waiting," it should also shift the focus from apocalyptic speculations to an attitude of constant vigilance in light of the nearness of Christ's coming.

939 ---. "Saint Paul et la parousie: 1 Thessaloniciens 4.13-5.11 dans l'exégèse moderne et contemporaine" (Unpublished Ph.D. Dissertation; Strasbourg: Université des Sciences Humaines de Strasbourg, 1992).

Traditional Protestant and Catholic exegesis, with its supernatural and literalistic presuppositions, discovered in 1 Thess 4:13-5:11 an essential eschatological teaching of Paul on the second coming of Christ in the endtime. The rise of the historical-critical method replaced this approach with a free investigation of this passage's meaning founded upon philological, grammatical, and historical study. This major transformation was reinforced by a growing rational criticism, which rejected supernatural events such as the return of Christ. It is no surprise that a variety of interpretative approaches (e.g., literary criticism, evolutionary theory, psychological explanations) has called into question the meaning of the pericope. Some today maintain the expectation of Christ's return, while others reinterpret it timelessly or existentially, or simply reject it entirely. Exegetes have shown special interest in the *Sitz im Leben* of 4:13-18, its place in Pauline eschatology (primitive stage?), its relationship to Jewish apocalyptic, Paul's use of early traditions, and the definition of the "Word of the Lord" in verse 15. But it is the hermeneutics of the text, particularly the meaning of apocalyptic eschatology, which divides most interpreters.

940 Kassing, Altfrid. "Der Tod im Leben des Christen nach dem Apostel Paulus," *LiMö* 25 (1959) 7-21.

Even though Paul did not reckon with his own death in the first two decades of his Christian life (1 Thess 4:13-18), his entire thought nevertheless emanated from the beginning from death and revolved around it.

941 Kettner, Edward G. "Time, Eternity, and the Intermediate State," *Concordia Journal* 12 (1986) 90-100.

The traditional view that the soul survives death and continues to exist in a disembodied state between death and resurrection, and during that time experiences either salvation or condemnation, has been increasingly challenged in recent times. Some have forwarded the idea that at death the individual moves from time into a timeless eternity, in which the resurrection has already taken place. A look at scripture's way of referring to death and time, however, shows that it never speaks of eternity as timelessness and clearly allows for the existence of an intermediate state.

942 Klijn, A. F. J. "1 Thessalonians 4:13-18 and Its Background in Apocalyptic Literature," *Paul and Paulinism: Essays in Honour of C. K. Barrett* (ed. Morna D. Hooker and Stephen G. Wilson; London: SPCK, 1982) 67-73.

1 Thess 4:13-18 can be explained entirely against the background of apocalyptic thinking. This applies not only to the question which the Thessalonians ask but also the answer which Paul gives. The problem at Thessalonica was a belief expressed in a number of apocalyptic writings (e.g., PssSol 17:50; 18:7; 4 Ezra 6:25; 7:27), namely, that survival until the end time was a special privilege. Thus some in the Thessalonian church wondered whether those believers who had already died would be somewhat at a disadvantage. Paul's answer was one which is also found in apocalyptic literature (e.g., 4 Ezra 6:20; 2 Bar 30:2; 51:13; Ps.Philo): at the end all people involved will partake in the events at the same time. At God's judgment there will be no earlier and later, but everything will happen simultaneously so that no one will be disadvantaged.

943 Löhr, Gebhard. "1 Thess 4:15-17: Das 'Herrenwort,'" *Zeitschrift für die neutestamentliche Wissenschaft* 71.3 (1980) 269-273.

On the basis of their styles, 1 Thess 4:15 and 1 Cor 15:15-52 must refer to the same "word of the Lord." There are two parts to the saying. The first refers to the moment: with a trumpet of God and a shout the Lord will come down from heaven and will raise those who are sleeping. The second refers to the participants: those who are living will be led in the clouds to a meeting of the Lord in the air. The second part may well have its background in Exod 19:17-25. The passage probably does not have to do with gnostics because of its apocalyptic-eschatological character.

944 Lüdemann, Gerd. "The Hope of the Early Paul: From the Foundation-Preaching at Thessalonika to I Cor. 15:51-57," *Perspectives in Religious Studies* 7.3 (1980) 195-201.

An exegetical study of 1 Thess 4:13-17 and 1 Cor 15:51-57 demonstrates that between Paul's first visit to Thessalonica and the time of writing 1 Corinthians his eschatological hope has undergone some changes. Paul shifts from a parousia-centered hope in which virtually all Christians will be alive at Christ's return to a resurrection-centered hope where survival has become an exception.

945 Magnien, P. M. "La Résurrection des Morts. D'après la première épître aux Thessaloniciens. Étude exégétique sur I Th. IV,13 - V,3," *Revue Biblique* 4 (1907) 349-382.

The members of the young Christian church in Thessalonica fell into desperation regarding their dead only because they wondered whether the deceased would be raised quickly enough to enjoy the graces of the messianic era--an era which they expected to come in the fashion of the millenarianist's writings of 4 Ezra and the Apocalypse of Baruch. Paul's words in 1 Thess 4:13-5:3, therefore, are not addressed to a church which had lost faith in the idea of the resurrection, but simply to one which was concerned with the times and dates (hence 5:1-3) with respect to their millenarian outlook.

946 Marxsen, Willi. "Auslegung von 1 Thess 4,13-18," *Zeitschrift für Theologie und Kirche* 66 (1969) 22-37.

A verse-by-verse analysis of 1 Thess 4:13-18 reveals that Paul is not primarily concerned with the resurrection of the dead but with the parousia. That Paul expected the resurrection of the dead is clear from the fact that he shared the Jewish belief of his day. But from the beginning the expectation of the parousia was foremost in his mind, and it was the main concern in his preaching to the Thessalonians. 1 Thess 4:13-18 should not be interpreted in light of 1 Corinthians 15, since the latter passage was written some years later and there was undoubtedly an evolution in Paul's thinking during this time. The phrase "we the living" (v 15) did not belong in the original text and an analysis of verses 16-17 shows that the resurrection of the dead is missing from the primitive wording. Had Paul been concerned with the resurrection, he would have made it a theme of his message.

947 Mason, John Philip. *The Resurrection according to Paul* (Lewiston, NY: Mellen, 1993).

The prevailing view that Paul's understanding of the resurrection arose primarily out of his experience of having seen the risen Christ Jesus fails to recognize the impact which apocalyptic tradition had on the apostle's thought. Paul inherited the connection of the resurrection of the dead with the day of the Lord's judgment from Jewish and early Christian apocalyptic traditions. Judaism also provided Paul with reflection upon the ethical implications of the resurrection of the dead. The Greek world of that day possessed a widespread pessimism about the fate of the dead. It is not surprising, then, that Paul expressed the Christian hope of the resurrection of the dead in terms borrowed from Jewish apocalyptic, even in the Greek setting of Thessalonica. In apocalyptic thinking, life after death was optimistically stated in terms of resurrection. The apocalyptic tradition which Paul cited in 1 Thess 4:16-17a provided the apostle with a temporal sequence and a depiction of glory of the last events.

948 Merklein, Helmut. "Der Theologe als Prophet: Zur Funktion prophetischen Redens im theologischen Diskurs des Paulus," *New Testament Studies* 38 (1992) 402-429.

What function does prophetic speech have in the theological discourse of Paul? The answer to this question is found in a study of 1 Thess 4:13-18. The prophetic utterance in this passage is limited to 4:15b with 4:16-17 consisting of elaborations of this utterance which make use of a variety of traditional apocalyptic motifs. A comparison of 1 Thess 4:13-18 with 1 Cor 15:50-58 points to clear parallels between these two passages. The function of prophetic speech is also illuminated by a study of 1 Cor 2:6-16 and Rom 11:25-36. For Paul revelation did not end with the kerygma. Prophecy was an important source of theological knowledge and the medium which makes theology relevant.

949 Meyer, Ben F. "Did Paul's View of the Resurrection of the Dead Undergo Development?" *Theological Studies* 47 (1986) 363-387.

In the debate over development in Pauline eschatology, there are two main positions. The maximalist position argues that Paul moved from a relatively crude, conventional affirmation of resurrection to a more refined conception of survival, and often characterizes this change as a transition from Jewish to Greek categories. The minimalist position doubts or denies any development, but frequently acknowledges the appearance of new, if minor, doctrinal elements in the later texts. A historical survey from Otto Pfleiderer (1873) to the present shows that current opinion on the relevant texts resists any consensus on the issue of development. An exegetical study of 1 Thessalonians 4, 1 Corinthians 15, 2 Corinthians 5 and Phil 1:23, however, supports the minimalist position and demonstrates that there is a total lack of persuasive evidence that Paul's teaching on the resurrection of the dead underwent significant development.

950 ---. "Paul and the Resurrection of the Dead," *Theological Studies* 48 (1987) 157-158.

Joseph Plevnick has recently argued (960) that the words "and thus we shall be with the Lord always" (1 Thess 4:17b) indicate entry into a new mode of existence. This suggests that the translation or assumption of believers is itself understood as transformative and is the functional equivalent of "we shall be changed" in 1 Cor 15:51. Therefore, there is no substantial development of eschatology between 1 Thessalonians and 1 Corinthians. What is new in 1 Corinthians 15, however, is Paul making explicit the "mystery" of the transformation of the living at the parousia as the counterpart of the resurrection of the dead.

951 Michaels, J. Ramsey. "Everything that Rises Must Converge: Paul's Word from the Lord," *To Tell the Mystery. Essays on New Testament Eschatology in Honor of Robert H. Gundry* (ed. Thomas E. Schmidt and Moisés Silva; Journal for the Study of the New Testament Supplement Series 100; Sheffield: JSOT Press, 1994) 182-195.

The "word of the Lord" (v 15a) to which Paul appeals in 1 Thess 4:13-18 is not to be found in verses 16-17, as most commentators assert, but in verse 15b ("we, the living...will not precede those who have fallen asleep"). Here Paul appeals to simple fairness as articulated in one of Jesus' well-remembered sayings recorded in Matt 20:16, "So the last will be first, and the first last." To Paul, this "word of the Lord" was a promise of equity or equality between the advantaged and the disadvantaged, in this case equity at the time of the parousia between the dead and the living.

952 Mounce, Robert H. "Pauline Eschatology and the Apocalypse," *Evangelical Quarterly* 46.3 (1974) 164-166.

There are some clear linguistic and conceptual parallels between the eschatology of the Thessalonian letters and the Apocalypse of John. The references in 1 Thess 4:13-18 to an archangel, a trumpet, and clouds are all paralleled in one way or another in Revelation. The parallels in 2 Thess 2:1-12 are even closer, especially with Revelation 13, 17, 19, and 20, and the emphasis on the Antichrist's blasphemy, demand for worship, supernatural and deceptive power, and destruction by Christ. Behind these two separate eschatological presentations, therefore, lay a common source of apocalyptic concept and imagery.

953 Neirynck, Frans. "Paul and the Sayings of Jesus," *L'Apôtre Paul. Personnalité, style et conception du ministère* (ed. A. Vanhoye; Bibliotheca ephemeridum theologicarum lovaniensium 73; Leuven: Leuven University Press, 1986) 265-321.

In the Pauline letters there are only two instances of an explicit reference to a command of the Lord (1 Cor 7:10-11; 9:14; see 1 Thess 4:15), but there is no quotation of the saying. Elsewhere there is no clear evidence for the conscious use of sayings of Jesus by Paul. Possible allusions to gospel sayings can be noted on the basis of similarity of form and context (e.g., 1 Thess 2:14-16; 4:8, 15-17; 5:2, 4, 13, 15) but a direct use of a gospel saying in the form it has been preserved in the synoptic gospels is hardly provable. Paul's knowledge of a pre-synoptic gospel, the Q-source, or pre-Q collections has not yet been demonstrated. Because of the paucity and the anonymity of the possible allusions and reminiscences, and because of their appearance together with other ethical teaching in the paraenetic sections, it remains doubtful whether Paul was using them as saying of Jesus.

954 Nepper-Christensen, Poul. "Das verborgene Herrnwort. Eine Untersuchung über 1. Thess 4,13-18," *Studia Theologica* 19.1-2 (1965) 136-154.

The closest Pauline parallel to 1 Thess 4:16-17 is 1 Cor 15:51-52, where the apostle, even if in another formulation, has made use of the same word of Jesus. In response to a question from the Thessalonians concerning the martyrs who have died because of their loyalty to Christ (v 14, διὰ τοῦ Ἰησοῦ), Paul cites a word of the Lord (v 15, the ground introduced by γάρ). The actual quotation is found in vv 16-17, verbatim in v 16a (beginning with ὅτι), and with modifications in vv 16b-17 (e.g., the "we" form). The quotation itself refers to the parousia, the resurrection, and those who will be alive at that eschatological event, but it is mostly the last of these three points which interests Paul here.

955 Omanson, Roger L. "Comings and Goings in the Bible," *The Bible Translator* 46.1 (1995) 112-119.

Translators of the New Testament into English need to pay more attention to the point of reference in translating Greek verbs of motion such as ἔρχομαι and ἄγω. For example, it needs to be made clear in 1 Thess 4:14 that Jesus *takes away from the earth* those Christians who were dead but have now been raised. Thus the future ἄξει in this verse should be rendered "will take back from earth." In conjunction with this translation of 4:14, one should translate the word ἅγιοι in 1 Thess 3:13 not as "saints" (i.e., deceased believers) but as "angels."

956 Parnham, F. S. "What is the Christian's Expectation?" *Evangelical Quarterly* 41.2 (1969) 113-115.

The New Testament presents the Christian's expectation as the one-time, visible, public, and glorious manifestation of the Lord, not some earlier, secret coming. This conclusion is supported by a study of the words ἀποκάλυψις ("revelation") and ἐπιφάνεια ("appearing") and how they function in significant passages (e.g., 1 Cor 1:7; 2 Thess 1:7; 1 Pet 1:5, 7, 13; 1 Tim 6:14; 2 Tim 4:1; Rom 8:19).

957 Peterson, Erik. "Die Einholung des Kyrios," *Zeitschrift für systematische Theologie* 7 (1930) 682-702.

In the eschatological section of 1 Thess 4:13-18 Paul uses the word ἀπάντησις to describe the "meeting" of the church, both the resurrected dead and the living believers, with the returning Christ. This word was a technical term in that day, referring to the ceremonial reception accorded to a distinguished person at their coming. This usage can be seen in the ancient sources, including papyri, inscriptions, Greek literature, and Latin texts. This understanding explains its use in 1 Thess 4:17, as well as other New Testament texts, and is endorsed by the understanding of the early church.

958 Plevnik, Joseph. "The Parousia as Implication of Christ's Resurrection: An Exegesis of 1 Thes 4,13-18," *Word and Spirit: Essays in Honor of David Michael Stanley on his 60th Birthday* (ed. Joseph Plevnik; Toronto: Regis College, 1975) 199-277.

1 Thess 4:13-18 is a consoling and comforting instruction concerning the participation of deceased believers in the parousia of Christ. The first part of Paul's argument (v 14) contains an extrapolation from the past saving event of Jesus' death and resurrection to the future presence of the faithful at his parousia. Here Paul makes use of an early creedal statement of the church and language which appears to recall the memory of Israel's exodus from Egypt. The second part (vv 15-17) is prefaced and characterized by "a word of the Lord" and gives an authoritative assurance about the participation of the deceased believers in that future event. Here Paul drew on a more general logion which had been attributed to Jesus and which he creatively adapted to the new situation. The parousia of the Lord is depicted in imagery from Old Testament and apocalyptic sources.

959 ---. *Paul and the Parousia. An Exegetical and Theological Investigation* (Peabody, MA: Hendrickson, 1997).

An exegetical study of Paul's references to the parousia (1 Thess 4:13-18; 5:1-11; 1 Cor 15:24-27; 15:51-53; Phil 3:20-21) and a theological analysis of the parousia from the soteriological-Christocentric, judicial, antagonistic, and ecclesiological aspects provides a two-fold means to grasp the apostle's understanding of this teaching and his use of apocalyptic imagery. If the gospel is to be relevant for the contemporary audience, these statements of Paul concerning the return of Christ must be expressed in the idiom of the present day. But before stripping Paul's language of its mythological imagery, their meaning and function in the particular context must be determined, in order to preserve the central truths which Paul propounded by means of these images.

960 ---. "The Taking Up of the Faithful and the Resurrection of the Dead in 1 Thessalonians 4:13-18," *Catholic Biblical Quarterly* 46.2 (1984) 274-283.

If, as the tenor of 1 Thess 4:13-18 suggests, Paul had already taught the Thessalonians that at the parousia of Christ they would all be assumed and gathered around the risen Lord forever, then the death of some of the faithful would obviously cause consternation in the church. It would be thought that the dead could not participate in the assumption--for one had to be alive to be assumed. Paul responds to this problem by showing that the deceased will be raised and participate fully with living believers in the parousia. The cause of grief in Thessalonica, therefore, was due not to the failure of Paul to teach the resurrection of the dead, but rather to the misunderstanding of his unique depiction of the believers' sharing in the parousia through their assumption.

961 ---. "The Ultimate Reality in 1 Thessalonians," *Ultimate Reality and Meaning* 12 (1989) 256-271.

The ultimate reality and meaning of existence, which is God himself and his kingdom, is taken for granted in 1 Thessalonians. Paul had earlier introduced the Thessalonians to this knowledge of God which involves God the Father, God's Son, the Holy Spirit as the Father's gift and the knowledge of God's will. At this stage of his ministry, Paul was greatly concerned with the ultimate fulfillment which he expected at the coming of the Lord from heaven in the endtime. While there are passing allusions to the ultimate fulfillment in the first half of the letter, it is in the second half, especially 4:13-5:11, where the picture of the parousia comes into full focus. Paul's imagery is not influenced by Hellenistic presentations of imperial parousias, as is commonly claimed, but presentations of assumptions in the Old Testament and apocalyptic writings.

962 Reese, James M. "A Linguistic Approach to Paul's Exhortation in 1 Thess 4:13-5:11," *SBL 1980 Seminar Papers* (ed. Paul J. Achtemeier; SBL Seminar Papers 19; Chico, CA: Scholars Press, 1980) 209-218.

Insights from linguistics and communication theory help the modern reader to hear Paul's message as he intended himself to be heard. In analyzing the communication act, one the most successful linguists has been Roman Jakobson, who identifies six factors in the "speech act": addresser, message, addressee, context, contact, and code. Each of these factors determines a different function of the language of communication, which functions are emotive, poetic, conative, referential, phatic, and metalinguistic. The application of this method to 1 Thess 4:13-18 and 5:1-11 reveals many linguistic factors in the text which are commonly overlooked or misjudged with respect to their function and significance.

963 Robinson, John A. T. "The Challenge of Thessalonians," *Jesus and His Coming. The Emergence of a Doctrine* (Nashville: Abingdon, 1957) 104-117.

Of the eschatological material in 1 and 2 Thessalonians, the more apocalyptic the passage, the remoter is its connection with anything in the Gospel tradition which may claim to be primitive or provide evidence for the teaching of Jesus, and *vice versa*. By the time of the earliest Pauline writings, the expectation of the parousia is already present in as fully developed form as it was ever to attain within the New Testament. Thereafter, the problem shifted to the *delay* of that which in itself was clearly defined, and to the relation between what were subsequently to be designated as two parousias.

964 Romeo, A. "'Nos qui vivimus qui residui sumus' (1 Thess. 4, 13-18)," *Verbum Domini* 9 (1929) 307-312, 339-347, 360-364.

It cannot be concluded from 1 Thess 4:13-18 that Paul expected the parousia in his lifetime. In fact, he is not dealing here at all with the timing of Christ's second coming. Rather, his concern is to comfort the Thessalonians by stressing the future reunification of currently living believers with their recently deceased loved ones at the parousia. A proper understanding of verse 15 shows that the participles ζῶντες and περιλειπόμενοι do not have a future but a present reference, and that the phrase εἰς τὴν παρουσίαν is not to be construed with περιλειπόμενοι but with φθάσωμεν. The crucial sentence should be understood to mean: "We, the currently living survivors (i.e., Paul and the grieving Thessalonians), will not encounter the Lord's appearance spatially ahead of (i.e., separated from) those who died before us." This interpretation essentially follows that of the church father Ephraem Syrus.

965 Rossano, Piero. "A che punto siamo con I Thess. 4,13-17?" *Rivista biblica* 4 (1956) 72-80.

After a brief review of the most common interpretations of 1 Thess 4:13-17, the article summarizes the argument of Anselm Wimmer (984). The article concludes with a translation of the passage which is in accordance with Wimmer's interpretation.

966 Rösch, K. "'Wir Lebenden, wir Übrigbleibenden' in 1 Thess. 4,15-17," *Theologie und Glaube* 10 (1918) 492-495.

967 Schenk, Wolfgang. "Auferweckung der Toten oder Gericht nach den Werken. Tradition und Redaktion in Mattäus xxv 1-13," *Novum Testamentum* 20.4 (1978) 278-299.

Although commentators differ radically in their opinions of the relation between 1 Thess 4:15-17 and the parable of the virgins in Matt 25:1-13, the semantic parallels suggest that a relationship between the two exists. Paul has altered the parable for his purposes, in the light of his statement of belief in verse 14 ("For since we believe that Jesus died and rose, thus also God will bring those who have fallen asleep through Jesus with him") and his typical use of the words of Jesus in post-Easter proclamation.

968 Schlier, Heinrich. "Auslegung des 1. Thessalonicherbriefes (4,13-5,11)," *Bibel und Leben* 4 (1963) 19-30.

Although it appears that Paul interrupts his paraenesis on holiness as fulfilling the will of God (4:1-12) only to return to this theme later in the letter (5:12-22), this is not the case. Instead, what the apostle writes in 4:13-18 and 5:1-11 is also an exhortation--for him a word of consoling exhortation.

969 Scott, J. Julius. "Paul and Late-Jewish Eschatology--A Case Study, I Thessalonians 4:13-18 and II Thessalonians 2:1-12," *Journal of the Evangelical Theological Society* 15.3 (1972) 133-143.

Parallels of literary form and doctrinal content, as well as verbal and conceptual similarities, exit between the major eschatological sections of the Thessalonian letters (1 Thess 4:13-18; 2 Thess 2:1-12) and the literature of Late Judaism. These parallels include such topics as the Messianic Age, the resurrection, archangels, the "sound of the trumpet," the rapture, the "gathering" of God's people, the Day of the Lord, and the Man of Lawlessness. These similarities, however, are superficial and the differences between Paul and the apocalyptic literature of his day are actually more significant. Although the apostle used some of the contemporary Jewish literary forms and terms, his thought is thoroughly and distinctively Christian.

970 Sordet, Jean-Michel. "La venue du Seigneur. Deux discours d'espérance à la lumière de deux hypothèses: 1 Thessaloniciens 4,13-18 et 2 Thessaloniciens 2,1-12," *Hokhma* 35 (1987) 35-57.

A comparative analysis of 1 Thess 4:13-18 and 2 Thess 2:1-12 shows that, although colored slightly by bizarre apocalyptic imagery, these two passages are an invitation to consider the hope resident in the proclamation of the resurrection and of the undeniable care which God has for the real problems of the world. Such a comparative study is also informative for the question of pseudepigraphy. The assumptions of many exegetes concerning the pseudepigraphy of 2 Thessalonians are not supported by the manner in which the material from 1 Thess 4:13-18 has been re-worked and rearranged in 2 Thess 2:1-12. In fact, the very manner in which this was accomplished strongly suggests that the material comes from the same pen, that of Paul.

971 Stein, Robert H. "Did Paul's Theology Develop? (1 Thess. 4:13-18)," *Difficult Passages in the Epistles* (Grand Rapids: Baker, 1988) 82-88.

Many insist that Paul's theology changed over the years so that what he taught in his early letters (1 Thessalonians) he no longer believed in his later ones. With respect to the parousia, Paul supposedly changed from the view that Jesus would return in his own lifetime (1 Thess 4:15, 17: "we who are alive") to the view that the second coming would not take place while he was still alive (Phil 1:19-26). An investigation of 1 Thess 4:15, 17, however, shows that there is no reason to conclude that Paul in these verses is teaching that he would personally live to participate in the parousia. On the contrary, within the text there are a number of reasons for denying that Paul sought to affirm that he would be alive when Christ returns. Although Paul's theology surely matured during his lifetime, there is no evidence for any substantial change.

972 Tondelli, Leone. "Qui residui sumus in adventum Domini (L'escatologia della I ai Thessalonicesi IV)," *Scuolo Catolicam* 55 (1937) 602-608.

973 Tuckett, Christopher M. "Synoptic Tradition in 1 Thessalonians?" *The Thessalonian Correspondence* (ed. Raymond F. Collins; Bibliotheca ephemeridum theologicarum lovaniensium 87; Leuven: Leuven University Press, 1990) 160-182.

Parallels between a number of passages in 1 Thessalonians (2:14-16; 4:8; 5:13; 5:15), especially 4:15-17 and 5:1-11, and in the gospels have caused many to believe that Paul had access to blocks of Jesus tradition. This conclusion, however, is unwarranted. At most Paul appears to have known one isolated tradition as a "Jesus tradition" in 5:2. The rest of Paul's claimed parallels can be adequately explained by his use of *other* traditions and his own ideas. Both Paul and the gospel traditions share a common fund of ideas and terminology from the Old Testament and Judaism, and this common background seems quite adequate to explain any overlap in language between Paul and the synoptic tradition.

974 Uprichard, Robert Edward Henry. "Exposition of 1 Thessalonians 4.13-18," *Irish Biblical Studies* 1 (1979) 150-156.

The specific problem to which Paul responds in 1 Thess 4:13-18 is whether Christians who die before the Lord's return will be at any disadvantage or even miss that great future event. Paul assures the Thessalonian believers that their dead will in no way be disadvantaged. The ground of such confident hope rests on two historical events and the implications of these events for believers: the death and resurrection of Christ (v 14), and the parousia of the Lord (vv 15-17).

975 Veldhuizen, A. van. "1 Thessal. 4:15,17," *Theologische Studiën* 29 (1911) 101-106.

Exegetes of 1 Thess 4:15, 17 must pay careful attention to the grammatical and lexical features of these verses. The presence of the personal pronoun "we" in the participial phrase "who are being left behind"--a phrase which is given twice--suggests a strong contrast with "those who have died." There is no warrant for concluding, however, that Paul believed that none of those included in the "we" would die before the parousia, including himself. A lexical analysis of the participle περιλειπόμενοι reveals that this word has the well-defined meaning of "survive" in the sense of a "stick retrieved from the fire." It always means "barely escaped but not yet out of danger." Thus, the "we" belong, for the time being, to the category of survivors. The "we" do not rejoice in surviving but rather mourn those of their dwindling numbers who have already been overtaken by death prior to Christ's return.

976 Vidal Garcia, Senen. "La fórmula de resurrección 'cristológica simple,'" *Salmanticensis* 27 (1979) 385-417.

The formula of 1 Thess 4:14 ("we believe that Jesus died and rose") apportions a christological meaning to the Christian hope, as well as an eschatological dimension, since it emphasizes Jesus' exaltation and his future coming as Savior. That christological-eschatological aspect is what serves as the foundation for the "Son of Man" sayings and the "maranatha" christologies, and this relationship, as well as the wording of the formula itself, evidences its origin within the Palestinian community. The formula also appears, though adapted to its context, in Rom 8:34b and 14:9.

977 Walvoord, John F. "1 Thessalonians 4: A Central Rapture Passage," *When the Trumpet Sounds* (ed. Thomas Ice and Timothy J. Demy; Eugene, OR: Harvest House, 1995) 251-259.

The almost universal assumption that prophecy cannot be interpreted literally is the major cause of the current confusion and diversity of views concerning the end times. A comparison of the rapture doctrine, as presented in 1 Thess 4:13-18, with the second coming of Christ, described in Revelation 19, makes it abundantly clear that the two events are quite different and do not occur at the same time, contrary to the common teaching of the church. The rapture involves the movement of the church from earth to heaven, whereas the second coming is a transition from heaven to earth.

978 ---. "Christ's Coming to Reign," *Bibliotheca Sacra* 123 (1966) 195-203.

The second advent of Christ is taught in the Old Testament passages of Deut 30:1-5, Zech 12:10-14, Dan 2:44-45 and 7:13-14. In the New Testament, Matt 24:27-30 points up the universal phenomena of the return, while Matt 25:31-46 depicts the judgment on the nations which will follow. The fact that the return of Christ is with his saints and that judgment will fall upon unbelievers and the lawless ones is established by the Thessalonian letters (1 Thess 3:13; 4:13-18; 5:1-4; 2 Thess 1:7-2:12). 2 Peter 2:1-3:17 portrays the apostasy which will immediately precede the return. Revelation 19 and 20, the capstone of the second advent, provides much detail on the tribulation. With the curse partially lifted, creation manifests great productivity. The second advent marks the end of the great tribulation period and ushers in the thousand years of peace made possible by the binding of Satan.

979 ---. "The Coming of Christ for His Church," *Bibliotheca Sacra* 123 (1966) 3-14.

The present age will culminate in the coming of the Lord for his church. Of the various views of the rapture, posttribulationism is unquestionably the most widely held. The arguments advanced in support of it, however, are unconvincing. The pretribulationist view of the rapture is scriptural and rests upon two premises: (1) the church is a body of saints distinct from those of other ages; (2) the tribulation is a future period of unprecedented trouble which will occur in the last half of Daniel's seventieth week, subsequent to the rapture. The evidence for pretribulationism is conclusive, and the thrust of such passages as John 14:1-3, 1 Thess 4:15-17, and 1 Cor 15:51-58 is to this point.

980 ---. "Posttribulationism Today. Part VIII: The Comforting Hope of 1 Thessalonians 4," *Bibliotheca Sacra* 133 (1976) 299-311.

Republished in John F. Walvoord, *The Blessed Hope and the Tribulation. A Historical and Biblical Study of Posttribulationism* (Grand Rapids: Zondervan, 1976) 94-107.

1 Thessalonians 4 does not help the cause of posttribulationism because its adherents have no explanation for the following questions: (1) How does a posttribulational rapture provide comfort to the sorrowing saints? (2) Why is Paul silent on the impending great tribulation? (3) Why is the rapture portrayed as an impending event? (4) What about the lack of a reasonable connection between this passage and the Olivet discourse? Paul is here introducing a new doctrine which distinguishes the rapture of the living saints from the second coming of Christ.

981 Ware, Phil. "The Coming of the Lord: Eschatology and 1 Thessalonians," *Restoration Quarterly* 22.1-2 (1979) 109-120.

The coming of the Lord is the central concern of Paul in 1 Thessalonians, especially in 4:13-18 and 5:1-11. These two units probably represent Paul's response to two specific questions: "What will happen to the Christians who have already died at Jesus' second coming?" and "When may we expect Jesus to come again?" While Paul's most direct teaching is found in these two sections, his interests in the second coming and other eschatological matters pervade the whole letter.

982 Waterman, G. Henry. "The Sources of Paul's Teaching on the 2nd Coming of Christ in 1 and 2 Thessalonians," *Journal of the Evangelical Theological Society* 18.2 (1975) 105-113.

The numerous parallels of words and expressions (e.g., "parousia," "the Lord himself," "from heaven," angels, trumpet, clouds) between Paul's teaching on the second coming of Christ in 1 and 2 Thessalonians (1 Thess 4:13-5:11; 2 Thess 1:3-2:12) and the teaching of Jesus in the Olivet discourse as recorded in Matthew 24-25, Mark 13 and Luke 21, point to the latter as a source, in oral or written form, of Paul's teaching. The close verbal resemblances, especially from Matthew's account, point to a written source used by Paul which may have antedated the writing of the gospel. Since Papias mentions the logia which he says Matthew composed in Hebrew (Aramaic) and which may have been a collection of the sayings and discourse of Jesus, it is an interesting possibility that this was the source which Paul used for his teaching in these letters on the second coming of Christ.

983 Wilcke, H. A. *Das Problem eines messianischen Zwischenreiches bei Paulus* (Abhandlungen zur Theologie des Alten und Neuen Testaments 51; Zürich: Zwingli Verlag, 1967) 109-147.

"Chiliasm," which is associated with the belief in the "between" reign of Christ, is not found in Paul. 1 Thess 4:13-18 and 1 Cor 15:20-28 make several points in this regard. In 1 Thess 4:16 the resurrection of Christ is the topic. On the basis of the grammar (the use of πρῶτον), one cannot posit two resurrections of Christians, of which the dead in Christ are part of the second. The context is one of grief experienced by the Thessalonians over those dead who believed, so there is no "chiliastic" perspective here, since there is no "between" reign evident. The meeting of Christ in the air does not indicate an interim period of one thousand years. The "word of the Lord" is probably from Jesus who, coming out of the same context, had no chiliastic thought.

984 Wimmer, Anselm. "Trostworte des Apostels Paulus an Hinterbleibene in Thessalonich (1 Th 4,13-17)," *Biblica* 36 (1955) 273-286.

Paul offers a number of words of consolation to those who remain behind after the death of members of the church in Thessalonica and in anticipation of the parousia. These words include statements about sleeping and death, those who are dead in Christ being raised first, the order of first-then, those who are left, and being caught up, among others.

985 Zedda, Silverio P. "Lo stato intermedio come partecipazione al mistero Pasquale, in S. Paolo," *Bibbia e Oriente* 8 (1966) 213-220.

It is widely recognized that Paul speaks of the intermediate state in 2 Cor 5:6-8 and Phil 1:21-24. What is not normally seen, however, is that earlier texts like 1 Thess 4:14, 16 and 1 Cor 15:18, 20, 23, while not speaking explicitly about the intermediate state, at least head in the same direction and demonstrate that Paul already has in mind the essential point of that condition, namely, that it is a life "with Christ" or "in Christ."

Other Relevant Sources:

449, 458, 499, 501, 513, 515, 516, 517, 529, 535, 552, 554, 565, 573, 590, 607, 640, 642, 668, 681, 859, 1144.

I. 1 Thessalonians 5:1-11

986 Aejmelaeus, Lars. *Wachen vor dem Ende: Die traditionsgeschichtlichen Wurzeln von 1. Thess 5:1-11 und Luk 21:34-36* (Suomen Eksegeettisen Seuran Julkaisuja 44; Helsinki: Finnische Exegetische Gesellschaft, 1985).

1 Thess 5:1-11 and Luke 21:34-36 both outline an apocalyptic scenario in which people await the end of time. There are numerous conceptual and other similarities between these two passages. They both contain language regarding the suddenness of the coming of the day of the Lord as well as a clear sense of the timing of the events associated with that day. These common elements point to a common traditions-history origin of the two passages.

987 Edgar, Thomas R. "The Meaning of 'Sleep' in 1 Thessalonians 5:10," *Journal of the Evangelical Theological Society* 22.4 (1979) 345-349.

The major opinion that καθεύδω in 1 Thess 5:10 refers to physical death is almost certainly wrong for the following reasons: (1) the biblical use of καθεύδω favors an interpretation other than physical death; (2) the verb γρηγορέω, which is contrasted with καθεύδω in the verse, nowhere else means physical life; (3) καθεύδω was used in the preceding verses of 5:6-7 without meaning death; and (4) the whole context (5:1-11) addresses the subject of vigilance, not physically living or dying. The verse means, then, that all believers, spiritual or not, will be caught up to meet the Lord when he comes. Believers are urged to be watchful but, even if they sleep, their hope is certain.

988 Focant, Camille. "Les Fils du Jour (1 Thess 5,5)," *The Thessalonian Correspondence* (ed. Raymond F. Collins; Bibliotheca ephemeridum theologicarum lovaniensium 87; Leuven: Leuven University Press, 1990) 348-355.

Although some do not hesitate to see 1 Thess 5:5 as a non-Pauline interpolation, others are more cautious and simply underscore the fact that the use of the phrase υἱοὶ ἡμέρας ("sons of the day") betrays an influence of the Synoptic tradition. It is also possible, however, that Paul himself was the creator of this new terminology, as a natural progression of thought from what he was trying to accomplish in 1 Thess 5:1-11. In its context, this phrase likely retains the eschatological sense of the "day of the Lord" from previous Jewish thought.

989 Förster, Gerhard. "1 Thessalonicher 5,1-10," *Zeitschrift für die neutestamentliche Wissenschaft* 17 (1916) 169-177.

1 Thess 5:1-10 is a statement that was not new to Paul, as he indicates in the expression "for you yourselves clearly know." The statement regarding the day coming as a thief in the night might reflect either Mosaic law or Greek law. If it is Mosaic law, it would indicate the day coming as a thief breaks into a house at night with destructive force. If it is Greek law, it would indicate the thief in the night profiting by the darkness of night. As words of the Lord, the Mosaic-law interpretation must be correct. Also, the

best reading of 5:4 is that of the plural "thieves" found in Codexes Alexandrinus and Vaticanus, rather than the singular "thief" found in Sinaiticus and other later uncials (so D F G).

990 Fuchs, Ernst. "Die Zukunft des Glaubens nach 1 Thess 5,1-11," *Glaube und Erfahrung: Zum christologischen Problem im Neuen Testament* (Tübingen: Mohr, 1965) 334-363.

A theological exposition of 1 Thess 5:1-11 moves from the indicative to the imperative on the basis of this passage moving from (1) belief to (2) life in Christ to (3) hope in God.

991 Gempf, Conrad. "The Imagery of Birth-Pangs in the New Testament," *Tyndale Bulletin* 45.1 (1994) 119-135.

Despite the patriarchal culture of first-century Palestine, male teachers such as Jesus and Paul, speaking or writing to ostensibly predominantly male audiences, used an image of pain which has never been felt by males: birth pangs. This image has been picked up by New Testament writers from the Old Testament and is used in a variety of ways. Sometimes the focus is on the "intensity" of the pain: it makes plain the acuteness of the pain and suffering. Yet other times the emphasis is on the "helplessness" of the sufferer. Elsewhere, there is portrayed a "productive" pain: a pain with a positive goal or outcome. Finally, there is a "cyclical" pain: an emphasis on a process which has already begun and must run its course.

992 Getz, Gene A. "Encourage One Another," *Yes God...I am a Creative Woman* (ed. Dorothy Dahlman and Bob Putman; Arlington Heights, IL: Harvest Publications, 1983) 103-113.

1 Thess 5:11 ("Therefore encourage one another and build each other up"), along with other scattered passages in the Thessalonian correspondence, indicates that one of the primary tasks of the church is to be engaged in mutual encouragement.

993 Harrison, William K. "The Time of the Rapture as Indicated in Certain Scriptures," *Bibliotheca Sacra* 114 (1957) 316-325.

Although the New Testament nowhere expressly declares whether the rapture will occur before or after the great tribulation, a clear conclusion can be reached from a careful analysis of the relevant biblical passages. 1 Thess 1:10 and 5:1-11, along with corresponding passages from the rest of the New Testament, show that "the wrath to come" must refer to the great tribulation and that 1 Thessalonians therefore establishes the position that the rapture of the church occurs before the great tribulation (this article is continued under the same title in *Bibliotheca Sacra* 115 [1958] 20-26; see 1118).

994 Hendrix, Holland Lee. "Archaeology and Eschatology at Thessalonica," *The Future of Early Christianity. Essays in Honor of Helmut Koester* (ed. Birger A. Pearson; Minneapolis: Fortress, 1991) 107-118.

The phrase "peace and security" (1 Thess 5:3) likely refers to Roman imperial sloganeering. The archaeological evidence suggests that there existed a distinctive sensitivity to propaganda about Roman rule on the part of the Thessalonians. Paul's citation of a slogan associated with Roman beneficence in his apocalyptic message to the Thessalonians appears to have been made in specific reference to the Thessalonian environment and to the experience of the city's inhabitants.

995 Hodges, Zane C. "The Rapture in 1 Thessalonians 5:1-11," *Walvoord: A Tribute* (ed. Donald K. Campbell; Chicago: Moody, 1982) 67-79.

1 Thess 5:1-11 teaches that Christ, at his coming, will deliver his people from the eschatological woes at their very outset so that those who have trusted him might live with him. Alternate explanations of this passage fail to grasp the unity of the argument in 5:1-11 and the way in which it unfolds the programmatic statement of 1:10 ("who delivers us from the wrath to come"). The "wrath" of 1:10 and 5:9 does not refer to eternal damnation but to the eschatological woes of the tribulation. This, along with a proper interpretation of the phrase "whether we are awake or sleep" (it describes not living and dead Christians but the states of watchfulness and unwatchfulness), does much to invalidate the posttribulational position. Thus the truth that the church will escape the tribulation by means of the rapture has firm roots in New Testament exegesis.

996 Holzmeister, Urban. "Das Gleichnis vom Diebe in den Ev. und beim Hl. Paulus," *Zeitschrift für katholische Theologie* (1910) 704-736.

997 Howard, Tracy L. "The Meaning of 'Sleep' in 1 Thessalonians 5:10--A Reappraisal," *Grace Theological Journal* 6.2 (1985) 337-348.

It has been claimed recently by some that καθεύδω in 1 Thess 5:10 refers not to physical death but "spiritual insensibility." The context, however, indicates that the word is used as a euphemism for death and that thus the majority view remains correct. This meaning is within the semantic range of the word and is supported by structural parallels between 1 Thess 4:13-14 and 1 Thess 5:9-11 in which καθεύδω is paired with κοιμάω. Paul in 5:10, therefore, returns to the issue which is behind the entire eschatological discourse beginning in 4:13, namely, the future of those who die in the Lord. Paul's response in 5:9-10 is the same as in 4:13-17: whether a believer is alive or has died, he will not experience any disadvantage at the parousia but will live with Christ.

998 Jonge, Henk J. de. "The Original Setting of the Χριστὸς ἀπέθανεν ὑπέρ Formula," *The Thessalonian Correspondence* (ed. Raymond F. Collins; Bibliotheca ephemeridum theologicarum lovaniensium 87; Leuven: Leuven University Press, 1990) 229-235.

The so-called "dying formula" (*Sterbensformel*) occurs eight times in Paul's authentic letters, though in slightly varying forms (1 Thess 5:10; 1 Cor 15:3; 2 Cor 5:14, 15 [2x]; Rom 5:6; 5:8; 14:15). This dying formula did not likely originate in the early church's celebration of the eucharist, as has often been claimed, but instead in the exhortatory homily of the earliest, Greek-speaking, Christian community, probably that of Jerusalem in the early thirties. This conclusion is suggested by an examination of the function of each particular instance of the formula in its literary context. The dying formula occurs in contexts in which the author wishes to highlight the new state of life to which Christians have been transferred--i.e., a paraenetic context.

999 Lautenschlager, Markus. "Εἴτε γρηγορῶμεν εἴτε καθεύδωμεν. Zum Verhältnis von Heiligung und Heil in 1 Thess 5,10," *Zeitschrift für die neutestamentliche Wissenschaft* 81 (1990) 39-59.

The verbs γρηγορεῖν and καθεύδειν are both used two times in 1 Thess 5:1-11. Most interpreters think that Paul uses this verbal pair in a different sense in 5:10 than he does in 5:6, based on how 1 Thess 4:13-18 is understood to refer to those who are left/living or sleeping at the parousia. However, a survey of the biblical usage of these words in both the Old and New Testaments, as well as an analysis of the structure of the passage in 1 Thessalonians, indicates that both verbs should be understood similarly. Rather than 5:10 referring to those who are alive or dead at the parousia, this verse, like 5:6, refers to those who are living in expectation of the parousia and not carelessly. The interpretation of 5:10, therefore, requires the sense "whether we live holy lives in anticipation of the parousia or whether we are negligent."

1000 Lövestam, Evald. "1 Thessalonians 5:1-11," *Spiritual Wakefulness in the New Testament* (trans. W. F. Salisbury; Lund: Gleerup, 1963) 45-58.

The wakefulness motif in 1 Thess 5:1-11 does not refer to mental alertness and watchfulness. Rather the admonition to "keep awake" means an exhortation to Christians not to let themselves be spiritually stupefied and choked by absorption in the present age of night, but to realize their position as sons of light and sons of the day, living in such a way as agrees with the day to come and thereby being ready for the parousia of the Lord. The thought of the readiness for the advent of Christ is central in this passage.

1001 ---. "Über die neutestamentliche Aufforderung zur Nüchternheit," *Studia theologica* 12 (1958) 80-102.

Of the five places in the New Testament where νήφειν ("be sober") appears in the New Testament, two of them are found in 1 Thessalonians: 5:6 and 5:8. There are also several places where cognate terms are used in the Pauline letters. This study considers all of these uses, as well as others in early Christian literature. Sobriety is bound with the idea of day and light, and stands in opposition to night and darkness in Thessalonians, as well as being used in a context of the language of weaponry and war.

1002 Lucchesi, E. "Précédents non bibliques à l'expression néo-testamentaire: 'Les temps et les moments,'" *Journal of Theological Studies* 28 (1977) 537-540.

The hendiadys "the times and the moments" appears twice in the New Testament: Acts 1:7 and 1 Thess 5:1. Although Dan 2:21 is usually seen to be the source of this phrase, it is better to look outside of the Bible for the source of the expression, especially to Philo of Alexandria. The lively diatribe in *Questions and Answers on Genesis* at 6:13 indicates a philosophical or possibly gnostic background to the use of the expression.

1003 Mattern, Lieselotte. *Das Verständnis des Gerichtes bei Paulus* (Abhandlungen zur Theologie des Alten und Neuen Testaments 47; Zürich: Zwingli Verlag, 1966) 77-86.

1 Thess 5:9 ("because God has not destined us for wrath but for the obtaining of salvation through our Lord Jesus Christ") follows an apocalyptic passage (1 Thess 4:13-18) in which the readers are to have hope, even though they have experienced death. Then 5:1-11 speaks of the day of the Lord. 5:8 speaks of living the Christian life in belief, love, and hope. 5:9 dwells on hope, grounded in the salvation which comes from Christ the savior. There is a clear either/or presented: wrath or salvation. Predestination in 5:9 is as in Rom 9:22-23: collective, not individual. Another passage in the letter, 1 Thess 1:10, is typical of the Pauline prayer, with affirmations of monotheism, the parousia, the resurrection of Jesus from the dead, and an apocalyptic dimension grounded in the same thought as Rom 5:9-10.

1004 Mayer, Bernhard. *Unter Gottes Heilsratschluss. Prädestinationsaussagen bei Paulus* (Forschung zur Bibel 15; Würzburg: Echter Verlag, 1974) 57-69.

Alongside study of Phil 2:12-13, 1 Cor 2:6-10a, 1 Cor 1:18, 2 Cor 4:3, 2 Cor 2:15, Rom 8:28-30, and Romans 9-11, there is a study of 1 Thess 5:9-10 in light of questions regarding the nearness of the parousia. In 1 Thess 4:13-18 Paul emphasizes those of the Christian community as sons of light--those who are characterized as belonging to the light and the day. This provides the foundation for what Paul says in 1 Thess 5:9-10. The holiness of Christians is grounded in the unqualified character of God. The eschatological holiness is effectual through the crucifixion and second coming of the returning Christ.

1005 März, Claus-Peter. "Das Gleichnis vom Dieb. Überlegungen zur Verbindung von Lk 12,39 par Mt 24,43 und 1 Thess 5,2.4," *The Four Gospels. Festschrift for Franz Neirynck* (ed. F. van Segbroeck; Bibliotheca ephemeridum theologicarum lovaniensium 100; Leuven: Leuven University Press/Peeters, 1992) 635-648.

The parable of the thief in Luke 12:39 (par. Matt 24:43) can be compared to 1 Thess 5:2, 4 in order to raise the general question of the contact of Pauline texts with the synoptic tradition, especially the possible reception of pre-synoptic Jesus tradition through the apostle. An investigation of this matter reveals that there is still much uncertainty regarding their relationship. It seems certain that the connection of Paul with the pre-synoptic tradition of Luke 12:39 and Matt 24:43 is detectable in the thief parable. It seems probable that Paul took up the thief parable already bound with the tradition of Luke 12:39. It is possible that the parable of the watching servant was already joined with the parable of the good and bad servant. In any case, it shows that Paul not only knew single words from the Jesus tradition but also a consolidated sayings source.

1006 Moffatt, James. "Ethnic Parallels to 1 Thessalonians, etc.," *Expository Times* 16 (1902) 568.

Parallels to four passages in the New Testament can be found in the writings of Plutarch and the Zoroastrian scripture: 1 Thess 5:6-8 and Plutarch, *de Iside* 6; 1 Thess 5:4-11 and Vendidad 18:23-25; Titus 2:5 and Plutarch, *Conjugalia Praecepta* 32; and James 3:4-6 and Plutarch, *de Garrulitate* 10.

1007 Nebe, Gottfried. *"Hoffnung" bei Paulus: Elpis und ihre Synonyme im Zusammenhang der Eschatologie* (Studien zur Umwelt des Neuen Testaments 16; Göttingen: Vandenhoeck & Ruprecht, 1983) 94-109, 164-168.

Two passages in 1 Thessalonians are especially important for the study of the vocabulary of hope in Paul: 5:1-11 and 2:19. The first passage, 1 Thess 5:1-11, presents eschatological hope, in which there is a process character to eschatological holiness. There are both past and future dimensions, both brought together in hope's process character. The second passage, 1 Thess 2:19, uses the language of hope, in which the final judgment is in view. Here hope is linked with the parousia.

1008 Plevnik, Joseph. "1 Thess 5,1-11: Its Authenticity, Intention, and Message," *Biblica* 60.1 (1979) 71-90.

1 Thess 5:1-11 is neither a later non-Pauline interpolation (G. Friedrich) nor Paul's anti-gnostic polemic (W. Schmithals, W. Harnisch), but the apostle's answer to the motives behind inquiring about the date of the Lord's day. Paul first threatens with disaster those who disregard the judgment day (vv 2-3), but then explains and corrects himself by repeatedly reassuring the faithful of their unchanged destiny for salvation (vv 4-5). In view of all of this, he calls believers to live vigilantly and soberly in constant readiness (vv 6-8), but also in the full assurance of salvation (vv 9-10). Paul's answer, therefore, avoids all speculation concerning the date of the end, destroys any quest for false security, and stresses responsibility even as he confirms the hope of salvation.

1009 Precedo Lafuente, Jesús. "El cristiano en la metáfora castrense de San Pablo," *Analecta Bíblica* 17-18.2 (1963) 343-358.

Military imagery is one of the prominent metaphors used by Paul to depict his ministry and the Christian life. The importance of this metaphor can be seen in 1 Thess 5:8 and Eph 6:14-17, where the believer's "armor" is used to encourage vigilance in the Christian life. The differences between the two passages indicate that the emphasis lies in the continuous use of the armor rather than in the specific correspondence between equipment and virtues. In the rest of Paul's letters, this imagery, which has some antecedents in the Old Testament, functions as an appropriate vehicle to represent the dignity of the Christian as well his total commitment to Christ. Consequently, life itself is seen in terms of a "militia Christi," where both the external and internal aspects of the battle are involved. This conflict is to be fought in light of the present juxtaposition of the two aeons and the future day of judgment.

1010 Renard, John. "Temple and Building: Pauline Images of Church and Community," *Review for Religious* 41 (1982) 419-431.

The temple and building images are the single most important and frequently used image of the church and community in the Pauline corpus (e.g., 1 Thess 5:11; 1 Cor 3:9-17; 6:19-20; Gal 2:18; Rom 8:9-11; 9:23; Col 2:6-7; Eph 2:19-22; 3:17). Even in those places where the noun "temple" or "building" is not found, these images are still expressed by the verb οἰκοδομεῖν ("to build"). Paul uses this verb to denote a particular task of an apostle in relation to the community which he serves and of which he is in some way a member.

1011 Rigaux, Béda. "Tradition et rédaction dans 1 Thess. 5.1-10," *New Testament Studies* 21.3 (1975) 318-340.

On the basis of problems with its terminology and theology, a number of recent scholars have proposed that 1 Thess 5:1-10 is inauthentic. By dividing the passage into its three parts (vv 1-3, 4-8a, 8b-10) and analyzing the theme of each and its redaction (the day of the Lord, vigilance, and Christian existence), it can be shown that the themes have been adapted according to the temporal situation, literary genre, and significance of their origins. In each part a large measure of the vocabulary and themes comes from Jewish apocalyptic speculation, perhaps already Christianized, but one can detect the redactional hand of Paul in adapting and transforming these notions. The source is not a baptismal catechesis, the influence of gnosticism, or the influence of Rom 13:11-14 or Luke 21:34, 36.

1012 Sáenz Galache, Mercedes. "'Dios no nos ha destinado a la cólera' (1 Tes. 5,9). Angustia existencial del hombre y premio escatológico de Dios," *La Ciudad de Dios* 187 (1974) 107-134.

Although humanity was created for the enjoyment of a supernatural life, the awareness of life under the power of sin, which is death, produces in humankind an existential anxiety. In response to this fear, late Judaism developed not only the doctrines of the resurrection and immortality, but, in the context of retribution theology, also hope for salvation in an eschatological kingdom. Drawing from these ideas, but enriched with the reality of Christ's resurrection, Paul gives a full solution to the human problem. This solution involves the resurrection of the dead as well as the transformation of those who will be alive at the moment of the parousia. Both the resurrected dead and the transformed living will join Christ in the inauguration of his kingdom here on earth. The parousia, therefore, is the event in which God will reward the righteous with the gift of life.

1013 Semmelroth, Otto. "'Erbauet einer den anderen' (1 Thess 5,11). Zur Wiedereroberung eines christlichen Begriffes," *Geist und Leben* 30.4 (1957) 262-271.

Modern piety shies away from the notion of "edification" because it sees in it the individualistic applications of previous generations. The notion, however, is a biblical one, chiefly Pauline, and it should connote the breadth of meaning which the biblical writers gave it. (1) In the Bible any human work of "building" (edification) is really a human participation in the creative activity of God; this is especially true of the Christian community as the building of God (1 Cor 3:9), built on the cornerstone which is Christ (Mark 12:10; 1 Cor 3:11). (2) The element of personal decision, in cooperation with grace, is not absent from the Christian concept of building up (edifying) the church and its individual members. (3) Nevertheless, such edification is also a form of community service within the church, whose members are living stones, built into a spiritual house (1 Pet 2:5).

1014 Vanderhaegen, Jean. "Espérer le jour du Seigneur. 1 Thess 5,1-6," *Assemblées du Seigneur* 64 (1969) 10-17.

The literal interpretation of 1 Thess 5:1-6 (i.e., that Paul is speaking of the end of the world and the cataclysms associated with it) is not justified. Since neither Paul nor the Old Testament prophets can be shown to believe in such a denouement to the world as we know it, Paul must instead be simply speaking of an end of this world, namely, the one which does not recognize the lordship of Jesus Christ. Paul's words, however, are culturally bound, and so it is important to strip away the Jewish apocalyptic level in his thinking in order to ascertain what it is that he truly means.

1015 Walvoord, John F. "Posttribulationism Today. Part IX: The Rapture and the Day of the Lord in 1 Thessalonians 5," *Bibliotheca Sacra* 134 (1977) 3-14.
Republished in John F. Walvoord, *The Blessed Hope and the Tribulation. A Historical and Biblical Study of Posttribulationism* (Grand Rapids: Zondervan, 1976) 108-121.

The "day of the Lord" is not a twenty-four hour day but rather an extended period of time. Based on Old Testament revelation, the day of the Lord is a time of judgment, culminating in the second coming of Christ, and followed by a time of special divine blessing to be fulfilled in the millennial kingdom. Nowhere in 1 Thessalonians 4 or 5 is the rapture specifically placed after the great tribulation and depicted as occurring at the time of the climax of the judgments which are brought on the world at the time of the day of the Lord. On the contrary, the Thessalonians are assured that their appointment is not a day of wrath but a day of salvation, a concept easily harmonized with the pre-tribulational interpretation.

1016 Yoder-Neufeld, Thomas Raye. *'Put on the Armour of God': The Divine Warrior from Isaiah to Ephesians* (Journal for the Study of the New Testament Supplement Series 140; Sheffield: Sheffield Academic Press, 1997).

The divine-warrior motif appears in Isaiah 59 as an already highly reflected and radically modified manifestation of a tradition ubiquitous in ancient, not least in biblical, religion. It pictures God as warrior judge in a fashion that draws on the mythological roots of the image, but also identifies the activity of the warrior with the exercise of conventional virtues. Wisdom of Solomon takes up the motif, accentuating its role within the scenario of the vindication of innocent victims and the defeat and destruction of victimizers, by bringing it into relation with the fate of the paradigmatic righteous person. The Divine Warrior is radically transformed by Paul in 1 Thessalonians 5 in light of his christological convictions. The motif is appropriated within a highly charged eschatological frame of reference, but not uncritically. Further, the Divine Warrior is both democratized and pacified. Nevertheless, the object of the Divine Warrior's attention remains the human community, as is clearly also the case in Isaiah and Wisdom of Solomon. Ephesians, finally, takes up the tradition with renewed critical creativity. As in 1 Thessalonians, the warrior is democratized but hardly pacified, since the enemies have now become the potencies of the gods. The construct of the armed deity at war with the human community in Isaiah and Wisdom of Solomon is now turned on its head. The transformation initiated by Paul is brought to completion by his student(s).

Other Relevant Sources:

385, 458, 501, 513, 516, 552, 554, 565, 573, 590, 640, 681, 689, 716, 876, 895, 907, 909, 916, 917, 923, 924, 927, 928, 931, 932, 933, 937, 938, 939, 945, 958, 962, 968, 973, 981, 982, 1038, 1144.

J. 1 Thessalonians 5:12-22

1017 Black, David Alan. "1 Thessalonians," *Paul, Apostle of Weakness. Astheneia and its Cognates in the Pauline Literature* (American University Studies: Series 7; Theology and Religion 3; New York: Lang, 1984) 22-53.

It is difficult in 1 Thess 5:14 to determine with certainty to whom Paul is referring in the designations τοὺς ἀτάκτους, τοὺς ὀλιγοψύχους, and τῶν ἀσθενῶν. Nevertheless, a good number of exegetical points strongly suggest that these three designations refer to three specific groups in the Thessalonian church, each of whom has been addressed at length earlier in the letter. The "idle" and "fainthearted" refer to the unemployed and mourning in the community who are addressed in 4:9-12 and 4:13-18 respectively. The identification of the "weak" likely refers to those Thessalonians who were in the need of steadfastness and perseverance in the midst of severe trials, and who are exhorted to watchfulness in 5:1-11. It is these believers who need help and support from their fellow Christians whom Paul has in mind in his command to the church to "help the weak."

1018 ---. "The Weak in Thessalonica: A Study in Pauline Lexicography," *Journal of the Evangelical Theological Society* 25.3 (1982) 307-321.

Most scholars interpret Paul's command to "help the weak" in 1 Thess 5:14 in terms of Pauline usage of the ἀσθεν– word group in his other letters. This interpretation, however, ignores the fact that 1 Thessalonians itself can provide the clue which makes the definition of "the weak" possible. An examination of the context of 1 Thess 5:12-22 within the letter as a whole and the words of verse 14 within 5:12-22 leads to the conclusion that "the weak" refers to those Thessalonians who, faced with severe persecution and the delay of the parousia, were in danger of giving up all hope. Paul probably had these Christians in mind when he exhorted the church to steadfastness and perseverance in 1 Thess 5:1-11.

1019 Broer, Ingo. "Das Ius Talionis im Neuen Testament," *New Testament Studies* 40 (1994) 1-21.

There are two approaches to the law of retaliation in the New Testament. 1 Thess 5:15 ("See that no one repays evil for evil") contains a negatively introduced form of the *Ius Talionis* (see also Rom 12:17 and 1 Pet 3:9).

1020 Cabiniss, Alan. "The Worship of 'Most Primitive' Christianity," *Journal of Bible and Religion* 26 (1958) 318-321.

Galatians, 1 and 2 Thessalonians, and 1 and 2 Corinthians, considered to be the earliest Pauline letters, provide the basis for discovering the organization and worship practices of "most primitive" Christianity. These letters show that the church at its earliest stage: (1) was divided into two orders, clergy and laity; (2) was empowered to impose censure and absolution; (3) followed an ecclesiastical calendar; (4) employed ceremonial acts such as the "holy kiss" and possibly incense and drama; and (5) had the public reading of Paul's letters, mutual prayer and blessing, a formulaic ending for its prayers, the recitation of the Lord's prayer, the congregational "Amen" response, and singing. Contrary to modern assumptions, early Christian worship was not at all plain and colorless but quite rich and adorned.

1021 Dunn, James D. G. "New Wine in Old Wineskins: VI. Prophet," *Expository Times* 85 (1973) 4-8.

Through the application of Joel's prophecy, the early Christian church believed that the gift of prophecy was no longer restricted to a few but available to the whole community. Taken to Hellenistic churches, prophecy was a novelty which Paul advised be controlled and evaluated. The problem of false prophesy cannot be addressed by the test of non-fulfillment but by a more dynamic means of discernment: it must honor Jesus and be edifying, in agreement with the guidelines given in 1 Thess 5:19-22.

1022 Frame, James Everett. "Οἱ Ἄτακτοι (1 Thess. 5.14)," *Essays in Modern Theology and Related Subjects: Gathered and Published as a Testimonial to Charles A. Briggs* (New York: Scribners', 1911) 191-206.

The use of ἀτακτεῖν and its cognates in the literature of that day indicates that there are two possible ways to understand οἱ ἄτακτοι in 1 Thess 5:14: "the disorderly" or "the loafers." An examination of the context, however, indicates that the latter meaning is preferred. This meaning is further strengthened by 2 Thess 3:6-11, where the problem with the loafers or idlers had become more acute and thus forced Paul to address their idle behavior in a more substantive manner. This errant lifestyle was due to a feverish excitement about the coming of the Lord.

1023 Fung, Ronald Y. K. "Charismatic Versus Organized Ministry? An Examination of an Alleged Antithesis," *Evangelical Quarterly* 52 (1980) 195-214.

The claim of Ernst Käsemann that the idea of an institutionalized ministry as presented in the Pastorals is diametrically opposed to the Pauline idea of a charismatic ministry cannot be maintained for the following reasons. First, an examination of Gal 6:6, 1 Thess 5:12, Rom 16:1, Col 1:7, 4:12, 17, Phil 1:1, and Acts 14:23 indicates that the Pauline communities were by no means amorphous associations without any clear concept of office. Second, Käsemann's analysis incorrectly assumes a succession of office that is institutionally guaranteed. Third, in Paul's thinking, charisma can find expression through offices, and offices must not be severed from charisma.

1024 Galitis, Georg A. "Der Weg der Vollendung. Eine exegetische Studie zu I. Thess. 5,14-28," *Theologia* 35 (1964) 65-86.

A detailed, word-by-word commentary on 1 Thess 5:14-28, with a short introduction to the historical context.

1025 Hänsel, F. M. A. "Über die richtige Auffassung der Worte Paul (1. Thess. 5,21f.)," *Theologische Studien und Kritiken* 9 (1836) 170-184.

The meaning of 1 Thess 5:21-22 is unclear. Investigation of the use of the word δοκιμάζειν in contemporary Greek writers indicates that it means "to test money changers." The early church fathers develop this notion in several ways. Some interpret 5:21 as referring to money changers; others attribute the words with this interpretation to Jesus; others attribute the words to Paul in the simple sense; and finally some attribute the words to Paul in conjunction with 5:21. These traditions of interpretation are maintained in the early church.

1026 Malherbe, Abraham J. "'Pastoral Care' in the Thessalonian Church," *New Testament Studies* 36 (1990) 375-391.

Paul in 1 Thess 5:14-15 is not, as is commonly held, characterizing three distinct groups within the church (i.e., the disorderly, the faint-hearted, and the weak). Rather, he is describing certain dispositions of character or psychological conditions to which he matches treatment appropriate to the particular case. In this manner, Paul exercises pastoral care over his Thessalonian converts by utilizing methods and traditions derived from moral philosophers who for centuries had been engaged in the moral reformation of people. In this psychagogic enterprise a major concern was to be discriminating in one's speech to one's auditor.

1027 Roetzel, Calvin J. "1 Thess 5:12-28: A Case Study," *SBL 1972 Proceedings* (ed. Lane C. McGaughy; 2 vols.; N.P.: Society of Biblical Literature, 1972) 2.367-383.

A number of structural and linguistic features argue for the assigning of 1 Thess 5:12-22 to the paraenetic section of the letter. Although Paul exercised a great deal of freedom in this and other closing paraenetic sections, it would be wrong to conclude that the material here is formless or that these sections have no common language or structure. There is also evidence that, despite the seemingly general nature of the exhortations, Paul has arranged and adapted these hortatory materials to fit the epistolary situation. The peace wish (vv 23-25) not only serves as a bridge between the paraenesis and letter closing but also summarizes a main concern of the letter. The apostolic pronouncement (v 27) underscores the apostolic character of the letter.

1028 Sauer, Jürgen. "Traditionsgeschichtliche Erwägungen zu den synoptischen und paulinischen Aussagen über Feindesliebe und Wiedervergeltungsverzicht," *Zeitschrift für die neutestamentliche Wissenschaft* 76 (1985) 1-28.

This thorough treatment of words for loving one's enemies and non-retribution deals with the major passages in the Gospels and the Pauline letters, including 1 Thess 5:15. The divergences of 1 Thess 5:15b from Rom 12:17a, a major Pauline passage on the topic, indicate that the Thessalonians' passage reflects a very early tradition.

1029 Schlier, Heinrich. "Auslegung des 1. Thessalonicherbriefes (5,12-28)," *Bibel und Leben* 4.2 (1963) 96-103.

Paul closes his first letter to the Thessalonians with a number of specific requests in 5:12-24. These requests are divided into three sections (vv 12-15, 16-22, 23-24), although they belong together and are not strongly joined to the previous section (using only δέ). The first section is concerned with those who administer the church; the second is addressed to all Christians in short commands; and the third is a prayer for the holiness of the believers and a word about the true God. Verses 25-28 constitute the postscript.

1030 Smith, Clay. "'Αδιαλείπτως Προσεύχεσθε: Is Paul Serious?" *Presbyterion* 22.2 (1996) 113-120.

In light of the options for interpreting the adverb ἀδιαλείπτως in Paul's letters, the preferred rendering when used in the context of prayer is "persistently" or "constantly." The range of meanings of ἀδιαλείπτως is broad, but since Paul's use of the adverb with reference to prayer appears to be consistent, it seems safe to draw conclusions with respect to 1 Thess 5:17 from his general use elsewhere. Paul's command to "pray constantly" should not be dismissed as an exaggeration nor interpreted literally to refer to uninterrupted praying. The apostle is rather encouraging believers to persist in the recognition of their dependence on God and to act accordingly: to pray. This type of prayer is both "unuttered and expressed," spilling forth from a thankful heart.

1031 Tragan, Pius R. "Un texte ancien sur l'organisation de l'Eglise (1 Thessaloniciens 5,12-13)," *Ministères et célébration de l'Eucharistie* (ed. P. Grelot; Sacramentum 1; Rome: Anselmiana, 1973) 149-180.

1032 Walton, Stephen John. "Paul in Acts and Epistles: The Miletus Speech and 1 Thessalonians as a Test Case" (Unpublished Ph.D. Thesis; Sheffield: University of Sheffield, 1997).

Paul's speech to the Ephesian elders at Miletus (Acts 20:18-35) is important for two interlocking debates: first, concerning the relationship between the portrait of Paul found in Acts and that derived from the letters; and second, concerning Luke's sources--specifically, whether Luke had knowledge of the Pauline letters. This thesis contributes to both debates by a careful examination of the speech, and a comparison with speeches by Jesus in Luke's gospel (to see how Lukan the Miletus speech is) and 1 Thessalonians (to see how Pauline the speech is). A comparison of the Miletus speech with 1 Thessalonians, especially the fifth chapter of that letter, reveals the presence of four major Miletus themes in Paul's letter to the Thessalonians, often using the same or similar vocabulary. The parallel is particularly clear in considering leadership, but it is also evident concerning suffering, money and work, and the death of Jesus. Thus, the Paul of this letter and the Paul of the Miletus speech sound very similar to each other--and these similarities extend to vocabulary and to manner and style of teaching.

1033 Ware, Kallistos Timothy. "'Pray without Ceasing': The Ideal of Continual Prayer in Eastern Monasticism," *Eastern Churches Review* 2 (1969) 253-261.

The command of Paul (1 Thess 5:17) to pray without ceasing was interpreted by the Messalians (late fourth and fifth centuries) as continual vocal prayer which eliminated all work, physical or intellectual. Abba Lucius' modified approach made continual prayer the task of the whole community in shifts or a repetition of short prayers while engaged in work. A more satisfying interpretation is to view prayer not essentially in vocal terms but as a state of the soul. In the Orthodox Church, prayer has three stages: of the lips, the mind, and the heart. Thus prayer grows increasingly inward until the grace of prayer without ceasing is attained. It is not a simple matter but is available to all--not only to the monastic.

1034 Unnik, W. C. van. "'Den Geist löschet nicht aus' (1 Thessalonicher 5,19)," *Novum Testamentum* 10.4 (1968) 255-269.

The difficulty in interpreting 1 Thess 5:19 ("Do not quench the Spirit") is that the passage is unique, with no exact parallel in the Pauline or other early Christian literature. Some texts such as Rom 12:11 and 2 Tim 1:6 shed light on the phrasing, and 1 Cor 14:39 on the noun πνεῦμα. Several extra-biblical passages are informative on the verb σβέννυμι, including Josephus, *Ant.* 11.40, 1 Esdras 3:20, and 4 Macc 16:4. The relation of the Spirit with charismatic experience is illuminated by the Old Testament, Acts, and Josephus, *War* 5.300ff. The linking of "quench" and "spirit" is found in Plutarch, *De*

Pythiae oraculis 17, although there is a question whether "spirit" is used in the same sense as Paul employs the term. Thus, in 1 Thess 5:19-20 Paul is probably exhorting believers not to quench the Spirit given to them by God out of a fear of appearing crazy in the eyes of other people.

1035 Zsolt, Geréb. "A Thesszalonikabeliekhez irott elsö levél ötödik részének magyaráta," *Református Szemle* 78 (1985) 308-314.
A verse-by-verse exposition of 1 Thess 5:16-28.

Other Relevant Sources:

549, 697, 895, 1104, 1182, 1183, 1187, 1188, 1194, 1197, 1199.

K. 1 Thessalonians 5:23-28

1036 Calkins, Arthur B. "La visión bíblica tripartita del hombre - clave para la vida cristiana," *Vida y Espritualidad* 7 (1991) 39-70.

1037 Carver, Frank G. "The Interpretation of 1 Thessalonians 5:23-24," *The Preacher's Magazine* 54.3 (1979) 49-53.
An examination of 1 Thess 5:23-24 in terms of its historical context, role in the letter as a whole, form, structure, and meaning shows that this closing "prayer-wish" summarizes the letter's concern with the continuing ethical transformation of the Christian through the sanctifying presence of God.

1038 Collins, Raymond F. "1 Thess and the Liturgy of the Early Church," *Biblical Theology Bulletin* 10.2 (1980) 51-64.
Republished in Raymond F. Collins, *Studies on the First Letter to the Thessalonians* (Bibliotheca ephemeridum theologicarum lovaniensium 66; Leuven: Leuven University Press, 1984) 136-153.
Paul's possible use of the liturgical traditions of the early church is evident in 1 Thessalonians, particularly in the opening greeting (1:1), the closing holy kiss and benediction (5:23-28), and some of the exhortations (5:1-11). It seems incontrovertible that the opening greeting and closing holy kiss of the letter derived from liturgical usage, that 1 Thessalonians was intended by Paul to be delivered in homiletic fashion to the church of Thessalonica, and that elements of a liturgical blessing are to be discerned in 3:11-13 and 5:23-24. A number of German scholars have argued that Paul incorporated elements of the primitive Christian baptismal liturgy into the exhortations of 5:1-11. But while it is clear that the apostle's letter was intended for public reading and that he employed motifs incorporated into the baptismal liturgy of the early church of later

times, the evidence does not warrant the conclusion that Paul was actually citing elements of a stylized baptismal liturgy.

1039 ---. "'... that this letter be read to all the brethren,'" *Louvain Studies* 9.2 (1982/83) 122-127.
Republished in Raymond F. Collins, *Studies on the First Letter to the Thessalonians* (Bibliotheca ephemeridum theologicarum lovaniensium 66; Leuven: Leuven University Press, 1984) 365-370.

The forceful nature of Paul's closing command in 1 Thess 5:27 ("I adjure you by the Lord that this letter be read to all the brothers") is rather surprising given the calm and positive tone found earlier in the correspondence. It may well be that the church at Thessalonica had not yet adopted the Jewish practice of reading the scriptures or Christian texts in its liturgical gatherings and that Paul, therefore, needed to introduce this novel practice in a forceful manner. The solemn injunction of 1 Thess 5:27 is echoed later in Col 4:16. This deutero-Pauline passage is an early indication that a letter to an individual church could become a letter for the Christian church as a whole, and is thus a milestone in the development of the idea of Christian scriptures and the New Testament canon.

1040 Dabek, O. Tomasz Maria. "Duch, Dusza i Cialo w 1 Tes 5,23," *Ruch biblijny i Liturgiczny* 40 (1987) 288-296.

An examination of the reference to "spirit, soul, and body" in 1 Thess 5:23.

1041 Festugière, A. M. "La trichotomie de I Thess. 5,28 et la philosophie grecque," *Recherches de science religieuse* (= *Science religieuse*) 20 (1930) 385-415.

Because of the pagan background of the Thessalonian converts, it makes sense that Paul would express himself in terms of their own language and understanding of the world. As a result, the trichotomy of 1 Thess 5:23 can be fruitfully examined in light of Greek philosophy and thought. The concept of the compositional division of human beings, discussed since Plato, can be traced throughout the history of Greek philosophy, and Philo of Alexandria provides much evidence that this concept had also entered into Hellenistic Jewish thought. In fact, it is probably from his Jewish roots that Paul takes and develops the concept such as he does. The apostle's usage and that of early Christianity, however, pulls the various ideas together in a way which had not been done before and gives the concept its highest expression.

1042 Klassen, William. "The Sacred Kiss in the New Testament. An Example of Social Boundary Lines," *New Testament Studies* 39 (1993) 122-135.

A survey of the kiss in ancient Judaism, Greco-Roman society, and the early church highlights its function as a means to publicly express reconciliation and so maintain the unity of the Christian community. The New Testament admonitions to practice the "holy kiss" (Rom 16:16; 1 Cor 16:20; 2 Cor 13:12; 1 Thess 5:26) or the "kiss of love" (1 Pet

5:14) stress the freedom to express without inhibition to all people of whatever background, rank, or gender, the ardor of love in any context. Thus the kiss was an outward act which affirmed the common bond of love experienced in the Christian community.

1043 Langevin, Paul-Émile. "L'intervention de Dieu, selon 1 Thess 5,23-24: Déjà le salut par grâce," *Science et Esprit* 41.1 (1989) 71-92.
Republished in *The Thessalonian Correspondence* (ed. Raymond F. Collins; Bibliotheca ephemeridum theologicarum lovaniensium 87; Leuven: Leuven University Press, 1990) 236-256.

A phrase-by-phrase examination of the closing benediction of 1 Thess 5:23-24 and an analysis of the relationships between the various elements of this passage and the rest of the letter allow two specific conclusions to be drawn: (1) the benediction acts as a synthesis of many of the major themes of the letter and conveys Paul's basic intentions; and (2) although the benediction might be brief, it is very significant in Paul's overall theological plan. It contains many of the themes from which later letters, such as Romans and Galatians, would profit.

1044 Manus, Chris Ukachukwu. "1 Thess. 5,27 and Related Passages: Reflections on the Ministry of the Lector in the New Testament Church," *Revue Africaine de Théologie* 10.20 (1986) 225-238.

1 Thess 5:27 ("I adjure you by the Lord that this letter be read to all the brothers") indicates that at a very early stage in Paul's ministry he imposed on his congregations the ancient Jewish practice of public reading of religious texts when they gathered together for worship. Similar injunctions in other letters purportedly written or named after him (2 Cor 1:13; Eph 3:4; Col 4:16; Rev 1:3) bear witness to this practice in the New Testament church.

1045 Mariani, Bonaventura. "Corpo - Anima - Spirito in San Paolo," *Euntes docete* 14 (1961) 304-318.

An analysis of the words σῶμα, σάρξ, ψυχή, and πνεῦμα in the writings of Paul shows that the apostle does not follow a well-defined and systematic psychology and anthropology. Instead, he uses terms that in some instances are borrowed from the popular philosophy and anthropology of the Hellenistic world, while in other instances show the influence of Jewish philosophy and anthropology. Paul's use of these key terms, although almost similar to the ideas of Philo, is not foreign to the doctrine of the Old Testament. The apostle considers humanity from a theological and moral aspect, not from a scientific viewpoint.

1046 Masson, Charles. "Sur I Thessloniciens V, 23. Notes d'anthropologie paulinienne," *Revue de Théologie et de Philosophie* 38 (1945) 97-102.

1 Thess 5:23 has long occupied the attention of theologians. There are two main interpretations of the passage, depending whether one takes "your spirit" to be the divine

Spirit in the human or the spirit of the human. On the basis of the liturgical character of the passage, seen especially in its parallelism, "your spirit" likely refers to the spirit of the person.

1047 McCaig, A. "Thoughts on the Tripartite Theory of Human Nature," *Evangelical Quarterly* 3 (1931) 121-138.

There are at least seven reasons why the trichotomist understanding of humanity is surely incorrect: (1) The creation account gives no suggestion of more than two constituent elements in humankind. (2) The biblical use of the relevant terms leads to the conclusion that "soul" and "spirit" are essentially one. (3) All the distinctions asserted by advocates of trichotomy are not supported by scripture. (4) The testimony of our own consciousness is that humans consist of two parts, not three. (5) There is a real basis in the nature of the soul for the twofold aspect which the scripture presents of the immaterial nature. (6) A special form of the two-fold aspect of soul and spirit appears in the antithesis between flesh and spirit. (7) The biblical texts often cited in support of trichotomy (1 Cor 2:14; 1 Thess 5:23; Heb 4:12; 1 Cor 15:44), when interpreted according to proper hermeneutical principles, are in agreement with the clear teaching elsewhere in scripture that humanity consists of two parts, body and soul.

1048 O'Callaghan, José. "¿Una nueva interpretación de 1 Tes 5,23?" *Studia Papyrologica* 4 (1965) 7-25.

1 Thess 5:23 is an important but problematic passage for the issue of anthropology. Exegetes from the patristic period interpreted this verse as teaching either a trichotomist or dichotomoist view of humanity. By contrast, modern exegetes, such as Masson (1046) and van Stempvoort (1051), tend to deny that 1 Thess 5:23 teaches anything about the makeup of humanity and instead focus on the verse's chiastic structure as the key to interpret properly its meaning. A new solution to this problem, however, is implied by two ancient letters in which the words "spirit," "soul," and "body" are mentioned together. These letters suggest that "spirit" should be interpreted as "moral attitude"--a meaning which fits well both the immediate and larger context of 1 Thess 5:23.

1049 Pitassi, Maria Cristina. "'Anima naturaliter mortalis?' L'interepretazione lockiana di 1 Tessalonicesi 5,23," *Letture della Bibbia e pensiero filosofico e politico moderno* (ed. Mario Miegge; Bologna: Edizioni Dehoniane, 1991) 87-99.

1050 Schweizer, Eduard. "Zur Trichotomie von 1. Thess 5,23 und der Unterscheidung des πνευματικόν vom ψυχικόν in 1. Kor. 2,14; 15,44; Jak. 3,15; Jud. 19," *Theologische Zeitschrift* 9 (1953) 76-77.

Xenocrates (third century BCE) defines spirit as divine, spiritual, and corporeal, while Philo (Isis and Osiris 360E: c. 100 CE) defines the human as soul and body. Thus the spirit has a divine element added. This is distinct from the bizarre three-part description of the human as spirit, soul, and body in 1 Thess 5:23. This points to a very important, early Greek conception of the human as both spiritual and somatic, and it does not originate in Jewish thought as many have posited for gnosticism, early Christianity, and the magical papyri. The two streams of Hellenism and Judaism had already flowed together much earlier.

1051 Stempvoort, P. A. van. "Eine stilistische Lösung einer alten Schwierigkeit in 1. Thess. V. 23," *New Testament Studies* 7.3 (1960/61) 262-265.

In 1 Thess 5:23 the words ὁλοτελεῖς and ὁλόκληρον should not be distinguished but taken to mean "entire" or "whole" in the sense of totality or integrity. Exegetes have also tried to clarify the meaning of the concepts of "spirit, soul, and body" by usually appealing to a trichotomous anthropology, when an appeal to a Semitic form of style is more appropriate. The passage is structured chiastically ("you" and "whole"; "whole" and "your spirit"), based upon synonymous parallelism with alliteration (ὁλοτελεῖς and ὁλόκληρον). Thus the second part of the sentence is normal, expressing a dichotomous position of soul and body.

1052 Veloso, Mario. "Contenido antropológico de 1 Tesalonisenses 5,23," *Revista Bíblica* 41.1-2 (1979) 129-140.

1 Thess 5:23, rather than describing the metaphysical existence of humankind, points to three different ways of manifesting one's whole being (spirit, soul, and body) which, through sanctification, attains the total harmony of the personality and receives a clear goal for the entire life: the coming of Christ. This brings as a result several helpful principles for psychotherapy: the psychic health as the expression of the balance and unity of the three manifestations of the human being; the confrontation with and liberation from sin; the search for an activity which is an expression of the whole personality; the possession of an objective for the total life; and the necessary relationship with the "God of peace" to attain and maintain this harmony.

1053 Weima, Jeffrey A. D. *Neglected Endings. The Significance of the Pauline Letter Closings* (Journal for the Study of the New Testament Supplement Series 101; Sheffield: JSOT Press, 1994).

The Pauline letter closings are carefully constructed units, shaped and adapted in such a way that they relate directly to--sometimes, in fact, even summarize--the major concerns and themes taken up in the bodies of their respective letters. In 1 Thessalonians, for example, Paul adapts the letter closing (5:23-28) so that it not only echoes three major themes of that letter (call to sanctified living; certainty of Christ's return; comfort in face of persecution) but also addresses the internal tensions in the Thessalonian church and encourages obedience and reconciliation. Similarly, in 2 Thessalonians, the letter closing (3:16-18) has been shaped to address the two major themes of that letter, namely, concern over Christ's return and conflict with the idlers. Paul's letter closings, therefore, aid in important ways our understanding of Paul's purpose, arguments, and exhortations--as well as our understanding of his readers and their historical situation(s).

1054 ---. "The Pauline Letter Closings: Analysis and Hermeneutical Significance," *Bulletin for Biblical Research* 5 (1995) 177-198.

The article evaluates the reasons why the Pauline letter closings have been ignored in the past and offers in response suggestive comments about their potential significance. This claimed significance of the Pauline letter closings is established by examining one of the closing conventions (the peace benediction) as it occurs in two of Paul's letters (1 Thess 5:23-24; Gal 6:16).

Other Relevant Sources:

836, 839, 841, 1024, 1027, 1029.

IV. Exegetical Treatments of 2 Thessalonians

A. 2 Thessalonians 1:1-2

1055 Goguel, Maurice. "L'énigme de la seconde épître aux Thessaloniciens," *Revue de l'histoire des religions* 71 (1915) 248-272.

There is nothing in 2 Thessalonians to provide grounds for contesting its Pauline origin. However, it is impossible that this letter had the same recipients as the first letter, as it seems to have been written at a date very close to 1 Thessalonians, making it superfluous if it was intended for the same place. Also, its dependence on the knowledge of the Jewish apocalyptic tradition shows that it cannot have been sent to a recently converted group of Gentiles. Thus, it is possible to furnish an alternative destination on the basis of these characteristics which do not fit with Thessalonica: 2 Thessalonians is actually the letter to the church at Berea.

1056 Knox, John. "A Conjecture as to the Original Status of II Corinthians and II Thessalonians in the Pauline Corpus," *Journal of Biblical Literature* 55 (1936) 145-153.

The desire to have the Pauline corpus contain seven letters led the editors to delete the openings of 2 Thessalonians and 2 Corinthians and to combine these letters with other letters to the same churches. When later in the middle of the second century a clearer distinction was felt appropriate at the points in Corinthians and Thessalonians where second letters so clearly began, the original openings were no longer available and thus new ones, mimicking the openings of the first letters (1 Thess 1:1 and 1 Cor 1:1-3), had to be composed. The openings of 2 Thessalonians and 2 Corinthians which are currently found in the New Testament, therefore, are later, non-Pauline additions.

1057 Michaelis, Wilhelm. "Der zweite Thessalonicherbrief kein Philipperbrief," *Theologische Zeitschrift* 1 (1945) 282-286.

Three points may be raised against E. Schweizer's hypothesis that 2 Thessalonians is a letter to Philippi (1061). The first is that good justification is needed for changing the address of a letter, and that the analogy with Eph 1:1 is not a true parallel. Second, a comparison of 1 and 2 Thessalonians does not indicate that they were composed at the same time, as Ephesians and Colossians appear to be. 2 Thessalonians does not appear to fulfil the requirements of a letter written to Philippi. Third, Schweizer's departure point with Polycarp's reference in *Phil* 11:3 does not hold in light of the other Pauline citations.

1058 Schulz, Anselm. "Gemeinde auf dem Weg. Auslegung des 2. Thessalonicherbriefes (1,1-12)," *Bibel und Leben* 8.4 (1967) 33-42.

The letter form is a personal form of communication which allowed Paul in 2 Thessalonians to reiterate the parameters of the faith to his young church. The letter opening (1:1-2) exhibits the style of its time and culture, reflecting also the brotherhood established by Jesus. The text of the letter extends from 1:3-3:16 and is divided into several major sections. The first is 1:3-12, concerned with introductory themes. This opening section consists of three parts: the thanksgiving and its basis (1:3-4); a word of comfort on the basis of past sorrow (1:5-10); and Paul's prayer for the Thessalonians (1:11-12).

1059 Schweizer, Eduard. "Replik," *Theologische Zeitschrift* 1 (1945) 286-289.

The response to the problems raised by W. Michaelis (1057) against the hypothesis that 2 Thessalonians is really a letter originally sent to Philippi (1061) can be brief. First, the analogy between Eph 1:1 and 2 Thessalonians holds if one looks at the situation in the late first century, where the letter was known as being addressed to the Laodiceans. Second, 1 and 2 Thessalonians do appear to be more similar than Ephesians and Colossians. Third, Polycarp does not use an introductory formula for his citations.

1060 ---. "Zum Problem des zweiten Thessalonicherbriefes?" *Theologische Zeitschrift* 2 (1946) 74-75.

Developing the comments of Ludwig Koehler regarding how doubtful traditions may endure even though they are wrong, one can see how traditions regarding 1 Corinthians endured in various places. Against the claim of Philippe Menoud that the use of Eph 1:1 to support the idea of 2 Thessalonians being a Philippian letter is not a certain analogy, it can be said that this is nevertheless the closest analogy which we have.

1061 ---. "Der zweite Thessalonicherbrief ein Philipperbrief," *Theologische Zeitschrift* 1 (1945) 90-105.

The letter of Polycarp to the Philippians (3:2) says that Paul wrote "letters" (plural) to this church, but we have only one. Furthermore, Polycarp's letter (11:3) cites Paul as being among the Philippians but then quotes a passage from 2 Thess 1:4. This evidence indicates that Polycarp knew more than one Philippian letter. W. Wrede (420) has already shown the difficulties with the eschatology of 1 and 2 Thessalonians. A consideration of these data leads to the conclusion that 2 Thessalonians was written at some time to the church in Philippi and not in Thessalonica.

Other Relevant Sources:

308, 314, 327, 389, 647, 648, 653, 655, 815.

B. 2 Thessalonians 1:3-12

1062 Artola, Antonio-Maria. "Le Christ se manifeste dans la communauté chrétienne. 2 Th 1,11-2,2," *Assemblées du Seigneur* 62 (1970) 75-80.

The four verses of 2 Thess 1:11-2:2 straddle two distinct sections of the letter, as this section amalgamates the end of the first chapter with the beginning of the second. The assignment of a chapter to the parousia, discussed in 2:1-12, was merited only to retain our attention. However, these four verses have doctrinal interest regarding the Christian community clearly manifesting the glory of God, and the false alarm which periodically upsets conscientious Christians.

1063 Aus, Roger D. "Comfort in Judgement: The Use of the Day of the Lord and Theophany Traditions in Second Thessalonians 1" (Unpublished Ph.D. Dissertation; New Haven: Yale University, 1971).

Writings roughly contemporary with 2 Thessalonians similarly describe an intermediary agent in theophany and/or Day of the Lord language as effecting the final judgment, as Jesus is described in 2 Thessalonians 1. The common situation in all these writings is one of distress or persecution. It was not atypical, therefore, for the author of 2 Thessalonians to describe Jesus as the coming judge using theophany traditions because of the situation of the letter. The addressees believe that the persecution which they are undergoing is part of the messianic woes. This leads them to believe that the Day of the Lord is in the process of coming or has come (2:2). The writer of 2 Thessalonians responds by stating in the first chapter that their persecution indeed has a positive value to it, even if it does not bring about the parousia. He comforts his readers in terms of a judgment theophany within the framework of an epistolary thanksgiving, stating that, although the Lord Jesus has not come yet, he definitely will come (1:7-10) and God's judgment concerning the persecuted and their persecutors will be just, even if it does not appear so now. The first chapter of the letter is thus not merely an introduction to the second chapter (as is commonly held) but deals in a pastoral way with what caused the Day of the Lord fervor, the persecution of the addressees.

1064 ---. "The Liturgical Background of the Necessity and Propriety of Giving Thanks according to 2 Thessalonians 1:3," *Journal of Biblical Literature* 92.3 (1973) 432-438. Republished in Roger D. Aus, *Barabbas and Esther and Other Studies in the Judaic Illumination of Earliest Christianity* (South Florida Studies in the History of Judaism 54; Atlanta: Scholars Press, 1992) 193-200.

Examples from Philo, Josephus, the Apostolic Fathers, and other ancient sources show that (1) the two phrases εὐχαριστεῖν ὀφείλομεν...καθὼς ἄξιόν ἐστιν ("We ought to give thanks...as it is fitting") in 2 Thess 1:3 (see also 2 Thess 2:13) are part of the Jewish prayer style, and that (2) these phrases fit their context very well. The two phrases express the necessity and propriety of thanking God precisely for the reasons given in 2 Thess 1:3-4, which are within a situation of suffering.

1065 ---. "The Relevance of Isaiah 66:7 to Revelation 12 and 2 Thessalonians 1," *Zeitschrift für die neutestamentliche Wissenschaft* 67 (1976) 252-268.
Republished in Roger D. Aus, *Barabbas and Esther and Other Studies in the Judaic Illumination of Earliest Christianity* (South Florida Studies in the History of Judaism 54; Atlanta: Scholars Press, 1992) 125-142.

Jewish interpretations of Isa 66:7 show that this verse was understood messianically precisely because of the "birth pangs" or "woes" associated with the Messiah's coming. Because the Jewish-Christian authors of Revelation and 2 Thessalonians were writing to severely persecuted Christian communities, these writers saw their situation as one of the messianic woes associated with the Day of the Lord, and thus employed Isa 66:7 and its neighboring verses to describe the coming of Jesus, who was soon to become king and judge over the entire world.

1066 Bassler, Jouette M. "The Enigmatic Sign: 2 Thessalonians 1:5," *Catholic Biblical Quarterly* 46 (1984) 496-510.

What is the referent, content, and significance of the ἔνδειγμα ("sign") in 2 Thess 1:5? Current scholarship, led by certain presuppositions about the Pauline authorship of this letter and a possible parallel with Phil 1:28, wrongly interprets the sign to be the church's steadfastness in the face of its sufferings. The words and context of this verse, however, suggest that it is the sufferings of the church *per se* which constitute a sign of divine justice. This interpretation is in keeping with a rabbinic theology of suffering. In this theological perspective (identified by the German word *Leidenstheologie*), suffering is not viewed as a sign of God's rejection but somewhat paradoxically as a sign of God's acceptance insofar as he offers through it an opportunity for his elect to receive in this age the punishment for their few sins, thus preserving the full measure of their reward in the age to come. At the same time suffering is also a sign of the absolute justice of God insofar as he insists on punishment even of his elect. A recognition of the presence of *Leidenstheologie* in this letter suggests further that "the one who restrains" (2 Thess 2:7) may be God himself, since he occasionally plays this role in texts which express this rabbinic theological perspective.

1067 Berger, P. R. "Lk 2:14: ἄνθρωποι εὐδοκίας. Die auf Gottes Weisung mit Wohlgefallen beschenkten Menschen," *Zeitschrift für die neutestamentliche Wissenschaft* 74 (1983) 129-144.

The phrase ἄνθρωποι εὐδοκίας in Luke 2:14 has a parallel in 2 Thess 1:11. Paul sees εὐδοκία as something to be accomplished.

1068 Beyer, A. "Zeugnisse des zweiten Thessalonicherbriefes," *Nach dem Gesetz und Zeugnis* 29 (1929) 496-497.

The Old Testament is informative for understanding the following passages from 2 Thessalonians: 1:7 and 2:7.

1069 Carson, Donald A. *A Call to Spiritual Reformation. Priorities from Paul and His Prayers* (Grand Rapids: Baker, 1992).

Three chapters examine three "prayer" passages in the Thessalonian letters: 2 Thess 1:3-12, under the heading "The Framework of Prayer" (pp 39-50); 2 Thess 1:1-12, "Worthy Petitions" (pp 51-63); and 1 Thess 3:9-12, "A Passion for People" (pp 79-94). The primary concern is to explain how these passages are applicable to believers today.

1070 Dunham, Duane A. "2 Thessalonians 1:3-10: A Study in Sentence Structure," *Journal of the Evangelical Theological Society* 24.1 (1981) 39-46.

Although the major editions of the Greek New Testament view 2 Thess 1:3-10 as consisting of one sentence, modern translations present the text in anywhere from one to nine sentences. Far from being unimportant, punctuation can impact the meaning and comprehension of a text in significant ways. 2 Thess 1:3-10 ought to be translated with new sentences beginning in verses 4, 6, 7b, and 10b. These proposed changes in punctuation both simplify and clarify the meaning of this passage.

1071 Fudge, Edward. "The Final End of the Wicked," *Journal of the Evangelical Theological Society* 27.3 (1984) 325-334.

The wicked will be utterly and eternally destroyed in hell rather than the traditional view that they will be immortalized to suffer unending conscious pain. The following factors can be cited in support of this challenging view: (1) the Old Testament uniformly speaks of the final destruction of the wicked, never their unending torment; (2) the intertestamental writings are mixed on the subject; (3) the New Testament language on the punishment of the wicked comes primarily from the Old Testament and should be interpreted with the Old Testament as a starting-place for its meaning; (4) the Pauline and other New Testament language, at face value, best describes total destruction; (5) the New Testament uses no language which compels a view of unending torment; and (6) common New Testament expressions signified in the Old Testament total destruction (worm, consuming fire, gnashing of teeth, smoke ascending forever, unquenchable fire, etc.) and there is no reason to change their meaning in the New Testament.

1072 Johnston, George. "'Kingdom of God' Sayings in Paul's Letters," *From Jesus to Paul: Studies in Honour of Francis Wright Beare* (ed. Peter Richardson and John Hurd; Waterloo: Wilfrid Laurier University Press, 1984) 143-156.

A survey of the eight "kingdom of God" texts in Paul's letters (2 Thess 1:5-12; 1 Thess 2:11-12; Gal 5:21; 1 Cor 4:20-21; 6:9-10; 15:50; Rom 14:17) reveals that the so-called "eschatological" or future dimension of the kingdom idea has been relegated to a fairly minor place, and its present fact has been translated instead into the great concept of spiritual life. "Kingdom of God" refers to God's royal redeeming work in each of the tenses; it should not be confined to ideas of future salvation in the resurrection life.

1073 Linder, J. R. "2 Thess. 1,5-6," *Theologische Studien und Kritiken* 40 (1867) 522-524.
An examination of 2 Thess 1:5-6 supports a deeper and fuller understanding of these verses, especially verse 6, where the verb ἀνταποδοῦναι should be rendered "to requite fully." This sense is supported by the surrounding verses.

1074 Schulz, Anselm. "Ausschauen in Nüchternheit. Auslegung des 2. Thessalonicherbriefes (1,11-2,12)," *Bibel und Leben* 7 (1966) 110-120.
The first of three brief expositions of 2 Thessalonians (see 1177, 1195), this article begins by discussing the prayer (1:11-12), which offers a model of a Christian intercession: the expression of thanks before God; the declaration of intention; and trust in the divine will. The actual request of the prayer is found in 2:1-3:16, which includes the imminent expectation of the parousia of Christ (2:1-12).

1075 Wichmann, W. *Die Leidenstheologie: Eine Form der Leidensdeutung im Spätjudentum* (Beiträge zur Wissenschaft vom Alten und Neuen Testament 4th Series 2; Stuttgart: Kohlhammer, 1930) 27-28.
2 Thess 1:4ff is only correctly understood from the perspective of the theology of suffering. It is a sign that correctly judges and that in the future all suffering will stop. There is thus a positive side to a theology of suffering.

Other Relevant Sources:

484, 695, 696, 697, 701, 834, 839, 905, 982, 1058.

C. 2 Thessalonians 2:1-12

1076 Alers, G. A. "ΤΟ ΚΑΤΕΧΟΝ en Ὁ ΚΑΤΕΧΩΝ (2 Thess. 2:6 en 7)," *Theologische Studiën* 6 (1888) 154-176.
τὸ κατέχον and its personal corollary, ὁ κατέχων, have been traditionally understood as (1) the power of the (Roman) state and its emperor(s); (2) judiciary institutions in general and the "good spirits" who exercise civil justice; and (3) the church of Christ and the Holy Spirit. Each of these interpretations, however, faces insurmountable problems. Only one view can overcome the difficulties of the other positions: τὸ κατέχον is to be understood not as a power but as a fact or condition, namely, that the temple of God (interpreted symbolically but not as the church) is not yet empty. God is still seated there, preventing the Antichrist from taking his place. God's rule is characterized by obedience to him rather than by legal or military institutions. When this obedience turns to general apostasy, then God, who himself is the "restrainer," departs (not as passive "taken out of the way") from among the midst of humankind, leaving the Antichrist to take openly and completely his place as God.

1077 Alford, Henry. "On the Prophetic Import of Ch. II. 1-12," *The Greek Testament: With a Critically Revised Text and a Critical and Exegetical Commentary* (4 vols.; London: Rivingtons, 1857) 3.55-69.

A historical survey of the various interpretations of 2 Thess 2:1-12 from the church fathers to the reformers to contemporary scholars reveals the very diverse ways in which this passage has been read. Those views which regard this prophecy as already having been fulfilled are to be rejected. Believers are to still look for the man of sin to appear immediately prior to the coming of the Lord. He will be the final and central embodiment of "lawlessness," that resistance to God and God's law which has been witnessed so many times already in partial and tentative eruptions. Similarly, the "apostasy," which has been foreshadowed by the Papacy, the rise of Mohammedism, and so many other events, also must still occur. These events are currently being hindered by the κατέχον and κατέχων--the principle of human government and those who exercise that power.

1078 Andriessen, P. "Celui qui retient la venue du Seigneur," *Bijdragen* 21.1 (1960) 20-30.

There is good evidence to believe that the whole of Paul's exposition in 2 Thessalonians refers exclusively to Christ and the obstacles which delay his return. This interpretation, suggested by J. Coppens (1094), is based on the fact that the phrase ἕως ἐκ μέσου γένηται (2:7) can mean "appear" as well as "disappear." There are many examples in scripture to sustain this interpretation and it seems to be more in harmony with the larger context. Thus ὁ κατέχων (2:7) would refer to the Antichrist who is now working in secret within the church, and the parousia must be delayed until he appears openly in his true light. Only then can the definitive struggle be engaged and the definitive victory of Christ be made manifest. On the other hand, τὸ κατέχον (2:6) refers to the general apostasy which is the secret work of the Antichrist and will immediately precede and accompany his personal appearance. Thus the "obstacle" and the "restrainer" of 2:6-7 refer not to some vague and hidden opposition to the Antichrist but rather to the double condition which must be fulfilled before the triumphant return of Christ.

1079 Aus, Roger D. "God's Plan and God's Power: Isaiah 66 and the Restraining Factors of 2 Thess 2:6-7," *Journal of Biblical Literature* 96.4 (1977) 537-553.
Republished in Roger D. Aus, *Barabbas and Esther and Other Studies in the Judaic Illumination of Earliest Christianity* (South Florida Studies in the History of Judaism 54; Atlanta: Scholars Press, 1992) 143-162.

Isaiah 66, an Old Testament text employed extensively in 2 Thessalonians 1, offers a solution to the perplexing problem of what and who are "holding up" the coming of the Day of the Lord in 2 Thess 2:6-7. The fact that a number of possible parallels between Isaiah 66 and 2 Thessalonians 2 can be found strengthens the likelihood that this Old Testament passage also provides the background of the κατέχειν factors in 2 Thess 2:6-7. Furthermore, the author of 2 Thessalonians shows knowledge of the Hebrew Old Testament and thus it is not surprising that he employed another expression from the Hebrew text of Isaiah 66 (66:9, עצר) to describe the restraining factors in 2 Thess 2:6-7. "That which retrains" (2:6, τὸ κατέχον) the day of the Lord and Jesus' return in glory is God's will or plan that the gospel first be preached to all the nations. "He who restrains" (2:7, ὁ κατέχων) is God himself, as in Isa 66:9. A table showing the use of various verses from Isaiah 66 in 2 Thessalonians 1-2 is appended.

1080 Bahnsen, Wilhelm. "Zum Verständniss von 2 Thess., 2, 3-12. Ein Beitrag zu Kritik des 2ten Thessalonicherbriefes," *Jahrbücher für protestantische Theologie* 6 (1880) 681-701.

A study of 2 Thess 2:1-12 indicates that Paul believed that the day of the Lord had already come, and was not something near or still future (see 2 Tim 3:1) and he had told the Thessalonians that. This letter corrects that misunderstanding by saying that the coming of the Lord is an event which is near but has not yet begun, thereby giving hope to the Christians.

1081 Barney, Kenneth D. "The Hinderer," *Conference on the Holy Spirit Digest* (ed. Gwen Jones; 2 vols.; Springfield, MO: Gospel Publishing House, 1983) 2.263-268.

The restraining force about which Paul speaks in 2 Thess 2:5-6 is the Holy Spirit. The mystery of iniquity has been at work ever since the fall but it is being held in check until God's strategic moment when the Holy Spirit will cease his unique hindering of evil through the body of Christ, which will be removed from earth by the rapture. When that restraint is "taken out of the way," the stage will be set for the apostasy and the revealing of the man of lawlessness.

1082 Barnouin, M. "Les problèmes de traduction concernant II Thess. II.6-7," *New Testament Studies* 23.4 (1977) 482-498.

Understanding 2 Thess 2:6-7 is difficult, and this difficulty is exacerbated by the traditional translation of these verses. Focusing on grammatical and syntactical evidence from Hellenistic Greek, especially that of the New Testament and of Plutarch, it is possible to give a better translation. The central difficulty of this passage revolves around the identity of the being who "restrains" (whether it is a person or thing). The evidence suggests that the phrase ἐκ μέσου γένηται does not refer to a final removal of this figure, but simply a substitution of someone/thing else for him/it.

1083 ---. "Un 'Lieu Intermédiaire' Mythique en 2 Thess 2.7," *New Testament Studies* 40.3 (1994) 471.

Despite the alternative proposals which have been made, evidence from gnostic writers and their opponents shows that the gnostic conception of "the intermediary" best explains the enigmatic phrase ἐκ μέσου γένηται in 2 Thess 2:7, even though the parallels are not exact. This phrase does not refer to the final removal of the restrainer but simply to a substitution of one figure for another.

1084 Bartelink, G. J. M. "ANTIKEIMENOΣ (Widersacher) als Teufels- und Dämonenbezeichnung," *Sacris Erudiri* 30 (1987/89) 205-224.

This article examines the use of the Greek word ἀντικείμενος ("opponent," "enemy") with particular attention to its function as a way of talking about Satan. The texts surveyed include the Septuagint, the New Testament (2 Thess 2:4; 1 Tim 5:14), Apostolic Fathers and Apologists, New Testament Apocrypha, and patristic writings (Clement of Alexandria, Origen, etc.).

1085 Berger, Martin. "Die Katechon-Vorstellung 2 Thess 2,6f. Dietrich Bonhoeffers Interpretation im Kontext der Rezeptionsgeschichte," *Protokolle zur Bibel* 5.1 (1996) 33-56.

After sketching the history of the interpretation of the κατέχων figure in 2 Thess 2:6-7, the article discusses its place in Bonhoeffer's theological reading of history as decay and situates his interpretation in the reception-history of the concept.

1086 Betz, Otto. "Der Katechon," *New Testament Studies* 9.3 (1963) 276-291.

Paul says in 2 Thess 2:6 that the community of Christians there knows the holy power (τὸ κατέχον) which holds off the entry of the last events. There have been many suggestions as to what this restraining force might be. The so-called Qumran Book of Mysteries (1Q27) and the book of Daniel (e.g., 9:24-27) point clearly to the restraining force being the Roman emperor. But could the emperor serve this function in Jewish literature? There is precedent in the recognition of Cyrus in Isa 45:1. Also, in light of Romans 13, it is possible to see the Roman emperor in this way in Paul's writings. If the apostle associated the restraining force with the emperor, his apocalyptic plan was made out of date by the passing of time. Claudius disappeared in 54 CE without the Antichrist or the endtimes coming. This strengthens the traditional linkage of the two letters. Even if they are not authentic, the thought still reflects Jewish tradition.

1087 Brown, Stephen G. "The Intertextuality of Isaiah 66.17 and 2 Thessalonians 2.7: A Solution for the 'Restrainer' Problem," *Paul and the Scriptures of Israel* (ed. Craig A. Evans and James A. Sanders; Journal for the Study of the New Testament Supplement Series 83; Studies in Scripture in Early Judaism and Christianity 1; Sheffield: JSOT Press, 1993) 254-277.

The methods of rhetorical criticism, mythopoetic imagery (traditional symbols and ideas), and "inner biblical exegesis" (earlier or original literary contexts) are combined in the attempt to identify the "restrainer" in 2 Thess 2:6-7. The first method involves a structural analysis of 2 Thess 2:1-12. The second method examines the concept of "the Middle" (2:7, ἕως ἐκ μέσου γένηται) in the biblical tradition. The third compares the structure of Isaiah 66 and 2 Thessalonians 1-2, showing how Paul's exposition honored the chiastic structure of this Old Testament passage. The results suggest that Isa 66:17 is the key verse behind the puzzle of 2 Thess 2:7. The article contains two appendices: one showing the parallel structures with intertextual correspondences in 2 Thess 2:3b-12; the other highlighting the parallels between 2 Thessalonians 1-2 and Isaiah 66.

1088 Bruce, F. F. "Paul and 'The Powers That Be,'" *Bulletin of the John Rylands University Library of Manchester* 66 (1984) 78-96.

In the expression "the powers that be" of Rom 13:1-7, Paul pictures principalities and powers as human rulers appointed by God. Both this passage and 2 Thess 2:1-12 (the restraining power is to be identified with the forces of law and order, represented by the Roman empire and embodied in the emperor) indicate that human government preserves law and order. Paul teaches that Christians are to respect their government, yield to its authority, and give it what it is due.

1089 Brunec, Michael. "De 'Homine peccati' in 2 Thess 2,1-12," *Verbum Domini* 35 (1957) 3-33.

The "man of sin" in 2 Thess 2:3 is to be identified not with an eschatological Antichrist but with the Pharisaic Judaism of Paul's own day. The main reasons for this conclusion are that the adversary in question must be considered contemporaneous with the apostle, and that the description given of this adversary fits that of the Pharisaic Judaism of Paul's day. These overall arguments can be supported by a fresh examination of many details in the text. For example, the ἀποστασία of 2:3 does not refer to a spiritual rebellion but to the physical departure of the church from Jerusalem at the beginning of the Jewish War. Or again, the epithet ἄνομος in 2:8 refers to the abuse of the law on the part of the Pharisees.

1090 Buzy, Denis. "L'adversaire et l'obstacle, II Thess. 2:3-12," *Recherches de science religieuse* 24 (1934) 402-431.

The problems of the parousia dominate the two letters to the Thessalonians. Two specific issues in 2 Thess 2:3-12, however, have always been especially problematic. The first concerns the concept of the Antichrist, and the second, the obstacle to the appearance of this figure. With reference to other literature in the New Testament, it is difficult to know if the Antichrist is a single person or a collective figure. The obstacle to the appearance of the Antichrist, however, is probably best understood as the proclamation of the gospel by the apostles, missionaries, and prophets of the church.

1091 Clark, Kenneth W. "The Meaning of ἐνεργέω and καταργέω in the New Testament," *Journal of Biblical Literature* 54 (1935) 93-102.

The verbs ἐνεργέω and καταργέω are typically translated in an inadequate and colorless manner which misses the vivid imagery that they had in their first-century Christian context. They are better rendered as "to infuse with supernatural spirit" (i.e., spirit-possession), or, in those situations where possession has already taken place, "to make supernaturally operative."

1092 Coppens, Joseph. "Le katechon et le katechon: derniers obstacles à la parousie du Seigneur Jésus," *L'Apocalypse johannique et l'Apocalyptique dans le Nouveau Testament* (ed. J. Lambrecht; Bibliotheca ephemeridum theologicarum lovaniensium 53; Leuven: Peeters/Leuven University Press, 1980) 345-347.

Following two previous articles on 2 Thess 2:1-12 (1093, 1094), it is possible to see that the sense of this passage is obscured largely as a result of many important and meaning-laden words being used in different senses within the chapter itself. When these different usages are examined and connections between verses eliminated simply on the basis of similar words being used, the whole chapter becomes fairly clear.

1093 ---. "Les deux obstacles au retour glorieux du Sauveur," *Ephemerides theologicae lovanienses* 46.3-4 (1970) 383-389.

The two obstacles to the glorious return of Christ are the mystery of iniquity and the man of sin. Contrary to the opinion of most scholars, 2 Thess 2:7-8 states that the man of sin by his actions is preventing the return of Christ in glory. This interpretation is supported by the fact that Paul is concerned, not with the manifestation of the man of sin, but with that of Christ. Furthermore, the beginning of the section of the discussion (2:6-12) returns to the first section (2:1-5), which is concerned exclusively with Christ's glorious revelation. In brief, verses 6-7 are a digression from the previous and following verses, and the "time" in view is actually only a marker of that digression, in effect saying, "now that you know what has been written here."

1094 ---. "Le 'Mystère' dans la théologie paulinienne et ses parallèles qumrâniens," *Littérature et théologie paulinienne* (ed. Albert-Louis Descamps; Recherches Bibliques 5; Paris: Desclée de Brouwer, 1960) 142-165.

In introducing into his vocabulary such terms as "revelation," "mystery," "knowledge," and "perfection," Paul constructs a tight unity, which has cognates in the literature discovered at Qumran. This article examines several parallels between Paul's writings and those from Qumran, including parallels to 2 Thess 2:1-12, especially 2:6-7. At Qumran, we find the term *Bₑnê* or *'Anšê haš-šahat* (CD 6:15; 13:14; 1QS 9:16; 10:19), which corresponds to the term υἱὸς ἀπωλείας ("son of destruction") from 2 Thess 2:3. In an appendix, 2 Thess 2:7 is examined, where it is suggested that it can actually refer to the coming of Christ, answering the three objections that (1) the verb ἀποκαλύπτειν is employed in the context of the return of the Antichrist in verse 3, (2) verse 7 is too distant from verses 2-3, where the return of Christ is indeed in view, and (3) the time in view is actually that of the Antichrist.

1095 Cothenet, Édouard. "La II Épître aux Thessaloniciens et l'apocalypse synoptique," *Recherches de science religieuse* 42 (1954) 5-39.

The apocalyptic eschatological outlook of the synoptic gospels, oriented toward the end of time, is different than the apocalyptic outlook of 2 Thessalonians. The apocalyptic traditions expressed in 2 Thessalonians are simply echoes of the predictions of Jesus concerning the chastisement of the Jewish people. This came about as a result of the Jewish persecution of Christians and was part of a response to the Jewish denial of Jesus' messianic status. This shows that Paul knew the form of the apocalyptic traditions which constituted the basis for the writer of the first gospel.

1096 Cowles, Henry. "On 'The Man of Sin,' 2 Thess. II.3-9," *Bibliotheca Sacra* 29 (1872) 623-640.

2 Thess 2:1-12 is Paul's response to believers in Thessalonica who wrongly interpreted his earlier words in 1 Thess 4:13-18 to mean that the return of Christ was imminent. Paul asserts that the parousia will not take place before the "man of sin" is revealed--a reference to a single individual and not to a corporate figure or indefinite succession of men who span the centuries. This individual is currently prohibited from coming by Christ who is the "restrainer/restraining power" referred to in 2:6-7.

1097 Cullmann, Oscar. "Le caractère eschatologique du devoir missionaire et de la conscience apostolique de saint Paul. Étude sur le κατέχον (-ων) de 2. Thess. 2:6-7," *Revue de l'histoire des religions* 16 (1936) 210-245.

Republished under the same title in Oscar Cullmann, *Des sources de l'Évangile à la formation de la théologie chrétienne* (Neuchatel: Delachaux et Niestlé, 1969) 51-75. Also republished in a German version as "Der eschatologische Charakter des Missionsauftrages und des apostolischen Selbstbewusstseins bei Paulus: Untersuchung zum Begriff des κατέχον (κατέχων) in 2 Thess. 2,6-7," *Vorträge und Aufsätze, 1925-1962* (ed. K. Fröhlich; Tübingen: Mohr/Siebeck, 1966) 305-336.

Although exegetes today are not privy to the knowledge of the original recipients of 2 Thessalonians, which would have illuminated the meaning of 2 Thess 2:6-7, they are not totally unable to understand what is going on in the letter. Limiting the question simply to the identity of the "restrainer," the best solution is that this is actually the proclamation of the gospel to the pagans. This is a natural development from Jewish eschatology and is in keeping with other primitive Christian writings, as well as with the writings of Paul himself. This concurrence with the letters of Paul allows two further conclusions to be drawn: (1) 2 Thessalonians is, in fact, probably Pauline; and (2) Paul's *eschatological* apostolic consciousness was more at the center of his theology than is often recognized.

1098 ---. "Wann kommt das Reich Gottes? Zur Enderwartung der christlichen Schriftsteller des zweiten Jahrhunderts," *Vorträge und Aufsätze, 1925-1962* (ed. K. Fröhlich; Tübingen: Mohr/Siebeck, 1966) 535-547.

On the basis of the exegesis of 2 Thess 2:6-7 presented in an earlier article (1097), interpretations of this passage in the following authors regarding the coming of the kingdom of God are explored: Pseudo-Clementine "Proclamation of Peter," Justin Martyr, Shepherd of Hermas, Epistle of Barnabas, and 2 Clement.

1099 Dawson, W. Bell. "The Meaning of 'Antichrist' in the Greek of the New Testament," *Evangelical Quarterly* 16 (1944) 71-73.

The preposition ἀντί, when combined with any office or position of authority, does not have its primary meaning of "opposite to" but "in place of." The title "Antichrist," therefore, emphasizes not the rebellious opposition of this figure to Christ but his deceptive claim to take the place of Christ as head or ruler.

1100 Dean, David E. "Martin Luther's View of the Antichrist," *Henceforth* 6 (1978) 85-97.

Luther's views of the Antichrist developed and broadened over three distinct periods of his life, using the term to refer to the Turks (Muslims), the pope, the Roman church and heretics in general. By the end of his life, Luther applied 2 Thess 2:3-12 exclusively to the pope but understood 1 John 2:18-22 as referring more broadly to any group that displaced the word of God and the gospel.

1101 Dixon, Paul S. "The Evil Restraint in 2 Thess 2:6," *Journal of the Evangelical Theological Society* 33.4 (1990) 445-449.

The traditional identification of "the restraint" (τὸ κατέχον) as good (e.g., the Roman Empire, the Holy Spirit, the church, Paul, the preaching of the gospel) is mistaken. Four exegetical considerations indicate that the restraint is evil, that the impersonal τὸ κατέχον refers to the mystery of lawlessness already at work, and that the personal ὁ κατέχων refers to Satan.

1102 Ernst, Josef. "Der eschatologische Gegenspieler im zweiten Thessalonicherbrief," *Die eschatologischen Gegenspieler in den Schriften des Neuen Testaments* (Biblische Untersuchungen 3; Regensburg: Pustet, 1967) 24-79.

In 2 Thess 2:1-12, Paul finally speaks of the eschatological opponent, the "man of lawlessness." But how did the author of 2 Thessalonians come to introduce this figure? It seems to reflect a relationship between the two Thessalonian letters (see 1 Thess 4:13-18) and the eschatological thought of his community. This figure is not an idea or community concept but an individual personality, held in check by God's plan for the parousia.

1103 Farrow, Douglas. "Showdown: The Message of Second Thessalonians 2:1-12 and the Riddle of the 'Restrainer,'" *Crux* 25.1 (1989) 23-26.

In coming to a new understanding of the perplexing problem of the "restrainer" in 2 Thess 2:1-12, it is important to recognize the following points. First, the distinction between τὸ κατέχον and ὁ κατέχων must not be overlooked: there are different referents for these terms. Second, the phrase ἕως ἐκ μέσου γένηται should not, as it typically has been, be taken to mean "until he [the restrainer] is removed out of the way" but rather "until he [the man of lawlessness] shall emerge out of the midst." The antecedent of this phrase is not the restrainer but the man of lawlessness. Thus, the matter of restraint involves a two-sided notion: as a holding back *both* of God's ultimate judgment *and* of the premature uncontrollable urges of lawlessness.

1104 Fee, Gordon D. "Pneuma and Eschatology in 2 Thessalonians 2.1-12: A Proposal about 'Testing the Prophets' and the Purpose of 2 Thessalonians," *To Tell the Mystery. Essays in New Testament Eschatology in Honor of Robert H. Gundry* (ed. Thomas E. Schmidt and Moisés Silva; Sheffield: JSOT Press, 1994) 196-215.

A careful study of 2 Thess 2:2, especially the difficult phrase ὡς δι' ἡμῶν ("as though through us"), suggests that someone speaking "by the Spirit" had interpreted a teaching of Paul to be that "the Day of the Lord has already come." Paul's solution to this inappropriate use of a "Spirit" utterance is found in 2:15 where the phrase διὰ πνεύματος is noticeably missing (compare the three phrases in 2:2) as he now urges them to hold fast to the "traditions" which they were taught. Thus the primary criterion for the testing of prophetic or spiritual utterances is how well it agrees with the traditions which Paul had taught, whether orally or in his letters. 1 Thess 5:19-22 leads one to think that Paul already earlier on had concerns about the Thessalonians' failure to be more perceptive about "Spirit" utterances.

1105 Feinberg, Paul D. "2 Thessalonians 2 and the Rapture," *When the Trumpet Sounds* (ed. Thomas Ice and Timothy J. Demy; Eugene, OR: Harvest House, 1995) 297-311.

Three of the most important issues in 2 Thess 2:1-12 with respect to the time of the rapture are as follows: (1) the relationship between 2 Thess 2:1 and Matt 24:29-31; (2) the silence of Paul about a pretribulational rapture in correcting false teaching in 2 Thess 2:2-4; and (3) the identity of the restrainer in 2 Thess 2:5-7. On these three key issues, there is no exegetical or theological matter which makes a pretribulational rapture impossible or even improbable.

1106 Fensham, F. C. "Wie en wat is die Antichris volgens Thessalonicense?," *Nederduitse gereformeerde Teologiese Tydskrif* 6 (1965) 159-169.

There are two main branches of thought regarding the Antichrist figure. One interpretation views the Antichrist as a representation of the evil forces already at work in this world which oppose both Christ and the church. The other interpretation holds that, while there will be an "antichrist" force at work in the end times, this force and all that is anti-Christian will culminate in one person. An exegetical study of 2 Thess 2:1-12, as well as other relevant passages, supports the latter position, namely, that the Antichrist will, in fact, appear in person at the end of time and that he will personify all the forces of evil.

1107 Freese, N. F. "Τὸ κατέχον und ὁ κατέχων (2 Thess. 2,6-7)," *Theologische Studien und Kritiken* 93 (1920/21) 73-77.

2 Thess 2:6-7 indicates that before the parousia of Christ the "mystery of lawlessness" must be fulfilled in two parts: the "apostasy" and the "revelation" of the "man of lawlessness." The apostasy is underway. The fulfillment of the second part of the mystery, however, remains until the man of lawlessness is revealed. There is thus the restraining moment for the fulfillment of this mystery and the parousia of Christ. This

clarifies the change from τὸ κατέχον to ὁ κατέχων. During the period before the fulfillment of the mystery there is an impersonal restraining force (v 6), but in verse 7 the man of lawlessness himself is this force.

1108 Fulford, H. W. "ἕως ἐκ μέσου γένηται (2 Thess. ii. 7)," *Expository Times* 23 (1911) 40-41.

It is generally held that the elliptical expression ἕως ἐκ μέσου γένηται implies destruction or overthrow. This sense is supported by the seemingly parallel phrase ἕως ἐκ μέσου ἀρθῇ (1 Cor 5:2; Col 2:14; Isa 57:2 [LXX]). A more exact parallel, however, can be found in the writings of Plutarch where this phrase denotes voluntary action. Paul, therefore, envisions the restrainer as retiring voluntarily from the scene of action instead of being forcibly removed. This understanding of 2 Thess 2:7 has important implications on the identity of the restrainer and the interpretation of the passage as a whole.

1109 Furfey, Paul Hanly. "The Mystery of Lawlessness," *Catholic Biblical Quarterly* 8 (1946) 179-191.

Very divergent meanings have been given to the phrase "the mystery of lawlessness" (2 Thess 2:7) in the patristic, medieval, Reformation, post-Reformation, and modern periods, thereby illustrating well the truth of Augustine's *dictum* concerning the "obscure words of the apostle." Nevertheless, a careful examination of the use of the word "mystery" in secular Greek texts, the Septuagint, and the New Testament, as well as a study of the larger context of 2:1-12 and the apocalyptic genre to which this passage belongs, suggests that the "mystery of lawlessness" refers to Satan's evil plan to frustrate as far as possible the redemptive work of Christ.

1110 Gatzweiler, Karl. "Der Paulinische Wunderbegriff," *Der Wunderbegriff im Neuen Testament* (ed. Alfred Suhl; Darmstadt: Wissenschaftliche Buchgesellschaft, 1980) 374-415.

2 Thess 2:9-10 is one of several Pauline passages related to the topic of "miracles" or "wonders." The phrase in 2 Thess 2:9 is introduced with the preposition ἐν, indicating the sphere and circumstance of these events. δύναμις refers not to the miracle but to the power. The adjective "all" modifies the first noun "power," not the following nouns, "signs and wonders," which are designated as "false." It is not surprising that Paul uses this kind of language here, since it is part of his understanding of the return of Christ. The apostle accepts a supernatural power as the source of these wonders. Such supernatural events function to make the arrival of the Antichrist public.

1111 Giblin, Charles Homer. "2 Thessalonians 2 Re-read as Pseudepigraphal: A Revised Reaffirmation of *The Threat to Faith*," *The Thessalonian Correspondence* (ed. Raymond F. Collins; Bibliotheca ephemeridum theologicarum lovaniensium 87; Leuven: Leuven University Press, 1990) 459-469.

Just over twenty years ago, in a monograph entitled, *The Threat to Faith* (1113), a new interpretation of the κατέχον/-ων in 2 Thess 2:5-7 was proposed: this enigmatic term alludes to a pseudo-charismatic spirit (of Dionysiac character) which "seized" or "possessed" the Thessalonians. Although some modifications to that previous study need to be made (e.g., 2 Thessalonians is not Pauline but pseudepigraphal; the "temple" in 2:4 is not a reference to the church but a symbolic construct; "and now" in 2:6 is not just logical but mainly temporal), its basic thesis is reaffirmed.

1112 ---. "Contra Periculum Imminens Fidei (2 Thess 2)," *Verbum Domine* 45 (1967) 23-31.
A summary of Charles Giblin's published dissertation (1113).

1113 ---. *The Threat to Faith: An Exegetical and Theological Re-Examination of 2 Thessalonians 2* (Anelecta Biblica 31; Rome: Pontifical Biblical Institute, 1967).
The purpose of 2 Thess 2:1-17 is to oppose a movement of false prophecy which had arisen in the Thessalonian church. The "man of lawlessness," though modeled by Paul on Antiochus Epiphanes, is a false prophet who is deceiving the community with a teaching about the Day of the Lord which he is passing off as the teaching of the apostle. τὸ κατέχον is not a restrainer of an "Antichrist" figure nor does he delay the coming of this figure or the Lord; rather, it is an impersonal reification of a demonic, Dionysiac, pseudo-prophetic force already at work in Thessalonica. Thus τὸ κατέχον represents a negative force which does not "restrain" but instead "seizes." This force and the "man of lawlessness" are both part of the "mystery of lawlessness." Sometimes the impersonal τὸ κατέχον is personalized as ὁ κατέχων because the evil force centered upon an individual prophet.

1114 González Ruiz, José María. "La incredulidad de Israel y los impedimentos del Anticristo, según 2 Tes. 2, 6-7," *Estudios Bíblicos* 10 (1951) 189-203.
A plausible hypothesis concerning the identify of the restrainer in 2 Thess 2:6-7 sees the archangel Michael as the one who restrains the coming of the Antichrist on behalf of the people of Israel--a hypothesis which can be supported with texts from Daniel and Revelation 12 and 20. In this view, what restrains the Antichrist is the prolonged unbelief of Israel, which is addressed especially in Romans 9-11. The advantage of this hypothesis over others which have been forwarded is that it explains the use of two genders to depict the restrainer. Furthermore, the fact that Paul had been persecuted in Thessalonica by the Jews is also a plausible explanation for why he could have included these motifs in his preaching to the church, as well as the mysterious tone in which he has mentioned them in the letter.

1115 Griffiths, J. Gwyn. "2 Thessalonians ii. 4," *Expository Times* 52 (1940/41) 38.
In the phrase ἐπὶ πάντα λεγόμενον θεὸν ἢ σέβασμα (2 Thess 2:4), which describes the "man of sin," most versions wrongly treat πάντα as a neuter plural instead of as a masculine singular, thereby resulting in a slightly inaccurate translation. A better rendering would be: "against every person who is called god or (every) thing which is worshipped."

1116 Gundry, Robert H. "Correction in 2 Thessalonians," *The Church and the Tribulation* (Grand Rapids: Zondervan, 1973) 112-128.

The typical pretribulational interpretation of 2 Thess 2:1-12 fails to explain a number of key issues in the passage, whereas the posttribulational view commends itself at every point. The Thessalonians mistakenly thought that Christ was about to return, that the day of the Lord was going to arrive in the immediate future. Paul reminds them that that event will not happen until *after* the apostasy and the revelation of the man of lawlessness. Those events will take place during the tribulation yet *before* the day of the Lord, for which Christians are to be alert. The identity of the restrainer remains an open question, although identification with the Holy Spirit remains the best explanation. Paul concludes the section with a restatement of Jesus' return to "slay" the "lawless one" and to "judge" those "who did not believe the truth" (2:8-12). From beginning to end posttribulationism characterizes the passage.

1117 Hamann, Henry P. "A Brief Exegesis of 2 Thess. 2:1-12 with Guidelines for the Application of the Prophecy Contained Therein," *Concordia Theological Monthly* 24 (1953) 418-433.

In order to combat the false teaching that the Day of the Lord had come--a teaching which caused some in the Thessalonian church to give up work--Paul asserts that the man of sin must be revealed prior to Christ's return. This diabolical counterpart to God's son through whom Satan works is the same figure who elsewhere in scripture is described as the Antichrist. He will exalt himself in the temple of God--the Christian church--in the midst of a religious apostasy. Yet the full power of his coming is currently being restrained by an impersonal and personal force--the law and those political leaders who embody that law. The classical Lutheran view that the Pope is the Antichrist is still a valid identification, since the essential marks of this rebellious figure are more clearly seen today than in the Reformation.

1118 Harrison, William K. "The Time of the Rapture as Indicated in Certain Scriptures," *Bibliotheca Sacra* 115 (1958) 20-26.

2 Thessalonians, particularly 2:1-12, confirms the conclusion reached in a study of 1 Thessalonians, namely, that the rapture will occur before the great tribulation. The "Day of the Lord" refers not to the coming of Christ itself but the great tribulation--an event which is "at hand." The removal of the church as the restraining force during the tribulation and the setting in of the apostasy are concurring events (this article continues an identically entitled article in *Bibliotheca Sacra* 114 [1957] 316-325; see 993).

1119 Hartl, Vinzenz. "ὁ κατέχων ἄρτι (2 Thess 2,7)," *Zeitschrift für katholische Theologie* 45 (1921) 455-475.

An exegesis of 2 Thess 2:6-7 indicates that Paul believed the "restrainer" to be a factor removed between 53 and 63 CE. It could be the temple as such, the Roman government, the civil order or something else, even James, the brother of the Lord and leader of the Palestine church, who had a high reputation with the Jews. Attempts to equate ὁ κατέχων with a person of high reputation and τὸ κατέχον with an institution cannot be proved.

1120 Holman, Charles L. "2 Thessalonians 2 (The 'Pauline Apocalypse')," *Till Jesus Comes. Origins of Christian Apocalyptic Expectation* (Peabody, MA: Hendrickson, 1966) 103-110.

2 Thess 2:1-12 demonstrates that in the first-century church there was a re-use and christological interpretation of traditional Jewish apocalyptic motifs. The "apostasy" which must precede the return of Christ most likely involves a religious rather than political rebellion. This rebellion will be promoted by the "man of lawlessness," an anti-god figure who is best traced to Daniel and who later became a traditional part of Jewish eschatology. Although it is impossible to determine with certainty the identity of the "restrainer" and "restraining force," there is good evidence that they refer to God and his intervening activity in the world.

1121 House, H. Wayne. "Apostasia in 2 Thessalonians 2:3: Apostasy or Rapture?" *When the Trumpet Sounds* (ed. Thomas Ice and Timothy J. Demy; Eugene, OR: Harvest House, 1995) 261-295.

The Greek term ἀποστασία in 2 Thess 2:3 has been interpreted in four different ways: (1) as an appositive to the "man of sin"; (2) as a passive "falling away" from the faith by either the church, Jewish people during the tribulation, or non-Christians as a whole; (3) as active revolt or rebellion; or (4) as the rapture of the church. Although the last view has not found much favor, it is supported by the meaning of ἀποστασία in Greek literature, the grammar of the passage, and contextual considerations in the Thessalonian letters. If ἀποστασία means departure, in the context of the departure of Christians before the day of the Lord, then the word corresponds with Paul's other terms to describe the deliverance of Christians from this world and their gathering to Jesus.

1122 Kaczewski, Józef. "To katechon--ho katechon (2 Tes 2,6-7). Krytyka nowych rozwiazan i wlasna propozycja," *Analecta Cracoviensia* 24 (1992) 153-170.

An exegetical analysis of 2 Thess 2:1-12 highlights the weaknesses of the various hypotheses concerning the identity of the κατέχον and κατέχων in verses 6-7. A better hypothesis is that the mysterious powers who hold back the parousia of the Antichrist are (1) faith, which allows Christians to persevere, and (2) Christ, who is both the master and the dispenser of this faith.

1123 Kern, Friedrich H. "Über 2. Thess 2,1-12. Nebst Andeutungen über den Ursprung des zweiten Briefes an die Thessalonicher," *Tübinger Zeitschrift für Theologie* 2 (1839) 145-214.

The language and context of 2 Thess 2:1-12 indicate that this letter could not have been written by Paul. There are striking parallels between the apocalyptic scenario in

2:1-12 with that found in Rev 13:3-10 and 17:8-14. The description of the man of lawlessness is dependent on the legend of Nero *redivivus*. Since Nero died in 68 CE, reliance on a myth which circulated after his death precludes the possibility that 2 Thessalonians was written by the apostle. Instead, it appears that the letter was written between 68 and 70 by a follower of the apostle who "paulinized" the apocalyptic material which he included in a letter based on 1 Thessalonians.

1124 Knox, John. "A Note on II Thessalonians 2:2," *Anglican Theological Review* 18 (1936) 72-73.

The clause ἐνέστηκεν ἡ ἡμέρα τοῦ κυρίου, which can be naturally taken only as referring to a present fact (the day of the Lord "has come" rather than "is at hand"), does not necessarily involve the conclusion that the Thessalonians were under the incredible misapprehension that the "day" had come, but only that the author of 2 Thessalonians understood that they were. This is the likely inference which a person like Paul (the probable author of the letter) would naturally draw from the news of the eschatological disturbances at Thessalonica which had reached him.

1125 König, Adrio. "Is die Teëhouer al uit die weg geruim?" *Nederduitse Gereformeerde Teologiese Tydskrif* 11.1 (1970) 36-44.

A survey of the various interpretations about the Antichrist illustrates how misguided and shortsighted the church has been through the centuries in identifying this figure. It has been claimed that the Antichrist is a political figure, a religious figure, a heresy, one who stands in opposition against God and the church, one who comes from within the church, and one who parades himself as Christ so as to mislead believers. A comparison of the position of Paul with that of John shows that Paul stresses the fact that the Restrainer of the Antichrist has not yet been removed (2 Thess 2:7), whereas John understands this figure as a present and as a plural reality (2 John 2). This does not necessarily indicate a difference in eschatology, for it is quite conceivable that the Restrainer disappeared in the period of at least twenty years which separates Paul's earliest letters from the letters of John. The description of the Antichrist by John as a plural phenomenon is confirmed by the witness of both the rest of the New Testament and the history of the church.

1126 Krodel, Gerhard A. "The 'Religious Power of Lawlessness' (*Katechon*) as Precursor of the 'Lawless One' (*Anomos*): 2 Thess 2:6-7," *Currents in Theology and Mission* 17.6 (1990) 440-446.

Three conclusions can be reached regarding the use and meaning of the verb κατέχω in 2 Thess 2:6-7: (1) the verb has essentially a hostile rather than beneficial sense in accordance with the apocalyptic genre of the whole passage; (2) the implied object of κατέχον is not the "lawless one" but "you"--the recipients of the letter whose faith and endurance have been praised (1:3-4); and (3) the "restraining person/force" refers to the religious/political powers within the empire, to its culture, and to its representatives who control, suppress, and lay claims upon the saints, and who "believe what is false" (2:11). The pseudepigraphal writer of 2 Thessalonians may well have chosen the vague word κατέχειν because some local magistrates had used it in connection with actions against Christians whom they felt needed to be "restrained."

1127 LaRondelle, Hans K. "The Middle Ages within the Scope of Apocalyptic Prophecy," *Journal of the Evangelical Theological Society* 32.2 (1989) 345-354.

Paul's theological interpretation and historical application of Daniel's eschatological Antichrist form an essential interpretative link between Daniel and Revelation. Paul's prophetic revelation in 2 Thess 2:1-12 provides the apostolic confirmation of the continuous-historical approach of Daniel's apocalyptic prophecies (rather than the contemporary-historical or futurist constructs). The apostle characterizes the coming Christian apostasy as a counterfeit cultic worship, authorized by a rival Messiah, who will rise within the Christian temple of God--the church--soon after the fall of pagan Rome (i.e., in the middle ages).

1128 ---. "Paul's Prophetic Outline in 2 Thessalonians 2," *Andrews University Semitic Studies* 21.1 (1983) 61-69.

Paul corrects the imminent expectation of the parousia in the church of Thessalonica by stressing a basic chronological order of the two major prophetic events: first, the revelation of the man of sin; then the revelation of Christ in glory. Paul derived his description of the Antichrist from a conflation of Old Testament revelations about anti-God powers (Daniel 7, 8-12; Ezekiel 28; Isaiah 11, 13) and Christ's teaching of apocalyptic events (Mark 13).

1129 Lietaert Peerbolte, Lambertus J. "The ΚΑΤΕΧΟΝ/ΚΑΤΕΧΩΝ of 2 Thess. 2:6-7," *Novum Testamentum* 39.2 (1997) 138-150.

Once 2 Thessalonians is recognized as a deutero-Pauline letter, a new solution is possible to the vexing problem concerning the κατέχον/κατέχων reference in 2:6-7. It is very likely that the vagueness of these terms is intentional and that the author did not refer to any identifiable object or being at all. Writing in a period after Paul's death to a congregation outside Thessalonica who would have been far less suspicious of a forgery than the church to which the letter claims to be sent, the author of 2 Thessalonians keeps his words extremely vague and so ingeniously obscures the reason for the postponement of the coming of the Day of the Lord. While in fact the pseudonymous writer himself has no answer either, he evokes the illusion among the readers of 2 Thessalonians that there is an answer, and that the Thessalonians knew it.

1130 ---. "The Man of Ungodliness: 2 Thessalonians 2,1-12 and Justin, Dialogue with Trypho 32 and 110," *The Antecedents of Antichrist. A Traditio-Historical Study of the Earliest Christian Views on Eschatological Opponents* (Supplements to the Journal for the Study of Judaism 49; Leiden: Brill, 1996) 63-95.

2 Thess 3:3-12 and Justin's *Dialogue* 32 and 110 prove that at the beginning of the second century CE a tradition existed concerning the coming of an eschatological opponent called the "man of ungodliness." This tradition was based on an interpretation of the prophecies of, at least, Daniel 7 and 11, which pertain to the coming of an eschatological tyrant. Its terminology was probably derived from the tradition on the eschatological climax of ungodliness, found in 2 Thessalonians and Matthew 24. Although there is no compelling evidence in the form of Jewish parallels, it is highly plausible that the tradition on the man of ungodliness was a Jewish tradition, although this assertion cannot be conclusively applied to the terminology also. The fact that Justin mentions the coming of the eschatological opponent in an offhand manner, without furnishing a long description of what will happen at his arrival, indicates that for Justin and his readers the coming of this opponent was a familiar expectation.

1131 Lofstrom, Elmer E. "Lawlessness and its Restrainer: A New Translation of 2 Thessalonians ii. 6-8," *Expository Times* 28 (1917) 379-380.

Much of the obscurity over 2 Thess 2:6-8 may be removed by a simple change in punctuation. If the phrase μόνον ὁ κατέχων ἄρτι is treated as a parenthetical comment, the translation of the passage is as follows: "for the mystery of lawlessness is already working (only there is he who is restraining it just now)--until it shall arise out of the midst, and then shall the lawless one be revealed." This connects the phrase ἕως ἐκ μέσου γένηται not with the personal restrainer but with the impersonal mystery of lawlessness which is already at work.

1132 Mackintosh, Robert. "The Antichrist of 2 Thessalonians," *The Expositor, 7th Series* 2 (1906) 427-432.

The key to understanding to whom Paul was referring as the "man of sin" is furnished by 1 Thess 2:14-16 and several passages of Acts which speak of the hostility of unconverted Jews towards the Pauline gospel. The "apostasy" (2:3) will involve the unmasking of the Jews as open enemies of God from whom the "man of sin" will emerge. This ungodly Judaism is being "restrained" (2:6, 7) in Paul's day from its full development by either the presence of suffering Christians in Jerusalem or, as is more commonly held, the power of Roman law.

1133 Marín, Francisco. "2 Tes 2,3-12. Intentos de comprensión y nuevo planteamiento," *Estudios Eclesiásticos* 54 (1979) 527-537.

Does 2 Thess 2:3-12 reveal anything about the first Christian communities' political commitment? Several interpretations (wrongly) suggest so, especially those which identify the restrainer as the Roman empire and the Antichrist as a future personage to appear at the end of time. A closer examination of the passage, however, demands a negative answer. Not only does a futuristic reading betray the church's consciousness of living in the absolute eschaton originated in Christ's resurrection, but also the "man of lawlessness" must be understood in a different way, namely, as the prototypical individual who becomes incarnate in every person who opposes God and his salvation. The "restrainer" also does not demand a political understanding, since it is God himself who restrains the wicked in order to allow humanity to come to salvation.

1134 ---. "Pequeña apocalipsis de 2 Tes 2,3-12," *Estudios Eclesiásticos* 51 (1976) 29-56.

2 Thess 2:3-12 echoes a specific tendency in the apocalyptic of the New Testament where the chronological uncertainty of the end has given place to the certainty of the judgment and to a parenthetical tone. This judgment has taken place in Christ's death and resurrection, which are elevated to the decisive moment upon which the future events depend. From that perspective, 2 Thess 2:3-12 has to do specifically with the judgment of the wicked (vv 3-4), which refers to a distributive singular rather than to an individual, and their followers (vv 10-12). The fact that the wicked can include each person opposing God invites a watchful behavior, since God's judgment is already present and is actualized at the end of each person's life. This ongoing presence of the judgment, which does not deny its future reality, is further supported by the reference to the parousia. Unlike other passages where the parousia refers to the final consummation, here it refers to the judgment in the cross and the consequent eschatological *presence* of the judgment of God (v 8) which parallels the *presence* of the iniquity in the world (v 9).

1135 McCall, Thomas S. "How Soon the Tribulation Temple?" *Bibliotheca Sacra* 128 (1971) 341-351.

Recent events and continuing tensions in the Holy Land raise the question of the erection of a Jewish temple. Biblically, there is reason to believe that there are two future temples: the "millennial" temple, which will be built by Jesus himself according to the details found in Ezekiel 40-48 and which will stand during his thousand year reign on earth; and the "tribulational" temple, which will be built and stand during the tribulation. Four passages in the Bible predict the desecration of the holy place (Dan 9:26-27; Matt 24:15-16; 2 Thess 2:3-4; Rev 11:1-2) and this expressly requires the existence of a temple. There are a number of strong incentives for the rebuilding of the temple which apply to both Christians (it will fulfill prophecy and should help in reaching Jews for Christ) and Jews (it will involve religious fulfillment and stabilize the state of Israel).

1136 McNamara, Martin. "The Revelation of the Messiah in the Targums and the Epiphaneia of Christ in St. Paul: 2 Thes 2,8; Tit 2,13; 1 Tm 6,14 etc.," *The New Testament and the Palestinian Targum to the Pentateuch* (Rome: Pontifical Biblical Institute, 1966) 246-252.

Despite the widespread use of the term ἐπιφάνεια in the Hellenistic world, it is quite probable that behind Paul's employment of this word in 2 Thess 2:8, 1 Tim 6:14, 2 Tim 1:10, 4:1, 8 and Tit 2:13 lies the Jewish concept of the revelation of the Messiah and of the kingdom of God. In this instance, Paul's doctrine and expression are dependent on the religion of his fathers rather than on any adaptation to his audience.

1137 Meulen, R. J. van der. "Veractualisering van de Antichrist," *Arcana Revelata. Een Bundel Nieuw-Testamentische Studiën aangeboden aan F. W. Grosheide* (Kampen: Kok, 1951) 69-76.

There are two questions concerning the nature and coming of the Antichrist: (1) Can it be concluded with certainty that evil will continue to increase and develop until it reaches a "ripening" or "apex"? (2) Does the New Testament support the notion of a personal Antichrist in whom all the anti-Christian strife of all ages will be concentrated? 2 Thess 2 answers the second question in the affirmative: a personal Antichrist will bring evil to its culmination. Other texts such as Matt 3:12, 9:37-38, 13:30 and John 4:35-38 also speak of a "ripening" of evil which will culminate in the Day of the Lord. Yet there are also the "daimonia of states," society, religion, and even the church, who set themselves up as absolute power and take on the prerogatives of divine authority. Rome was thus perceived in New Testament times as the Antichrist.

1138 Miguens, M. "L'Apocalisse 'secondo Paolo'," *Bibbia e Oriente* 2.4-5 (1960) 142-148.

A comparison of the apocalyptic section of 2 Thess 2:3-12 with other apocalyptic texts in the New Testament sheds light on many of the exegetical difficulties found in this Pauline passage. Paul seeks to correct a false claim that the day of the Lord had come by asserting that the "apostasy" and "man of lawlessness" must come first. This evil figure is probably an allusion to the Roman emperor as a representative of the temporal power of the world. The "mystery of lawlessness" already at work in the world refers to the persecutions currently experienced by the church and the false teachings which are beginning to spread. God is mercifully postponing the day of Christ's return in order that humanity will have more time to repent and believe.

1139 Moran, John W. "Is Antichrist a Man?" *American Ecclesiastical Review* 92 (1935) 578-585.

In apocalyptic writings an individual may represent a group. Thus, athough Paul in 2 Thess 2:1-12 speaks of the "man of lawlessness," the apocalyptic genre of this passage allows for the view that the apostle is not thinking of an individual but a collection of men extending from his day to the end of the world. This interpretation is supported by the teaching of Jesus who spoke of "false Christs and false prophets" (Matt 24:11-13, 24) and of John (1 John 2:18). There is a distinction, however, between the first Antichrists and those at the end of the world. The latter will have the special assistance of Satan and be able to work false wonders so as to seduce even the elect. That which restrains the appearance of the final Antichrists are the preachers and the proclamation of the gospel.

1140 Moreland, Donald D. "The katechon: A Proposal for the Translation and Interpretation of 2 Thessalonians 2:6-7 in its Literary and Historical Context" (Unpublished Ph.D. Dissertation; Paris: Faculté Libre de Théologie Protestante, 1986).

The "restrainer" is a solidarity of persons activated by Satan who use all types of deception to gain divine honor and power in the church. The spirit of the restrainer is ancient but reveals itself in a new way vis-à-vis the gospel of salvation revealed in Jesus Christ. The old legalism is transmuted into Christian form. The achievement of official recognition of divine authority in the church by the papacy is the revelation of the "katechon"--the man of lawlessness, not because all popes have advocated lawlessness as a way of life, but because their official system of theology is a legalistic one which sets aside the New Testament gospel and because their self-exaltation has been promoted by lawlessness and resulted in the spiritual enslavement of countless people.

1141 Mussner, F. "Das Buch Judith und die neutestamentliche Antichristidee," *Trierer Theologische Zeitschrift* 72.4 (1963) 242-245.

There is a probable link between Judith and 2 Thessalonians. Statements concerning Nebuchadnezzar are made in Judith (3:8; 6:2b) which correspond to Paul's description of the Antichrist (2 Thess 2:4). The reason is that Nebuchadnezzar was conceived as a meta-historical figure representing the secular power which, from time to time in history but especially in the final onslaught of the Antichrist, fights against God and his people.

1142 Nestle, Eberhard. "2 Thess. 2. iii.," *Expository Times* 16 (1905) 472-473.

It is commonly claimed that 2 Thess 2:3 distinguishes two sequential events which will precede the final coming of the Lord: first, the apostasy, and then the revealing of the man of sin. The words of Paul, however, do not justify this distinction. For it has been generally overlooked that ἡ ἀποστασία is nothing else but a translation of the Hebrew בליעל, as is also the phrase ὁ ἄνθρωπος τῆς ἀνομίας.

1143 Orchard, J. Bernard. "Ellipsis and parenthesis in Gal 2:1-10 and 2 Thess 2:1-12," *Paul de Tarse. Apôtre du Notre Temps* (ed. A.-L. Descamps, L. de Lorenzi, and G. Benelli; Série monographique de "Benedictina": Section paulinienne 1; Rome: Abbaye de S. Paul, 1979) 247-258.

There are some striking parallels in style and thought-process between Gal 2:1-10 and 2 Thess 2:1-12, even though they deal with quite different subject matter. In addition to exhibiting the same directness of approach, sensitivity to those addressed, emotional depth, and power of description, both passages make the same use of parenthesis, ellipsis and anacoluthon. The clue to understanding Paul's "asides" and ellipses is simply to pay careful attention to the main drift of his argument and the life-situation of his addressees. Thus, in order to understand the difficult ellipsis of 2 Thess 2:7b, it is only necessary to carry forward in one's mind the unexpressed apodosis of 2:3b, namely, "the day of the Lord will not come."

1144 ---. "Thessalonians and the Synoptic Gospels," *Biblica* 19 (1938) 19-42.

The eschatological discourse of Matthew--and not that of the other Synoptic Gospels--provides the appropriate background and *milieu* for rightly understanding Paul's teaching of the parousia. In fact, there are compelling reasons for believing that the literary relationship between the eschatological material in 1 and 2 Thessalonians

(1 Thess 2:14-16; 4:16-17; 5:1-7; 2 Thess 1:7-10; 2:1-12) and Matthew 24-25 is closer than generally recognized. The parallel between 2 Thess 2:3, 7 and Matt 24:34 suggests a new hypothesis regarding the meaning of Paul's mysterious terms τὸ κατέχον and ὁ κατέχων. "That which restrains" is the present unfulfillment of the prophecy about the destruction of Jerusalem and the terrible events which will accompany its desolation. "The restrainer" is the archangel Michael, the patron of Israel, who defends the city of Jerusalem until the moment pre-ordained by God for the manifestation of the final reprobation of the ancient temporal kingdom of Israel, signified by the total destruction of Jerusalem and its temple at the orders of Titus.

1145 Pate, C. Marvin. "2 Thess 2:1-12: Anti-Christ Versus Christ: The Garden of Eden Revisited," *The Glory of Adam and the Afflictions of the Righteous. Pauline Suffering in Context* (Lewiston, NY: Mellen, 1993) 291-312.

The divine struggle between the Antichrist ("the lawless one") and Christ depicted in 2 Thess 2:1-12 is a struggle thoroughly immersed in Adamic theology. In this passage Paul relates to the reader the dark side of the *Urzeit-Endzeit* schema whereby the Antichrist, the eschatological personification of the serpent in the garden, attempts to counter Christ's reclamation of Adam's lost dominion and glory. Furthermore, the people of God will share in Christ's, the true Adam's, dominion and glory because they have suffered for him. The Adamic theology which undergirds 2 Thess 2:1-12 suggests the reason why a number of passages in the Thessalonian letters link so closely suffering and glory: righteous suffering restores Adam's lost glory.

1146 Pax, Elpidius. "2 Thess 2,8-10," ΕΠΙΦΑΝΕΙΑ. *Ein religionsgeschichtlicher Beitrag zur biblischen Theologie* (Münchener Theologische Studien; Munich: Karl Zink, 1955) 221-228.

1147 Powell, Charles E. "The Identity of the 'Restrainer' in 2 Thessalonians 2:6-7," *Bibliotheca Sacra* 154 (1997) 320-332.

In light of the chiastic structure of 2 Thess 2:1-17 and the emphases in this passage, the restrainer refers to the ministry of the Spirit (ὁ κατέχων) through the church as believers pursue their mission of preaching the gospel (τὸ κατέχον) to the world. When their mission is accomplished, they will be gathered together with Christ and live forever with him (1 Thess 4:17; 5:9-10; 2 Thess 2:1). Then, following the rapture, the lawless one will be revealed in the tribulation period and will rule, and the Holy Spirit will operate through the two witnesses (Rev 11:3-13), the 144,000 (Rev 7:1-8), and other tribulation saints in preaching the gospel.

1148 Preez, J. du. "Op soek na die betekenis van 'ὁ ναὸς τοῦ θεοῦ' in 2 Thessalonisense 2:4," *Nederduitse Gereformeerde Teologiese Tydskrif* 22 (1981) 91-95.

The phrase "the temple of God" in 2 Thess 2:4 has been variously interpreted to refer to the temple in Jerusalem, a heathen place of worship, heaven, the church of

Christ, and a material building on earth. Following the suggestion of G. Wohlenberg (190), one should understand this phrase in far broader terms than merely referring to the temple in Jerusalem, while at the same time avoiding the ever present danger of spiritualizing the text. The temple motif effectively brings together everything that can be seen as being a part of God's sanctuary, namely, the heavens and earth and everything in service of God.

1149 Reimpell, J. C. "Das κατέχειν im 2. Thessalonicherbrief," *Theologische Studien und Kritiken* 60 (1887) 713-736.

In light of the great debate concerning the nature of the "restrainer" of 2 Thess 2:7, including claims that this figure refers to the Roman emperor as well as other claims about which it is not possible to be certain, a thorough biblical discussion is warranted. The evidence indicates that the subject and the power of the restrainer do not come from a basis in the realms of the state, but are to be found in the sphere of the church. This understanding clarifies the language used and is consonant with the biblical basis of the concept. As a result, the apostle's language has a practical meaning of great significance, both for the Thessalonians and for all time.

1150 Robinson, D. W. B. "II Thess. 2,6: 'That which restrains' or 'That which holds sway'?" *Studia Evangelica II* (ed. Frank L. Cross; Texte und Untersuchungen zur Geschichte der altchristlichen Literature 87; Berlin: Akademie Verlag, 1964) 635-638.

It is usual to take κατέχειν in 2 Thess 2:5-6 as meaning "restrain" and, consequently, as having for its implied object "the man of lawlessness." It is preferable, however, to render κατέχειν as "hold fast," "possess," or "occupy." With this translation, it becomes reasonably certain that τὸ κατέχον is a title for the occupying or possessing power, i.e., Rome. As a consequence, it is no longer necessary to think of τὸ κατέχον and ὁ ἀνόμος as opposed to one another. Paul is not introducing a second cryptic term, meaningful only in relation to the first, but rather is explaining the identity of the principal eschatological figure ("the lawless one"). Rome and its human representative, the emperor, have power and "hold sway" for a time until they are removed.

1151 Rouiller, Grégoire. "Le mystère d'iniquité. Étude de 2 Thess 2:1-17," *Les Échos de Saint-Maurice* (St-Maurice, 1972) 68.

1152 Schippers, R. *Mythologie en Eschatologie in 2 Thessalonicenzen 2:1-17* (Amsterdam: Vrije Universiteit, 1961).

In 2 Thess 2:1-17 Paul makes use of an apocalypse in order to refute his opponents' mythologizing approach to the eschaton. The Thessalonians were being misled by those who, in gnostic fashion, claimed that the kingdom had already come spiritually but "the people have not recognized it" (Gospel of Thomas 51, 113). Ever since the Antiochian school, exegetes have been confident that the "postponement of events" was itself a definitive precursor or sign of the eschaton. Consequently, they held that Paul and other

New Testament writers viewed the Antichrist as the "organic end-product of a universally Christianized and then de-Christianized world" in an "end-of-history" manner. Such exegesis is based on several apparent problems which can be eliminated by viewing the parousia in connection with the Old Testament promises concerning the regathering of all Israel in the land. Material from Daniel, Maccabees, and the Dead Sea Scrolls sheds light on the nature of the apostasy and the identity of the man of lawlessness. It is best to regard the events, persons, and institutions referred to in the text as representing recurring agents in the "hidden" plan of God by which, in each dispensation, he sovereignly allows and even uses "lawlessness" to serve his purposes but also restrains it in order to gather into his fold the full number of those sealed for redemption.

1153 Schmid, Josef. "Der Antichrist und die hemmende Macht (II Thess. 2:1-12)," *Theologische Quartalschrift* 129 (1949) 323-343.

2 Thess 2:1-12 is difficult to understand because: (1) it seems that the readers already knew of it from previous instruction; (2) Paul speaks of this theme in no other place in his letters; and (3) it relies upon apocalyptic language. To understand this passage one must determine who the "son of destruction" and the "restraining force" are. For Paul, who lived in the burning expectation of the near end of the age, the Antichrist as the son of destruction was an individual whose manifestation would come as a sign of the coming of Christ. A distinction is not to be made between an impersonal and personal restraining force, since their grounding is the same.

1154 Schneider, E. E. "Mysterium iniquitatis. Das heilige Geheimnis der Sünde," *Theologische Zeitschrift* 19.2 (1963) 113-125.

The "mystery of iniquity" (2 Thess 2:7) is not the Antichrist, since mystery in the New Testament is always applied to God's work in Christ. A sacred mystery does lie hidden in sin, but it is a mystery which according to God's plan is worked out on us, in us, and for our good. The divine intent is that, through the pain caused by the knowledge of our guilt and the realization of our utter helplessness, we may turn back, believe the incredible, and learn to obey God.

1155 Shaw, R. H. "A Conjecture of the Signs of the End," *Anglican Theological Review* 47 (1965) 96-102.

Since the earliest days of the church (e.g., Irenaeus, Hippolytus), it has been common to find a close connection between Mark 13 and 2 Thessalonians 2. But although Paul's eschatological remarks can be made to dovetail those of Jesus, a number of differences exist between these two discussions. For example, Jesus foretold many false Christs but Paul only one. Jesus saw false Christs at the time of the fall of the temple and after, but Paul only at the time of the end of the world. Jesus said nothing about a false Christ being accepted or displayed as God, but Paul saw the false Christ in the place of God. Therefore, there is no direct connection between Mark 13 and 2 Thessalonians 2.

1156 Sirard, Leas. "La parousie de l'Antéchrist, 2 Thess 2,3-9," *Studiorum Paulinorum Congressus Internationalis Catholicus 1961* (Analecta Biblica 17/18; 2 vols.; Rome: Pontifical Biblical Institute, 1963) 2.89-100.

An important part of understanding Paul's statements about the Antichrist in 2 Thess 2:1-12 is a proper analysis of the verbs ἀποκαλύπτειν (2:3) and κατέχειν (2:6-7), which are used to describe his future "revelation" and his present "hindrance." It seems that, for Paul, the true sign of the end times should be the fall of the kingdom of Satan--a fall which precedes very closely the advent of the new kingdom which will arrive in a very unexpected fashion.

1157 Spadafora, Francesco. "L'Ostacolo e l'Avversario," *Divinitas* 29 (1985) 261-274.

In 2 Thess 2:1-12 Paul communicates to the faithful Thessalonians who faced violent persecution by Jews (see 1 Thess 2:14-16) the prophecy of Jesus about the imminent destruction of Jerusalem (see Matthew 24). This prophetic approach to the text is preferable to the eschatological interpretation, which contends that Paul was referring to the end of the world. The obstacle and the adversary are the persecutions and trials being suffered by the new Christians at the hands of Jewish opponents.

1158 Stephenson, Allen M. G. "On the Meaning of ἐνέστηκεν ἡ ἡμέρα τοῦ κυρίου in 2 Thessalonians 2,2," *Studia Evangelica IV* (ed. Frank L. Cross; Texte und Untersuchungen zur Geschichte der altchristlichen Literatur 102; Berlin: Akademie Verlag, 1968) 442-451.

It has come about in the past century for a variety of reasons that the verb ἐνέστηκεν in 2 Thess 2:2, which once was commonly translated as "is imminent," is now almost universally rendered "is present," "is come," or even "has come." But though ἐνέστηκεν literally means "is present," this translation is logically impossible in the context of 2 Thess 2:2. Paul must be using this word as a sort of rhetorical hyperbole to express as vividly as possible the idea of the day of the Lord being immediately around the corner. Another possibility is that the usage here is analogous to the common use of a Greek present verb in a future sense.

1159 Stephens, D. J. "Eschatological Themes in II Thessalonians 2:1-12" (Unpublished Ph.D. Dissertation; St. Andrews, Scotland: University of St. Andrews, 1976).

1160 Stepien, Jan. "Drugi znak paruzji w eschatologii s'w. Pawla," *Ruch Biblijny i Liturgiczny* 15.2 (1962) 65-72.

An analysis of the notion of an Antichrist in 2 Thess 2:1-12 reveals that this figure is not Satan, nor an abstraction of an anti-divine force, nor a collective figure. Rather, he is a specific, individual person who appears as an envoy of Satan at the end of the world shortly before the return of Jesus and mimics Christ. The Pauline notion of an Antichrist has its roots in Dan 11:36, Isa 14:13-14 and Ezek 28:2-9.

1161 Strobel, Adolf. *Untersuchungen zum eschatologischen Verzögerungsproblem auf Grund der spätjüdisch-urchristlichen Geschichte von Habakuk 2,2ff* (Novum Testamentum Supplements 2; Leiden: Brill, 1961) 98-116.

The dilemma of the meaning of the "restraining force" requires a study of 2 Thess 2:1-12 on the basis of coherence with known traditions, and consideration of the unity of the section. The idea must be rejected that there is not a Jewish apocalyptic influence on the idea of the "restraining force," as von Dobschutz proposed. The restraining force is God, reflecting the assumptions of Hab 2:3. In an excursus on the authenticity of the letter, an argument is made for Pauline authorship on the basis of its conceptual imagery and the nature of the vocabulary of the section not being clearly different from the apostle's use of similar vocabulary in other letters. Linguistic items in 2 Thessalonians which have been claimed to be non-Pauline are similar to the terminology used in Romans 1-2.

1162 Thomas, Robert L. "A Hermeneutical Ambiguity of Eschatology: The Analogy of Faith," *Journal of the Evangelical Theological Society* 23.1 (1980) 45-53.

The analogy of faith has long been considered a standard hermeneutical guideline. Its careless use, however, has produced many illegitimate exegetical conclusions, especially in biblical passages dealing with eschatology. A safeguard against this abuse is a strict application of the grammatical-historical approach to exegesis. Such an approach is well illustrated in 2 Thess 2:3. In light of grammatical and historical considerations, the passage has the following sense: "The day of the Lord is not present unless first in sequence within that day there has come the apostasy and following this apostasy's beginning the revealing of the man of lawlessness." Rather than the two events preceding the day of the Lord, as has so often been suggested, these are happenings which compose the early stages of that day after it has begun. By observing the non-occurrence of these, the Thessalonian readers could rest assured that the day whose early stages are so characterized had not yet begun.

1163 Thornton, Larry R. "Salvation in the Tribulation in Light of God's 'Working unto Delusion,'" *Calvary Baptist Theological Journal* 3 (1987) 26-49.

Many dispensationalists have concluded, on the basis of 2 Thess 2:1-12, that those who have heard the truth of the gospel and refuse to believe before the return of Christ will have no opportunity to convert during the seven years of tribulation. A study of salvation during the time of tribulation in light of God's "working unto delusion" (v 11), however, shows this conclusion to be unfounded.

1164 Townsend, John T. "II Thessalonians 2:3-12," *SBL 1980 Seminar Papers* (ed. Paul J. Achtemeier; SBL Seminar Papers 19; Atlanta: Scholars Press, 1980) 233-250.

The author of 2 Thessalonians in the apocalyptic section of 2:1-12 seems to be drawing upon some kind of source in which the "restraining force/person" is probably a known figure. The "temple" in verse 4 is likely the Jerusalem sanctuary and this suggests that this apocalyptic section must stem from before 70 CE. The masculine κατέχων is probably to be identified with either the man of lawlessness or God, simply because these are the only two persons mentioned in the passage before the introduction of the "restraining force/person." Issues that cannot be answered definitively include various points of grammar in verses 6-7 and a specific identification of the "restraining force/person."

1165 Trilling, Wolfgang. "Antichrist und Papsttum: Reflexionen zur Wirkungsgeschichte von 2 Thess 2:1-10a," *Begegnung mit dem Wort. Festschrift für Heinrich Zimmermann* (ed. Josef Zmijewski and Ernst Nellessen; Bonner biblische Beiträge 53; Bonn: Hanstein, 1980) 251-271.

The question must be asked whether the figure of an "eschatological opponent" or an "Antichrist" has any theological relevance today. 2 Thessalonians 2, one of the most important passages in the New Testament on this subject, provides a strong figure of the Antichrist, one which was taken up and concretized in the Reformation. It provides a model of a human or super-human person who appears at the parousia of Christ.

1166 Ubbink, J. Th. "ὡς δι' ἡμῶν (2 Thess 2,2) een exegetisch-isagogische puzzle?" *Nederlands theologisch tijdschrift* 7 (1953) 269-295.

The older part of the Thessalonian congregation had misunderstood Paul's eschatology in his first letter to them. In their grief over the martyrdom of fellow believers, some were claiming that Paul himself had written in 1 Thessalonians that the day of the Lord had come. Paul counters this error in 2 Thessalonians and appends in typical fashion his personal signature to show the authenticity of this letter. Thus, there is no reason to conclude from the words of 2 Thess 2:2 (ὡς δι' ἡμῶν) the existence of a forged letter claiming to come from the apostle. The phrase ὡς ὅτι found at the end of this verse can express cause ("because"), or introduce an actual situation ("that"), or a hypothetical situation ("as if"). Although context must ultimately decide the intended meaning, the same phrase in 2 Cor 5:19 is clearly being used to describe an actual situation. This is also the sense of ὡς ὅτι in 2 Thess 2:2.

1167 Walvoord, John F. "Will Israel Build a Temple in Jerusalem?" *Bibliotheca Sacra* 125 (1968) 99-106.

It is clear from Matt 24:15, supported by Daniel, 2 Thessalonians 2 and Revelation 13, that the scriptures anticipate a future temple with a sacrificial system which will be underway at the time when the man of lawlessness comes to exercise authority, desecrate the temple, and establish himself as an object of worship. The sacrifices offered in this temple are not to be confused with the sacrifices mentioned in conjunction with the millennial temple of Ezekiel 40-48.

1168 Watt, P. B. van der. "Die Antichris en sy Tyd," *Nederduitse Gereformeerde Teologiese Tydskrif* 8 (1967) 7-11.

The Antichrist described in 2 Thess 2:1-12 is a future person and should not be interpreted as some have done as a movement or ideology. The parousia of the Antichrist is an actual future event which signals that the time of Christ's return is near. This personal figure will be an exponent and product of a fallen sinful world.

1169 Weinrich, William C. "Antichrist in the Early Church," *Concordia Theological Quarterly* 49 (1985) 135-147.

Early Christian notions of the Antichrist derive from two principal sources: (1) traditional depictions of opponents of God and his people mediated through such biblical texts as Daniel, Ezek 28:2 and 36-38, Isa 14:13-14, 2 Thess 2:1-12 and Revelation; and (2) a more specifically Christian image of the Antichrist as the opponent of Jesus, the Christ of God. The majority opinion of the church fathers is that Paul's reference to the temple of God refers to the Jerusalem temple which will be rebuilt by a Jewish pseudo-Messiah who comes from the tribe of Dan. Although the fathers do apply the Antichrist idea to contemporary persons and parties (heretics, persecutors, schismatics), the figure of the Antichrist in his fullness remains a distinctly future, eschatological reality.

1170 Whiteley, Denys Edward Hugh. "Teaching Peculiar to 2 Thessalonians," *The Theology of St. Paul* (Philadelphia: Fortress, 1964) 234-240.

Three issues in 2 Thess 2:3-7 have caused much debate: the identity of the "apostasy," the "man of lawlessness," and "the restrainer." Paul was certain that some kind of rebellion in the religious sphere was about to occur before the end came, but he did not know what specific form it would take. The "man of lawlessness" was not, for Paul, an abstract principle of evil but a concrete, though indeterminate, human being. But while the apostasy and man of lawlessness were future events and thus, somewhat understandably, not specific in Paul's mind, this is not the case with the "restrainer," whose work was currently in operation when the apostle wrote 2 Thessalonians. The traditional explanation which identifies the restraining force with the Roman empire is the most defensible of the various positions which have been forwarded.

1171 Wilkinson, Thomas L. "The Man of Lawlessness in II Thessalonians," *The New Testament Student and His Field* (ed. John H. Skilton and Curtiss A. Ladley; Philadelphia: Presbyterian and Reformed Publishing, 1982) 124-149.

Paul's figure of the man of lawlessness is to be seen as an individual who will appear at the end time just prior to the parousia of Christ. His significance is to be seen in his opposition to Jesus Christ, against whom he presents a counter claim of faith. He does appear to be presented as a false prophet, but he transcends that category completely by his claim to deity. No military-political features are overtly and demonstrably present, yet they cannot be entirely excluded. The man of lawlessness is not in existence at present, though he is related to the present economy of evil, in that both he and it are included in the Satanic activity which opposes God's plan of salvation by a counter plan of evil. The man of lawlessness, however, is not himself Satan, but derives his power from him. Though he undoubtedly appears as a concentration of evil, yet he himself remains with the race of humankind.

1172 Wuest, Kenneth S. "The Rapture - Precisely When?" *Bibliotheca Sacra* 114 (1957) 60-69.

The evidence from the prophecy of Revelation, 2 Thessalonians 2, the promise given to the Philadelphian church (Rev 3:10), and the imminence of the rapture all supports a pretribulation, premillennial position. There is nothing in the Bible which indicates that the church will either enter or pass through the tribulation.

1173 Yates, Roy. "The Antichrist," *Evangelical Quarterly* 46.1 (1974) 42-50.

Although the actual name "Antichrist" is found only in the Johannine letters, the idea is much more widespread, especially if one understands the force of the *anti* as indicating opposition as well as a false claim. Three New Testament passages which are especially important on this subject are 1 John 2:18, 2 Thess 2:3-10 and Revelation 13. Paul's "man of sin" presents an insoluble problem of interpretation, but he certainly saw Satanic power as ultimately manifested in a tyrannous human power totally disassociated from God. Revelation 13 likewise depicts all the world's perverted political power concentrated and raised to a peak of union and opposition against God, Christ, and the church. Satan himself is operative in this lie, and outlasts all human movements and powers which depend on him.

Other Relevant Sources:

321, 376, 378, 383, 406, 464, 496, 568, 573, 618, 627, 640, 797, 905, 924, 925, 928, 952, 969, 970, 982, 1062.

D. 2 Thessalonians 2:13-17

1174 Artola, Antonio-Maria. "'Prière et apostolat.' 2 Th 2,16-3,5," *Assemblées du Seigneur* 63 (1971) 76-81.

2 Thess 2:16-3:5, despite its brevity, contains much doctrinal and paraenetic significance. It exhorts, first of all, fidelity in the faith. It also highlights in a concrete manner the force of communal prayer for the spread of the faith. Finally, it underlines particularly that the project of God with regard to the believer is the source that all follow.

1175 Merk, Otto. "Überlegungen zu 2 Thess 2,13-17," *Nach den Anfängen fragen. Herrn Prof. Dr. theol. Gerhard Dautzenberg zum 60. Geburtstag an 30. Januar 1994* (ed.

C. Mayer, K. Müller, and G. Schmalenberg; Giessen: Selbstverlag des Fachbereichs Evangelische Theologie und Katholische Theologie und deren Didaktik, 1994) 405-414.

1176 Otzen, Povl. "'Gute Hoffnung' bei Paulus," *Zeitschrift für die neutestamentliche Wissenschaft* 49.3-4 (1958) 283-285.

The claim of Franz Cumont (*Lux Perpetua* [Paris: Geuthner, 1949]) that the phrase ἐλπὶς ἀγαθά (2 Thess 2:16) is a technical expression connected with the Demeter-Persephone cult is incorrect. One of the two proofs to which Cumont appeals is 2 Thess 2:16. Before writing 2 Thessalonians, Paul visited the cities of Thessalonica, Athens and Corinth, where the Eleusinian mysteries were well known and also traces of Demeter worship have been found. There, it is claimed, Paul found in the common speech the phrase "good hope" as an expression for the expectation of beatitude after death.

1177 Schulz, Anselm. "Die Kunst zu trösten. Auslegung des 2. Thessalonicherbriefes (2,13-3,3)," *Bibel und Leben* 7.3 (1966) 179-185.

The second of three brief expositions of 2 Thessalonians (see 1074, 1195), this article continues the discussion of Paul's request. The discussion begins with an insertion. The insertion begins with a word of thanks (2:13-14), a call for standing firm (2:15), a prayer wish (2:16-17), a request for intercession (3:1-2), and a statement of the true God being Christ (3:3).

1178 Vander Stichele, Caroline. "The Concept of Tradition and 1 and 2 Thessalonians," *The Thessalonian Correspondence* (ed. Raymond F. Collins; Bibliotheca ephemeridum theologicarum lovaniensium 87; Leuven: Leuven University Press, 1990) 499-504.

Explicit (the term παράδοσις) and indirect (the verb παραλαμβάνω) evidence concerning the terminology of tradition in the Thessalonian correspondence shows that there are four relevant texts: 1 Thess 2:13; 4:1; 2 Thess 2:15; and 3:16. A closer look at their context makes it clear that there is a striking similarity in place and formulation between 1 Thess 2:13 and 2 Thess 2:15 and between 1 Thess 4:1 and 2 Thess 3:6. The structural agreement and the terminological affinity between 1 and 2 Thessalonians can hardly be accidental. It looks as if the second letter used the first letter as a model. But similarity does not imply identity. There is a stronger emphasis on tradition in 2 Thessalonians. This does not necessarily mean that Paul is the author of both letters, but rather that the author of 2 Thessalonians truly tries to imitate the authentic Paul.

Other Relevant Sources:

363, 450, 695, 836, 839, 876, 1064, 1111, 1113, 1151, 1152.

E. 2 Thessalonians 3:1-5

1179 Dewailly, Louis-Marie. "Course et gloire de la parole (II Thess., III, 1)," *Revue Biblique* 71.1 (1964) 25-41.

2 Thess 3:1 is a seemingly simple verse with few interpretive difficulties. Nevertheless, it provides a strikingly first-hand picture of the needs of Paul and his cohorts. The two elements of the prayer for which he asks the Thessalonian church regarding the spread of "the message of the Lord," namely, speed and honor for the spread of the gospel, are telling in that they are linked very closely to the needs of the apostle and his fellow workers. The delivery of Paul and his fellow workers from opposition (3:2), the strengthening of the Thessalonian church in the face of the "evil one" (3:3), Paul's confidence that the Thessalonians are following his commands (3:4) and that they will be led by God's love and Christ's perseverance (3:5), all speak of an opposition to the message that unifies the diverse elements of this prayer.

Other Relevant Sources:

836, 1174, 1177.

F. 2 Thessalonians 3:6-15

1180 Ahsmann, Piet. "'Wie niet wil werken moet ook maar niet eten'. 2 Tessalonicenzen 3,10," *Schrift* 64 (1979) 146-152.

The saying in 2 Thess 3:10 ("If anyone will not work, let him not eat") represents the viewpoint of the author of 2 Thessalonians, who, like Paul, is attempting to come to terms with the delay of the parousia and wishes to ground the church in an economic lifestyle which is suitable to stable long-term growth. The borrowing of citations from 1 Thessalonians (particularly 2:9) is one of the tell-tale marks that this letter is deutero-Pauline. Nevertheless, the saying in 3:10 may well have been one that Paul could have spoken and is used here to counter the excesses of those "false apostles" who presume on the good graces of the Christian community, by living in idleness on grounds of an outdated claim of dominical (or apostolic) authority for an imminent parousia and mendicant life-style. The issues in 2 Thessalonians are typical of the tension throughout the history of the church between the need for radical conversion on the one hand and maintenance of the status quo on the other.

1181 Artola, Antonio-Maria. "L'Apôtre-ouvrier se donne en modèle. 2 Th 3,7-12," *Assemblées du Seigneur* 64 (1969) 71-76.

The section of 2 Thess 3:7-12 does not lack topicality. In effect, it reveals to us the conviction of Paul, not solely for the labor of Christians in view of assurance of their proper maintenance, but, more than that, for the actual work that is given to a minister of the Lord.

1182 Aune, D. C. "Trouble in Thessalonica: An Exegetical Study of I Thess 4:9-12, 5:12-14 and II Thess 3:6-15 in Light of First Century Social Conditions" (Unpublished Th.M. Dissertation; Vancouver: Regent College, 1989).

Most commentators have understood the problems of idleness and disorder alluded to in 1 Thess 4:9-12, 5:12-14, and 2 Thess 3:6-15 to be eschatological in nature. There is compelling evidence, however, that the trouble in the Thessalonian church was social rather than eschatological. Many causes for the problems of disorder and idleness present themselves when important background information about the social and economic situation of first-century Thessalonica and the social dynamics in the Thessalonian church are taken into account. Very likely, the ones causing the trouble in Thessalonica were artisans and manual laborers who took advantage of the generosity of other, wealthier members in the community of faith. These "disorderly brothers" seem to have disregarded important societal norms about the benefactor/beneficiary relationship by acting as if they were entitled to support from others in the church. Paul admonishes them to work with their hands so that they can support themselves and become responsible members of the community.

1183 Dormeyer, Detlev. "Das Verständnis von Arbeit im Neuen Testament im Horizont der Naherwartung," *Hervormde Teologiese Studies* 45.4 (1989) 801-814.

The New Testament seems to present conflicting ideas about work: on the one hand, believers should be industrious (2 Thess 3:10); on the other hand, they should evade work (see Matt 6:25). This theological study explores the Old Testament, Jewish, Greek and New Testament background to these differing concepts about work and concludes that they can be harmonized in light of Jesus' proclamation of the coming kingdom of God.

1184 Jewett, Robert. "Tenement Churches and Communal Meals in the Early Church: The Implications of a Form-Critical Analysis of 2 Thessalonians 3:10," *Biblical Research* 38 (1993) 23-43.

Alongside the traditional category of "house churches," there is evidence in the Pauline letters for the existence of "tenement churches," which met without the sponsorship of a patron in the living or working spaces of *insula* buildings. Thus whereas house churches had an upper- or middle-class patron, the tenement churches consisted entirely of the urban underclass (see Rom 16:14-15). A system of "agapaic communalism" appears to have provided the support for the sacramental meals in such churches, contrasting with the "patriarchalism of love" in house churches. A tenement-church structure in which communal meals were being provided by the members themselves is the only form of early Christian congregational life for which the regulation in 2 Thess 3:10 could actually be considered absolutely essential. The references to work and community support in 1 Thess 2:9 and 4:9-12 are most easily understood in light of the hypothesis that at least some of the Christian groups in Thessalonica were having difficulty maintaining support for a tenement-church system.

1185 ---. "Tenement Churches and Pauline Love Feasts," *Quarterly Review* 14 (1994) 43-58. Republished with slight revisions in Robert Jewett, *Paul the Apostle to America: Cultural Trends and Pauline Scholarship* (Louisville, KY: Westminster/John Knox, 1994) 73-86.

The majority of early Christians lived in the apartment buildings called *insulae* in the inner cities rather than in private villas. Thus, in addition to "house churches," there appears to have existed "tenement churches," which were more communally structured and met without the sponsorship of a wealthy patron. The admonition in 2 Thess 3:10b ("If anyone does not want to work, let him/her not eat") points in the direction of a communally supported system of love feasts in the church at Thessalonica.

1186 Judge, Edwin A. "Cultural Conformity and Innovation in Paul: Some Clues From Contemporary Documents," *Tyndale Bulletin* 35 (1984) 3-24.

On the basis of his writings and in comparison to pagan authors, Paul must be set in opposition to Marx. The apostle does not hold the formal structure of society in his day to be systematically oppressive. Nor does he suggest that its violent overthrow would be in principle in the positive interest of humankind. The Thessalonian letters, with their demand that people work to support themselves, show how he reacted against parasitic aspects of the system. The Corinthian letters reveal a head-on confrontation with the mechanisms by which it imposed social power defined as moral superiority. Paul's positive response was to build a remarkable new construction of social realities which both lay within the fabric of the old ranking system and yet transformed it by a revolution in social values.

1187 Kurichialnil, John. "If Any One Will Not Work, Let Him Not Eat," *Biblebhashyam* 21.3 (1995) 184-203.

The eschatological hope which the Thessalonian Christians had in the return of Christ made some of the believers impatient, irresponsible, and lazy. This led Paul to issue his command of 2 Thess 3:10: "If anyone will not work, let him not eat." This command suggests that earning one's livelihood by honest work is a necessary requirement of moral Christian living. This notion is completely in agreement with the theme of work found in the Old Testament, the activity of Jesus and his disciples, and both the example and teaching of Paul.

1188 Menken, Maarten J. J. "Paradise Regained or Still Lost? Eschatology and Disorderly Behaviour in 2 Thessalonians," *New Testament Studies* 38.2 (1992) 271-289.

The reproach in 2 Thess 3:6-12 of "walking without order and not according to the tradition" may allude to Gen 3:17-19, a passage understood in Jewish tradition as God's imposition of the obligation upon humankind to work hard in order to eat. The content of the eschatological error combatted in 2 Thess 2:1-12 is that the parousia of the Lord had taken place. The conduct of the ἄτακτοι of 3:6-12 stems from this eschatological error, which presumed that the return of Christ meant the restoration of paradise and the annulment of the curse of Gen 3:17-19.

1189 Moffatt, James. "2 Thessalonians iii. 14, 15," *Expository Times* 21 (1909) 328.

The similarity of the expression used by the emperor Marcus Aurelius (6.20) with that of Paul in 2 Thess 3:14-15 but given for a quite different purpose or goal highlights the sharp contrast between Stoic individualism and the Christian sense of obligation toward a fellow believer.

1190 Moulton, H. K. "Tired of Doing Good?," *The Bible Translator* 26.4 (1975) 445.

2 Thess 3:13 and Gal 6:9 should be considered together since the message of both verses is the same. The use of the prepositions "in" and "of" in various English translations of these verses ("Let us not be weary *in* welldoing"; "Let us never tire *of* doing good") has proved confusing, for it suggests that Paul is questioning his readers' desire to keep on doing right. The apostle, however, is addressing their attitude and wants to ensure that they will do what is right cheerfully all the time.

1191 Pytel, Jan. "Religijne i spoleczne aspekty pracy w Pismach Pawlowych," *Studia theologica Varsaviensia* 20.2 (1982) 97-104.

An analysis of a number of passages in Paul's letters (including 1 Thess 2:9; 4:11; 2 Thess 3:8-12) which deal with the issue of work demonstrates that labor in the eyes of the apostle contains much religious value. It not only perfects the human being but also allows a person to help the poor and those who work full time on behalf of the gospel. Paul himself is a good example of a proper work ethic. He works manually and can provide for himself, thereby ensuring his independence. The apostle in turn appeals to his readers to have their own occupation and to avoid the idlers. All of Paul's theology of labor can be summed up in the sentence: "If any one will not work, let him not eat" (2 Thess 3:10).

1192 Quacquarelli, Antonio. "Note sulla esegesi di 2 Th. 3,10 nella letteraratura monastica antica," *Mémorial Dom Jean Gribomont (1920-1986)* (ed. Y. de Andia; Studia ephemeridis "Augustinianum" 27; Rome: Institutum Patristicum Augustinianum, 1988) 503-519.

An analysis of how 2 Thess 3:10 was interpreted in the early church.

1193 Romaniuk, Kazimierz. "Les Thessaloniciens étaient-ils des paresseux?" *Ephemerides theologicae lovanienses* 69 (1993) 142-145.

Ronald Russell's interpretation of 2 Thess 3:6-12 (1194), in which he looks to a sociological analysis relying upon an Epicurean and even gnostic understanding of this passage, opposes the traditional eschatological explanation as to why some believers in Thessalonica gave up work. Russell's sociological interpretation, however, is not warranted on two grounds. First, he fails to consider the powerful influence which the expectation of the parousia had in the early church. Second, he has fallen victim to sociological exegesis--a method which can be criticized for being anachronistic and overly optimistic about its conclusions.

1194 Russell, Ronald. "The Idle in 2 Thess 3:6-12: An Eschatological or a Social Problem?" *New Testament Studies* 34 (1988) 105-119.

Although the problem of idleness in the Thessalonian church (2 Thess 3:6-12) has often been given an eschatological explanation--either the idleness was found to be rooted in a belief in the imminence of the parousia or the "enthusiastic radicalism" resulting from a somewhat gnostic form of realized eschatology--the evidence best supports a sociological reason. Some of the sociological reasons proposed thus far (i.e., Greco-Roman disdain for manual labor, Epicurean philosophical tradition, the moralist's advice on a proper occupation) reflect upper class Hellenistic life. These proposals, however, founder on the fact that the Pauline churches were composed primarily of believers from a lower social position (the poor, slaves, artisans, freedmen) with a minority from higher social levels in positions of leadership. The unemployed urban poor often came into the Christian community seeking client-benefactor relationships without attempting to support themselves.

1195 Schulz, Anselm. "Die Pflicht des Christen, zu arbeiten. Auslegung des 2. Thessalonicherbriefes (3,4-3,18)," *Bibel und Leben* 7 (1966) 256-264.

The third and concluding part of a brief exposition of 2 Thessalonians (see 1074, 1177), this article gives attention to the issue of laziness and idleness. Paul's discussion of this issue falls into several parts, including first a discussion of his two introductory themes of confidence and preparation (3:4-5), his strict command to avoid laziness (3:6), the example of the apostle (3:7-9), the command to work (3:10-12), additional wisdom (3:13-15), and a peace wish (3:16). The letter concludes with greetings and the grace wish (3:17-18).

1196 South, James T. *Disciplinary Practices in Pauline Texts* (Lewiston, NY: Mellen, 1992).

An examination of Pauline texts which address the issue of discipline (1 Cor 5:1-8; 2 Cor 2:5-11; Gal 6:1; Rom 16:17, Phil 3:2; 2 Thess 3:6-15; Eph 5:3-14; several texts from the Pastorals) leads to the following conclusions: (1) in cases involving community members, discipline was salvific in intent as well as protective of the community; (2) discipline could take a variety of forms, from shunning to expulsion; (3) Paul left it to the community to decide what specific action to take, except in extreme cases; (4) early Christian discipline was derived from the gospel, which brought the community into existence, and not from pagan or Jewish models; and (5) discipline served the vital functions of social control and boundary maintenance.

1197 Spicq, Ceslaus. "Les Thessaloniciens 'inquiets' étaient-ils des paresseux?" *Studia theologica* 10 (1956) 1-13.

The verb ἀτακτεῖν, the adjective ἄτακτος, and the adverb ἀτάκτως are employed only by Paul in the New Testament and only in his two letters to the Thessalonians. As a result, the meaning of this word-group is somewhat difficult to establish. There are two main branches of interpretation of this word-group: (1) a reference to the undisciplined, who live their lives in disorder, and (2) a reference to the lazy or unemployed. An investigation of the use of this word-group in literary texts, papyri, and inscriptions shows that it never refers to those who are lazy, although either the undisciplined, the negligent, or the unemployed may be in view.

1198 Storm, Melvin R. "Excommunication in the Life and Theology of the Primitive Christian Communities" (Unpublished Ph.D. Dissertation; Waco, TX: Baylor University, 1987).

This study examines excommunication in light of the life and concerns, both practical and theological, of the Pauline, the Matthean, and the Johannine communities. Chapter one examines 2 Thess 3:6-15 and concludes that the problem found therein probably embodied several factors: (1) the typical Greek disdain for manual labor, (2) an eschatological misunderstanding, and (3) the hostility of the working class toward the wealthy. As to the method of discipline, the following three-step procedure was carried out in the early church: (1) admonition, (2) avoidance, and (3) disassociation.

1199 Winter, Bruce W. "'If a Man Does Not Wish to Work...' A Cultural and Historical Setting for 2 Thessalonians 3:6-16," *Tyndale Bulletin* 40 (1989) 303-315.
Republished with minor changes in Bruce W. Winter, *Seek the Welfare of the City. Christians as Benefactors and Citizens* (First-Century Christians in the Graeco-Roman World; Grand Rapids: Eerdmans, 1994) 41-60.

The problem of idleness in Thessalonica has a sociological rather than an eschatological cause. In the face of famines in Macedonia at this time, some members of the Thessalonian church sought the patronage of wealthy Christians for the purpose of obtaining money to buy grain or receive handouts. Subsequent to the writing of 1 Thessalonians, Paul learned that some who did not wish to work had reverted to a patron-client relationship. This required him to address the problem at greater length than in the previous letter.

1200 Zorn, C. M. "II Thess. 3:6,14,15," *Theologische Quartalschrift* 23 (1926) 236-239.

Other Relevant Sources:

549, 662, 663, 674, 680, 707, 708, 738, 739, 740, 741, 1022.

G. 2 Thessalonians 3:16-18

Other Relevant Sources:

469, 836, 1053.

INDEX OF AUTHORS

NEW TESTAMENT TOOLS AND STUDIES

edited by

BRUCE M. METZGER, PH.D., D.D., L.H.D., D. THEOL., D. LITT.

and

BART D. EHRMAN, PH.D.

VOL. XI *Studien zum Neutestamentlichen Briefformular,* von Franz Schnider und Werner Stenger. 1987. ISBN 90 04 08414 2

VOL. XII *Strukturale Beobachtungen zum Neuen Testament,* von Werner Stenger. 1990. ISBN 90 04 90113 0

VOL. XIII *Life of Jesus Research: An Annotated Bibliography*, by Craig A. Evans. 1989. ISBN 90 04 09180 7

VOL. XIV *A Key to the Peshitta Gospels*; vol. I: *ʾĀlaph-Dalath*, by Terry C. Falla. 1991. ISBN 90 04 09354 0

VOL. XV *Text and Interpretation: New Approaches in the Criticism of the New Testament*, edited by P. J. Hartin and J. H. Petzer. 1991. ISBN 90 04 09401 6

VOL. XVI *An Index to Periodical Literature on the Apostle Paul,* by Watson E. Mills. 1993. ISBN 90 04 09674 4

VOL. XVII *The Gospel of John as Literature: An Anthology of Twentieth-Century Perspectives,* edited by Mark W. G. Stibbe. 1993. ISBN 90 04 09848 8

VOL. XVIII *Nag Hammadi Texts and the Bible: A Synopsis and Index,* edited by Craig A. Evans, Robert L. Webb and Richard A. Wiebe. 1993. ISBN 90 04 09902 6

VOL. XIX *Studying the Historical Jesus: Evaluations of the State of Current Research,* edited by Bruce Chilton and Craig A. Evans. 1994. ISBN 90 04 09982 4

VOL. XX *The New Testament in Greek,* IV. *The Gospel According to St. John,* edited by the American and British Committees of the International Greek New Testament Project. Volume One: *The Papyri,* edited by W. J. Elliott and D. C. Parker. 1995. ISBN 90 04 09940 9

VOL. XXI *Comparative Edition of the Syriac Gospels: Aligning the Sinaiticus, Curetonianus, Peshîṭtâ and Ḥarklean Versions,* by George A. Kiraz; 4 volumes. Vol. 1: Matthew; Vol. 2: Mark; Vol. 3: Luke; Vol. 4: John. 1996. ISBN 90 04 10419 4 (set)

VOL. XXII *Codex Bezae.* Studies from the Lunel Colloquium, June 1994, edited by D. C. Parker and C.-B. Amphoux. 1996. ISBN 90 04 10393 7

VOL. XXIII *Bibliography of Literature on First Peter,* by Anthony Casurella. 1996. ISBN 90 04 10488 7

VOL. XXIV *Life of Jesus Research: An Annotated Bibliography,* by Craig A. Evans. Revised edition. 1996. ISBN 90 04 10282 5

VOL. XXV *Handbook to Exegesis of the New Testament,* edited by Stanley E. Porter. 1997. ISBN 90 04 09921 2

VOL. XXVI *An Annotated Bibliography of 1 and 2 Thessalonians,* by Jeffrey A.D. Weima and Stanley E. Porter. 1998. ISBN 90 04 10740 1